British national identity and opposition to membership of Europe, 1961–63

MANCHESTER
1824

Manchester University Press

British national identity and opposition to membership of Europe, 1961–63

The anti-Marketeers

Robert F. Dewey, Jr.

Manchester University Press

Manchester and New York

distributed in the United States exclusively
by Palgrave Macmillan

Copyright © Robert F. Dewey, Jr. 2009

The right of Robert F. Dewey, Jr. to be identified as the author of this work has been
asserted by him in accordance with the Copyright, Designs and Patents Act 1988.

Published by Manchester University Press
Oxford Road, Manchester M13 9NR, UK
and Room 400, 175 Fifth Avenue, New York, NY 10010, USA
www.manchesteruniversitypress.co.uk

Distributed in the United States exclusively by
Palgrave Macmillan, 175 Fifth Avenue, New York,
NY 10010, USA

Distributed in Canada exclusively by
UBC Press, University of British Columbia, 2029 West Mall,
Vancouver, BC, Canada V6T 1Z2

British Library Cataloguing-in-Publication Data
A catalogue record for this book is available from the British Library

Library of Congress Cataloging-in-Publication Data applied for

ISBN   978 0 7190 7871 2   *hardback*

First published 2009

18 17 16 15 14 13 12 11 10 09   10 9 8 7 6 5 4 3 2 1

Typeset in Warnock Pro
by R. J. Footring Ltd, Derby, UK
Printed in Great Britain
by the MPG Books Group

To Mom and Dad, Helen, Susan and Gabriel

Contents

Acknowledgements

Dr E. H. H. Green of Magdalen College, Oxford, was my supervisor, mentor and friend. He died in September 2006, long before this book was published. But the project would not exist without Ewen. From the gestation of the original idea through to the completion of a rough draft of the manuscript he pushed me to address the topic with greater breadth and complexity. He was an unfailing source of inspiration, through the excellence of his own work, his qualities as a teacher and by virtue of the bravery and dignity he demonstrated in confronting life's hardships. It was my great honour to be Ewen's first DPhil student – there should have been many more.

Researching this topic raised an abundance of challenges. The most daunting of these included the necessity of consulting every copy of the *Daily Express* between 1961 and 1963 on microfilm at the National Newspaper Library. This entailed innumerable and interminable rush-hour journeys on the coach between Oxford and Victoria and travel on the Northern Line between central London and Colindale. I cannot in good conscience recommend this exercise to anyone, but the help provided by the staff at Colindale made this bearable and worthwhile. My research also benefited from the skilful assistance of the librarians, archivists and staffs at the British Library, the BBC Written Archives Centre at Caversham, the Bodleian Library, Oxford, the House of Lords Records Office, the Labour History Archive and Study Centre in Manchester, the Liddell Hart Centre for Military Archives at King's College, London, the Imperial War Museum, the Wren Library at Trinity College, Cambridge, the University of Birmingham Library, University College London Library, and the New York Public Library. Every effort has been made to secure copyright for quotations included in the book and I am grateful to the various archivists and trustees who provided permissions. I must also thank the entire team at Manchester University Press for their great efficiency and care in shepherding this book to publication.

I benefited from contact with other historians and political scientists encountered during the course of research and at conferences, including Peter Catterall, George Wilkes, Stuart Ward, Nick Crowson and Oliver Daddow, who shared insights on a host of topics relating to the first application debate and Euroscepticism in general. In this regard the observations of Ted Bromund, in particular, were invaluable. I must also thank Piers Ludlow and Nick Owen, who, as examiners, provided essential comments on the thesis version. A postdoctoral fellowship sponsored by the European Commission at the Maxwell School of Citizenship and Public Affairs at Syracuse University provided a welcome oasis for further reflection and I am therefore grateful to Margaret Herman, Director of its Global Affairs Center, Mitchell Orenstein, Director of the Center for European Studies, and especially Craig Parsons, former Director of the European Union Center. I must also thank original participants in the first application debate for their willingness to submit to lengthy interviews or provide written correspondence and I was most obliged to Lord Jenkins and Michael Foot, not only for their time and recollections, but for their enthusiastic support of the project.

The value of friendship, and my inordinate good fortune in that respect, was never more apparent than in the pursuit of this project. Dave Gavaghan and Elaine Welsh, Tim and Julie Fish, Kate Charles and Keith Rose, the Bennetts, the Tupous, Tom Evans, Sebastian Rosato and Clare Brant were incomparable hosts at various stages of research. So too were David Hagan and John McCarthy, who cast aside all conventional wisdom regarding houseguests by providing accommodation in spare corners of their West Kensington flats for months on end. Other crucial supporters included Sir Bryan Cartledge and Professor Paul Slack, his successor as Principal at Linacre College, Oxford. I also appreciate the support provided by my colleagues in the History Department at DePauw University. And I am, as always, grateful to my friends at Colgate University, including Gloria Vanderneut and John LeFevre, and will forever be indebted to Professor Jerry Balmuth of the Philosophy Department for adopting me as one of his undergraduate advisees and for being the most resolute champion of the 'life of the mind'.

Finally, and most importantly, this book is dedicated to my mother and father, my sister Helen, my wife Susan and son Gabriel. That gesture is an inadequate measure of the love I feel for them and my immense appreciation for all the sacrifices they have made on my behalf. My parents' and sister's tolerance for and unyielding belief in the importance of this lengthy process were steadfast and always encouraging. Susan provided morale boosts and gentle pushes when they were needed and wisdom derived from her own scholarly endeavours and publishing experiences. Gabriel simply lit up my world with his little smile. In countless ways their love made it possible for me to pursue a dream and, for that reason, the fruits of this labour are as much theirs as mine.

Abbreviations

AB	Arthur Bryant (Papers)
ACML	AntiCommon Market League
AP	Lord Avon Papers
BBC	British Broadcasting Corporation
BBC WAC	British Broadcasting Corporation Written Archives Centre
BBK	Lord Beaverbrook Papers
BD	John Biggs-Davison (Papers)
BHL	British Housewives' League
BNP	British National Party
CAB	Cabinet Files
CAP	Common Agricultural Policy
CCO	Conservative Central Office
CDS	Campaign for Democratic Socialism
CIA	Commonwealth Industries Association
CND	Campaign for Nuclear Disarmament
COA	Central Office Agent
COO	Chief Organisation Officer
CPA	Conservative Party Archives
CRD	Conservative Research Department
ECSC	European Coal and Steel Community
EDC	European Defence Community
EEC	European Economic Community
EFTA	European Free Trade Association
Euratom	European Atomic Energy Community
FBI	Federation of British Industries
FBM	Forward Britain Movement
FO	Foreign Office
GATT	General Agreement on Tariffs and Trade
HG	Hugh Gaitskell (Papers)
HMD	Harold Macmillan Diaries

KBO	Keep Britain Out
LEL	League of Empire Loyalists
LPA	Labour Party Archives
LRD	Labour Research Department
MF	Michael Foot (Papers)
NATO	North Atlantic Treaty Organisation
NFU	National Farmers' Union
OECD	Organisation for Economic Co-operation and Development
OEEC	Organisation for European Economic Co-operation
PLP	Parliamentary Labour Party
PREM	Prime Minister's Files
PRO	Public Record Office
TUC	Trades Union Congress
UN	United Nations
WEU	Western European Union

Introduction

On 24 January 1962 Prime Minister Harold Macmillan appeared on television to deliver a broad assessment of Britain's prospects for the coming year. In the midst of a souring economy and 'pay pause' controversy, he urged Britons to do 'a little bit extra' to 'earn' their place in a changing world.[1] He tempered that challenge, however, by offering assurances about the sanctity of Britain's traditional spheres of influence, its associations with the Commonwealth, the United States and Europe. Audience research exposed this as one of Macmillan's less convincing party political broadcasts. Amidst complaints about 'empty platitudes', one viewer described it as '"no more cheering than a candle in the fog"'.[2]

Public reactions apart, the speech was revealing in both its contents and its omissions. Though the Government had proffered Britain's first application to join the European Economic Community (EEC) six months earlier, the ongoing negotiations for membership scarcely featured in the Prime Minister's observations. Yet in a brief aside, one that made no direct mention of the Common Market, Macmillan counselled,

> There's one thing I think people mustn't be frightened about. Some people think that if you enter into one of these alliances or groupings, you will lose your identity. Well of course if you enter into any kind of a contract, a treaty, if you join a club … you hand over to the common pool something

---

[1] H. Macmillan, Conservative Party political broadcast, 24 January 1962, British Broadcasting Corporation Written Archives Centre, Caversham (hereafter cited as BBC WAC), Film 35/36; *The Times*, 25 January 1962; H. Macmillan, *At the End of the Day, 1961–63* (London, 1973), p. 52.

[2] BBC Audience Research Department Memo, 21 February 1962, BBC WAC, T 32/1 (440/1). Indeed, the bulk of those who were predisposed to share the Prime Minister's point of view were unimpressed, as were the 49 per cent who described themselves as 'open-minded'.

of your own liberty. But that doesn't mean that if we join one of these, that
Britain will cease to be Britain or British people to be British.[3]

However opaque the context, Macmillan's comments were clearly
designed to assuage fears about the perceived threat EEC membership
posed to national sovereignty and national identity.

Macmillan's thoughts thus constituted a reluctant response to the
subjects of this study, the opponents of Britain's first attempt to join the
EEC, between 1961 and 1963. As we shall see, the counterpoint to the
Prime Minister's cautious public posture on the Common Market was an
enthusiasm among these early Eurosceptics, known as 'anti-Marketeers',
for making Britishness the focal point. One week before Macmillan's
speech, for instance, Rene MacColl of the *Daily Express* wrote,

> Loss of identity is a disturbing condition in an individual. Cause for
> lively alarm. How much worse for a nation! A nation which – like Britain
> today – finds itself being elbowed out of its own way of doing things ... by
> the hidden persuaders inspired by Bonn, Paris and Rome.[4]

This was a typical salvo from the most voluble of the opponents. But it
was also emblematic of the primacy accorded national identity by the
anti-Marketeers.

In a broader sense Macmillan had bared one of Britain's fundamental
dilemmas over Europe. Essentially, this was the challenge of reconciling
a policy based upon a revised vision of Britain's international standing
with those sections of the public that subscribed to and in many cases
cherished older definitions of Britain's place in the world. Indeed, the
anxieties of that constituency were summarised only days later by Robin
Day, a presenter on the *Gallery* programme, broadcast by the British
Broadcasting Corporation (BBC). In a discussion with Sicco Mansholt,
a Vice-President of the European Commission, Day suggested, 'deepest
of all is the feeling that we shall, sooner or later, be sinking our national
identity into a new super-state of Europe, and thereby abandoning our
position in the Commonwealth and our freedom to conduct our own
foreign policy'.[5]

Studies of Britain's first application to join the Common Market and
the policy evolution that preceded it have tended to privilege the 'high
political' realm, that 'half-closed world peopled by senior politicians, civil

---

[3] Macmillan, Conservative Party political broadcast, 24 January 1962.
[4] *Daily Express*, 16 January 1962.
[5] *Gallery* programme, 1 February 1962, BBC WAC, Film 13/14. In January 1963 a
Crossbow article similarly noted that 'people in every party are equally and under-
standably nervous at the possible loss of national identity upon British entry to
the Common Market'. G. Pears, 'A Question of National Identity', *Crossbow*, 6:22
(January–March 1963), p. 37.

servants and publicists',[6] in Whitehall, Westminster and Brussels, over the 'low politics' of Fleet Street leader columns, national and regional pressure groups, and individual activists. Britain's self-regard, insofar as it features in such analyses, is generally cast in the realm of diplomacy, policy formation and, to a lesser extent, parliamentary politics. Traditionally this body of work has exhibited two notable trends. First, a prevailing orthodoxy characterises Britain as the 'awkward', 'reluctant' or 'detached' partner in the story of European integration.[7] A second and often related subplot has involved an attempt to identify the point at which Britain 'missed the bus', 'boat' or 'train' leading to European unity.[8]

These lines of enquiry are entirely logical. On the one hand, they reflect the structure of a policy process that was overwhelmingly conducted at official level. In the case of Britain's first application, for example, Lord Windlesham observed that 'public debate opened at the moment when the final crucial stage of decision-making closed'.[9] On the other hand, they are also natural, given the broad patterns of Britain's interaction with the early movement for European unity. In May 1950, the Labour Government declined involvement in discussions of the Schuman Plan, which led to the creation of the European Coal and Steel Community (ECSC). The same year, Britain steered clear of talks about the creation of a European Defence Community (EDC). No British officials were present at Messina in June 1955, when ministers from the ECSC member states conferred about the creation of a customs union. Instead, a minor Board of Trade official initially observed but later withdrew from the follow-up meetings, which took place in the form of the Spaak Committee. Britain was thus absent from a process that ultimately led to the ratification of the Treaty of Rome by 'the Six'

---

[6] M. Bentley and J. Stevenson (eds), *High and Low Politics in Modern Britain* (Oxford, 1983), p. 1.

[7] S. George, 'The Awkward Partner: An Overview', in B. Brivati and H. Jones (eds), *From Reconstruction to Integration: Britain and Europe Since 1945* (Leicester, 1993), pp. 179–90; S. George, *An Awkward Partner: Britain in the European Community*, 2nd edn (Oxford, 1994); S. George (ed.), *Britain and the European Community: The Politics of Semi-Detachment* (Oxford, 1992); S. Greenwood (ed.), *Britain and European Integration Since the Second World War* (Manchester, 1996); H. Young, *This Blessed Plot: Britain and Europe From Churchill to Blair* (London, 1998); J. W. Young, *Britain and European Unity, 1945–1992* (London, 1993); D. A. Gowland and A. Turner, *Reluctant Europeans: Britain and European Integration, 1945–1998* (Harlow, 2000).

[8] Examples include M. Charlton, *The Price of Victory* (London, 1983); S. Bulmer, 'Britain and European Integration: Of Sovereignty, Slow Adaptation and Semi-Detachment', in S. George (ed.), *Britain and the European Community: The Politics of Semi-Detachment* (Oxford, 1992), pp. 1–29. See also R. Denman, *Missed Chances: Britain and Europe in the Twentieth Century* (London, 1996); E. Dell, *The Schuman Plan and British Abdication of Leadership in Europe* (Oxford, 1995); E. Roll, *Where Did We Go Wrong? From the Gold Standard to Europe* (London, 1995).

[9] Lord Windlesham, *Communication and Political Power* (London, 1966), p. 29.

(Belgium, France, Germany, Italy, Luxembourg and the Netherlands) in 1957 and the formal birth of the European Economic Community and the European Atomic Energy Community (Euratom) in January 1958.

The British Government's response to Messina was Plan G, an attempt to secure trade arrangements with the EEC that preserved sovereignty and Commonwealth trade preferences, ducked the external tariff and excluded agriculture. But attempts to sell this alternative free trade area to the Six failed by the autumn of 1958 and left Continental suspicions of British motives in its wake. In 1959 Britain joined the European Free Trade Association (EFTA) of the outer 'Seven' countries, which included Austria, Denmark, Norway, Portugal, Sweden and Switzerland. But by the end of 1960, the costs of exclusion from the EEC, both political and economic, weighed upon Macmillan as he assessed Britain's world role in the context of a new 'Grand Design'. A decision to seek membership soon followed and, after convincing the Cabinet and canvassing Commonwealth capitals, a formal announcement was made on 31 July 1961. Eighteen months of prolonged negotiations followed until the French President, General Charles de Gaulle, halted the proceedings in January 1963.

These events have attracted rigorous scholarly attention following the release of official documentary evidence under the 'thirty-year rule'. James Ellison and Jacqueline Tratt inspected the upper reaches of the decision-making and policy processes that carried Britain's search for a free trade area and Macmillan's decision to seek EEC membership. Wolfram Kaiser's dissection of British policy up to 1963 concluded that the Government's actions were not so much 'awkward' as manifestations of a tactical pattern described as 'using Europe and abusing Europeans'. Piers Ludlow broke new ground by analysing the negotiation of Britain's first application from a Brussels perspective.[10] Alan Milward's 'official history' challenged the assumptions underpinning the 'missed bus' thesis by placing Britain's European stance between 1945 and 1963 in the context of broader strategic priorities relating to national security and prosperity.[11]

But the high political approach is especially ill-suited to analysis of the opposition to entry. For one thing, it risks imposing a template of Euroscepticism as a parliamentary phenomenon upon an anti-Market

---

[10] J. Ellison, *Threatening Europe: Britain and the Creation of the European Community, 1955–58* (Basingstoke, 2000); J. Tratt, *The Macmillan Government and Europe: A Study in the Process of Policy Development* (London, 1996); W. Kaiser, *Using Europe, Abusing Europeans: Britain and European Integration, 1945–63* (London, 1996); N. P. Ludlow, *Dealing With Britain: The Six and the First UK Application to the EEC* (Cambridge, 1997). See also essays in W. Kaiser and G. Staerck (eds), *British Foreign Policy, 1955–64: Contracting Options* (London, 2000).

[11] A. Milward, *The UK and European Community: Vol. 1, The Rise and Fall of a National Strategy 1945–1963*, Government Official History Series (London, 2002).

movement that orchestrated its most significant arguments and achievements outside Westminster. It is tempting for instance to accept Hugo Young's conclusion that Hugh Gaitskell was the 'first of the Eurosceptics'.[12] But this obscures the fact that the Labour leader's 'thousand years of history' speech arrived fourteen months after Macmillan announced Britain's application. In fact, the primary lines of opposition, ones Gaitskell used to dramatic effect, had been moulded and articulated by others during the interim.

In addition, the 'high politics' outlook risks unqualified acceptance of the characterisations supplied by pro-entry advocates. They were eager to consign the anti-Market movement to a lunatic fringe or, as one contemporary described it, 'an unholy alliance of Empire Loyalists and fellow travellers'.[13] Thus, while the observation that the anti-Marketeers presented an 'extreme and extremely emotional case'[14] is largely correct, it is nonetheless incomplete. Although anti-Marketeerism was invariably emotive, it was not uniform. Distinguishable shades of opposition ranged between outright xenophobia and rejections of membership carefully deduced from the terms of entry.

The Westminster orientation, in particular, also narrows evaluation of the movement through judgements of its political efficacy. Superficially, its impact seemed indeterminate and therefore inconsequential because de Gaulle's veto rather than domestic obstruction terminated Britain's application. David Cannadine, for example, described Lord Beaverbrook's *Daily Express* crusade against entry as 'ill judged and ultimately ineffective'.[15] But this misses a crucial point. As the following chapters contend, dissent of that variety was not so much 'ill judged' as inevitable, because the anti-Market world-view was beholden to versions of Britishness that were fundamentally incompatible with membership of Europe. Ultimately, therefore, top-down approaches are problematic because they furnish an incomplete appraisal of attitudes and indirect influences.

One of the remaining gaps in the study of Britain's first application is a comprehensive examination of the role of its opponents and the precise nature of anti-Marketeer sentiment. Traditionally they have been defined by partial accounts dating from the 1960s. Thus, while Miriam Camps' detailed survey referenced domestic attitudes, it took a dismissive view

---

[12] Young, *This Blessed Plot*, pp. 161–2.

[13] H. McClaren, 'Anti-Market: Profile of a Lobby', *Crossbow*, 6:21 (October–December 1962), p. 13. For examples of this tendency see J. Critchley, 'The Flat Earthers', *Spectator*, 25 May 1962, p. 677; H. Fairlie, 'The Earl of Sandwich's Crew', *Spectator*, 31 August 1962, p. 296.

[14] N. Davies, *The Isles: A History* (Oxford, 1999), pp. 924–5. Similar points are made in M. Camps, *Britain and the European Community, 1955–1963* (London, 1964), p. 506; N. Beloff, *The General Says No: Britain's Exclusion from Europe* (London, 1963), pp. 175, 178.

[15] D. Cannadine, *History in Our Time* (London, 1998), p. 247.

of the opponents of entry[16] and little notice of their activities outside Westminster. Three years after de Gaulle's veto, Lord Windlesham provided a more effective starting point by analysing public opinion and the pressures aligned both for and against the EEC application, with especial emphasis on the limited impact of the AntiCommon Market League (ACML) and Common Market Campaign. But this analysis was restricted to a single chapter in *Communication and Political Power*[17] and its conclusions about pressure group influence were formulated without access to subsequently released documents, which, this study concludes, indicate that the impact of anti-Marketeers in particular was more complex than the polls suggested. Robert Lieber's examination, though more thorough, was primarily directed towards gauging the influence wielded by elite opinion and 'sectional' pressure groups like the Trades Union Congress (TUC) and Federation of British Industries (FBI) as the European issue developed political salience. Robert Pfaltzgraff presented wider documentation of anti-Market forces but only within selected chapters of his work on British policy between 1957 and 1967.[18]

More recent studies have begun to redress the balance by providing thoroughly researched explorations of key sub-themes in the first application debate. George Wilkes and Stuart Ward, for instance, have analysed the resonance of the Commonwealth issue.[19] Nick Crowson probed the intertwining of anti-Market sentiment and local circumstances in the November 1962 South Dorset by-election.[20] Ted Bromund has investigated the 'Empire lobby', the FBI and the National Farmers' Union (NFU) between 1956 and 1963. For that reason the latter organisation is omitted from this study but also because, unlike the other pressure groups that will feature in Chapter 4, it enjoyed a client relationship

[16] Camps, *Britain and the European Community*, pp. 504–5.

[17] See ch. 6, 'Public Opinion and the Common Market', in Windlesham, *Communication and Political Power*, pp. 153–80.

[18] R. J. Lieber, *British Politics and European Unity: Parties, Elites and Pressure Groups* (Berkeley, 1970); R. L. Pfaltzgraff, Jr., *Britain Faces Europe* (Philadelphia, 1969).

[19] G. Wilkes, 'The Commonwealth and British European Policy: Politics and Sentiment, 1956–63', in A. May (ed.), *Britain, the Commonwealth and Europe: The Commonwealth and Britain's Applications to Join the European Communities* (Basingstoke, 2001), pp. 53–81. See also G. Wilkes (ed.), *Britain's Failure to Enter the European Community, 1961–63: Crises in European, Atlantic and Commonwealth Relations* (London, 1997). For discussion of the consequences of Britain's application for the Dominion relationship see S. Ward, *Australia and the British Embrace: The Demise of the Imperial Ideal* (Melbourne, 2001). See also S. Ward, 'Anglo-Commonwealth Relations and EEC Membership: The Problem of the Old Dominions', in Wilkes (ed.), *Britain's Failure*, pp. 178–99; and S. Ward, 'A Matter of Preference: Britain, Europe and the Erosion of the Old Commonwealth Relationship', in May (ed.), *Britain, the Commonwealth and Europe*, pp. 156–80.

[20] N. J. Crowson, 'Lord Hinchingbrooke, Europe and the November 1962 South Dorset By-election', *Contemporary British History*, 17:4 (winter 2003), pp. 43–64.

with the Government. Indeed as Bromund has demonstrated, the NFU sought to avoid antagonising the Conservative leadership and decided against playing the patriotic card despite its distaste for the EEC.[21] Other scholarship has helped contextualise the anti-Marketeers within the lengthier discourse of opposition to Europe. Both Nick Crowson and Anthony Forster, for example, have criticised the tendency to define Euroscepticism as a phenomenon of the late 1980s and 1990s.[22] Crowson thus incorporates Tory anti-Marketeers in his analysis of the post-war Conservative Party and European integration. Forster's broad survey of Euroscepticism adds Labour anti-Marketeers to the mix but his study, unlike Crowson's, is almost entirely the product of secondary sources. In any event, the chronological ambitions of both works allowed only intermittent focus upon the first application debate.[23]

This study is distinguished by its attempt to provide the first book-length analysis of the opposition aligned against Britain's initial application to the join the EEC and the following chapters are constructed with four overriding intentions. First, the book extends beyond existing scholarship by providing a comprehensive rendering of the views and activities of the anti-Market movement. In particular, it emphasises 'low political' protest and populism of the kind exercised by Fleet Street crusaders, pressure groups, expert pundits, constituency activists, independent parliamentary candidates, pamphleteers, letter writers and maverick MPs, among others.

Second, the book's distinctive analytic framework situates objections to Europe in the context of national identity. The central argument contends that constructions of Britishness, whether reflexive or calculated, conscious or unconscious, dominated both the genesis and the subsequent transmission of anti-Market sentiment. It was a process facilitated in part by traditional 'us' versus 'them' comparisons that juxtaposed Britons against Continental 'others'. It also included manifestations of what Michael Billig conceptualised as 'banal nationalism',[24] in which the 'unwaved flags' and symbols of nationhood were conveniently mobilised or manipulated to serve the anti-Market cause. Thus, while a reverence

---

[21] T. Bromund, 'From Empire to Europe: Material Interests, National Identities and British Policies Towards European Integration, 1956–63' (unpublished PhD dissertation, Yale University, 1999), pp. 256–7. For the full survey of the NFU see pages 134–259. The NFU is also discussed in Pfaltzgraff, *Britain Faces Europe*, pp. 95–8, and Lieber, *British Politics and European Unity*, pp. 45–54, 83–5 and 117–32.

[22] N. J. Crowson, *The Conservative Party and European Integration Since 1945* (New York, 2007), p. 7; Anthony Forster, *Euroscepticism in Contemporary British Politics* (London, 2002), p. 2.

[23] See, in particular, Crowson, *The Conservative Party*, ch. 6, 'The Conservative Sceptic', pp. 152–87; and Forster, *Euroscepticism*, ch. 2, 'Opposition to Europe, 1945–69', pp. 10–31.

[24] M. Billig, *Banal Nationalism* (London, 1995).

for national sovereignty and a desire to protect British agriculture and to preserve Commonwealth connections featured prominently, the anti-Market discourse was frequently a political expression of deeper anxieties about Britain's 'imagined community'.

Third, the book demonstrates that the impact of the anti-Marketeers was greater than previously suggested but less than its proponents hoped, precisely because the overwhelming reliance upon national sentiment was simultaneously the movement's greatest strength and greatest weakness. On the one hand, a 'nation before party' spirit animated superficial co-operation, influenced public opinion and shaped the political calculations of the Labour and Conservative parties. On the other hand, emotive arguments, particularly those articulated in xenophobic form, further marginalised the anti-Market case. What is more, the unity implied by invoking collective belonging dissolved because the national symbols and perceptions which supported its claims were imagined in disparate ways.

Finally, and in keeping with its bottom-up orientation, research for this study deliberately engaged official archives as a destination of last rather than first resort. As the bibliography indicates, it relies to a great extent upon a disparate and often unconventional body of anti-Market pamphlets, newsletters, petitions, speeches, correspondence and other materials. Extensive use is also made of personal papers of prominent anti-Marketeers, including Lord Beaverbrook, Sir Arthur Bryant and Viscount Montgomery, among others, the Conservative and Labour Party archives, BBC transcripts and, above all, issues published between 1961 and 1963 of the *Daily Express*, the most vocal critic of Britain's application.

The content of the book is further shaped by two structural considerations. It should be noted from the outset that the chapters which follow eschew a chronological format in favour of one organised around categories of opposition. In this regard, it partly replicates the strata of a protest that was fractured by means, personalities and ideological dispositions. The structure, however, is prescribed by analytic considerations. Removing the arguments from a political narrative facilitates a closer inspection of ideas in the anti-Market rationale.

In addition, references to anti-Marketeers are registered in the broadest sense. Thus, while there is much to distinguish anti-Market forces from opposition to the European Community and European Union in the decades that followed, this study accepts Anthony Forster's call for a broader use of the term Euroscepticism, 'as a particular manifestation of a school of sceptical thought about the value of Britain's involvement with moves toward supranational European integration'.[25] The detailed implications of that chronological extension, however, largely lie outside

---

[25] Forster, *Euroscepticism*, p. 2.

the contours of this study. Of greater significance therefore is the lateral extension of the definition with regard to anti-Marketeers and a slight revision to include 'schools of sceptical thought', a distinction which better captures the wide spectrum of anti-Market ideologies, identities, pressures and opinions. The analysis thus incorporates both notable and obscure groups and individuals who self-consciously aligned themselves with the movement and offered strident objections to British entry. That category included, for example, individuals like Lord Beaverbrook and John Paul, founder of the ACML. But the study also includes those who were wary of being identified with the anti-Market lobby, as in the case of former Prime Minister Anthony Eden, and others, like the historian C. E. Carrington, whose gradually evolved positions were pursued independently and predicated upon the available terms of entry rather than outright hostility to membership or latent anti-Europeanism.

Before a detailed analysis of the opponents of EEC membership is undertaken in subsequent chapters, an opening chapter presents a series of motifs which help illuminate the construction of British identities and the patriotic dimensions of the anti-Market discourse. It contends that while post-war nationalism is generally conceptualised as the outpost of extremism, a greater understanding of the phenomenon is gained from acknowledging its pervasive and therefore 'banal' relationship with the conduct of everyday life. The chapter also accounts for the dynamic through which British identities were constructed and subsequently reaffirmed. Of particular note is the propensity for 'us' and 'them' distinctions derived from comparative national typologies. Prominent benchmarks of British identity, particularly as they related to the anti-Market discourse, are also discussed.

Chapter 2 undertakes the most comprehensive examination to date of the *Daily Express* campaign against Britain's application. The chapter commences by placing the last of Lord Beaverbrook's crusades in the context of his enduring dominance over *Express* affairs, his penchant for Empire causes and a British identity defined by Dominion relationships. But it also clarifies the roles played by the *Express* staff in pursuit of the cause and demonstrates how the paper's 'common man' orientation was uniquely suited to the transmission of populist patriotism, in what became the most effective vector of anti-Market sentiment. A second section accounts for the dimensions and conduct of the campaign as manifest in the pages of the *Express*, its bid for influence outside Fleet Street and its relationships with other anti-Marketeers. The third part of the chapter argues that the *Express* articulation of an expansive British 'us' was reliant upon the juxtaposition of a foreign 'them' in European as well as Commonwealth contexts. A final section details the exploitation of identity themes as they related to everyday life and the issues of sovereignty, agriculture and Beaverbrook's lifelong pursuit of Empire Free Trade.

Chapter 3 provides new research on the pronouncements of anti-Market pundits. These included the historians C. E. Carrington, A. J. P. Taylor and Sir Arthur Bryant, as well as the economists James Meade, Roy Harrod and E. J. Mishan, and the political scientist William Pickles, at the London School of Economics. The chapter discusses the origins of their dissent and differentiates between the intractable sceptics and those whose opposition evolved from a 'wait and see' position. It highlights the divergence of opinions as the pundits contemplated historic and future Commonwealth roles and the relative merits of free trade and protectionism. But it also contends that a broad anti-Market consensus, irrespective of academic discipline, venerated national 'independence' and interpreted the Common Market's ambitions as political rather than economic. That orientation, it is suggested, invited comparisons rooted in the certainties of history, institutions and national character. As a result, technical and detached lines of reason were frequently overtaken by the rhetoric of sentiment and patriotism.

Those divisions and inclinations are more evident in Chapter 4, which expands upon existing scholarship detailing the activities of opposition pressure groups. The opening section charts the affairs of organisations defined as 'single-issue groups', ones that formed for the explicit purpose of fighting British membership. These included the ACML, Keep Britain Out (KBO) and the Forward Britain Movement (FBM). Ideological predilections for the imperial Conservative, free trade Liberal and Labour socialist traditions, respectively, it is suggested, limited their co-operation, helped define their agendas and featured in their patriotic invocations of the national interest. The second half of the chapter journeys further towards the political and nationalist margins by dissecting anti-Market fervour among 'multi-issue groups' that attached the cause to their existing programmes. It considers youth and women's groups, Protestant conspiracy theorists and Commonwealth lobbies. It also examines associations on the far right, such as the League of Empire Loyalists (LEL) and True Tories, and their counterparts on the left, the Communist Party of Great Britain and the Campaign for Nuclear Disarmament (CND).

Finally, Chapter 5 scrutinises the politics of the anti-Market issue as it related to the Labour and Conservative parties, national identity and the shape of the domestic debate. It is divided into three sections. The first takes Gaitskell's 'thousand years of history' speech at the October 1962 Labour Party conference as its starting point. It shows that, whatever Gaitskell's personal convictions, his politicisation of the domestic debate in patriotic terms shrewdly summarised the position of the growing anti-Market lobby. The section charts Labour's stance as it evolved from a 'wait and see' position, determined by fears that the Common Market issue would divide the party. It also reveals the nature of party factions, including Lord Attlee's anti-Market contributions and allegiances to the concept of a multiracial Commonwealth. In addition it discusses

Labour's robust defence of national planning prerogatives, a stance that antagonised Continental socialists. The second section of Chapter 5 discusses the machinations of dissenting Tory MPs, their organisation, rhetorical emphasis on Commonwealth and sovereignty themes and Macmillan's fears for Conservative unity. It will also look outside the Commons to the views of Tory grandees like Anthony Eden and Lord Montgomery of Alamein and show how anti-Market sympathies helped unseat a Conservative candidate at the South Dorset by-election for the first time since 1906. The third and final section evaluates the politics of propaganda. It reveals that, by adopting a cautious approach to the claims of anti-Marketeers, and by failing to engage the public with a campaign in support of entry, the Government created the scenario it hoped to avoid, namely, a hardening of public opinion against entry. The chapter reveals that Conservative Central Office's secret polling confirmed the trend in the late summer of 1962 and exposed just how far populist anti-Market forces had succeeded in creating public anxieties about threats to Britain's national character. The chapter concludes by showing that the anti-Market advances forced the Government into a publicity campaign in support of entry, one that directed most of its energies towards countering the sceptical claims.

Since the book lacks a narrative format and pursues a specific anti-Market focus, it is perhaps worth briefly reviewing the chronology of Britain's application. Macmillan claimed in retrospect, and his opponents at the time believed, that the Common Market application represented a 'turning point'[26] in British history. But whatever the historic stakes, the Government's announcement of its intention to apply on 31 July 1961 waived drama in favour of caution and conditions. After nine months of consultations with the Six, Macmillan told the Commons, Britain intended to submit an application for membership under Article 237 of the Treaty of Rome.[27] Britain would negotiate, he said,

> with a view to joining the Community if satisfactory arrangements can be made to meet the special needs of the United Kingdom, of the Common-wealth and of the European Free Trade Association.... These negotiations must inevitably be of a detailed and technical character, covering a very large number of the most delicate and difficult matters. They may, there-fore, be protracted and there can, of course, be no guarantee of success.[28]

In the debates that followed, vocal opponents on both sides of the House aired their views, including Conservative MP Anthony Fell,

---

[26] Macmillan, *At the End of the Day*, p. 1.

[27] Article 237 of the Treaty of Rome set out the provisions for EEC expansion, under which prospective countries submitted applications for membership.

[28] *Parliamentary Debates*, Commons, 5th Series, vol. 645, 31 July 1961, col. 930.

who referred to the Prime Minister as a 'national disaster'.[29] But the Commons ultimately voted 313 to 5 in favour of Macmillan's decision. Approximately twenty Conservative MPs abstained, along with the bulk of the Parliamentary Labour Party (PLP), whose leadership had adopted a noncommittal position 'on the fence'.

A confluence of domestic circumstances appeared favourable to Macmillan's endeavour. These included the support of the FBI, financial interests in the City of London and provisional approval from the TUC. In Parliament, as we shall see in Chapter 5, Macmillan was wary of internal dissent. But only one Conservative MP had voted against the Government and a partisan edge to the Common Market debate languished until the autumn of 1962. The Liberals had favoured joining the EEC since the late 1950s and adopted a resolution calling for negotiations at their 1960 annual conference. Hugh Gaitskell, sensing Labour divisions over Europe and recovering from the party's bruising debates over unilateral disarmament and Clause IV, immediately adopted a 'wait and see' position. Thus, though anti-Market factions forwarded their arguments at their respective party conferences in the autumn of 1961, motions against entry were easily defeated.

Meanwhile, Fleet Street editorial support for an entry policy had evolved since 1960 and by the summer of 1961 included *The Times* and *Sunday Times*, the *Mail*, *Mirror*, *Financial Times*, *Guardian*, *Observer* and *Telegraph* as well as other publications such as *The Economist*, *Encounter* and the *Spectator*. The lone voices of dissent among Fleet Street's major players emanated from the Beaverbrook stable.[30] Pro-entry pressure groups had also stirred in anticipation of the announcement. In January 1961 the Common Market Campaign was organised under the leadership of Lord Gladwyn, Roy Jenkins and Peter Kirk. In May it drafted a document in support of accession that was signed by 140 prominent officials, parliamentarians, economists, academics, journalists and business leaders.[31]

Other omens were more ambiguous. As pollsters discovered, the persistence of a sizeable and potentially capricious 'undecided' constituency was a defining characteristic of the domestic debate. Even the narrow *Daily Express* question 'Are you for or against Britain joining

---

[29] *Parliamentary Debates*, Commons, 5th Series, vol. 645, 31 July 1961, col. 934.

[30] In addition to Beaverbrook's *Express* newspapers, a clutch of smaller publications also protested against entry. These included the *Daily Worker*, *Reynolds News*, *New Statesman* and *Tribune* as well as the free trade oriented *City Press*. See G. Wilkes and D. Wring, 'The British Press and Integration: 1948 to 1996', in D. Baker and D. Seawright (eds), *Britain For and Against Europe: British Politics and the Question of European Integration* (Oxford, 1998), pp. 190–2.

[31] *The Times*, 25 May 1961. It also commenced publication of *Common Market Broadsheet* in July 1961. The Common Market Campaign was an offspring of the Federal Union, an organisation created in 1938 to study and promote federalism.

the Common Market?' yielded 'uncommitted' responses that ranged between 33 and 38 per cent from August 1961 to January 1963.[32] Gallup polls showed that support for membership hovered between 40 and 50 per cent through much of the period, but fluctuations in opinion tended towards a hardening against entry.[33] In addition, anti-Market organisations quickly materialised. The FBM staged its first press conference in June 1961, KBO formed in August and the ACML commenced its public meetings in October. Their early arguments, like those forwarded by the *Daily Express*, exploited patriotic sentiment and narrowed the points at issue to a choice between Commonwealth and Common Market.

Darker clouds loomed on the horizon. For one thing, Macmillan had gone on record with pledges, however ambiguous, to secure 'satisfactory' terms for EFTA, British agriculture and the Commonwealth. Given its past record, Britain also needed to demonstrate the sincerity of its approach. Most of all, Macmillan knew he had to overcome the suspicions and obstruction of the French President, General de Gaulle.

In his 10 October 1961 opening speech to the Six in Paris, Edward Heath, the Lord Privy Seal and leader of Britain's delegation to the negotiations, outlined his country's requirements for special consideration.[34] Entry talks began in Brussels on 8 November but there was little demonstrable progress through the spring of 1962. Negotiators faced difficulties in rationalising the needs of Commonwealth countries. These included the question of temperate zone foodstuffs exported by Australia, Canada and New Zealand. But the developing economies of the New Commonwealth also sought special consideration for their manufactures, raw materials and agricultural products. The Six, meanwhile, were preoccupied with internal negotiations over the creation of the Common Agricultural Policy (CAP) until mid-January 1962. But that in turn exercised leaders of the NFU, because the agreed CAP formula generated agricultural subsidies by way of levies rather than through the British system of guaranteed prices and deficiency payments. It also played into the hands of anti-Marketeers, who propagated fears that the Continental system heralded dearer food prices for British consumers.

An initial breakthrough in the negotiations arrived at the end of May 1962 with an agreed formula for the gradual implementation of the

---

[32] For examples of its polls results see *Daily Express*, 30 December 1961, 28 February, 24 March, 25 September, 21 December 1962 and 22 January 1963.

[33] Social Surveys (Gallup Poll) Ltd, 'British Attitudes to the EEC, 1960–63', *Journal of Common Market Studies*, 5 (1966), pp. 49–61; J. Spence, 'Movements in the Public Mood: 1961–75', in R. Jowell and G. Hoinville (eds), *Britain into Europe: Public Opinion and the EEC, 1961–75* (London, 1976), pp. 19–23. See also J. Moon, *European Integration in British Politics, 1950–63: A Study of Issue Change* (Aldershot, 1985), pp. 205–7.

[34] Subsequently published as *The United Kingdom and the European Economic Community*, Cmnd 1565 (London, 1961).

Common External Tariff on Commonwealth manufactures, up to 1970. But the conundrums of British domestic agriculture and temperate zone exports remained intractable. Despite hints of progress and marathon negotiating sessions, talks were suspended for the summer holidays on 5 August. With further meetings postponed until October, Macmillan faced the prospect of hosting the Commonwealth Prime Ministers' Conference with only a partial outline of the terms of entry.

Unfortunately for the Government, the first advances in Brussels had coincided with a deterioration of public confidence. At its 5 July meeting, the Cabinet observed a 'noticeable swing in public opinion' against British membership.[35] Indeed, a *Daily Mail* poll in late June pointed to a 20 per cent decrease in the support for entry since April.[36] The anti-Market movement, as we shall see, had gathered momentum throughout the spring and summer of 1962. The *Daily Express* pushed its protest to greater heights with calls for a general election and articles written by prominent opponents. A proliferation of anti-Market literature included *A Call to the Commonwealth* by Conservative MPs Peter Walker and Derek Walker-Smith, as well as *A Choice for Destiny* by Sir Arthur Bryant.[37] The FBM, meanwhile, hosted an all-party 'Britain–Commonwealth–EFTA conference' in the House of Commons committee rooms in July and rallies in support of the Commonwealth were scheduled for late August and early September.

Though the attitude of the Commonwealth Prime Ministers during the 10–19 September meetings was 'rather more critical than had been expected',[38] the Government finessed a final communiqué out of revised statements. In fact, the final document left Britain free to decide on entry without requiring approval from a further Commonwealth meeting.[39] By this time, however, the Common Market issue was acquiring its partisan contours. In the immediate aftermath of the conference Macmillan and Gaitskell made television appearances on consecutive nights. Aware of the application's faltering public image, the Prime Minister issued a forceful statement of the Government's case for entry. Gaitskell replied with the first expression of his claim that British entry on available terms would mean the 'end' of both the Commonwealth and Britain's

---

[35] Public Record Office, Kew, London, Cabinet Files (hereafter cited as PRO, CAB) 128/36, Part II CC 44(62), 5 July 1962.

[36] *Daily Mail* poll reprinted in the *Daily Express*, 4 July 1962.

[37] P. Walker and D. Walker-Smith, *A Call to the Commonwealth: The Constructive Case* (London, 1962); A. Bryant, *A Choice for Destiny: Commonwealth or Common Market* (London, 1962).

[38] F. Bishop, memo to PM, 'Commonwealth Conference – Cabinet', 19 September 1962, Public Record Office, Kew, London, Prime Minister's Files (hereafter cited as PRO, PREM) 11/3662.

[39] 'Meeting of Commonwealth Prime Ministers, 1962 – Final Communiqué', copy in PRO, PREM 11/3652.

'thousand years of history'.[40] Any doubts about Labour's emerging position evaporated in the following two weeks. On 29 September it released its statement of the five conditions for entry, while Gaitskell again evoked the 'thousand years of history' during his notorious patriotic address to the Labour Party conference at Brighton on 3 October.[41]

Gaitskell's attack galvanised Conservative unity, as evident during the overwhelming defeat of the party's anti-Marketeers at its Llandudno conference. But continuing Labour attacks, lack of resolution in Brussels, a November by-election loss at South Dorset, attributed to anti-Marketeer influence, and rising anxiety about the terms in Fleet Street and elsewhere bred pessimism, especially when combined with the Government's other mounting difficulties. Polls at the end of November, Macmillan confided in his diary, put the Government ten percentage points behind Labour.[42]

The 'special relationship' with the United States and de Gaulle's attitude towards British entry were ongoing features of Britain's diplomacy with France. But in December those two issues peaked, just as talks in Brussels were stalling, this time over British agriculture. On 15–16 December, Macmillan met with de Gaulle at Rambouillet, where Britain's orientation towards Europe was discussed, as it had been at Chateau de Champs in June 1962. But on this occasion French antipathy was clearer. In the meantime, America had announced the cancellation of its Skybolt missile project, a weapon Britain planned to purchase after the demise of its own Blue Streak programme in 1960. When Macmillan reached a deal with President Kennedy for the purchase of Polaris missiles, only days after Rambouillet, the agreement provided de Gaulle with an opportune vindication of his questions about Britain's ties to the United States. Presented with a similar offer from Kennedy, de Gaulle dutifully declined.

Below the worsening relationship between Macmillan and de Gaulle, those responsible for securing agreements negotiated with greater haste. Earlier in December, the Mansholt Committee had been charged with finding a way through the agriculture impasse. But de Gaulle arrested the proceedings at a press conference at the Elysée Palace on 14 January 1963. Britain's links to EFTA, the United States and the Commonwealth and the unique character of its agricultural support system, he contended, made it unsuitable for membership. In a summation of his

---

[40] *The Times*, 22 September 1962.

[41] Labour Party National Executive Committee, *Britain and the Common Market* (London, 1962). Gordon Brown, when Chancellor of the Exchequer, perhaps unintentionally set the same number of conditions for British adoption of the single currency.

[42] Harold Macmillan Diaries, Department of Special Collections and Western Manuscripts, Bodleian Library, Oxford (hereafter cited as HMD), 29 November 1962, MS Macmillan dep. d. 47.

reasoning, he suggested that 'the nature, the structure, the very situations that are England's differ profoundly'[43] from those of Europe. A fortnight later, despite diplomatic attempts to save the negotiations, Britain's first application collapsed. 'De Gaulle is trying to dominate Europe', a frustrated Macmillan told Kennedy. 'It is the end – or at least the temporary bar – to everything for which I have worked for years'.[44]

<hr />

[43] *The Times*, 15 January 1963.
[44] H. Macmillan to President Kennedy, 28 January 1963, quoted in Macmillan, *At the End of the Day*, p. 366.

1

National identity and Britishness

Analysis of national identity is overwhelmingly a process of deconstruction. But any study acknowledging the complexities of patriotic sentiment must also involve a process of reconstruction. In other words, it is one thing to label manifestations of nationalism as extremist, insular or derived from fallacious assumptions and quite another to examine their pervasiveness and appeal. The following discussion of national identity, envisaged as a series of leitmotifs rather than a rigid analytic structure, is designed to help illuminate the synergy between nationalist thought and anti-Market activism in the chapters that follow. In the process, it addresses the following questions. First, what theoretical constructs might help account for the endurance of nationalism in a globalising era? Second, what mechanisms facilitated the imagination of British identities and what dynamics sustain visions of national uniqueness? Finally, what particular components of British identity were manifest in the first application debate or lent themselves to manipulation in the anti-Market discourses?

Post-1945 nationalism – the theoretical perspective

The need to reconcile an age of globalisation with the persistence of nationalist fervour poses the greatest challenge to any consideration of nationalism and national identity after 1945. Some analysts regard the dichotomy as a feature of the decreasing validity and relevance of nation states. The acceleration of economic interdependence, the internationalisation of trade, technological and communications innovation, and the globalisation of political issues, not to mention wholesale shifts in the patterns of cultural consumption, have all been cited as symptoms of the nation state system in decline. A host of multinational acronyms, including the UN, GATT, IMF, NATO, NAFTA and, for the purposes of this study, the EEC and latterly the EU, are offered as institutional proof. Concurrently, however, one must account for the national aspirations of post-colonial states as well as the nationalist movements within 'established' states. Is it possible to reconcile the two apparent contradictions? What is the condition of nationalism in the older nation states? How might theoretical answers to those questions contribute to an understanding of why the integrative agenda of the EEC provoked such strong nationalist reactions among those who opposed British membership?

A notable 'modernist' interpretation offered by Eric Hobsbawm ascribed nationalism to the grand era of nation building and regarded its current incarnations as negative, spasmodic kicks against an encroaching and inevitable globalisation. In the 1992 edition of *Nations and Nationalism Since 1780*, he contended that 'nationalism, however inescapable, is simply no longer the historical force it was in the era between the French Revolution and the end of imperialist colonialism after World War II'.[1] With the superseding of national economies, nation states will be seen 'primarily as retreating before, resisting, adapting to, being absorbed or dislocated by the new supranational restructuring of the globe. Nations and nationalism will be present in this history, but in subordinate, and often rather minor roles.'[2]

Though compelling, this modernist and Marxist interpretation is limited by a tendency to dismiss nationalism as a misplaced energy or false consciousness, rather than analysing its contemporary manifestations. But Hobsbawm's work raises two further difficulties. First, any theory binding the fate of nationalism to economic reductionism underestimates the importance of social or cultural factors. In an alternative vision, Ernest Gellner acknowledged the forward march of industrial and economic development and subsequent degree of cultural congruence. But, given the intricacies of industrial culture and its links to the political realm, he predicted a modification rather than the elimination of nationalism,[3] one in which it 'persists, but in a muted, less virulent form'.[4] Anthony Smith was more critical of economic determinism's failure to adequately address 'the historic cultural and social components of ethnic organisation and identity',[5] as well as of 'modernist' views equating nationalism with the rise of the nation state. His broader reading of national identity points to the enduring significance of pre-national bonds, characterised as 'looser collective cultural units' or 'ethnies',[6] to whom modern nations are indebted.

---

[1] E. Hobsbawm, *Nations and Nationalism Since 1780* (Cambridge, 1992), p. 169.
[2] *Ibid.*, p. 191.
[3] E. Gellner, *Nations and Nationalism* (Oxford, 1983), p. 119.
[4] *Ibid.*, p. 122.
[5] A. D. Smith, *Nations and Nationalism in a Global Era* (Cambridge, 1995), p. 72.
[6] *Ibid.*, p. 47. See also A. D. Smith, *National Identity* (London, 1991) and 'National Identity and the Idea of European Unity', *International Affairs*, 68:1 (1992), pp. 55–76.

Smith reconciles the globalisation and fragmentation dichotomy by attributing both phenomena to the same source. Ironically, closer contact between nations, as in the example of European integration, 'encourages' rather than discourages 'ethnic and historical comparison and proliferation of fragmenting ethnic nationalisms'.[7]

The second major difficulty with the 'decline of nationalism' thesis is its predilection for consigning nationalism to the fringe. Hobsbawm, for instance, laments the descent of nationalism into xenophobia, 'which rarely ever pretends to be more than a cry of anguish or fury'.[8] In fact, this view of nationalism, as distinct from a laudable civic-minded patriotism, passes almost unquestioned. Older 'established' nations customarily regard nationalism as the preserve of foreign or irrational elements. Thus, according to widespread belief, 'The English do not need nationalism nor do they like it'.[9] This might be defined as one of the most ironic of English conceits, a nationalist sentiment exposed by the process of its denial. Domestically, nationalist outbursts are also seen as the preserve of the desperate or irrational. That aspect of the modernist framework is especially problematic for this study, because it reinforces the tendency to relegate anti-Marketeers to an irrelevant extreme.[10] In this case, in other words, theory further marginalises the political margins.

A fundamental understanding of nationalism must acknowledge the extent to which national identity lies at the heart of contemporary existence. Benedict Anderson claims that 'nation-ness is the most universally legitimate value in the political life of our time'.[11] For Anthony Smith, despite their occasions of excess, 'the nation and nationalism remain the only realistic basis for a free society of states in the modern world'.[12] The most compelling view suggests that, far from waning, nationalism is so much a part of our world-view as to defy recognition. 'Banal nationalism' as defined by Michael Billig involves a complex of 'ideological habits' in which the nation is 'flagged' via politics, culture and the common aspects of daily life. It is called nationalism because it is devoted to representations of nationhood and it is 'banal' by virtue of its familiarity.[13]

---

[7] *Ibid.*, p. 145. See also P. Hassner, 'Beyond Nationalism and Internationalism: Ethnicity and World Order', *Survival*, 35:2 (summer 1993), pp. 59–60.

[8] Hobsbawm, *Nations and Nationalism*, p. 170.

[9] R. Colls and P. Dodd (eds), *Englishness: Politics and Culture, 1880–1920* (London, 1986), p. i.

[10] In a more recent example, *The Economist*'s view of nationalism at the height of the 1996 'Beef War' suggested 'Something embarrassing is happening in Britain. If it goes no further it could perhaps be ignored by this island's more thoughtful inhabitants and by Britain's European neighbours as merely, well, the last desperate gamble of a fading government.' *The Economist*, 25 May 1996.

[11] B. Anderson, *Imagined Communities: Reflections on the Origins and Spread of Nationalism* (London, 1983), p. 3.

[12] Smith, *Nations and Nationalism in a Global Era*, p. 147.

[13] Billig, *Banal Nationalism*, p. 6.

As a leitmotif that underscores some of the discussion of identity in the chapters that follow, Billig's conception of the 'banal' is especially helpful because it retrieves nationalism from the margins and from moments of exception. 'The metonymic image of banal nationalism', Billig writes, 'is not a flag which is being constantly waved with a fervent passion; it is the flag hanging unnoticed on the public building'.[14] A host of banal signifiers, including press, money, language, postage, songs and imagined homelands, all point to a conception of national place and reinforce a sense of natural order. Thus, it would be wrong to assume that nations progress beyond nationalism and the need for national symbols. In fact, a national identity, properly considered, 'is a form of life, which is daily lived in the world of nation states'.[15]

The ubiquity of banal nationalism is also significant because it speaks to the ease with which anti-Marketeers played the national card. In other words, opposing Europe on patriotic grounds did not necessitate a complicated search for flags to wave, because so many were readily at hand. Those included the grand themes invoked by anti-Market agitators such as parliamentary sovereignty, Dominion allegiance or World Wars sacrifice. But it also meant that the *Daily Express*, for example, could call upon symbols from daily life, such as cuisine or the British policeman, and juxtapose them against the traditions of European 'others'. Nor did the meanings attached to symbols or symbolic rhetoric require much explication. When he noted how Prime Minister John Major effortlessly invoked the phrase '"thousand years of history"' in a 1992 speech on sovereignty and the Maastricht Treaty, Billig might just as easily have referenced Hugh Gaitskell's use of the same phrase thirty years earlier at Labour's Brighton conference. 'He could refer to a thousand years of national history without mentioning any historical detail', Billig wrote:

> These were commonplaces in themselves. It was enough to remind the audience (or 'us') that 'we' have existed for a thousand years in 'our' unique manner. The speaker could presume that his audience would well understand, or recognize, that the nation possessed its own distinctive national identity.[16]

Those examples are also notable because they highlight the importance Billig accords media and politicians in the process of 'flagging' nationhood. If 'political discourse, which is grounded in the national context ... and employed in the practice of representation' and 'newspapers, like politicians claim to stand in the eye of the country',[17] then

---

[14] *Ibid.*, p. 8.
[15] *Ibid.*, p. 69.
[16] *Ibid.*, p. 72.
[17] *Ibid.*, pp. 98, 114.

those forums offer an ideal vantage point for examining national themes in the European debate. That is particularly relevant for analysis of anti-Marketeers, who were so thoroughly immersed in identity questions.

But there are dangers in overstating the effortlessness of mobilising banal nationalism. The most prominent flags of national representation in the Common Market debate did not wave themselves. It should also be noted that 'not all flags are waved … in the same vigorous manner'.[18] Thus, while the anti-Marketeers proved adept at manipulating banal symbols, their most spirited banners were sometimes also ethnocentric. Moreover, national symbols could be accorded different meanings both among those who propagated the messages and among those who consumed them. Though pro-Marketeers were far less likely to invoke patriotic symbolism, it was nonetheless the case that the banal trappings of the World War II experience, for example, could provide either a rationale for EEC entry or grounds for rejecting membership. Similarly, hoisting the Commonwealth banner was by no means a guarantor of unity among anti-Marketeers. As we shall see, Commonwealth advocates split between those who accorded primacy to its newer members and those who championed kinship relationships with the older Dominions.

Imagining Britishness

Prior to examining elemental components of Britishness, the dynamic through which those elements are imbued with meaning and assimilated into versions of national identity deserves attention. First, if nations are 'imagined communities', as Anderson suggests,[19] contemporary national identity is a function not merely of an original imagination but also of the extent to which the nation is re-imagined. Thus, nationalism, as Smith argues, is best understood as a process that incorporates the 'attainment and maintenance of autonomy, unity and identity',[20] interspersed with moments of more intense reflection, self-awareness or insecurity. This is also consistent with the dynamism described in Billig's assertion that nations are not simply imagined but reproduced daily.

Second, as recent historical debate has shown, the meaning of British history is subject to considerable temporal variation.[21] The same, however, might be said of identity. In fact, such is the complexity of British consciousness that some objections to European membership owe more

---

[18] *Ibid.*, p. 103.

[19] Anderson defined the nation as 'an imagined community – and imagined as both inherently limited and sovereign'. *Imagined Communities*, p. 4.

[20] Smith, *Nations and Nationalism*, pp. 148–9.

[21] D. Cannadine, 'British History as a "New Subject"', in A. Grant and J. K. Stringer (eds), *Uniting the Kingdom? The Making of British History* (London, 1995), p. 24.

to the experience of Flanders or Dunkirk and veneration of 'the thousand years of history' than to the implications of the Treaty of Rome or the eventualities of Maastricht.

Third, an acceptance of the continuing presence of nationalism must by extension recognise the electoral imperatives by which all parties attempt to align their policies with a proclaimed pursuit of the national interest. One of the conundrums for this study, however, is the difficulty of determining whether objections to Common Market membership constituted instinctive, emotive reactions of national identification or cynical, politically motivated appeals. On occasion, personal reactions appeared to transcend political interest, creating improbable anti-Market alliances and muting the partisan edges of the Common Market debate until the autumn of 1962. In other instances, multiple cases for and against European entry have led to contentious and politicised battles over the legitimacy of patriotic credentials. As Michael Foot (later a leader of the Labour Party but a rebellious backbencher in the early 1960s) complained, 'We on the left are very resentful of these bloody Tories who try to come along and pinch patriotism as if the bloody thing belonged to them'.[22]

Fourth, allegiance to the nation does not preclude other forms of identification. Smith has distinguished between a 'pervasive, collective' identity and more individualistic, 'situational' identities conditioned by various factors, including region, family, class, religion and ethnicity.[23] Thus, Britishness, understood as a 'superimposed'[24] identity, coexists with sub-national, regional or local loyalties. Accepting this duality does not necessitate exclusive choices. In fact, British identity displays both collective and situational aspects in varying degrees. On the one hand, Britishness has been described as a collective but somewhat distant abstraction reflected in relations with the outside world and bound up with diplomatic, military, imperial and institutional images and symbols.[25] On the other hand, Britishness is 'a source of personal identity ... an occasional rather than a constant presence'.[26] As subsequent chapters will show, the most vociferous opponents of the first application subscribed to a range of keenly imagined versions of collective Britishness. But their voices were also augmented by the inclusion of those for whom

---

[22] Interview with Michael Foot, 27 October 1998. This statement resembles George Orwell's contention that 'Patriotism has nothing to do with Conservatism. It is actually the opposite of Conservatism, since it is a devotion to something that is always changing and yet is felt to be mystically the same.' G. Orwell, *The Lion and the Unicorn: Socialism and the English Genius* (1941, London, 1982 edn), p. 115.

[23] Smith, *Nations and Nationalism*, pp. 123–4.

[24] L. Colley, 'Britishness and Otherness: An Argument', *Journal of British Studies*, 31:4 (October 1992), p. 316.

[25] R. Samuel (ed.), *Patriotism: The Making and Unmaking of British National Identity* (London, 1989), vol. 1, p. xiii.

[26] *Ibid.*, p. xv.

a particular situation, namely the implied external threat of the Treaty of Rome, aroused an identifiably British reaction.

Fifth, Britishness may, ironically, be sustainable precisely because of, rather than in spite of, the vague or limited nature of its earliest definitions. Lawrence Brockliss and David Eastwood have questioned the extent to which Linda Colley's early 'Britons'[27] subscribed to a pervasive cultural identity. Accordingly, the cohesion of the eighteenth- and nineteenth-century Union 'depended not on the creation of a hegemonic British identity but on the availability of institutions and symbols which offered a means of identifying with Britain'.[28] If we extend Brockliss and Eastwood's logic, the historic predominance of multinational state allegiance over cultural considerations may indeed help account for the ability of a British identity to survive the intervening centuries and, more recently, the end of Empire, accession to the EEC and membership of the European Union, despite the worst fears of the anti-Marketeers. Thus, the viability of Britishness as an identity may rest not in the imposition of a flattening Britishness from above, but rather in the ability of its multinational components to secure viable positions within the British state which allow for the continued fulfilment of both situational and collective identities.

Finally, nationalists imagine themselves and their nations as unique and the anti-Marketeers were no exception. Despite their claims, however, national uniqueness does not exist *a priori*. Rather it is conceptualised, more often than not, from an 'us' versus 'them' process of comparative differentiation. Thus, if the imagined community emerges from positive claims of who 'we' are, it arises equally from negative comparisons.[29] 'Quite simply', Linda Colley observed, 'we usually decide who we are by reference to who and what we are not'.[30] That process is therefore contingent. As Billig notes, in order to imagine '"our" nation in all its particularity, it must be imagined as a nation amongst other nations ... an international context which needs to be imagined every bit as much as does the national community'.[31]

While a persistent belief in national uniqueness is characteristic of patriotism in established European nations, Britain has been singled out as a particularly 'awkward partner'. According to the thesis, Britain's 'awkward' reputation and lack of *communautaire* spirit derives from unique circumstances, actual or imagined, a shared complicity of external and domestic considerations. But the 'awkward partner' claim, with its implication of a British *Sonderweg* or unique historic path, has invited

---

[27] L. Colley, *Britons: Forging the Nation 1707–1837* (New Haven, 1992).

[28] L. Brockliss and D. Eastwood (eds), *A Union of Multiple Identities, the British Isles c. 1750–1850* (Manchester, 1997), p. 195.

[29] E. Said, *Orientalism* (New York, 1978), p. 54.

[30] Colley, 'Britishness and Otherness', p. 311.

[31] Billig, *Banal Nationalism*, p. 83.

criticism. According to Wolfram Kaiser, 'the *Sonderweg* thesis of British post-war history adopts the myth, created by the British political elite, of British exceptionalism'.[32] Kaiser is correct to highlight the exaggerations of British uniqueness. But exceptionalism as a belief represents assumptions of a pervasive nature, beyond a mere national vision created and imposed by a high political subset. Likewise, the notion of British uniqueness as an analytic device is merely the partial fulfilment of a legacy of Whiggish historicism, if not the entire tradition of writing national histories. Less nationally inclined comparative historicism has also highlighted the extent to which Britain's semi-detached developmental path was different from that of its European neighbours,[33] even if the notion of a *Sonderweg* was overplayed by historians.[34] Kaiser is also correct to condemn the *Sonderweg* methodology for its absence of a comparative European perspective.[35] Ironically, however, such criticism misses the paradox. A *Sonderweg*, even if it discourages comparative analysis, owes its very existence to a comparative context.

The components of Britishness

This section is not designed to facilitate a full deconstruction of Britishness into its constituent parts. In addition to being incomplete, such a catalogue could diminish the extent to which identity might be imagined as collective while also underestimating the banal dimensions of experience, memory and socialisation. The intention instead is to illustrate some major components and complexities of 'imagined' Britishness that contributed to the conduct of the European debate and the trajectory of anti-Market dissent in particular. That process also serves as a reminder that Britishness is a collection of identities rather than a singular, monolithic entity.[36] As we shall see, the forces aligned against EEC membership could venerate similar symbols of Britishness but invest them with entirely different values or meanings, a tendency which may help explain the lack of unity within the movement as a whole.

Uncertain definitions

In the early 1960s, challenging questions about Britain's international role and domestic fitness were paralleled by a creeping unease with the definition of 'British', as reflected in the subtleties of terminology. There

---

[32] Kaiser, *Using Europe*, p. 211.
[33] N. Davies, *Europe: A History* (Oxford, 1996), p. 13; T. Nairn, *The Break-Up of Britain: Crisis and Neo-Nationalism* (London, 1977), pp. 14–19.
[34] Brockliss and Eastwood, *A Union of Multiple Identities*, pp. 207–8.
[35] Kaiser, *Using Europe*, p. xvii.
[36] A. Barnet, 'After Nationalism', in Samuel (ed.), *Patriotism*, vol. 1, pp. 148–9.

is danger in placing undue emphasis on the significance of language. Indeed, to speak of Britain or Great Britain was often simply a matter of linguistic convention. The term applied to a range of imagined intentions, from isolationist Little England to expansive Greater Britain. Nonetheless, a tendency to demand greater precision from the term 'Britain' exposed emerging fault lines in the domestic, Commonwealth and European contexts of identity along which future debate would spread.

In 1941 George Orwell observed 'that we call our islands by no less than six different names, England, Britain, Great Britain, the British Isles, the United Kingdom and, in very exalted moments, Albion'.[37] For, Orwell however, internal differentiations were a 'minor point',[38] much less important than the two nations, rich and poor. Yet, by the 1960s, disputes over meaning betrayed uncertainties. A. J. P. Taylor's Preface to *English History 1914–1945* recognised the extent to which the previous generation's broad use of the term 'England' was subject to a 'more rigorous' nomenclature in 1965. Taylor lamented that 'whatever word we use lands us in a tangle'[39] and dismissed the problem by writing an English history in the Whiggish, Anglo-centric tradition of the Oxford Series. He incorporated what he labelled the 'lesser breeds' of Scotland, Wales and Ireland 'when they made a difference in English affairs as they often did. So no one minded my pedantry.'[40] Of course, subsequent historians objected to Taylorian pedantry, criticising both the terminology and the assumptions from which it emerged. In the following decade, J. G. A. Pocock's 'Plea for a New Subject'[41] highlighted the desire for a more inclusive historical consideration of Britishness, on a four-nations model.[42]

Uncertainty over the definition of 'British' was equally apparent in the fundamental reassessments occasioned by decolonisation. In official circles a 1961 suggestion from Duncan Sandys, the Secretary of State for Commonwealth Relations, that Commonwealth countries adopt usage of the noun 'Britain' and adjective 'British' rather than 'United Kingdom'[43] aroused a degree of unease requiring Cabinet-level discussion. For Norman Brook, the Cabinet Secretary, questions of definition amounted

---

[37] Orwell, *The Lion and the Unicorn*, p. 47.

[38] *Ibid.*, p. 47.

[39] A. J. P. Taylor, *English History 1914–1945* (Oxford, 1965), p. v.

[40] A. J. P. Taylor, *A Personal History* (New York, 1983), p. 236.

[41] See in particular, J. G. A. Pocock. 'British History: A Plea for a New Subject', *Journal of Modern History*, 47:4 (December 1975), pp. 601–28. See also essays by J. G. A. Pocock and D. Cannadine in A. Grant and K. J. Stringer (eds), *Uniting the Kingdom? The Making of British History* (London, 1995).

[42] For examples, see Colley, *Britons*; Davies, *The Isles*; H. Kearney, *The British Isles: A History of Four Nations* (Cambridge, 1989); K. Robbins, *Great Britain: Identities, Institutions and the Idea of Britishness* (London, 1998).

[43] Note on discussion between PM and Commonwealth Secretary, 20 January 1961, PRO, PREM 11/3652.

to more than 'a minor matter of nomenclature'. His catalogue of reservations included both the legalistic insufficiency of the term 'Britain' and its omission of Northern Ireland. Of greater concern, however, was the likelihood of causing offence among both the Dominions, 'where there are still many people who like to think of themselves as "British" and new Commonwealth members who might associate the terms with an attempt to revive an imperial spirit'.[44] By the time of the 1962 Commonwealth Conference, 'British' terminology had been officially adopted, but not until after consultation with the Prime Ministers of Canada, Australia and New Zealand.

The implications of application to and eventual membership of the European Community forced Britons to confront their European credentials. However, the fundamental question of Britons as Europeans is significant as much for its presence as for its absence in the political discourse. In the first application debate, anti-Marketeers seized upon the logical extremes of membership, the *Daily Express* bleakly asking readers, 'Do you want to be British?'[45] The doomsday scenarios of the anti-Marketeers were matched by the Macmillan Government's cultivated nonchalance over the consequences of membership. When not avoiding the issue publicly, Macmillan soft-pedalled the political implications of the Treaty of Rome for national identity. In the debates that followed his 31 July 1961 presentation of application intentions to the Commons, Macmillan assured his audience, 'I am bound to say that I do not see any signs of the members of the Community losing their national identity because they have delegated a measure of their sovereignty'. Of federalism he noted, 'Europe is too old, too diverse in tradition, language and history to find itself united by such means'.[46]

The historic schizophrenia in Britain's European policy is overwhelmingly characterised by an unwillingness to redefine Britishness in an integrated European framework. The architects of entry policy assumed Britons would eventually need to be taught to be 'good Europeans'.[47] But as David Marquand complained, 'no-one managed to invent a new British identity centred upon a new European destiny. Edward Heath tried, but failed. No-one else even tried.'[48] During the first application debate, as we shall see in Chapter 5, British policy was constrained by

---

[44] N. Brook to Home Secretary, 27 March 1961, PRO, PREM 11/3652.

[45] *Daily Express*, 6 January 1962.

[46] Macmillan, *At the End of the Day*, pp. 22–3. For a fuller text of his 2 August 1961 speech see *Parliamentary Debates*, Commons, 5th series, vol. 645, cols 1482–91.

[47] E. Heath to H. Macmillan, 7 February 1961, PRO, FO 371/158264/12, quoted in Kaiser, *Using Europe*, p. 150.

[48] D. Marquand, 'How United Is the Modern United Kingdom?', in A. Grant and K. J. Stringer (eds), *Uniting the Kingdom? The Making of British History* (London, 1995), p. 288.

the need to prove European credibility in Brussels while maintaining patriotic British credentials at home.

History

In the summation of his case against the outmoded nation state, Uwe Kitzinger noted, 'A nation's identity is not imposed on it by the past'.[49] The implication of a choice about 'who we are' accords well with the theoretical notion of nations as manufactured or imagined. This contrasts, however, with practical beliefs in the deep significance of 'who we were'. The past, if not an agent of imposition, is nonetheless a profound force of condition.

If the community is imagined, so too is the conceptualisation of its own past. The relative youth of nation states thus contrasts with the belief in the timelessness of nations.[50] Hence the apparent contradiction between the birth of the British nation state in 1707 and a broader reverence for the 'thousand years of history'. National history straddles the paradox. Chronicles of the past legitimise the ancient aspects of belonging, codify the uniqueness of national mythology and celebrate the previous sacrifices upon which the present and future depend. If nationalism is assumed to incorporate a 'complex dialectic of remembering and forgetting',[51] then historians, as custodians of the past, are inevitably crucial to the process.[52]

History as a transcendence of the present is nonetheless, in its narrative assumptions, a product of its time. It is also a product of its own methodological past. At the time of the first application, populist British histories were notable for the preponderance of Anglo-centric, Whig assumptions. As we shall see in Chapter 3, the recruitment of historians such as Arthur Bryant and A. J. P. Taylor to the anti-Market cause had significant consequences for the context of the European question. In particular, opposition to Europe was reinforced by both the breadth of populist historical interpretations and the depth of an ageing tradition, rich with established symbols, myths and assumptions. Yet, if the celebratory histories of national institutions, destiny and character seemed increasingly out of touch with contemporary realities, its hold nonetheless remained considerable.[53] Even recently, the spirit of the traditional national story and the patriotism of Thatcher and Major

---

[49] U. Kitzinger, *The Second Try: Labour and the EEC* (Oxford, 1968), p. 48.

[50] Anderson, *Imagined Communities*, pp. 11–12.

[51] Billig, *Banal Nationalism*, p. 37; E. Hobsbawm and T. Ranger (eds), *The Invention of Tradition* (Cambridge, 1983), p. 13.

[52] R. Samuel, *Theatres of Memory* (London, 1994), pp. x, 430; P. Mandler, *History and National Life* (London, 2002), p. 13.

[53] D. Cannadine, 'British History', pp. 13–17.

resonated more with Prime Minister Stanley Baldwin's inter-war odes to Englishness[54] than the pleas of Pocock for a more expansive and sophisticated consideration of British history.

Generation

To speak of a particular national memory is misleading if it is taken to imply a concrete consensus sensed equally across time among the members of the nation. The plural, national memories, allows for subjectivity and the importance of personal experience and is therefore more appropriate. Nonetheless, we generally tend to designate and classify beliefs or experiences as typical of a particular age or generation. A typology of the ages, not entirely unlike the 'us' and 'them' of nationality, thus gives rise to the 'post-war generation', 'Edwardians', 'Victorians', and so on. Reference to 'the sixties', for instance, conjures images of a generational sea change. Yet, for some contemporary analysts, the early 1960s typified an enduring ebb tide. Anthony Sampson's *Anatomy of Britain*, published in 1962, for example, highlighted the sense of a burdensome legacy and creeping malaise. In his concluding chapter Sampson wrote, 'All through this book I have felt haunted by the Victorians, who invented so many of the institutions which we now work'.[55] But he also differentiated his surroundings as suffering, 'unlike the Victorians, from an oppressive lack of innovation and zeal'.[56]

A break from the ethos of the past was crucial to supporters of the Common Market application in particular. For many pro-Europeans, membership of the Common Market would offer a welcome shock, however vaguely defined, to a British system perceived as complacent. Roy Jenkins, appearing in a debate on the BBC's *Panorama* programme one week before the formal announcement of Britain's intention to apply, supported membership 'because I think what we need at the present time in this country is a shake-up. I think we've got insular, inward looking and sluggish.'[57] The corollary of presenting membership as a forward-thinking policy was a depiction of anti-Marketeers as beholden to a previous age. Thus, in the same debate, Jenkins described his fellow

---

[54] For accounts of inter-war British identity see K. Lunn, 'Reconsidering "Britishness": The Construction and Significance of National Identity in Twentieth Century Britain', in B. Jenkins and S. Sofos (eds), *Nation and Identity in Contemporary Europe* (London, 1996), pp. 83–100; S. Nicholas, 'The Construction of National Identity: Stanley Baldwin, "Englishness" and the Mass Media in Inter-War Britain', in M. Francis and I. Zweiniger-Bargielowska (eds), *The Conservatives and British Society, 1880–1990* (Cardiff, 1996), pp. 126–46.

[55] A. Sampson, *Anatomy of Britain* (London, 1962), p. 620.

[56] *Ibid.*, p. 638.

[57] *Panorama*, 24 July 1961, BBC WAC, Film No. 31/32.

panellists, Michael Foot and Viscount Hinchingbrooke, as 'nostalgic old imperialists'.[58]

Likewise, at diplomatic level, Macmillan's attempt to convince France of Britain's European credentials hinged partly upon the presentation of the Common Market application as the natural policy of a new generation. It was a point Macmillan emphasised on at least two occasions during his meetings with de Gaulle at Chateau de Champs in June 1962.

> It was in his view clear that Britain was ready to accept the policy of closer association with Europe. This was perhaps less true among the older generation, but the young were no longer attracted by the ideals of Empire which had thrilled the generation brought up on Kipling and they were looking for a new vision. This they would find in the European ideal.[59]

The meaning accorded to events, myths or symbols is conditioned by one's proximity to them. The personal, experiential aspect of identity thus helps explain the seemingly irrational or unexpected, whether it be Gaitskell's Brighton speech or Beaverbrook's persistence. As we shall see, much anti-Market sentiment betrayed an older nostalgic British identity precisely because so many of its exponents were themselves products of an earlier age.

Geography

If identity involves fundamental questions of 'who we are' or 'who we were', it is equally influenced by perceptions of 'where we are'. Ironically, Britain is both more and less than Metternichian 'geographic expression'. In strict cartographic terms, 'Britain' is insufficient compared with the more inclusive 'United Kingdom of Great Britain and Northern Ireland'.[60] And yet the most expansive definitions of British soil, kinship and citizenship have extended well beyond the Isles proper to include imperial lands and subjects. The geographic component of identity thus holds a unique duality, defined on the one hand by physical bounded space and on the other by what Edward Said described as an 'imaginative geography'.[61]

Imagined geography, crucial to the formulation of 'us', is equally notable for the construction of conceptual boundaries and categorisation of others. According to the axiom celebrated in poetry and prose, Britain's separation from the Continental landmass shaped the development and

---

[58] *Ibid.*
[59] Record of Conversation at Chateau de Champs, 3 June 1962, PRO, PREM 11/4019.
[60] Billig, *Banal Nationalism*, p. 78.
[61] Said, *Orientalism*, p. 54.

destiny of the 'offshore islanders'. Far more important than the separation is its imagined meaning, the manner in which that separation is endowed with significance. This may help explain why the English, for instance, attributed a different set of characteristics to the Irish, their other 'offshore island' neighbours. Thus, the breach of the divide, symbolic or otherwise, by immigrant, bomber, tunnel or treaty has been interpreted in varying degrees as a threat to British identity. A contemporary reference to Common Market opponents as 'Flat Earthers'[62] perhaps unintentionally highlighted the imagination–geography link. For the Little England tradition in particular, the Treaty of Rome amounted to the violation of a natural order pre-ordained by the physical geography of the English Channel, guaranteed by the inviolability of the nation state and sanctified by its inevitable historically imagined product, the 'thousand years of history'.

Commonwealth/Empire

Nowhere are the depth and significance of the imperial experience in the British psyche more ambiguous than in the apparent contradiction between the historic experience of Pax Britannica and the process of decolonisation. For most analysts, the Empire was crucial to the imagining of Britishness, and debate, where it exists, generally centres upon questions of degree. For some, Britain's historic uniqueness from the European 'other', real or imagined, lay in the experience of Empire.[63] For others, the soul, if not the very existence, of Great Britain depended upon inextricable links to the imperial domain. According to David Marquand, Empire amounted to a British 'vocation, their reason for being British as opposed to being English, Scots or Welsh. Shorn of Empire, "Britain" had no meaning'.[64]

But what of decolonisation? Superficially, domestic experience of the 'Wind of Change'[65] would appear to contradict the implied depth of attachment to imperial adventure. Apart from its pace and scale, decolonisation was notable for the relative lack of domestic political trauma.[66] In reality, however, the comparative absence of disruption

---

[62] Critchley, 'The Flat Earthers', p. 677.
[63] Brockliss and Eastwood, *A Union of Multiple Identities*, p. 208; Colley, 'Britishness and Otherness', pp. 324–35; Davies, *Europe*, p. 13; Nairn, *The Break-Up of Britain*, pp. 19–24, 69–70.
[64] Marquand, 'How United Is the Modern United Kingdom?', p. 288.
[65] The phrase was used by Macmillan in his 3 February 1960 speech to the South African Houses of Parliament and referred in particular to the growth of nationalism in Africa and to the emergence of independence movements in general. For a full text of the speech see H. Macmillan, *Pointing the Way, 1959–1961* (London, 1972), pp. 473–82.
[66] Robbins, *Great Britain*, pp. 302–3.

suggests an assemblage of diverse rather than shallow imperial meanings. As the differentiation and allegiances implicit in the distinction
between the Dominions and New Commonwealth suggested, the variety
of imaginative and experiential Empire visions[67] tempered the overall
impact of imperial decline.[68]

The first application debate mirrored the ambiguous significance of
Empire and Commonwealth. Inevitably, Commonwealth interests loomed
large in the negotiation process. In the wake of a stormy Commonwealth
Economic Consultative Council meeting at Accra in September 1961,
Macmillan described the Commonwealth presence as 'the crucial issue
in the negotiations'.[69] Yet, as a strategic question, the Commonwealth
exercised rather less power than the rhetoric of the public debate implied.
In fact, with the exception of Accra and the 1962 Commonwealth Conference, much of the application process is notable for the absence of
co-ordinated Commonwealth agitation. Commonwealth quiescence
was partly secured by Government issue management, a process which
included opaque pledges to Commonwealth interests, emphasis on the
conditional nature of the application and a focus on political rather than
economic motivations. More importantly, however, a lack of unity within
the Commonwealth itself meant that opposition, when it did exist, was
fragmentary in nature. The fundamental alterations to Empire occasioned by decolonisation were manifest in the composition and outlook
of the Commonwealth. For a Dominion leader like Australian Prime
Minister Bob Menzies, change destroyed the cosy familiarity of the old
structure. In a letter to Macmillan he wrote, 'The plain English is that
the new Commonwealth has nothing like the appeal for us that the old
one had. It appears to have no instinct for seeking or obtaining unity.'[70]
Ultimately, Commonwealth leaders seemed largely resigned to British
entry or were placated by Macmillan's pledges to obtain 'satisfactory'
arrangements. As a result, overseas opposition focused more on the
terms of entry than on the principle of British membership.

Whatever the international realities of the New Commonwealth,
domestic aspects of the European debate suggested the lingering
vitality of the Commonwealth to British identity. In a September 1961
Gallup poll, 48 per cent of respondents rated the Commonwealth as
most important to Britain, while the United States and Europe lagged

---

[67] J. M. MacKenzie, *Propaganda and Empire: The Manipulation of British Public
Opinion, 1880–1960* (Manchester, 1984), pp. 1–2. See also J. M. MacKenzie, 'The
Popular Culture of Empire in Britain', in J. M. Brown and W. R. Louis (eds), *The
Oxford History of the British Empire: Vol. 6, The Twentieth Century* (Oxford, 1999),
pp. 213–31.
[68] Robbins, *Great Britain*, p. 303.
[69] H. Macmillan to E. Heath, 14 September 1961, PRO, PREM 11/3560.
[70] R. Menzies to H. Macmillan, 15 January 1962, PRO, PREM 11/3665.

behind, with 18 and 19 per cent, respectively.[71] For anti-Marketeers the Commonwealth was a central, and in many cases the primary, motivation for objection to Europe. The proximity of European overtures to decolonisation facilitated emotional if simplistic criticisms of British foreign policy. 'Commonwealth not Common Market' became the most prominent slogan of an opposition that equated the British application with a betrayal of Commonwealth obligations. Domestically, as we shall see, differentiation between the 'Old' and 'New' Commonwealth was equally manifest in competing anti-Market rationales. Inevitably, the Dominions featured most prominently in a sentimental approach typical of the *Daily Express*. The timeworn Beaverbrook plea for Empire Free Trade, an ill-defined structure that encouraged imperial free trade within the secure confines of an external tariff, owed more to his failed 1929–31 Empire Crusade and the spirit of Joseph Chamberlain than the realities of post-war politics. Its Greater Britain approach emphasised racial, linguistic, institutional and historic unity. A second vision, typical of Labour opposition, equated a multicultural Commonwealth more with an internationalist future than an imperial past. Accordingly, a wider grouping based on British democratic ideals and expanded patterns of trade offered global rather than insular regional solutions to questions of peace and prosperity.

Sovereignty

For all its historic resonance, the idea of a Commonwealth trade alternative only flickered in vague plans at the margins of the first application debate and had all but vanished by the time of British entry. In contrast, the implications of integration for national sovereignty have emerged as the most enduring feature of Britain's European debate. To some degree, the political volatility of the sovereignty issue is a measure of anti-Marketeer and Eurosceptic success in portraying integration as a threat to an unwritten constitution, Parliament, monarchy, judicial system and the components of self-governance. To a greater extent, however, sovereignty lends itself to deeper imaginative truths, relating to national identity. If we assume the nation to be 'an imagined political community and imagined as both inherently limited and sovereign',[72] then suggestions of federalism appear to challenge the definition of 'us' at its most fundamental level. Moreover, integration clashed with identity because national institutions, most often aligned with parliamentary democracy, were frequently upheld as keystones in the evolution of Britain and virtues of Britishness. Those institutions were perceived as

---

[71] Social Surveys (Gallup Poll) Ltd, 'British Attitudes', p. 53.
[72] Anderson, *Imagined Communities*, p. 6.

offering the basis for a collective relationship with the British state, one that transcended local and regional identities.

Set in a Common Market context, British institutions were credited with preserving national uniqueness because they were comparatively non-European in character. Popular reverence for Britain's democratic achievement held sway for many on both the left and the right. As a result, Britain's parliamentary model was upheld as offering superior structural and philosophical lessons for recently defeated Europeans and newly independent territories alike.

There is disagreement about just how important sovereignty was to British policy. David Marquand, like the devotees of the 'awkward partner' thesis, sees the diffusion of power to European institutions as anathema to the traditional sensibilities of British policy makers.[73] For Wolfram Kaiser, government posturing on the sovereignty issue is all about domestic considerations. 'A large majority of the Conservative governing elite', he claims, 'has never cared much for the concept'.[74] In fact, the divergent assessments, taken together, point to the truth. The dilemma presented by European integration is embodied in a clash between the practical realities of international politics and the popular understanding of the sovereignty concept.[75] If the European project is dedicated to the preservation of the nation state,[76] then a flexible interpretation of sovereignty is imperative for its success. Thus, for a pro-European like Roy Jenkins,

> the real issue is not how you can preserve the greatest degree of that rather sterile concept of sovereignty but rather how you can most increase the country's influence.... And I don't see – committed long-term European that I am – the full federal form of the United States of America ever working in Europe. The differences are too great.[77]

But the pragmatic version of sovereignty collides not only with its orthodox conceptualisation but also with the potency of that concept in the public mind. As Ulf Hedetoft argues, 'sovereignty is the central building block in the wall of national identity', where people do not distinguish 'between sovereignty as an attribute of the state and as their own cultural property'.[78]

---

[73] Marquand, 'How United Is the Modern United Kingdom?', p. 284.
[74] Kaiser, *Using Europe*, p. 209.
[75] U. Hedetoft, 'The State of Sovereignty in Europe: Political Concept or Self-Image', in S. Zetterholm (ed.), *National Cultures and European Integration* (Oxford, 1994), pp. 13–48.
[76] A. Milward, *The European Rescue of the Nation State* (London, 1992).
[77] Interview with Lord Jenkins of Hillhead, 18 November 1998.
[78] Hedetoft, 'The State of Sovereignty', p. 17.

The anti-Marketeers, as we shall see, thus capitalised by depicting sovereignty as an all-or-nothing proposition and the EEC as a supranational federalist bogey. Nor was this lost on the Government, whose unease was exacerbated by voices from abroad. In November 1962, a time of increased public opinion concerns, Macmillan's private secretary, Philip de Zulueta, complained,

> One thing which does rather worry me at the moment are the number of speeches which are being made particularly by members of the Commission explaining how inevitable political federation is if we go into the Common Market.... If you saw Monsieur Monnet you might be able to impress upon him that this sort of talk now is very unhelpful to the cause of European unity since it alarms the people in this country.[79]

Throughout the entire first application episode, as will become evident in Chapter 5, fears about the actual threat to sovereignty were superseded by the Government's unwillingness to discuss the topic in public.

Religion

The extent to which a religious dimension is included within a national identity depends largely upon whether religion is held to be an institutional, formal or primary component. If nationalism is accepted as an ostensibly modern and secular phenomenon,[80] it would be expected to display a decreasing debt to religion over time. The British case is no exception. Linda Colley's account of early British identity suggested that, by virtue of its juxtaposition against Continental and specifically French Catholicism, 'Protestantism was the foundation which made the invention of Great Britain possible'.[81] While the exact depth and unity of Protestant British identification are open to question,[82] there is no doubt about a religious component to the early British 'we'/European 'other' formula. Nor was religion absent from British identities in the century that followed the Act of Union, whether conditioned by a Nonconformist conscience, Ulster Unionism or the notion of the Church of England as a Tory pillar. But what of a religious dimension to Britishness in the second half of the twentieth century? If, as Colley suggests, 'God

---

79 P. de Zulueta to H. Macmillan, 14 November 1962, PRO, PREM 11/3796. At the time Monnet was President of the Action Committee for the United States of Europe, a lobbying organisation he had founded in 1955.
80 Billig, *Banal Nationalism*, p. 77.
81 Colley, *Britons*, p. 54. For a longer view on the role of religion and vernacular, see Adrian Hastings' critique of Hobsbawm, Gellner and the 'modernists'. A. Hastings, *The Construction of Nationhood: Ethnicity, Religion and Nationalism* (Cambridge, 1997), pp. 4–5, 35–65.
82 Brockliss and Eastwood, *A Union of Multiple Identities*, p. 1.

had ceased to be British',[83] how might an enduring religious aspect be manifest in the British 'us' before the Common Market 'them'?

The continuing relevance of the religion and identity question owes less to formal religion than to a more banal legacy of cultural antecedents. While guarding against a depiction of nationalism as the inevitable, necessary beneficiary of religious decline, the secular avenue does provide nationalism with religious–cultural impulses.[84] Creation mythology, mysticism, self-sacrifice, ritual and paths to immortality feature in the development and persistent vanities of national uniqueness. If God was no longer British, there was nonetheless a profound legacy of divine grace and subscription to a 'chosen people' designation, articulated in both subtle and overt forms. Surprisingly, appeals to a Protestant 'us', normally confined to Ulster politics, appeared at the edges of the debate over Europe. A hybrid of centuries-old religious prejudice and fundamentalist biblical scholasticism combined with contemporary politics to fuel a small but adamant anti-Europeanism. The ominously titled Treaty of Rome and the prominence of Christian Democrat leaders in the EEC heralded papal domination among Protestant conspiracy theorists. Less explicit but more prevalent anti-Marketeer appeals drew upon instances of quasi-religious exception. As we shall see, Beaverbrook's opposition to the Common Market was proclaimed a crusade, pursued with evangelical zeal and couched in a spirit of moral superiority. More commonly, the experience of war, particularly the miracle of Dunkirk and the profound triumph of good over Nazi evil, suggested an element of divine grace.

War

Nowhere is the conception of an 'other' more potently defined than in war and a military dimension is regarded as central to the genesis and re-imagining of British identity. For Linda Colley, Britain 'was an invention forged above all by war'.[85] Accordingly, Britishness as a collective identification emerged from the protracted eighteenth-century conflict with France and the subsequent development of Empire, during which Britons thought in terms of commonality rather than division.

The twentieth-century experience of total war, and World War II in particular, is overwhelmingly cited as a mitigating factor against early British participation in the European project and the absence of a more *communautaire* spirit. In this critique, Britain's World War II experience was insular despite the global dimensions of the conflict, because of the symbolic values attached to 'the Blitz' and the Battle of Britain in particular. That 'Britain alone' triumphalism buttressed a

---

[83] Colley, *Britons*, p. 374.
[84] Anderson, *Imagined Communities*, pp. 11–12.
[85] Colley, *Britons*, p. 5.

sense of national uniqueness, elevated distinctions between Britons and Continental 'others', and affirmed the perception of an extra-European dimension to national interest.[86] For some historians, the longevity of those themes in the patriotic discourse of both the experience of war and the experience of war as remembrance is taken as proof of their depth. A number of variations play on the critical theme. For Ken Morgan, Britain's ongoing fixation with victory framed an inability to embrace post-imperial modernity.[87] Whereas war experience featured prominently in the minds of the vanquished, 'Great Britain, almost uniquely in the contemporary world, has remained cribbed, cabined and controlled by recollections of victory'.[88] For Wolfram Kaiser, the mobilisation of populist, nostalgia-ridden prejudices remains part of a wider, more obstructive and politically motivated 'British tradition of using Europe and abusing Europeans'.[89] In February 1999, Germany's Minister of Culture suggested that 'There is only one nation in the world that has decided to make the Second World War a sort of spiritual core of its national self, understanding and pride'.[90]

The reality of British war memories is perhaps rather more complex than these judgements suggest. Nonetheless, critics are correct to highlight the central importance of war memories and imagery. If, indeed, British youths are 'so immersed in war-movie clichés that their attitudes as well as their language ... are conditioned to the point of being knee-jerk reactions',[91] this might be taken as a sign of just how banal and therefore easily manipulated the World War II experience has become.

The extent to which a 'never again' mentality featured in the thinking of both pro- and anti-Marketeers revealed the intensity of the British experience of both World Wars and the fact that banal nationalism informed both sides of the first application debate. For anti-Marketeers, the war provided emotionally charged fodder, blending recent memory with a seamless historicism in which Hitler and Mussolini appeared as heirs

---

[86] For examples see D. Reynolds, 'Britain and the New Europe: The Search for Identity Since 1940', *Historical Journal*, 31:1 (1988), p. 227; Robbins, *Great Britain*, pp. 48, 53; Young, *Britain and European Unity*, p. 169.

[87] K. O. Morgan, 'The Second World War and British Culture', in B. Brivati and H. Jones (eds), *From Reconstruction to Integration: Britain and Europe Since 1945* (London, 1993), p. 33.

[88] *Ibid.*, p. 45. For more of his views on World War II in the post-war political psyche see K. O. Morgan, *Britain Since 1945. The People's Peace*, 3rd edn (London, 2001), pp. 3–28.

[89] Kaiser, *Using Europe*. For a shorter exposition of his thesis see W. Kaiser, 'Using Europe and Abusing the Europeans: The Conservatives and the European Community, 1957–1994', *Contemporary Record*, 8:2 (1994), pp. 381–99.

[90] *The Times*, 14 February 1999.

[91] *Guardian*, 16 February 1999. For contemporary analysis of German stereotypes in the British press see the essays by H. Husemann, J. Brooker and D. Head in E. Rainer (ed.), *Stereotypes in Contemporary Anglo-German Relations* (London, 2000).

of the Armada and Napoleon. But the war featured in the pro-Common Market position as well. In the winter of 1962, Macmillan offered Bob Menzies the political rationale behind the British application:

> By folly and weakness on the one side, and incredible wickedness on the other, Europe has twice pulled itself to pieces in a single generation.... Of Germany you can never be sure. There are some fine with good ideas; but owing to the tragic defeat of the two legions of Varus in the first century and the fact that the Romans retired from the Elbe to the Rhine, there is always a streak of barbarism in the German people. It is a kind of smouldering fire which can easily be fanned up into a roaring flame.
> It is for this reason, apart from any economic question, that I have very slowly come to the conclusion that we ought, and indeed that we must, try to have a political influence in Europe.[92]

How far Macmillan subscribed to such a historical rationale, intended as it was for a sceptical Commonwealth leader, is open to question. In proposing membership as an antidote to fears over Germany, Macmillan was no doubt trying to spike the guns of the opponents. However, the political justification indicated a negative reasoning for entry and implied a profound lack of trust. The language and attitude, whether rooted in fear or playing up to fear, betrayed the considerable weight of the recent past and traditional typology of the 'other'.

Conclusion

Nationalism in modern nations amounts to more than an occasional patriotic impulse or fringe xenophobia. Far from decaying at the margins of society before globalising intrusions, nationalism has become a defining element of contemporary existence. The inconspicuous nature of such nationalism is symptomatic of the depth of its assimilation. Nationalism, as Michael Billig has argued, is banal by virtue of being pervasive.

Thus, Britishness amounts to more than the experience of a European 'other' in its genesis, perpetuation and contemporary manifestations. But the rise of the EEC and the implications of membership cast British identities into realms of doubt and crystallised perceived uncertainties. Admittedly, the Britishness of the anti-Marketeers generally involved the preservation of specifically imagined national identities rather than the re-imagining of new ones. The extent to which this was the case is perhaps best highlighted by the paucity of alternatives offered to the denounced Common Market. This is not to suggest that Britishness was an overwhelmingly Conservative concept. Leftist opponents campaigned

---

[92] H. Macmillan to R. Menzies, 7 February 1962, PRO, PREM 11/3665, T/51/62.

against British entry on what they considered fundamentally sound socialist and patriotic grounds. In fact, a proliferation of unlikely partnerships across the political divide indicated that elements of Britishness were indeed banal. As Macmillan remarked in his memoirs, 'The new alliance between the extreme Right and extreme Left was very queer. It was ridiculed by someone who said he had lived to see "Butskell" replaced by "Silverbrooke".'[93]

---

[93] Macmillan, *At the End of the Day*, p. 26. See also HMD, 5 August 1961, MS Macmillan dep. d. 43. The 'Silverbrooke' term paired Labour MP Sidney Silverman with Conservative MP Viscount Hinchingbrooke.

2

The *Daily Express* and the anti-Market campaign

Since 17 July 1933 a red cartoon Crusader has adorned every copy of the *Daily Express*. Bearing a sword and the shield of St George, the Crusader rises from the upper right corner of the headline in tribute to the Empire Free Trade aspirations of its one-time owner, Max Aitken, Lord Beaverbrook. The *Express* enhanced the tradition in 1951 by shackling its Crusader in chains. The restraints, Beaverbrook promised, would remain until a Tory Government with an Empire policy governed Britain. The emergence of the Common Market debate in 1961, however, further animated Beaverbrook and Crusader alike. In a renewed and vigorous attack on perceived enemies of the Commonwealth, Beaverbrook pledged 'I will take the chains off the Crusader the day the Common Market is beaten'.[1]

As both symbolic device and barometer of literal intent, Beaverbrook's chained icon affords convenient access to the world-view of the *Daily Express*. Spiritually, the Crusader manifested an ethos of moralistic dissent and a quest through battle for honour, if not immortality. Moreover, as the public knew, the Crusader's implied meanings accorded with the character and aspirations of its owner. Cartoon representations of an armour-clad Beaverbrook begged comparisons. Was the Crusader Don Quixote or bold knight-errant?

In fact, the imposition of chains suggested a further analytic duality. For the *Daily Express*, shackles symbolised the failure of successive British Governments to secure unity and prosperity through Commonwealth policy. But from a detached perspective, the Crusader might be regarded as a prisoner of his own restraints. In a national identity context, for instance, the Crusader appears ensnared by the representation of a distinctive British national identity increasingly at odds with its contemporary surroundings.

---

[1] Beaverbrook to F. Bidlake, 26 June 1962, Lord Beaverbrook Papers, House of Lords Records Office, London (hereafter cited as BBK) F/3.

Beaverbrook's shackled knight and his campaign against British membership of the EEC derived from a devotion to the imperial vision of Joseph Chamberlain. Empire was an *Express* template as well, one that predated Beaverbrook's ownership, from November 1916. In April 1900 the first edition of Arthur Pearson's *Daily Express* had declared 'Our policy is patriotic; our party is the British Empire'.[2] After assuming control of the paper, Beaverbrook campaigned for imperial unity, with slight thematic variations, until his death in 1964.

Beaverbrook's disciples linked the Common Market to a demonology of unfulfilled Commonwealth trade options. Accordingly, the 1932 Ottawa Agreements, the 1945 US loan, the 1947 General Agreement on Tariffs and Trade (GATT) and restrictions imposed by the 1961 loan from the International Monetary Fund (IMF) had all distracted Britain from its path to greatness.[3] Following as it did on the heels of Suez and the 'Wind of Change', the Common Market application added further links to the chains. Beaverbrook complained to Prime Minister Harold Macmillan, 'This policy runs against the faith of the *Daily Express* in the Commonwealth, a traditional and ineradicable clause in our creed'.[4]

Despite its loose employment of the terms 'Empire' and 'Commonwealth', the underlying *Express* focus was clear. The real Commonwealth, the Beaverbrookian 'us', was equated with the white Dominions. Identification with the older Commonwealth was a function of ethnicity, shared history and kinship. Readers of the Beaverbrook press encountered Britons, Canadians, New Zealanders, Australians and many white inhabitants of Africa as members of a family. A. J. P. Taylor presented a good example in the *Sunday Express*:

> Call it sentiment, emotion, anything else you like. The fact remains that the nations of the Commonwealth are our brothers and sisters, and that foreign countries are not. The fact is true in the most literal sense. Millions of people in Canada, in Australia and in New Zealand are our relations by blood. When they or their ancestors left this country, they did not cease to be British. They went to the colonies or the Dominions in order to remain British. They took with them an allegiance to our institutions, to our soil, to our common past.[5]

Other *Express* writers suggested that an elevation of European over Commonwealth priorities would lead to the termination of British identity and nationhood. *Sunday Express* editor John Junor concluded,

> When the Commonwealth is finished, so is Britain. There then is the extent of our peril. It is real and deadly. It is quite certain that the next

---

[2] *Daily Express*, 24 April 1900.
[3] *Daily Express*, 10 October 1961.
[4] Beaverbrook to H. Macmillan, 28 November 1961, BBK C/235.
[5] *Sunday Express*, 3 December 1961.

few months will decide whether the Empire that started with the first Elizabeth is to end with the second.[6]

The 'Commonwealth not Common Market' slogan had meanings that exceeded mere questions of trade.

Yet the imperial components of an imagined British 'us' must not obscure the extent to which *Express* identity was also shaped by its perceptions of the wider world. *Daily Express* identity was a nationally imagined product of belonging and not belonging, in equal measure. Thus, while the definition of a Beaverbrookian 'us' depended upon a Dominion-inclusive conception of Greater Britain, it likewise required the juxtaposition of a foreign 'them'. As we shall see, a variety of 'others' provided contextual variations but invariably led to equations of Britishness versus otherness.

British identity composed in opposition to the Common Market was product and process in the exploitation of an 'us' and 'them' dichotomy. 'Cross the English Channel tomorrow and you will be abroad', the *Express* claimed. 'Cross to the other side of the earth ... you will be at home'.[7] Beaverbrook's crusade, however, amounted to more than an exercise in self-affirmation or bias against foreign association. At its logical extremes the Common Market imperilled a British 'way of life'. According to George Gale,

> Britain is required to lose itself in Continental Europe the spirit of whose laws and temper of whose political institutions are radically different from and inferior to our own.... The identity of this country is infinitely too valuable a possession to ourselves and our children, to Europe, to the Western Alliance, to the world, for it to become lost in the Continental land-mass.[8]

Historical treatments of Beaverbrook's life devote little attention to his anti-Market campaign. The well known contradictions and ambiguities of Beaverbrook's persona have muddied the waters. As one of his former employees suggested, 'To pin him down is like trying to trap a globule of quicksilver with your thumb'.[9] Beaverbrook's character inspired strong reactions from his contemporaries. The BBC's Lord Reith wrote of him, 'To no one is the vulgar designation "shit" more appropriately applied'.[10] But Beaverbrook collected loyal, if sometimes unlikely

[6] *Sunday Express*, 22 October 1961.

[7] *Daily Express*, 6 August 1961.

[8] *Daily Express*, 1 August 1962.

[9] A. Draper, *Scoops and Scandals: Memoirs of a Fleet Street Journalist* (London, 1988), p. 56.

[10] Lord Reith quoted in R. Allen, *Voice of Britain: The Inside Story of the Daily Express* (Cambridge, 1983), p. 109.

devotees. A. J. P. Taylor, his official biographer, 'loved him more than any man I ever met'.[11] Michael Foot looked upon Beaverbrook as a second father.[12] The dominance of admirers and former employees among the ranks of biographers led to a preponderance of anecdote over analysis.[13] In most accounts, Beaverbrook's post-war activities have appeared as a *dénouement*, with his final crusade adding a brief coda. Chisholm and Davie's[14] comprehensive biography, for instance, devotes approximately one page to the 1961–63 campaign.

Yet, as this chapter argues, the *Daily Express* campaign deserves more extensive consideration, precisely because its significance lies beyond either its viability or the immediacy of its political impact. The ultimate importance of the campaign emerges instead from the philosophical traditions and banal assumptions framing its construction, content and deployment. The zealous objections to the Common Market were the political expression of deeper imperatives, forced upon the world-view of the *Express* by a particular vision of 'imagined community'. In this regard, the Crusader wielded a double-edged sword. At one edge, Beaverbrook propaganda was employed in attack, a conscious manipulation of symbols for explicit political ends. At the other edge, the Crusader's sword defended a British identity imagined in minute detail. To use Michael Billig's metaphor (see Chapter 1), the *Daily Express* waved its flags with vigour in part because it found so many unwaved flags at its disposal.

This chapter evaluates the roots, nature and centrality of national identity issues employed by the *Express* during its pursuit of the anti-Market campaign. The first section argues that *Express* opposition was imperative, given Beaverbrook's editorial control and his vision of British identity. But, as we shall see, staff collusion and assumptions about the audience also shaped the message. Second, the chapter examines the parameters and methods of Beaverbrook's campaign, both within and outside Fleet Street. The third section details the extent to which the *Express* definition of a British 'us' overwhelmingly required the comparative presence of a foreign 'them'. A fourth section examines manipulation of the banal components of identity, both as a defence of a

---

[11] A. J. P. Taylor, *Beaverbrook* (London, 1972), p. 632.

[12] M. Foot, 'Beelzebub', in L. Gourlay (ed.), *The Beaverbrook I Knew* (London, 1984), p. 81.

[13] T. Driberg, *Beaverbrook: A Study in Power and Frustration* (London, 1956); D. Farrer, *G – For God Almighty: A Personal Memoir of Lord Beaverbrook* (London, 1969); Gourlay, *The Beaverbrook I Knew*; P. Howard, *Beaverbrook: A Study of Max the Unknown* (London, 1964); C. M. Vines, *A Little Nut Brown Man: My Three Years with Lord Beaverbrook* (London, 1968); A. Wood, *The True History of Lord Beaverbrook* (London, 1965). Each author was either in the personal employ of Beaverbrook or employed by Beaverbrook Newspapers Ltd. Beaverbrook even reviewed the manuscripts of work by Driberg and Howard before publication.

[14] A. Chisholm and M. Davie, *Beaverbrook: A Life* (London, 1992).

British way of life and as part of a discourse on issues of national sovereignty, agriculture and Commonwealth trade. The chapter concludes by highlighting the tensions and contradictions inherent to the campaign.

The 'Voice of Britain'

As the self-proclaimed 'Voice of Britain', the *Daily Express* spoke by nature and design to an imagined 'Middle Britain' rather than 'Middle England'. Commercial imperatives played a part, especially since northern and Scottish editions had been published since the late 1920s. As *Express* veteran Chapman Pincher noted, 'there was no alternative when the paper had big sales in Scotland and Wales'.[15] Terminology suggested that it was also a matter of banal assumptions. According to John Junor, editor of the *Sunday Express* from 1954 to 1986, reference to Britain or Great Britain in the early 1960s was 'simply a matter of using the language of the day'.[16] But Beaverbrook was fountainhead of the *Express* approach in both its conscious and its unconscious forms. His personal identity and methods of control, the complicity of the *Express* staff and assumptions about the nature of the audience all heralded an expansive definition of Britishness.

'The Proprietor'

The close resemblance between Beaverbrook's opinions and those displayed in the *Daily Express* measured the strength of 'the Proprietor's' convictions as well as the manner of their imposition. Although Beaverbrook had, by 1961, long since claimed to have retired from a supervisory role, archives relating to Beaverbrook Newspapers Ltd reveal the octogenarian press baron's attention to minute management details and continuing dominance over all aspects of newspaper production. Beaverbrook tormented his directors, editors and journalists with criticisms, dictated leader articles, set salary levels, railed against 'unreasonable' expenditure, suggested new formats for layout and advertising, perused circulation figures and monitored the competition.[17]

Beaverbrook exacted conformity with his wishes through various methods, though none of these required his presence in Fleet Street. The telephone was the instrument of primary control and editors were subject to consultation at all hours, whether at home, at El Vino's or

---

[15] Correspondence with Chapman Pincher, 31 May 1998.
[16] Interview with Sir John Junor, 19 November 1996.
[17] Correspondence relating to the management of Beaverbrook Newspapers for 1961–62 can be found in BBK H/213–25.

inside the 'Black Lubianka'.[18] For less immediate but equally important matters, Beaverbrook dictated questions and orders into his Sound-scriber machine. These messages were subsequently typed onto small strips of paper by secretaries and forwarded to their destinations with the implicit demand for a prompt reply. Above all, Beaverbrook ruled by expectation, and perhaps in the early 1960s by reputation. A deferential nod accompanied staff references to Beaverbrook as 'the Lord', 'the Principal Reader', 'the Chief Reader', 'the Proprietor' and 'the Old Man'. *Express* writers knew that pleasing the general public was secondary to pleasing the single reader above.[19]

The incorporation within the *Express* of sub-national British identities paralleled Beaverbrook's self-image. By all accounts he imagined himself foremost as Canadian.[20] Born in Ontario and raised in New Brunswick, Max Aitken amassed his fortune early in life as an investor and business opportunist. But Aitken's move from Nova Scotia to Britain in 1910 was ostensibly a permanent departure. The observation that he took great pride in his native accent[21] suggested a conscious dedication to Canadian credentials. In Britain, he remained a consistent advocate for Canadian affairs. He spoke of returning 'home' throughout his life and obtained a Canadian passport when they were first offered, in 1947. Late in life he donated large sums to the University of New Brunswick and other causes in the province.

Scottish parentage rooted Beaverbrook's ancestral history on British soil and further legitimised the coexistence of Canadian and British identities. The son of a Presbyterian clergyman, his outlook carried spiritual overtones as well. Colleagues[22] and critics alike struggled to reconcile Beaverbrook's ruthless character with his conspicuous use of devotional themes. His articles, letters and messages to staff bristled with biblical allusions and moral certainties. In an act that suggested either secular professional sympathy or an intense egotism, Beaverbrook penned a life of Christ entitled *The Divine Propagandist*.[23] The stylistic 'God on our side' righteousness of the *Express*, contrived or not, was an

---

[18] El Vino's bar was a Fleet Street institution and received its share of custom from Beaverbrook's senior staff. As Bob Edwards and others have related, however, it was by no means a 'safe' area. Editors and journalists were summoned to the phone behind the bar to accept calls from Beaverbrook. The art deco *Express* building constructed on Fleet Street in the 1930s was labelled the 'Black Lubianka' by its numerous detractors.

[19] Chisolm and Davie, *Beaverbrook*, p. 576; J. Junor, *Memoirs: Waiting For a Midnight Tram* (London, 1990), p. 87.

[20] R. Edwards, *Goodbye Fleet Street* (London, 1988); Howard, *Beaverbrook*, p. 159; Taylor, *Beaverbrook*, p. 170; interview with Sir John Junor, 19 November 1996.

[21] Howard, *Beaverbrook*, p. 17.

[22] Edwards, *Goodbye Fleet Street*, p. 95; Howard, *Beaverbrook*, p. 151.

[23] Lord Beaverbrook, *The Divine Propagandist* (London, 1962).

entrenched pillar of the Beaverbrook ethos. To Macmillan's half-hearted entreaties for Common Market lenience, Beaverbrook replied, 'As well ask us to repudiate the Presbyterian Church as give up the cause'.[24]

Though based in London's corridors of power, Beaverbrook felt like an outsider before the peculiarities of English social class delineation.[25] If anything, a sense of exclusion may have bolstered his allegiance to Dominion Britishness. Thus, a Canadian who referred to the House of Lords as the 'House of Make Believe'[26] was nonetheless a knight, peer, press baron, member of two wartime Cabinets, advisor to Bonar Law, arch enemy of Stanley Baldwin, confidant of Winston Churchill and imperial policy gadfly. Beaverbrook's involvement in British life and politics was neither contradictory nor incompatible with his primary Canadian identification. In fact, with one foot in each of two worlds Beaverbrook imagined a third, a 'Greater Britain'.

The messengers

As the last of Fleet Street's great barons, Beaverbrook's direction of *Express* affairs was unique by early 1960s standards and the anti-Market campaign was no exception. Beaverbrook stamped his convictions on his newspaper and, as a result, was equated with the propagation of all *Express* views. The 'Voice of Britain', however, was more chorus than soloist and subscription to an overwhelmingly 'British' or 'Greater British' format owed much to *Express* staff acquiescence and complicity.

The appeal of the *Daily Express* to an expansive imagined Britain owed much to the efforts of its key employees. Traditionally, the recruitment of editors mirrored Beaverbrook's own status outside English class traditions.[27] An American, Ralph Blumenfeld, set the paper's populist tone early in the century. E. J. Robertson, an employee of thirty-six years, and Beverly Baxter, a long-serving managing editor, were both Canadians. John Gordon, *Sunday Express* editor from 1928 to 1954, was a Scots Presbyterian who rose from humble origins in Dundee. His successor, John Junor, began life in a Glasgow tenement. Despite his Tory orientation, Beaverbrook's unorthodox instincts led to the recruitment of journalists almost irrespective of political allegiance. *Tribune* was a favourite hunting ground,[28] so much so that Beaverbrook offered monetary assistance when the publication experienced financial difficulties. 'Where shall we get our recruits without *Tribune*?', Beaverbrook

[24] Beaverbrook to H. Macmillan, 28 November 1961, BBK C/235.

[25] Chisolm and Davie, *Beaverbrook*, p. 453.

[26] Beaverbrook to J. Junor, message undated, BBK H/217.

[27] Taylor, *Beaverbrook*, p. 174.

[28] *Tribune* alumni in Beaverbrook's employ at one time or another included Ian Aitken, Tom Driberg, Bob Edwards, Michael Foot and Robert Millar.

reportedly asked a protesting E. J. Robertson.[29] Under Beaverbrook's oppressive gaze the diverse backgrounds and political orientations made for an odd but successful mix.

The pursuit of the anti-Market campaign elicited three distinct responses from the *Express* staff. For a small group of non-believers the crusade required traditional compliance with the wishes and style of the owner. Not all Beaverbrook's 'outsiders' were necessarily 'insiders' to his imagined version of Greater Britain. By the early 1960s, ageing imperial diatribes found decreasing resonance among the staff. As Chapman Pincher confided, 'apart from the leader writers and, perhaps, the Parliamentary reporters, nobody gave a damn about Empire Free Trade'.[30] By some estimates, George Malcolm Thomson, one of Beaverbrook's most trusted leader writers, 'didn't believe in anything'[31] and regarded his role with utmost 'cynicism'.[32] Thomson's skill, however, lay in his ability to replicate 'the Proprietor's' language on the leader page and his contributions reinforced the Beaverbrook aura in propaganda messages.

A second group incorporated those who leaned in anti-Market directions but who failed to embrace the cause with the urgency demanded by Beaverbrook. Political principles placed *Daily Express* editor Bob Edwards, a socialist and *Tribune* alumnus, in an awkward position in 1961. But like other leftists on the staff, he reconciled his socialist instincts with the broad spirit but not the imperialist particulars of the crusade. Ostensibly this was achieved by subscribing to a definition of British interests that embraced the Commonwealth in its multiracial entirety rather than through the narrow kinship of Beaverbrook's Dominions.[33] Yet not all were pleased with Edwards' commitment to the cause. Beaverbrook's son Max, a director at Beaverbrook Newspapers, complained to his father, 'He has no idea of the Common Market and says so'.[34]

In fact, editorial tensions that arose during the campaign were components of broader management issues. Roger Wood replaced Edwards in 1962 but was also criticised for giving insufficient priority to Commonwealth and Common Market affairs.[35] It was their misfortune to have assumed responsibilities at a time when cracks appeared in the self-confidence of the *Express* organisation. Beaverbrook's complaint was typical of a rising concern among upper management in early 1962: 'The *Daily Express*', he wrote, 'is languishing, languishing through want of some drive or energy that doesn't seem to be going into it at

[29] Beaverbrook quoted by Taylor, *Beaverbrook*, p. 598.
[30] Chapman Pincher, written correspondence, 31 May 1998.
[31] Interview with Sir John Junor, 19 November 1996
[32] R. Edwards, written correspondence, 8 November 1996.
[33] Edwards, *Goodbye Fleet Street*, p. 82.
[34] M. Aitken to Beaverbrook, 15 January 1962, BBK H/221.
[35] M. Aitken to Beaverbrook, 31 July and 18 August 1962, BBK H/221; Beaverbrook to R. Wood, 5 March 1962, BBK H/225.

the present time'.[36] Sales figures for 1961 showed continued if tapering growth towards a daily circulation of 4,328,000, second only to the *Mirror*'s 4,561,000.[37] But the departure from the *Daily Express* editorship of Arthur Christiansen in 1957 had left a void. In the last four years of Beaverbrook's life the editorship passed from Edward Pickering (Christiansen's successor) to Bob Edwards to Roger Wood and back to Edwards again.

A third group fully embraced the anti-Market cause. *Sunday Express* editor John Junor, in particular, played rather more than Sancho Panza to Beaverbrook's Quixote. Junor was subject to the demands of 'the Proprietor'[38] but managed the intrusions with more dexterity than anyone else on the staff.[39] Similarities of outlook contributed to a largely successful relationship. Scottishness for both men was central to the conceptualisation of a British identity. Junor shared Beaverbrook's philosophical optimism and vision of 'rugged, radical imperialism'.[40] He adopted the anti-Market cause and continued in Eurosceptic mode for the remainder of his career.

Excessive anti-Market zeal among a group of editors, cartoonists and leader writers even produced occasional strains. Michael Cummings' political cartoons often exceeded the ferocity of the leader writers and the opinion column. Beaverbrook took occasional issue with attacks on the Tories[41] but greater concerns emerged over the cartoonist's mischievous treatment of Charles de Gaulle.[42] In August 1962 Max Aitken informed Beaverbrook, 'I have warned the editors about being too anti-French. This is an easy situation to slip into – the spearhead generally comes from Cummings.'[43] Leader writer James McMillan, though a newcomer to the *Express* in 1961, quickly established himself as a Beaverbrook patriot. Between the commencement of the campaign and February 1962, he personally addressed more than twenty-five meetings

---

[36] Beaverbrook to T. Blackburn, undated, probably 22 February 1962, BBK H/222.

[37] Figures from Royal Commission on the Press, *Report – Royal Commission on the Press, 1961–62,* Cmnd 1811 (London, September 1962), p. 174.

[38] Among other things, Junor complained of having to accompany Beaverbrook on his ritualistic business walks 'every goddamned morning'. Interview with Sir John Junor, 19 November 1996.

[39] Edwards, *Goodbye Fleet Street,* p. 64.

[40] Junor, *Memoirs,* pp. 60, 166. For another perspective see P. Junor, *Home Truths: Life Around My Father* (London, 2002), pp. 54–5.

[41] M. Cummings, *On the Point of My Pen: The Best of Cummings* (Portsmouth, 1985), p. 6.

[42] According to the legend, de Gaulle was so incensed by Cummings' treatment of Pierre Laval's execution that he formally complained to the British Government. For Cummings' version of the incident see Allen, *Voice of Britain,* p. 161.

[43] See BBK H/220. As we shall see, the campaign intentionally spared de Gaulle the normally hostile typology of the European other, not least because the General held the key to British exclusion from the Common Market.

and debates sponsored by local organisations such as the Glasgow Parliamentary Association, Brighton Businessmen and the Liverpool Institute of Export. Beaverbrook, however, objected to commitments beyond Fleet Street. McMillan declined further speaking invitations after being warned, 'The real medium for making headway against the Common Market is the *Daily Express*.... I am against the small meeting with divided opinion bandying to and fro, and of little interest in the great game of public opinion.'[44]

The audience

Beaverbrook's management style led *Express* writers to construct articles with the 'Principal Reader' in mind. The ramifications of this were considerable. Playing to expectation reinforced the extent to which the 'Voice of Britain' was the voice of 'the Proprietor'. It also amplified a tone of unity and self-referential verity. Uncompromising and simplistic opinions were offered as truths, with assurances of moral authority. If *Express* convictions differed from those offered by contemporary wisdom, competitors or the Government of the day, so much the better. Most importantly, such an approach meant that Beaverbrook's assumptions about his audience and collective identity governed the approach of the *Express* to its readers. Thus, overtures to the British 'us' or 'we' found expression in the language of 'you' and 'yours'. The primary propaganda pamphlet produced by the *Express*, for instance, was entitled *You and the Common Market*.[45] Page 1 propaganda routinely included titles such as 'Europe and You', 'Germany and You', 'You Should Know' and 'You Be the Judge'.[46]

Beyond personalising its approach, 'you' linguistics cultivated a material dimension to national identity, a sense of belonging through ownership. Historically, a consumerist orientation typified most of the paper's approaches to the public. Beaverbrook offered material salvation through imperial unity, equated prosperity with happiness and promoted competition as religion in a fashion that accorded well with the emergence of an acquisitive post-war society. Indeed, the *Express* originally coined the 'You've never had it so good' slogan attributed to Macmillan in the 1959 election campaign.[47] By implication, Beaverbrook suggested, 'You can have it even better!'

Links between ownership and national identity emerged as potent themes. A materialist outlook most often led to depiction of the Common

---

[44] Beaverbrook to J. McMillan, 8 February 1962, BBK H/220.
[45] *Daily Express, You and the Common Market* (London, 1962).
[46] *Daily Express*, 2 August 1961, 31 March 1962, 3, 5 January 1963, 4 January 1963.
[47] H. Evans, *Downing Street Diary: The Macmillan Years, 1957–63* (London, 1981), pp. 39–40.

Market as a contravention of imperial economic destiny and a threat to the affluence of individual Britons. A spirit of ownership also provided subtle edges to the mystical aspects of belonging. Beaverbrook's Britons were encouraged to regard themselves as the inheritors and therefore owners and guarantors of British tradition, sovereignty, institutions and symbols. The Treaty of Rome thus presented a threat to Britons' ownership of a prized possession, their own national identity.

Individualist and materialist patriotism enhanced the populist credentials of the *Express* by suggesting a transcendence of class distinctions. Much has been made of the absence of class in the paper's appeal to its audience.[48] Indeed, one-third of its readers were drawn from the A and B social groups, with 39 per cent in the C1 category and the remainder in C2 and D1.[49] Beaverbrook championed expansionist principles as an antidote to divisions. He wrote:

> It has been said that the *Daily Express* appeals to the middle class mind. That is not so. It appeals to a particular kind of mind in every class.… We appealed to the character and temperament which was bent on moving upward and outwards and which was not trammelled by any doctrinaire conception in its view of national needs and opportunities.[50]

The most important aspect of the *Express* approach to its audience lay in a 'common man' orientation. The celebration of daily life and average Britons had important implications for identity. By removing London from the geographical locus of its imagined readership, the *Express* offered admission to a broader spectrum of British interests. Arthur Christiansen, a long-serving *Express* editor, had refined the 'common man' approach[51] by imagining two prototype readers, '"the man in the back streets of Derby"' and '"the man on the Rhyl Promenade"'.[52] The reference points became so entrenched that Christiansen's staff presented him with framed pictures of a Derby back street and the Rhyl Promenade when he retired in 1957. A social and geographic parallel was adopted at the *Sunday Express* and later featured in John Junor's frequent homage to Auchtermuchty.

---

[48] Allen, *Voice of Britain*, p. 17; A. C. H. Smith, *Paper Voices: The Popular Press and Social Change, 1935–65* (London, 1975), p. 238; Taylor, *Beaverbrook*, p. xi.

[49] Edwards, *Goodbye Fleet Street*, p. 98. See also Junor, *Memoirs*, pp. 87, 222. The Institute of Practitioners in Advertising verified the claim in a 1961 readership survey. It showed that 1,700,000 *Express* readers were drawn from the A and B categories. See *Daily Express*, 11 October 1961.

[50] Beaverbrook quoted in Taylor, *Beaverbrook*, p. 175.

[51] For more on Christiansen's 'common man' approach see Allen, *Voice of Britain*, pp. 17, 39–42, 66; L. Chester and J. Fenby, *Fall of the House of Beaverbrook* (London, 1979), pp. 20, 23; D. Edgar, *Express '56 : A Year in the Life of an Express Journalist* (London, 1981), pp. 104–5.

[52] Allen, *Voice of Britain*, p. 39.

The range of *Express* objections to Common Market membership was facilitated in part by its focus upon everyday affairs. The inclusion of women's concerns, in particular, extended the scope of banal symbolism. Not surprisingly, such appeals functioned within socially conservative boundaries and the common woman typically featured as the common man's wife. Consumerism infused the early 1960s women's pages with fashion, travel and housekeeping themes. Articles bore titles like 'Are supermarkets too impersonal?' and 'Just how thrifty can a woman be?'[53] The housewife entered the pantheon of British institutions. Anne Edwards' spirited defence of the 'English lady' suggested that:

> There isn't any doubt that French women dress better, Italian women cook better, American women housekeep better and every other brand of woman is sexier than she is. She is inflexible as Florence Nightingale still, even if it's only about the right way to prune the roses. And as positive as ever that she and hers are the backbone of the country and that their method of doing things will eventually save us.[54]

Hearth-and-home considerations were central to articulations of the national spirit. In July 1962, for instance, the *Daily Express* asked its readers to identify the location of Britain's 'true heritage'. Top prize was given to a woman who equated her home and its roots with the essence of England, while an additional prize was awarded to a woman who found Britain best represented in the simple life of her town.[55] As we shall see, the extension of such themes to include 'dear food' and cost-of-living issues was but a short step for architects of the anti-Market campaign.

To sum up, *Express* patriotism owed much to both unconscious assumptions and the conscious manipulation of banal national identity. Beaverbrook's presence was overwhelming, but management style alone fails to account for the scale and depth of conviction of the paper's anti-Market campaign. Staff believers, subscribing to Beaverbrookian ideas, either wholesale or in part, also contributed to the tenor of anti-European sentiment. Assumptions about the nature of the readership were equally important. By appealing to Britons as individuals and consumers, as owners of a precious identity and as members of a wider collective, the *Express* sought to mobilise a self-affirming and politically dynamic patriotism.

---

[53] *Sunday Express*, 8 and 22 January 1962.
[54] *Sunday Express*, 18 February 1962.
[55] Letters to the *Daily Express*, 2 July 1962.

The parameters of the campaign

Indications of *Express* opposition to a British application emerged in the summer of 1960 and blended with existing biases against association with Europe or surrender of imperial responsibilities. But in the spring and summer of 1961 an increased urgency accompanied claims of a Commonwealth sell-out. A tip from an unnamed but well placed source alerted the *Express* to the imminence of Macmillan's announcement two and a half weeks before its delivery.[56] On 30 July, the day before Macmillan's presentation to the Commons, the *Express* told readers 'There has not been such a moment in 900 years. Not since the Norman Conquest has anything taken place to change the status of Britain so shatteringly and irrevocably.'[57] Two days later the paper warned 'Let the politicians and pressure groups beware'.[58] The following day a box at the bottom of page 1 entitled 'Europe and You' set 'Preservation of the Commonwealth, Protection of Agriculture and Maintenance of National Sovereignty' as 'essential national interests' and basic grounds for opposition ('propaganda boxes' are discussed below, under '*Express* methods').[59]

The campaign's framework, like all *Express* undertakings, reflected the dichotomies of Beaverbrook style and method. On the one hand, a spirited attack on the Common Market invoked great themes while locating objections in the slightest of details. Its ferocity suggested a contravention of fundamental principles and the risks were elevated to include the defining elements of national consciousness. On the other hand, however, the campaign was restrained both by a desire to pursue the cause independently and by an allegiance to Fleet Street propaganda.

Beaverbrook, the external campaign and its limits

Though frequently abroad, Beaverbrook maintained enthusiastic control over anti-Market operations[60] in spite of, or because of, advancing age and failing health. Like its 1929–31 Empire Crusade predecessor, a cause Beaverbrook pursued in the pages of the *Daily Express* and through sponsorship of independent parliamentary candidacies, the anti-Market campaign bore an ad hoc appearance. More importantly, Beaverbrook's imperial message had altered little during the three intervening decades. On this occasion, however, Beaverbrook's anti-Market activities were largely confined to newsprint propaganda forums and techniques, with

---

[56] D. Clark to E. Pickering, 12 July 1961, BBK H/216.

[57] *Daily Express*, 30 July 1961.

[58] *Daily Express*, 1 August 1961.

[59] *Daily Express*, 2 August 1961.

[60] Robert Edwards, written correspondence, 8 November 1996; Sir John Junor, interview, 19 November 1996; Taylor, *Beaverbrook*, p. 647; Vines, *A Little Nut Brown Man*, p. 32.

occasional forays beyond restricted to commitments of *Daily Express* resources and personnel.

The campaign directed considerable time, money and effort towards external propaganda. Following a reader's suggestion, the *Express* produced and distributed 35,000 window stickers bearing the 'Commonwealth not Common Market' slogan. Of these, 18,000 were sent in direct response to reader requests and another 17,000 to representatives for distribution within specified markets and trade shows.[61] In November 1961, on the recommendation of George Malcolm Thomson, a personal letter bearing Beaverbrook's signature was drafted for an intended audience of church ministers, the editors of local newspapers and chambers of commerce. The letter, defining a clear choice between Commonwealth and Europe, requested support for the campaign. 'By speech, by the written word, informal meetings and in casual conversation', the recipients were urged, 'you can do much to enlighten the public'.[62] More than 54,000 letters had been posted by the end of 1961. The effort elicited a disappointing response, however, and by the third week of January 1962 the *Express* offices had received only 400 replies. Tom Blackburn, *Express* Newspapers' general manager, attempted to console Beaverbrook by suggesting that 'Although the replies are very small indeed it doesn't say that the letter wasn't effective. The public are still bewildered on which way to go Common Market wise.'[63]

The traditional art of pamphleteering produced more positive results. In January 1962 the *Express* published 200,000 copies of *You and the Common Market* for a target audience of MPs, editors, NFU officials and farmers. Seventy-five per cent of the copies were distributed for sale, with the remaining 50,000 withheld to fulfil readership requests. Three days after the initial date of sale, central booksellers reported having sold up to 50 per cent of stock.[64] Similar energies were directed towards the production of full-page anti-Market advertisements for publication in provincial newspapers. These reproduced the *Daily Express* appeals of Lord Attlee, Viscount Montgomery and Beaverbrook for a wider British audience. Typical of these was the production of Beaverbrook's 'You and the Common Market' solicitation in May 1962. At a cost of some £13,000, the advertisement featured in more than thirty provincial papers, with a combined circulation of 8,205,000.[65]

---

[61] T. Blackburn to Beaverbrook, 6 June 1962, BBK H/224; M. Aitken to Beaverbrook, 18 July 1962, BBK H/221.

[62] Beaverbrook draft letter, undated, BBK H/218.

[63] T. Blackburn to Beaverbrook, 20 January 1962, BBK H/222.

[64] T. Blackburn to Beaverbrook, 2, 5, 17 and 20 January 1962, BBK H/222.

[65] T. Blackburn to Beaverbrook, 24 May 1962, BBK H/223; T. Blackburn to Beaverbrook, 7 June and 13 August 1962, BBK H/224. The *Express* was forced to organise placement of the advertisement itself when agents Colman, Prentice and Varley refused, on the grounds that they were the acting advertising agency for Conservative Central Office.

The anti-Market campaign differed somewhat from its Empire Crusade predecessor in the comparative absence of backroom intrigue and political mischief. Beaverbrook admitted to one reader, 'The fight may not be as lively as during the Empire Crusade before the war, but I regret I can do nothing more to make it so'.[66] Garfield Weston, a fellow Canadian and head of the baking and milling conglomerate Associated British Foods, explored alternative avenues. Like Beaverbrook, Weston's career featured a brief stint in Parliament, extensive imperial investments and high-profile British holdings, including Allied Bakeries and Fortnum and Mason. Most importantly, shared political convictions made both men champions of imperial causes and sworn enemies of the Common Market.[67] While Beaverbook thanked Weston for the 'measures you have taken to turn our expectations into substance',[68] the precise extent of Weston's activity is unclear. He facilitated interaction between Beaverbrook and Arthur Bryant[69] and sought to exploit his contacts with John Diefenbaker, the Canadian Prime Minister. Beaverbrook remained somewhat distant,[70] however, and discouraged Weston's attempt to arrange meetings with Gaitskell during the 1962 Commonwealth Conference.[71]

Despite numerous requests for financial assistance, Beaverbrook restricted his donations to a small clutch of anti-Market pressure groups. Publicity within the pages of the *Express* was supplemented with cheques for the ACML, the FBM and the Commonwealth Industries Association (CIA). In most instances Beaverbrook wrote cheques of £100 or £200 but in each case instructed his financial secretary to obtain a full refund from the *Daily Express* coffers.[72]

A combination of factors shaped Beaverbrook's reluctance to pursue the campaign beyond the pages of the *Daily Express*. Age may well have limited some of his usual zeal. To a reader requesting the creation of a new party, Beaverbrook confessed 'I am an old man now in my eighty-fourth year, and I could not embark on such a tremendous undertaking.... Now I must leave the task to younger men.'[73] Internal memos reveal provisional discussion of by-election politics and independent candidacies, including possible runs by *Express* writer Bob Pitman[74] and, as we

---

[66] Beaverbrook to E. Bidlake, 26 June 1962, BBK F/3.
[67] Interview with Garry H. Weston, 24 September 1998.
[68] Beaverbrook to G. Weston, 27 May 1962, BBK C/323.
[69] Beaverbrook to G. Weston, 2 June 1962, BBK C/323. See also correspondence between Weston and Arthur Bryant in Sir Arthur Bryant Papers, Liddell Hart Centre for Military Archives, King's College, London (hereafter cited as AB Papers) H/4.
[70] Edwards, *Goodbye Fleet Street*, p. 147.
[71] Beaverbrook to G. Weston, 14 September 1962, BBK C/323.
[72] See correspondence between Beaverbrook and A. G. Millar and T. Blackburn, 27 March, 17 April 1962, BBK H/223, and on 1, 30 and 31 August 1962, BBK H/224.
[73] Beaverbrook to R. S. Rawle, 22 December 1962, BBK F/4.
[74] T. Blackburn to Beaverbrook, 17 June 1961, BBK H/215.

shall see in Chapter 4, John Paul, President of the ACML. But those ventures faltered in the planning stages before fears of lost deposits and a lack of organisational support. Both West Lothian and West Derbyshire, for instance, were rejected.[75] As Beaverbrook responded to one reader, 'There is no shortage of money but there is a considerable dearth of candidates suitable for the job'.[76] Ultimately, Beaverbrook settled for *Daily Express* coverage of by-election campaigns with favourable reports and analysis accorded to select anti-Market candidates.

An unwillingness to shoulder by-election risks was coupled with an apparent reluctance to share the anti-Market stage. Beaverbrook declined all speaking invitations, most notably a request for his presence at a rally at the Albert Hall organised by the umbrella organisation the AntiCommon Market Union, on the grounds of age and illness.[77] Even within the pages of the *Express*, James McMillan was instructed to avoid excessive devotion to smaller anti-Market meetings.[78] When recommending pressure groups to activist readers, Beaverbrook invariably restricted his endorsements to either the ACML or the FBM.

Express methods

A reluctance to push beyond newsprint parameters stemmed primarily from Beaverbrook's regard for the *Express* as the most important forum for dissent. His most illuminating pronouncement on crusading methods is found in an August 1962 memo to his son Max:

> Newspapers like people must have a reason for living. Our reason is and has been the development of Britain by and through overseas associations. For half a century Britain has hesitated between seeking association with Europe or closer relations with the Commonwealth. Now her Government has decided on Europe. But her people are for the Commonwealth.... But in a battle between the Government and the people, the people always win. Always report the news. Be brief. And do not hesitate to make news. Not fabrication. The Empire Crusade was an occasion when the *Daily Express* made news. So is the campaign against the Common Market.[79]

Irrespective of its political intent, the *Express* campaign also functioned as an act of self-affirmation at a time when the components of messianic, imperial identity found decreasing resonance with conventional opinion. By placing the sovereign determination of national

---

[75] M. Aitken to Beaverbrook, 30 April 1962, BBK H/221; Beaverbrook to B. J. Allison, 4 June 1962, BBK F/4.
[76] Beaverbrook to L. D. Hills, 17 August 1962, BBK F/3.
[77] Beaverbrook to L. Smythe, 20 June 1962, BBK F/3.
[78] Beaverbrook to J. McMillan, 27 February 1962, BBK H/220.
[79] Beaverbrook to M. Aitken, 24 August 1962, BBK H/221.

interest in the hands of 'the people' rather than the Government, the paper aspired to patriotically transcendent ground. But the crusade was also self-aggrandising by nature and sought external reactions, positive or negative. Common Market dissent allowed for differentiation from the rival *Daily Mail*, reiterated a commitment to propaganda over commercial considerations and facilitated claims to the status of 'The Voice that is Independent'.[80]

The anti-Market offensive was Beaverbrook's chief obsession between 1961 and 1963. In general, Common Market articles featured almost daily, though not at the expense of news reporting. Coverage, however, affirmed Beaverbrook's reputation as a 'master of the black art of ink'[81] and the aptitude of the *Express* for ruthless propaganda. An anti-Market bias was imposed through a variety of presentational techniques. If such methods lacked subtlety they were nonetheless detailed and comprehensive.

The *Express* seized opportunities to apply a negative slant to European news. Internal Common Market difficulties such as falling rates of growth or political wrangling over the CAP were presented as evidence of fundamental and dangerous weakness. Domestic reports blurred distinctions between those offering outright opposition to the entire Common Market project and those objecting to the projected terms of agreement. Likewise, the implied emphases in headlines or article titles did not necessarily correspond with the exact content of the news or precise intent of guest authors. Harold Wilson, for example, is unlikely to have chosen 'I say there is still time to save the Empire'[82] as the title for his article on the Commonwealth. Similar techniques led to criticism from the Press Council in June 1962 for use of a 'misleading'[83] Common Market headline.

Wherever possible, the *Express* tethered the Commonwealth to its reports on Europe. This was inevitable, given the paper's historic allegiance to imperial causes. International news in the *Sunday Express*, for instance, originated from the appropriately named 'Empire and Foreign News Desk'. But the inclusion of Dominion topics, and Canadian ones in particular, was also a product of recurrent cultivation. Beaverbrook's influence shaped opinion columns dedicated to a tradition of Canadian friendship forged in wartime bravery, financial support and the 'intangible bonds' of collective belonging.[84] Dominion leaders knew

---

[80] *Daily Express*, 12 December 1961. See also 8 December 1961 and 17 August 1961.

[81] Howard, *Beaverbrook*, p. 13.

[82] *Sunday Express*, 10 June 1962.

[83] General Council of the Press, *The Press and the People: The 9th Annual Report of the General Council of the Press* (London, 1962), p. 43.

[84] *Sunday Express*, 19 August 1962. For other examples see opinion columns in *Daily Express*, 2 December 1961 and 26 June 1962; *Sunday Express*, 1 July 1962; and *Daily Express* propaganda box, 19 August 1961.

that evidence of their scepticism towards British entry would provide the *Express* with newsworthy items and quotable propaganda. In a speech defending Commonwealth preference during a visit to London, Australian Prime Minister Robert Menzies warned Macmillan that 'the noise that will come from the Commonwealth will be such as to exhaust even the vocabulary of the *Daily Express*'.[85] Duly impressed, the *Express* reported the remarks the following day and also incorporated the quote in a 'propaganda box' the following month.[86] The 1962 Commonwealth Prime Ministers' Conference provided a rich, if disorganised, seam of opposition material and the *Express* extracted maximum value for its news and leader pages.[87]

Negative Common Market imagery was imposed through a conscious manipulation of language. Words such as 'surrender', 'price', 'concession', 'failure', 'defeat' and 'betrayal' invariably accompanied references to British entry and the projected domestic and Commonwealth consequences. Staff members appeared to compete with each other in a campaign promoting alternative labels for the Common Market. Chapman Pincher alone offered Beaverbrook 'The European Coalition', 'The European Anschluss', 'Common Denominator', 'Common Auction', 'Common Melting Pot', 'Common Vortex', 'Common Cauldron' and 'Doomsday Club' and was pleased by Beaverbrook's adoption of 'The European Axis'.[88] George Thomson suggested recasting the Treaty of Rome as the 'Black Pact'.[89] A similar philosophy governed the approach to Britain's team of negotiators. Norman Smart railed against the 'tri or bilingual' cosmopolitanism of Britain's 'Five Flying Knights', who thrived in the 'cloak and dagger' cocktail atmosphere of Brussels, with little regard for the Commonwealth or 'sweet farmlands of Britain'.[90] The Lord Privy Seal, nicknamed 'Lord Heath of Brussels', emerged as the most frequent target for charges of duplicity. His announcement of the plan to eliminate preferences for Commonwealth manufactures was thus described as 'one of the most humiliating retreats in British diplomacy … unconditional surrender!'[91]

The most striking manifestations of Beaverbrookian propaganda emerged on the front page in the form of what are best described as 'propaganda boxes'. Designed for high impact, the small, bold typeface boxes offered alarmist objections to Common Market membership on all conceivable grounds. The boxes stood independently, reflected recent

[85] *Daily Express*, 13 June 1962.
[86] *Daily Express*, 16 July 1962.
[87] See especially *Daily Express* coverage, 10–13 and 18–21 September 1962.
[88] C. Pincher to Beaverbrook, 14 and 21 June 1961, BBK H/218.
[89] G. Thomson to Beaverbrook, 16 July 1961, BBK H/218.
[90] *Daily Express*, 9 March 1962. See also 'Intelligence Report', *Daily Express*, 13 November 1962.
[91] *Daily Express*, 31 May 1962.

news or ran in a particular thematic series. Topics included Dominion war debts, Commonwealth kinship, British uniqueness, threats to the standard of living, ominous Articles within the Treaty of Rome, the cost of entry, employment and food prices. Primary responsibility for the construction of propaganda boxes fell to Robert Millar, another of Beaverbrook's former *Tribune* men.[92] Staff memos, however, reveal the participation of others, including Roger Wood, James McMillan and Robert Pitman. Naturally, Beaverbrook assumed a primary role in reviewing and amending them, as well as suggesting further topics for consideration.[93]

As the employment of cartoonists like Osbert Lancaster, Carl Giles and Michael Cummings suggested, Beaverbrook believed in the importance of visual images. Giles, best known for his Middle England portrayals of the 'Giles Family', rarely entered the Common Market political fray. But when called upon to do so, his efforts were perfectly in keeping with the *Daily Express* spirit. In one such example Giles showed dark, moustachioed, Italian troops, complete with organ grinder's monkey, substituting for British soldiers during the Changing of the Guard at Buckingham Palace.[94] Cummings, who 'couldn't ask for a better subject than the Common Market',[95] drew countless leader-page caricatures featuring de Gaulle, Adenauer, Macmillan and Heath, with Kennedy frequently lurking in the background. Though he had little contact with the cartoonist, Beaverbrook was 'delighted' with Cummings' efforts and made 'extensive use' of the drawings.[96]

By virtue of its hardened convictions and vast circulation, the 'Voice of Britain' also operated as the *de facto* voice of the anti-Market lobby. In an attempt to lend its campaign an air of authority and respectability the *Express* sought out high-profile dissenters to write on its leader page. The specific content of articles by guest authors will be dealt with in later chapters. For the moment it should be noted that the recruitment drive met with mixed results. To their credit, the editors largely succeeded in gathering the highest-profile objectors available at the time. The incongruous composition of the group highlights the ideological breadth of opposition but also suggests a paucity of choices. Ironically, the left offered the most prominent guest authors. Harold Wilson and Lord Attlee both contributed pieces to the *Sunday Express*. Historian A. J. P. Taylor, who wrote for the *Sunday Express* under annual contract, gladly addressed Commonwealth and Common Market themes. On the

---

[92] R. Edwards, written correspondence, 8 November 1996.
[93] R. Wood to Beaverbrook, 31 January 1962; and Beaverbrook to R. Pitman, 3 July 1962, BBK H/225.
[94] *Daily Express*, 14 October 1962.
[95] M. Cummings to Beaverbrook, 6 December 1961, BBK H/213.
[96] Beaverbrook to M. Cummings, 3 March 1962, BBK H/220.

Conservative side Viscount Hinchingbrooke, Viscount Montgomery and Anthony Fell, among others, submitted their written opinions to the cause. William Pickles, a professor at the London School of Economics, underscored economy and sovereignty issues, while Oliver Smedley presented the free trade case against Common Market protectionism.

Other targets of the *Express* recruiting drive either declined the opportunity or subscribed to incompatible views. These included Sir Harry Legge-Bourke and Lord Fisher,[97] as well as Julian Amery, who disappointed Beaverbrook by failing to carry his father's banner into the fray.[98] As we shall see in the following chapter, Sir Arthur Bryant was 'deeply touched' by Beaverbrook's overtures but chose to pursue his strident anti-Market views through the *Sunday Times* and *Illustrated London News*.[99] Lord Lambton's draft submission for publication in the *Express* was rendered unprintable by its reference to Beaverbrook's 'extreme line' and its personal attacks upon Harold Macmillan.[100] Viscount Alexander of Hillsborough, an outspoken anti-Marketeer and correspondent with Beaverbrook, probably eliminated himself from consideration by expounding Catholic conspiracy theories centred on papal plots and Kremlin–Vatican alliances.[101] Overall, the shortage of prominent dissenters was less a reflection of *Express* failings than a symptom of the dilemma faced by the anti-Market movement as a whole. If anything, the comparative absence of celebrity accomplices only steeled the resolve at the *Express*, heightening the presumed national responsibility implicit in its mission.

The *Express*, Hugh Gaitskell and Harold Macmillan

The hardening of Labour's Common Market policy in the autumn of 1962 increased both the likelihood and necessity of an association with 'the Proprietor'. Soon after the Labour Party conference, Michael Foot wrote to Beaverbrook, 'Politics are now made infinitely more exciting. Our old friend Gaitskell is off the fence and on the right side and I am sure he can never clamber back on again.'[102] With the *Daily Mirror* and the rest of

---

[97] D. Marks to Beaverbrook, 13 April 1962; and R. Wood to Beaverbrook, 2 July 1962, BBK H/225.

[98] Beaverbrook to J. Amery, 3 May 1962, BBK C/4. Julian Amery was MP for Preston North and Secretary of State for Air at the time of the first application. He was the son of L. S. Amery, a Colonial Secretary under Baldwin (1924–29) who, like Beaverbrook, was a disciple of Joseph Chamberlain and a great inter-war champion of tariffs and imperial destiny.

[99] A. Bryant to Beaverbrook, 8 July 1962, BBK C/76.

[100] Lord Lambton draft article; Beaverbrook to Lambton, 3 July and 17 August 1962, BBK C/200. See also C. Wintour to Beaverbrook, 4 July 1962, BBK H/268.

[101] For examples of Alexander's anti-Catholicism see correspondence in BBK C/2.

[102] M. Foot to Beaverbrook, 8 October 1962, BBK C/137.

Fleet Street offering outright or conditional support for British entry, only the *Daily Express* could provide Gaitskell with sympathetic leader-page coverage before a mass readership. For Beaverbrook, an association with Gaitskell offered the *Daily Express* campaign a sharper parliamentary focus and, perhaps, greater 'trouble-making' opportunities.

Links between Labour and the *Express* had developed throughout 1962. In January, Chapman Pincher helped Labour expose a Communist agent in its ranks by putting George Brown in touch with the heads of MI5 and MI6.[103] Shortly thereafter, Pincher relayed a message from Brown to Beaverbrook that affirmed Commonwealth safeguards as the linchpin of Labour's European approach and added Patrick Gordon Walker's suggestion that the party was moving in an anti-Market direction.[104] In February, Harold Wilson wrote a leader-page article in the *Daily Express* advocating the development of a Commonwealth alternative.[105] In subsequent months Wilson contributed articles to the *Sunday Express* that decried the development of a European nuclear deterrent, highlighted the betrayal of the Commonwealth and called for an election on the Common Market issue.[106] Meanwhile, Bob Pitman, an *Express* writer, Labour Party member and former socialist candidate, composed a strident anti-Market pamphlet entitled *British Trade Unions and the Common Market*.[107]

Those connections notwithstanding, the *Express* had maintained a steady critique of Labour's 'wait and see' policy. The leader page praised Gaitskell and Labour MP Manny Shinwell for showing faith in the Commonwealth at the 1961 Labour Party conference but warned of the constant threat posed to the party's patriotic credentials by the wavers of the 'Red Flag'. 'Only under the Union Jack', it counselled, 'can the Party move forward to triumph'.[108] Front-page coverage of Gaitskell's

[103] C. Pincher to Beaverbrook, 23 January 1962, BBK H/225. According to Pincher's letter, Arthur Bax of Labour's press and publicity department had been identified as a Communist agent following tips from a Russian defector to US authorities. Bax resigned on 22 January but Pincher avoided writing on the subject for fear of libel charges.

[104] C. Pincher to Beaverbrook, 5 and 14 February 1962, BBK H/225.

[105] H. Wilson, 'A New Deal Now for the Commonwealth', *Daily Express*, 26 February 1962.

[106] Harold Wilson's articles for the *Sunday Express* included: 'I Say There Is Still Time to Save the Empire', 10 June 1962; 'Macmillan Must Call an Election Now', 16 September 1962; 'Is Macmillan Ready to Drop His Bluff at Last?', 14 October 1962; 'Danger!... The German Finger Is Reaching for the H-Bomb Trigger', 13 January 1963.

[107] R. Pitman, *British Trade Unions and the Common Market* (London, 1962). It is unclear who funded the pamphlet's publication. It is mentioned in James McMillan's correspondence with Beaverbrook, making it likely that the *Express* covered printing costs.

[108] *Daily Express*, 4 October 1961.

8 May 1962 speech featured a headline that referred to 'Mr. (Facing-both-ways) Gaitskell'.[109] The 3 June leader advised that a failure to 'Come off the fence!' put his political standing and personal honour at risk.

Harold Macmillan believed that Gaitskell had sold out to Beaverbrook.[110] In reality, Gaitskell understood the dangers of co-operation but felt that he could maintain an independent standing.[111] Beaverbrook's correspondence fails to reveal just how far he and Gaitskell conspired on political matters. Information and ideas were clearly exchanged, however, through the agency of Garfield Weston.[112]

The points of shared empathy derived most obviously from Commonwealth themes. In the run-up to the Commonwealth Prime Ministers' Conference Gaitskell put his views to *Express* writer George Malcolm Thomson, who dutifully forwarded the comments to Beaverbrook. Gaitskell called the negotiated terms of entry 'an insult to the nation's intelligence' and argued that if the Prime Minister abandoned negotiations, he would appear to be following Labour. Alternatively, if Macmillan adhered to the developing course, Gaitskell predicted greater trouble would arise within Conservative ranks.[113] The *Express* took those views to heart and proclaimed Gaitskell's television broadcast on 21 September 1962 'the most effective political appearance yet seen on television in Britain'.[114] The *Sunday Express* printed an interview with Gaitskell the following week, during which he again pressed the issue of Britain's 'disappearance' should it join the Common Market and the Government's abandonment of the Commonwealth under the influence of the City of London and the United States.[115] The *Express* quoted extensively from Gaitskell's speech at the party's Brighton conference and praised Gaitskell for speaking on behalf of the people. 'On this issue', it concluded, 'the verdict at Brighton is the verdict of the nation'.[116]

Meanwhile, despite enjoying pro-entry editorial backing in Fleet Street, Harold Macmillan's uneasy relationship with the press[117] surfaced in frequent diary entries complaining of unfairness and inaccuracies. Journalists, he told Harold Evans, were like painters: 'Unless their work

---

[109] *Daily Express*, 9 May 1962.
[110] HMD, 15 October 1962, MS Macmillan dep. d.47.
[111] Alistair Hetherington Diary, 27 September 1962, in P. M. Williams, *Hugh Gaitskell* (Oxford, 1982), p. 738.
[112] H. Gaitskell to Beaverbrook, 12 December 1962, BBK C/139.
[113] G. M. Thomson to Beaverbrook, 10 September 1962, BBK H/225.
[114] *Daily Express*, 22 September 1962.
[115] *Sunday Express*, 30 September 1962.
[116] *Daily Express*, 4 October 1962. An accompanying cartoon showed Gaitskell draped in Britannia costume with Macmillan running up a gangplank wearing a beret and leaving behind a suitcase labelled '1000 Years of History'.
[117] A. Horne, *Macmillan: Vol. 2, 1957–1986* (London, 1989), p. 262. See also HMD, 6 August 1961, MS Macmillan dep. d.43.

is controversial, exaggerated, distorted, they arouse no interest'.[118] Ironically, Macmillan enjoyed cordial relations with Beaverbrook and support from the *Express* on many issues.[119] But as Macmillan knew and Beaverbrook affirmed, Common Market policy formed a great chasm. To Beaverbrook he confessed 'I never hoped that anything called the Treaty of Rome would be acceptable to you'.[120]

Having served with Beaverbrook at the Ministry of Supply during the war, Macmillan understood Crusader politics and assumed those manipulative powers would be unleashed against the Common Market application. Macmillan thus adopted a conciliatory approach, mixing gratitude for past support with occasional complaints about *Express* articles and cartoons.[121] If Macmillan's special consultations with newspaper editors failed to include those from the *Express* or *Evening Standard*,[122] that reflected an understanding relationship with Beaverbrook and a recognition that the editors answered to a higher authority. Thus, despite a threat to remove his support for Macmillan's Government in June 1962,[123] Beaverbrook ultimately remained loyal. 'I cannot really be too hard on Macmillan', he confided to Lord Lambton.[124]

The most severe criticisms of Macmillan's leadership invariably originated at the *Sunday Express*. Its editor, John Junor, thought him 'phoney as a five-bob note' and famously resigned in a temporary protest against Beaverbrook's failure to attack Macmillan over the Profumo scandal.[125] A June 1961 'Crossbencher' column in the *Sunday Express* predicted that in the year 2061 Oxford undergraduates would face examination questions comparing Macmillan to Lord North. In addition to repeated calls for and predictions of an imminent general election, the leader page

---

[118] H. Macmillan quoted in Evans, *Downing Street Diary*, p. 63.

[119] See for example HMD, 3 February and 1 June 1962, MS Macmillan dep. d. 44, 46.

[120] H. Macmillan to Beaverbrook, 9 April 1962, and Beaverbrook to Macmillan, 11 April 1962, BBK C/235. See also Beaverbrook to Macmillan, 7 March and 16 June 1962, BBK C/235.

[121] See for instance Beaverbrook to Macmillan, 13 June and 28 November 1962, BBK C/235; Macmillan to Beaverbrook, 27 November 1962, BBK C/235. Macmillan's displeasure with cartoonists is mentioned in Beaverbrook to A. Eden, 24 January 1961, Special Collections, University of Birmingham Library, Lord Avon Papers (hereafter cited as AP) 23/8/34.

[122] Lambton to Beaverbook, 14 February 1961; Beaverbrook to Lambton, 17 February 1961, BBK C/200.

[123] In an interview, Beaverbrook noted that the *Express* had 'always supported Macmillan' but warned, 'If the Government persists in the project known as the Common Market, I must oppose the Conservatives. That is my decision.' Beaverbrook interviewed by *Sydney Sunday Telegraph*, 3 June 1962. Excerpts reprinted in the *Express*, 4 June 1962.

[124] Beaverbrook to Lambton, 17 August 1962, quoted in Taylor, *Beaverbrook*, p. 648.

[125] Junor, *Memoirs*, pp. 113, 123; Taylor, *Beaverbrook*, p. 662. Macmillan himself stepped down soon after, clearing the way for Junor to return to duty at the *Sunday Express*.

declared open hostility to Macmillan's leadership in July 1962 under the title 'Parting of the Ways'.[126] Beaverbrook's loyalty held sway, however, and in December 1962 'Crossbencher' grudgingly conceded that 'One thing and one thing only utterly rules out an anti-Macmillan revolt. The fact that even if he is not the best possible Tory Prime Minister, he is the only one they have got.'[127]

Defining the British 'us'

The process of comparative differentiation implicit in the response to the Common Market revealed the presence of a broad set of identity-defining assumptions. Naturally, the campaign discourse focused upon thematic details of Common Market membership, with frequent reference to the Commonwealth context. But the process revealed just how far the narrowly inclusive parameters of a British 'us' depended upon a correspondingly exclusive definition of 'them', encompassing a vast range of complex international relationships. Viewed in its totality, the *Express* crusade pointed to a wider Battle for Britain, in which British identity featured as both the means and the end.

Great Britain – the nation state in the international context

The reaction of the *Express* to 'Europe' was largely informed by an older isolationist tradition. The paper remained an unrepentant supporter of Munich and appeasement. In retrospect, the 1939 promise to Poland was characterised as a 'foolish guarantee' to a nation which 'by its intransigence plunged us into war'.[128] The *Express* also opposed the US loan and Marshall Aid, as well as British participation in the Western European Union (WEU) and EFTA. With regard to the Cold War, the paper advocated British development of an independent nuclear deterrent and the return of the Rhine Army. 'Leave heavyweight fighting to the heavyweights', Corelli Barnet's article reasoned.[129] A champion of lost causes,

---

[126] *Sunday Express*, 29 July 1962. For an example of *Sunday Express* election calls, see J. Junor, 'Macmillan Must Call an Election Now', 22 October 1961; W. Sendall, 'An Autumn Election?' and 'May Election Likely', 8 July and 14 October 1962; H. Wilson, 'Macmillan Must Call an Election Now', 16 September 1962. See also opinion page columns, 16 and 23 September 1962, and coverage of H. Gaitskell's election request, *Sunday Express*, 30 October 1962.

[127] *Sunday Express*, 2 December 1962. The *Express* took a somewhat repentant line soon after, reminding readers that critiques of the Government were an 'inevitable part of the democratic process ... these criticisms should not be misunderstood'. *Daily Express*, 20 December 1962.

[128] *Daily Express*, 16 August 1961.

[129] *Daily Express*, 8 January 1962.

the *Express* also revelled in its relative isolation in Fleet Street. Staking its claim as a solitary voice of journalistic dissent paralleled a glorifying 'Britain alone' orientation.

The *Express* remained sensitive to charges of isolationism and reacted to Macmillan's characterisation of the anti-Marketeers as 'Little Englanders'. 'Nonsense!', it cried. Britain's destiny lay in its status as 'the centre and force of a Commonwealth that spans the globe and outnumbers the population of the Common Market by four to one'. It added:

> It is advocates of union with the Six who are the 'isolationists', the Little Europeans who cannot see beyond the Continent. The answer to Europe is not withdrawal behind the channel but advance towards the Commonwealth – towards the splendid alternative.[130]

Shifting attention from 'Little Englanders' to 'Little Europeans' and from 'Splendid Isolation' to the 'splendid alternative' was a typical example of *Express* table-turning, an act in keeping with Beaverbrook's unorthodox perception of the outside world.

If the patriotic line of the *Express* papers figured in a framework of traditional responses, it was equally symptomatic of the dichotomy described by A. D. Smith, namely, a nationalist response to globalising trends.[131] The Common Market threat to national sovereignty and Empire coalesced with wider fears for the established nation state before the combined forces of internationalism and new nationalism. Thus, the United Nations (UN) was also a target of Beaverbrook's venom. Alternatively referred to as 'malignant', 'benighted' and 'farcical', the UN entered the world of *Express* demons because it empowered the new nationalist voices of crumbling empires. A list of enemies that included Archbishop Makarios, Nehru and Jomo Kenyatta, among others, gave concrete form to the differentiation between 'our' constructive patriotism and 'their' dangerous, undemocratic and unstable nationalism. A UN vote condemning Britain's Rhodesian policy (seventy-three to one) was thus depicted as a 'disgraceful onslaught' led by Britain's 'tormentors'.[132] UN action in Katanga was labelled 'Blitzkrieg.... Not since Hitler has there been such cold blooded aggression.... Even the methods are the same.'[133] Britain's £10 million UN levy provided the inevitable material affront. The leader page counselled immediate withdrawal and the application of UN levy funds to the defence of Commonwealth interests.[134]

---

[130] *Daily Express*, 22 January 1963. See also *Daily Express* opinion page, 25 October 1961 and 12 December 1962.
[131] Smith, *Nations and Nationalism*, p. 145.
[132] *Daily Express*, 29 June 1962.
[133] *Daily Express*, 14 September 1961.
[134] *Daily Express*, 1 January 1963.

The post-war emergence of the United States as a superpower produced conflicting sentiments. Despite misgivings as a Canadian patriot, Beaverbrook remained largely in favour of the Anglo-American alliance. His views may have been conditioned in part by wartime experience in Washington or subscription to a historicism envisioning a British legacy in the American success story. As a North American businessman, Beaverbrook may also have empathised with the spirit of American capitalism and consumerism. Or perhaps, like many other believers in Churchill's circle, he viewed Atlanticism as a path to influence. The *Express* consistently portrayed Macmillan as a partner in joint exercises of Anglo-American diplomacy. The meeting between Kennedy and Macmillan in Bermuda was thus a conference of 'the Big Two' and the *Express* rejoiced that 'goodwill and strength will march together in the Anglo-American Alliance'.[135]

The *Express* pages of the early 1960s generally divorced America as a cultural and entertainment phenomenon from America as a hegemonic and at times oppressive pursuer of national self-interest. Every copy of the *Express* included a 'This Is America' column, which offered brief synopses of light politics, human-interest stories, spectacular crimes, star personalities and the latest trends. The 'rags to riches' spirit of Horatio Alger loomed large in personality stories, perhaps as a reinforcement of Beaverbrook's own creation myth.[136]

But below a general enthusiasm for the 'special relationship' lurked unease with the America of Abadan and Suez, an opponent of Empire and supporter of the Common Market. When Dean Acheson, the former US Secretary of State, told a West Point audience in December 1962 that 'Britain had lost an empire and ... not yet found a role', the *Express* attacked his 'denigration of Britain's role in the world'. Yet the editors directed anger in equal measure at the British Government's willingness to cast aside Commonwealth assets and at its failure 'to harness the talent and native genius of the people'.[137] An article by Lord Attlee entitled 'We're Still a Great Power' reiterated faith in Anglo-American friendship and excused America's increased tendency to treat Britain as just another European state. 'Who can blame them', he wrote, 'when they see us going cap-in-hand, begging to be allowed to join their Common Market'.[138] The culmination of the Polaris/Skybolt controversy (see Introduction) two weeks after Acheson's comments compounded worries about Britain's worth in American eyes. In subsequent months, articles

---

[135] *Daily Express*, 23 December 1961.
[136] The *Daily Express* referred to John Glenn as 'America's Columbus', 21 February 1962. Mickey Mantle personified the 'rag to riches' dream, 17 April 1962.
[137] *Daily Express*, 7 December 1962. See also 8 December 1962. For the text of Acheson's speech at West Point see *The Times*, 11 December 1962.
[138] *Daily Express*, 7 December 1962.

bearing the phrases 'sell out', 'given up' and 'given away' reinforced a sense of capitulation, a final affront as America shoved Britain towards a diminished role in a Common Market.[139]

Beaverbrook's Britons – the 'us' and 'them' of Empire

Nowhere were doubts over the 'Great' in 'Great Britain' more apparent than in the question of decolonisation. The Empire liquidation lament was a well rehearsed *Express* refrain[140] by the early 1960s but the Common Market application provided further insult to imperial sensitivities. As we have seen, the assertion by the *Express* and its defence of 'us' drew primarily upon a Dominion-derived understanding of the British collective. Time and again the theme emerged in news articles and the leader page. Labour motions for the dissolution of the Southern Rhodesian Federation amounted to a 'slight against our kith and kin'.[141] The *Express* deplored exclusion of Natal sugar growers from Commonwealth markets because 'no people are more stubbornly British than those of Natal'.[142] The text of Heath's October 1961 opening speech in Brussels, which was deliberately withheld from Commonwealth leaders before being leaked, was branded 'a betrayal of brotherhood'.[143]

National obligations implied by kinship were in turn bolstered by a language of debt. With 'Remember Gallipoli' rhetoric the *Express* acknowledged blood debts in a World Wars discourse of ultimate sacrifice. One such homage noted that 'Oceans separate their homelands from each other and Britain.... Yet they came, and tens and hundreds of thousands came with them, to fight for a country they had never seen. Just because that country was Britain.'[144] Honour applied to material obligations as well and readers were supplied with frequent testimonials to wartime generosity. Inevitably, those included Canada's £275 million gift, £160 million interest-free loan and £460 million mutual aid supplies.[145]

The definition of Dominion kinship stood in greatest relief when juxtaposed with the 'other' members of the Commonwealth. Significantly, while Dominion references conjured a crusading vision for the future, the remainder of the Empire or New Commonwealth formed part of a less relevant, rose-coloured past. The Beaverbrook press glorified adventurism abroad in nostalgic terms that suggested cultural and ethnic superiority. In the week preceding the release of the film *Lawrence*

---

[139] See for example *Daily Express*, 19 April 1962.
[140] For examples see *Daily Express* opinion columns for 9 February, 28 October and 2 November 1962.
[141] *Daily Express*, 4 December 1962.
[142] *Daily Express*, 7 December 1961.
[143] *Daily Express*, 25 November 1961.
[144] *Daily Express*, 16 July 1962.
[145] See for instance *Daily Express*, 19 August 1961.

of Arabia, the *Express* serialised 'the century's greatest adventure story'.[146] Sentimental tributes accompanied coverage of decolonisation. An *Express* photo-news feature on Ugandan independence incorporated William Blake as it mourned 'At midnight tomorrow, the Union Jack will be lowered from its flag pole here and Uganda, this green and pleasant land, will become independent'.[147] A January 1963 article on Malta opened with the image of a 'warm January sun set over this corner of the British Empire'.[148] The Southern Cameroons was described as a 'West African banana land', where regrets for Britain's departure tempered the jubilation of independence.[149]

The question of citizenship was conspicuously absent, despite the tributes to Commonwealth unity. Coverage of the Commonwealth Immigration Bill, for instance, was extensive during the second half of 1961. But the leader pages avoided explicit articulations of a British 'us' and alien 'them'. The editors, however, made their racial preferences clear through subtle contrivances of presentation. Thus, a leader entry applauding Government tolerance of Irish immigrants was placed next to an article on the 'savages' and horrors of the Congo.[150] Eleven days later further coverage of the immigration debate was followed by a small article reporting the arrival of 104 jobless Jamaicans on a charter to Gatwick.[151] Concrete evidence of the underlying attitude towards New Commonwealth immigration was explicitly revealed in Beaverbrook's correspondence with his son. In January 1961 Max Aitken wrote to his father,

> I think your suggestion that we should limit all immigration into Britain is right. I am entirely in favour of this; in some ways it strikes at the basis of Empire, but there is little doubt that the Commonwealth countries are unloading refugees upon us who have no intention of working here at all, but going straight on to national assistance.... I do not think this is a subject we want to give prominence in our newspapers but the facts might be interesting.[152]

Ironically, a perception of kinship based on a history of emigration from Britain to the Commonwealth was negatively reinforced by immigration from the Commonwealth to Britain.

In the context of the 'Wind of Change', a Britishness reliant upon Dominion connections seemed increasingly tenuous. As always, the

---

[146] *Daily Express*, 10–14 December 1962.
[147] *Daily Express*, 8 October 1962.
[148] *Daily Express*, 17 January 1963.
[149] *Daily Express*, 2 October 1961.
[150] *Daily Express*, 7 November 1961.
[151] *Daily Express*, 18 November 1961.
[152] M. Aitken to Beaverbrook, 3 January 1961, BBK H/214.

persistence of such an identity in the *Express* owed much to Beaver-brook's influence and the traditional defence of an unfulfilled vision. An expansive Britishness allowed for the continuing allegiance to sub-national identities as well as membership, illusory or not, of a collective that exceeded national borders. Racial distinctions played a significant role and were used more commonly than many, in retrospect, would care to admit.[153]

The European 'them'

While the campaign was framed by assumptions about Britain's place-ment in a global context, it was primarily informed by a typology of the European 'other'. As always, the paradigmatic 'us' and 'them' discourse figured prominently and objections to Common Market membership produced a wealth of negative imagery. An opinion piece that could only have been dictated by Beaverbrook or mimicked by Thomson declared:

> Weep for the Tories! The banners of Joshua are trailing in the mire. Mr. Macmillan describes Britain as the offshore islands of Europe.... But, Britain, drawing strength from the Empire, has always exceeded every country on the Continent in power, influence and prestige.[154]

Beneath revulsion for the Common Market project in its entirety lurked particular distinctions about the leading European players and the relative merits of patriotism and nationalism. De Gaulle's resurrec-tion of past grandeur for application to the French present, for instance, earned him the steadfast admiration of the *Express* opinion page. In part this amounted to identification through wishful thinking, the desperate hope that the General might save Britain from itself. In July 1961 Beaverbrook mused, 'I hope de Gaulle will succeed in excluding Britain from the European set-up, thus throwing her entirely on her Empire resources'.[155]

The French President's national greatness ethos was frequently com-pared with the patriotic insufficiencies of the Macmillan Government. Of course, France was European and therefore subject to the scepticism accorded all foreigners. But in de Gaulle the *Express* located funda-mental values of national pride and national self-interest. In fact, the notable qualities mentioned in descriptions of him, 'courage, patriotism, and a magnificent disregard for difficulties',[156] resembled British vir-tues. De Gaulle was credited with a comprehension of Britain's national

---

[153] Interview with Michael Foot, 27 October 1998.
[154] *Daily Express*, 14 June 1962.
[155] Beaverbrook to C. Pincher, 18 July 1961, BBK H/218.
[156] *Daily Express*, 24 August 1962.

interests that escaped most British politicians. His rejection of Polaris missiles and dedication to the development of an independent nuclear deterrent was called a 'French Lesson'.[157] His re-election in November 1962 was hailed as 'the triumph of the patriot over those who discount patriotism. That is what gives it a special significance. And not for France alone.'[158] The *Express* further identified with the General on imperial issues. Sympathetic coverage of his 'Algerian problem' contrasted ungrateful backward subjects with the modernising and civilising influences of colonial rule.[159]

While extolling Gaullist patriotism, the *Express* denounced German nationalism as historically and therefore inevitably prone to excess. War memories featured throughout the Beaverbrook press as entertainment, analytic tool and propaganda material. In the opening months of 1961 alone, the *Sunday Express* serialised stories on de Gaulle, Mussolini and Rudolf Hess. But Germany, of all the Axis powers, was set aside for special treatment. According to one Fleet Street rumour, Beaverbrook ordered all writers to refer to the World Wars as 'The First German War and The Second German War'. 'Which makes Lord Beaverbrook's campaign', one television commentator joked, 'the Third German War'.[160]

Express materialism incorporated economic performance both as a component of identity and as a measure of the intentions of the 'other'. Beaverbrook capitalised on traditional suspicions and fears about German competition. The *Express* projected economics as a substitute for defeated militarism by linking alleged economic ambitions to the World Wars experience. Accordingly, German exporters would use the Common Market to dismantle British industry, control a captive market and destroy the Empire. Thus, in Chancellor Adenauer's claim that maintenance of a Commonwealth trade bloc was incompatible with Common Market membership, 'Germany's purpose is the same as it was in two World Wars'.[161]

Stereotypes of German national character lent themselves to fears of a resurgent power in Europe and the spectre of war over the building of the Berlin Wall. The *Express* relentlessly depicted an untrustworthy Germany, bent on the recovery of lost territories and unification. The Berlin question was a cause deemed 'not consistent with the temper and outlook of the British race'.[162] The *Express* version of history justified what the paper believed to be Khrushchev's decision to build the Wall, given 'the long history of Teutonic invasions ending in the unparalleled pillage

[157] *Daily Express*, 28 December 1962.
[158] *Daily Express*, 27 November 1962.
[159] See *Daily Express* opinion column, 25 January and 20 February 1962, for examples.
[160] ITV transcript, 'What the Papers Say', 29 March 1962. Copy in BBK H/223.
[161] *Daily Express*, 10 March 1962.
[162] *Daily Express*, 13 October 1961.

of the last war'.[163] Hints from the national chairman of the German Free Democrats, Dr Erich Mende, that his party was willing to talk to the Soviets, awakened fears that Germany might cut a secret deal with Russia for the purposes of reunification. Ensuing *Express* hysteria managed to incorporate references to the Rapallo Treaty of 1922 as well as the 1939 Soviet–Nazi pact.[164] In early January 1962 it ran a photo of Stalin and Ribbentrop and warned that 'From Frederick the Great through Bismarck to Hitler the Germans have repeatedly deserted the West for the East'.[165]

Express opinion was well known in Germany and in January 1962 Beaverbrook successfully provoked his own German 'war', a skirmish with *Bild Zeitung*.[166] Given its German Free Democrat sympathies, Herr Springer's paper took exception to the wilder claims in the *Express* about secret Russian 'deals'. 'We Germans Are Finally Fed Up', *Bild* protested. The *Express* countered with allegations that Herr Springer's papers were guilty of spreading 'Nazi-like propaganda'[167] and added continuous assertions belittling the East German threat. In a further turn of Macmillan's 1959 re-election theme it claimed that 'The West Berliners are well fed, well housed and as free as ever. They have never had it so good.'[168] Again this was too much for *Bild Zeitung*, which told its three million readers that 'The *Daily Express* is known for its hatred of Germany. It has a frightening lack of instinct … to claim in the face of the wall that life was never so good for us is either malicious or stupid.'[169]

Banal nationalism and grand issues of Common Market membership

Beyond the manipulated conceptions of 'us' and 'them', the *Express* cultivated public fears by depicting British identity under siege. In the broadest sense, Common Market membership implied the swamping of the British Isles as a historic, cultural and political entity.

> How important then to realise that the drive for British market entry is not primarily concerned with economics. The aim is to submerge Britain's identity with that of foreigners in Europe. Do you want to be British? Or are you willing that you and your children should belong to some British-French-German-Italian hotchpotch?[170]

---

[163] *Daily Express*, 22 November 1961.
[164] *Sunday Express*, 10 December 1961.
[165] *Daily Express*, 5 January 1962.
[166] On Beaverbrook's orders, all criticism by *Bild Zeitung* was printed in full in the *Express*. Beaverbrook to M. Aitken, 19 January 1962, BBK H/220.
[167] *Daily Express*, 17 January 1962.
[168] *Daily Express*, 31 January 1962.
[169] *Bild Zeitung*, quoted in *Daily Express*, 6 February 1962.
[170] *Daily Express*, 6 January 1962.

Influencing the man on the street required a diminished aura of high politics and a detailed celebration of the British way of life. In this regard one of the most potent features of the *Express* campaign lay in its conscious elevation of the unconscious or banal components of Britishness.

In keeping with its dedication to Rhyl and Derby man (see above), ominous aspects of Common Market membership were couched in implications for everyday living. The impartial British police officer, referred to as the 'pride of Britain. And the envy of the rest',[171] was thus contrasted with the Continental 'traditions' of arbitrary intervention, extremism and fascism. Daily bread occupied particularly hallowed ground and one's dinner plate became a benchmark of patriotism in articles protesting against the faddish pretensions of foreign foods. 'Let's forget the croissants and coffee and settle for the traditional breakfast of bacon and eggs, lashings of porridge and plenty of the thickest darkest marmalade we can find.'[172] Rene MacColl presented the imposition of metric measurement as an alien precursor of darker threats:

> Centigrade for Fahrenheit, octals for shillings, and presumably before long we'll be driving on the right side of the road. A cricket pitch is 22 yards long. Come now – what's that in metres? As far as I'm concerned a firkin is still nine gallons, and I don't care what the Common Market chums make of that.... This could be the sunset of the British way of life.[173]

Page 1 propaganda boxes raised scaremongering to new heights by incorporating everything from the borough council to car ownership. Freedom of labour movement lent itself to visions of mass nomadic migrations.[174] Trade unionists were warned, 'If Britain enters the Common Market foreigners will swarm here'.[175] Obscure European laws implied new levels of subjugation before faceless 'foreign agents'.[176]

The anti-Market political agenda obliged the *Express* to address the constitutional and diplomatic aspects of the Rome Treaty. But exploration of the grand issues of membership in no way dimmed treatment of the consequences for ordinary citizens. Detailed threats to daily life pointed upwards to negotiations in Brussels and at the same time grounded high political themes that were otherwise clouded by complex detail or remote diplomacy. Thus, popular historicism, personal economics, individual liberty and collective belonging infused the treatment of national sovereignty, agriculture and Commonwealth trade concerns.

---

[171] *Daily Express*, 3 July 1962.
[172] *Daily Express*, 19 February 1962.
[173] *Daily Express*, 16 January 1962.
[174] *Daily Express*, 30 November 1962.
[175] *Daily Express*, 5 February 1962.
[176] *Daily Express*, 7 April 1962. See also 11–12 June 1962.

National sovereignty

Beaverbrook's 'Commonwealth not Common Market' orientation must not obscure the profound importance the *Express* attached to issues of national sovereignty. In fact, the campaign vehemently defended the concept before all prospective incursions. The populist strength of the *Express* defence drew primary sustenance from its absolute definition of national sovereignty as 'our most precious possession – the Freedom and Independence of our people'.[177]

In general, sovereignty appeared as an inviolable historic right rather than as an abstract principle. Crown-in-Parliament sovereignty, the legacy of a revolt against Rome, was thus emphasised in the context of Anglo-European relations. The *Daily Express* claimed the Magna Carta, Trafalgar and the Reform Bill as testaments to British independence,[178] while the *Sunday Express* invoked the Armada, Napoleon and World War II. Before the ominous Treaty of Rome, it claimed, Britain faced the spectre of rule from 'a council on the Continent'.[179] The spirit of the entire agreement was presented as anathema to British sensibilities and more in keeping with the Continent's 'tradition of absolutism and unbridled government'.[180] In his *Sunday Express* column, A. J. P. Taylor compared the Common Market to the German *Zollverein*, equating the price of membership with an end of independence for individual states. 'Within thirty years', he wrote, 'many of them ceased to exist and the rest were marching under Prussian orders'.[181] Recent history informed dark assumptions about the Rome Treaty's ultimate goals. 'Shall we join the Dictators?', the *Express* asked.[182] 'Questions of Sovereignty' propaganda boxes prophesied 'Britannia can only enter Europe in chains', forecast an end to British authority over taxing and spending, and envisioned the transfer of trade decisions to Common Market bureaucrats.[183] The *Express* reinforced the sense of constitutional violation by declaring the secretive negotiating process undemocratic. It championed populist principles by repeatedly calling for an election or referendum on the Common Market issue.[184]

The expansive definition of sovereignty meant that any threat to Parliament also presented risks for the Crown. On the principle of monarchy and its accompanying imperial and constitutional connotations,

---

[177] *Daily Express*, 29 March 1962.
[178] *Daily Express*, 30 March 1962.
[179] *Sunday Express*, 18 June 1961.
[180] *Daily Express*, 29 September 1962.
[181] *Sunday Express*, 2 July 1961.
[182] *Daily Express*, 29 August 1962.
[183] *Daily Express*, 15 December 1962. See also 14 and 17 December 1962.
[184] For examples, see *Daily Express* opinion column 12 October and 19 November 1962.

the *Express* remained steadfastly loyal. It worried about the fate 'of the magic and mystique of the Queen's authority'.[185] Playing to the obvious importance of the monarchy for many of its readers, it warned 'Well may the Government fear the wrath of its supporters if ever they are required to sing not the present national anthem but "God Save Professor Hallstein"'.[186]

The philosophic support of the *Express* for the monarchy, however, clashed with Beaverbrook's traditional distrust of hereditary institutions.[187] Thus, while the Queen herself was accorded utmost loyalty and admiration, the extended monarchy received less generous treatment. In particular John Gordon at the *Sunday Express* criticised the Royal Family's extravagant use of helicopters, yachts and planes. 'Expenditure on minor royals', he complained, 'is rising far above what most people consider reasonable and even generous'.[188] Prince Philip emerged as a primary target and Beaverbrook took personal exception to his public support for British Common Market membership.[189] So there was little surprise when, during a trip to South America in March 1962, the Prince exclaimed 'The *Daily Express* is a bloody awful newspaper. Full of lies, scandal and imagination. It is a vicious paper.'[190] The outburst appeared in other papers and generated a parliamentary motion against Beaverbrook's treatment of the Royal Family. Despite the controversy the Prince remained an *Express* target.[191]

Agriculture

In one of its few stands on behalf of producer interests, the campaign also defended the British farmer. The sustenance and growth of British agriculture had always been central to the *Express* mission.[192] But the emergence of the Common Market as a challenge to British farmers, and small farmers in particular, pushed agricultural concerns to the fore. To this end *Farming Express* was founded in June 1960. Ostensibly a protest against the ominous 'betrayal' of British agriculture 'in view of the dangerous movement for making Britain a province of Europe',[193] *Farming*

[185] *Sunday Express*, 10 September 1961.

[186] *Daily Express*, 11 September 1961. Dr Walter Hallstein was the first President of the European Commission, serving from 1958 to 1967.

[187] Allen, *Voice of Britain*, pp. 63, 88; Edgar, *Express '56*, p. 125.

[188] J. Gordon to Beaverbrook, undated, January 1961, BBK H/217.

[189] Howard, *Beaverbrook*, pp. 141–2. See also Beaverbrook's *Sunday Express* article 'This Is Why I Believe What I Believe', 6 May 1962.

[190] *Daily Express*, 21 March 1962.

[191] For examples see *Daily Express*, 11 August 1962 and 5 June 1963.

[192] M. Aitken statement on *Farming Express*, quoted in *Daily Express*, 28 November 1961.

[193] *Farming Express*, 23 June 1960, quoted in *Sunday Express*, 18 February 1962.

Express was a 'fly by night activity'[194] and a persistent money loser. None-theless, its incorporation of *Daily Express* propaganda techniques included the distribution of 35,000 'Fight the Common Market' window stickers and the provision of speakers for agricultural meetings.[195]

The *Express* defended farming interests in part because the issue conformed to Beaverbrook's protectionist inclinations. It was a point he emphasised in a memo to *Daily Express* editor Edward Pickering:

> Our policy is protectionism wheresoever applied. Wherever we can keep out the foreigner we wish to do so. Whosoever applies for protection in relation to agriculture whether it is for agriculture's production or pro-duction that is consumed by agriculture, we must be on the side of the angels and the angels were protectionists. Never depart from that general principle.[196]

As the articles of Ed Trow and others suggested, the *Express* valued farming not only as an occupation but also as a way of life. In par-ticular it emphasised the fate of the small farmer, though such appeals frequently lacked a supporting economic logic. Before economists' sug-gestions that there were too many small and therefore inefficient farms, Trow replied 'I say there are too many economists'.[197] Despite an interest in the patriotic facets of small farms, the *Express* generally resisted temptations to romanticise the British landscape and country lifestyle. In fact, farming was portrayed as a competitive and progressive industry. Trow celebrated the higher quality of farm shows at the Olympia Exhibi-tion Centre by noting that 'The bowler hat and rolled umbrella brigade is being forced out of the British farm show. For the first time since the war, a national farm show has set out to cater for the men who really matter.'[198] Bountiful harvests were credited to the improved land management techniques of post-war farmers.[199] 'In a single generation the farmers have increased total output by 80% with a labour force that has fallen by half.'[200] Numerous articles celebrated the benefits of robust agricultural production.[201]

A vigorous endorsement of British agricultural interests and the existing price support structure demanded a corresponding indictment of Europe's system of agricultural price reviews. The *Express* rejected the CAP because it failed to address the unique character and 'special

---

[194] Interview with Sir John Junor, 19 November 1996.

[195] E. Pickering to Beaverbrook, 16 July and 5 June 1962, BBK H/225.

[196] Beaverbrook to E. Pickering, 12 March 1962, BBK H/225.

[197] *Daily Express*, 30 January 1963.

[198] *Daily Express*, 23 October 1962.

[199] For example see *Daily Express*, 12 November 1962.

[200] *Daily Express*, 30 June 1963.

[201] For example see *Daily Express* opinion column, 12 December 1961.

difficulties'[202] faced by British farmers. The European design for agricultural funding via penalties on food imports, and in Britain's case
Commonwealth imports, offered further affront. The *Express* described
the system as intolerable and concluded that 'money taken by Britain
from Canada would be used to finance agriculture in Europe! What a
preposterous notion!'[203]

Empire Free Trade and 'dear food'

The fight on behalf of British farming and the Commonwealth pointed to
the personal apex of Beaverbrook's anti-Market trinity, the final mobilisation of his lifelong commitment to Empire Free Trade. Under variations
on that theme, a dream of Greater Britain coalesced in an amalgam of
imperial glorification, banal patriotism, boundless prosperity, agricultural defence, 'common man' consumerism and anti-Europeanism. As
a Beaverbrook priority, the Commonwealth trade mantra was a well
rehearsed, sentimental and easily applied alternative to the Common
Market. But the appeal was compromised by problems of presentation
and outdated or insufficient detail.

Whatever its real or imagined relevance, the notion of Empire Free
Trade as an alternative to Britain's membership of the Common Market
summoned ghosts from the earlier Empire Crusade and beyond. Justification for the pursuit of a Commonwealth trade policy relied upon
a historicism of treachery and loss. Robert Peel's reluctance to retain
protectionism in 1846 and Arthur James Balfour's inability to embrace
the imperial trade cause in 1903 were both linked to electoral failure
and subsequent years of aimless opposition.[204] Stanley Baldwin's refusal
to grant preference for Commonwealth meat producers and 1938 agreements to remove duties on foreign wheat were highlighted as gross
betrayals of the spirit of the Ottawa Agreements.[205] A *Sunday Express*
book review eulogised Neville Chamberlain as a man of patriotic vision
whose 'proudest achievement was the policy of protection and Empire
trade by which he hauled Britain back to prosperity'.[206]

The story of unfulfilled Commonwealth trade options was accompanied by an Empire Free Trade strategy that was historic in its own
right. By his own admission, Beaverbrook never actually met his hero,
Joseph Chamberlain.[207] But Empire Free Trade, as Beaverbrook acknowledged, was the policy of Chamberlain 'renewed, renamed and re-shaped'

---

[202] *Sunday Express*, 22 July 1962.
[203] *Daily Express*, 16 January 1962.
[204] *Daily Express*, 8 May 1962.
[205] *Daily Express*, 12 September 1962.
[206] *Daily Express*, 26 November 1961.
[207] Lord Beaverbrook, *Resources of the British Empire* (London, 1934), p. 100.

to suit his own imperial crusade. Thus, whereas Chamberlain spoke of imperial preferences, Beaverbrook imagined a complete preference system of free trade within the confines of a British, Dominions and Commonwealth system.

During his 1929–31 Empire Crusade, Beaverbrook proclaimed the campaign 'a movement that will save the British race'.[208] Thirty years later the stakes and strategic formula remained largely the same. In a *Sunday Express* article entitled 'This Is Why I Believe What I Believe', he wrote: 'It is my firm belief that the Common Market ... will in effect destroy the system of Imperial Preference, and on that account the structure of the British Empire or Commonwealth'.[209] Beaverbrook's articulation of the path to Empire Free Trade remained embedded in the earlier campaigns. In the 1934 edition of *Resources of the British Empire*, his 'practical formula' accorded 'First place to the home producer in the home market. Second place to other Empire producers. Third place to the foreigner.'[210] Beaverbrook offered no apology for the lack of detailed specificity, claiming 'The case for Empire Free Trade does not depend upon ingenious pleading. It is founded upon the facts of Imperial trade.... It needs no further arguments.'[211] In fact, during the entirety of its anti-Market crusade the *Express* never authoritatively presented the logistics for a system of preferences. The only blueprint to appear in the pages of the *Express* was excerpted from *A Call to the Commonwealth*,[212] a document produced by two Tory MPs that articulated an inclusive, multiracial definition of Commonwealth interests. Beaverbrook's *Sunday Express* article on the 'stomach tax' offered little vision and even less optimism: 'We will fight but if we lose this struggle against folly and wickedness then our last hope is that Canada may be willing to take up the leadership of the British Empire that the British Government is determined to abdicate'.[213]

Apart from any historical perspective, Empire Free Trade policy in the early 1960s required justification as a pillar of national interest and identity, the antithesis of Common Market membership. The *Express* never shied from reminding the Government of its imperial identity and obligations. William Barkley claimed that 'The odd thing is that here in 1961 we are faced with the same unresolved dilemmas of 30 years ago. Still the Tory Party without Empire or Commonwealth, is nothing as was once said.'[214] Extension of the argument prophesied a party split along a Commonwealth–Europe fault line and carried an implicit threat that the

[208] Lord Beaverbrook, *My Case for Empire Free Trade* (London, 1930), p. 24.
[209] *Sunday Express*, 6 May 1962.
[210] Beaverbrook, *Resources of the British Empire*, p. 12.
[211] *Ibid.*, p. 14.
[212] Walker and Walker-Smith, *A Call to the Commonwealth*.
[213] 'A Statement by Lord Beaverbrook', *Sunday Express*, 11 February 1962.
[214] *Daily Express*, 25 November 1961.

Express might revoke its traditional support for the Tories.[215] Wherever possible the stakes were raised by portraying Britain's application as a stark choice between Europe and the Commonwealth, between surrender and an embrace of national destiny. 'A whole misguided chapter of enthusiasm for Europe and coolness towards the Commonwealth would be ended in an instant. One decision alone is essential – the decision by the people and their leaders to *Make Britain great again!*'[216]

The relevance of Empire Free Trade, and indeed the Commonwealth itself, required a portrayal of Commonwealth trade as the natural and progressive path to British prosperity. But prevailing trends in the comparative growth of trade with the Commonwealth and Europe were not favourable. To compensate, the *Express* made reference to short-term trade variations but ignored the long-term negative trends. The editors seized upon trade figures for the fourth quarter of 1962, for instance, which demonstrated an increase in exports to the Commonwealth and a corresponding fall in exports to the Six.[217]

Most importantly, the *Express* resurrected the historic 'dear food' issue in a banal and consumer-orientated discourse. The 'stomach tax' was an old bogey, 'the ancient liberal slogan'[218] that undermined Joseph Chamberlain and latterly Beaverbrook's own Empire Crusade. But rather than banish the food price debate, Beaverbrook exorcised the demon by expropriating the label and inverting its meaning for anti-Market purposes. Front-page propaganda boxes thus invested affordable food with a patriotic value. The cheap bread loaf, redolent of the Chamberlain era debate, re-emerged with food price increases[219] as a symbolic consequence of European membership. Accordingly, the EEC demanded taxes on inexpensive Commonwealth imports to coddle inefficient French wheat producers with the inevitable result, 'YOUR FOOD WILL COST YOU MORE!'[220] NFU predictions of 10 per cent increases in food prices if Britain joined[221] featured prominently, as did warnings of 'the foreign giant looming over breakfast'.[222] A hearth-and-home Britishness was central to an appeal incorporating women and family. 'Housewives Beware! … If Britain enters Europe experts estimate that food prices will soar by 4s in the £. A rise of nearly 8s per week in the food bill for every man, woman and child in the country!'[223] There were also reminders for the Government of the readership's electoral inclinations. Successive

---

[215] *Daily Express*, 28 July 1962.
[216] *Daily Express*, 12 December 1962.
[217] *Daily Express*, 3 January 1963.
[218] *Daily Express*, 22 June 1962.
[219] *Daily Express*, 19 March 1962.
[220] *Daily Express*, 22 June 1962.
[221] *Daily Express*, 9 January 1963. See also 22 January 1963.
[222] *Daily Express*, 7 November 1962.
[223] *Daily Express*, 18 December 1962.

propaganda boxes in January 1963 warned the Tory Party's workers, MPs, contributors and candidates of imminent political fall-out from any attempt to 'substitute dear French food for cheap Commonwealth fare'.[224]

For the *Express* the likely abandonment of Commonwealth preferences was a 'disaster'[225] and its realisation 'a dreadful surrender'.[226] But by the early 1960s preferences in Empire Free Trade form were no longer a viable proposition. Despite the depth of his commitment, Beaverbrook was under no illusions about the prospects for his imperial cause. Disappointed by the terms of the 1932 Ottawa Agreements, he pledged 'The Crusade goes on and on until the goal is reached'.[227] But the growing futility of Empire Free Trade privately haunted him from the early 1950s.[228] Six months prior to Macmillan's Common Market application, Beaverbrook discouraged Lord Balfour's bid for a 'Commonwealth First Movement', claiming that 'The movement to which you and I have dedicated our political lives has come to an end. And we should not waste time and effort in the language of the hustings in "beating a dead horse".'[229] In May 1962 Beaverbrook took an apologetic tone with his readers when he claimed his sole 'regret' in life was 'that I have failed in my struggle for political and commercial union of the British Empire'.[230]

The appearance of the phrase 'Empire Free Trade', however infrequent, owed its presence to Beaverbrook's continuing dominance over the construction of *Express* opinions. Its previous failures, contemporary relevance or prospects for attainment were of little consequence. The cause transcended its plausibility because its architect had become its physical embodiment. For Beaverbrook, Empire Free Trade was not an alternative path, it was the only path. Its inclusion was an imperative dictated by a personal pattern of political opposition, by a particular historic frame of reference and ultimately by a subjectively imagined vision of British national identity.

Conclusion

De Gaulle's press conference of 14 January 1963 brought a temporary respite in the anti-Market battle. 'Non!' read the *Express* headline, 'De Gaulle blocks the way'.[231] In an accompanying page 1 cartoon, Cummings

---

[224] *Daily Express*, 7–10 January 1963.

[225] *Sunday Express*, 13 May 1962.

[226] *Daily Express*, 28 July 1962.

[227] Beaverbrook, *Resources of the British Empire*, p. 73.

[228] See Beaverbook letter to J. W. Brittain, 14 February 1952, as well as a December 1954 message to shareholders quoted in Taylor, *Beaverbrook*, pp. 602, 614.

[229] Beaverbrook to Balfour, 1 January 1961, BBK C/22.

[230] *Sunday Express*, 6 May 1962.

[231] *Daily Express*, 15 January 1963.

depicted de Gaulle as a gendarme stopping Kennedy and Macmillan in vehicles bearing Polaris missiles and the Common Market application, respectively. Once again, the *Express* suggested, de Gaulle was offering Britain lessons in the pursuit of national greatness.[232] A fortnight later the final collapse of talks led to the rejoicing headline 'Glory, Glory Hallelujah! It's All Over. Now Forward.'[233] Naturally, the *Express* opinion page highlighted its solo efforts and championed 'the right to take credit for a sound policy which was in the end, supported by most of the people in the country'.[234]

Beaverbrook's personal response to de Gaulle's veto was ambiguous. According to his secretary, Colin Vines, the event passed without great celebration at Cherkeley Court, Beaverbrook's estate in Surrey.[235] There are a number of possible reasons for Beaverbrook's reticence. First, he was privy to de Gaulle's intentions well in advance[236] and probably came to terms with its meaning before the General's press conference. Second, Beaverbrook appeared rather less inclined than the *Express* to accept personal credit for the defeat of Britain's application. Indeed, his realisation that the veto owed far more to French objections than the *Express* campaign[237] was coupled with a certainty that future British applications would follow:

> Of course it was those who rallied round the banner who made the posi-
> tion impossible for the Government here. They have seized on the de
> Gaulle way out, but if they had not found that way we would have crushed
> their movement. The struggle is not yet over. But we have won the first
> campaign.[238]

Primarily, however, Beaverbrook's reserve stemmed from personal reflections which placed the Common Market battle in the context of a lifelong quest for imperial unity. During an interview in 1964 with the *Telegraph*, he openly wept when questioned about the failure of the Empire Crusade. 'I was unworthy', he confessed. 'I thought I could carry on the great policy of Joe Chamberlain. But I failed, you know. I failed.'[239]

---

232 *Sunday Express*, 20 January 1963.
233 *Daily Express*, 30 January 1963.
234 *Daily Express*, 31 July 1963.
235 Vines, *A Little Nut Brown Man*, p. 148.
236 C. Pincher, *Pastoral Symphony* (Shrewsbury, 1993), p. 49.
237 Taylor, *Beaverbrook*, p. 655.
238 Beaverbrook to C. Gunner, 2 February 1963, BBK F/4. See also Beaverbrook to Lambton, 4 April 1963, BBK C/200.
239 H. Massingham interview with Lord Beaverbrook, quoted in Taylor, *Beaverbrook*, p. 667.

Viewed in retrospect, the chained Crusader provides a most appropriate symbol of Beaverbrook's anti-Market campaign, a cause shackled by tensions both in its methods and in its imagined version of British national identity. For all its expansive sentimentality and idealistic certainties, incompatible dualities restrained Beaverbrook's crusade. Many contradictions arose because the campaign, like its Empire Crusade predecessor, relied upon 'the Proprietor's' whim rather than any grand design. Beaverbrook preached a full attack on the Common Market but circumscribed its pursuit almost entirely within the confines of Fleet Street. The *Express* claimed *de facto* chairmanship of the movement against membership but seemed reluctant to share the platform. Beaverbrook ran the campaign but publicly disavowed any responsibility for its conduct. He condemned the Government but spared the Prime Minister. Above all else, the *Express* claimed to speak for Britain while telling Britons exactly what they ought to think.

The anti-Market campaign was also chained by tensions between the imagined community as a fixed historic vision and the imagined community as on ongoing proposition. Beaverbrook's exposition of contemporary Britishness relied heavily upon an idealised version of uniqueness that set Britain's experience of Empire against 'other' national histories. But as the basis of a glorious past the Beaverbrookian definition was increasingly remote. Its imagination depended upon the continuing retrieval of an unfulfilled ethos culled from the age of Joseph Chamberlain. Thus, the centrality of an imperial past was temporally problematic because its continuing relevance demanded a process of imaginative reaffirmation. As a contemporary proposition, that vision was at odds with the 'Wind of Change' political realities, as well as with the application to join Europe. Moreover, as a proposition for destiny, Beaverbrook's New Jerusalem was a work in progress. The achievement of his ideal imagined community was contingent upon the salvation of a Dominion unity whose realisation decreased with its extension into the future.

Ultimately, however, *Express* Britishness was posited as a unified collective and claimed populist currency in spite of, and because of, its intrinsic dualities and inconsistencies. Opposing the Common Market on the basis of national identity and national interest allowed the *Express* to transcend party politics, incorporate seemingly disparate voices, exploit traditional values and symbols, and provide the basis for genuinely populist opposition. At a time when the membership issue was largely de-politicised, Beaverbrook filled a void with the unorthodox and powerful resources of patriotic sentiment. Where the Government issued assurances or avoided discussion of the political or economic consequences, Beaverbrook offered a Pandora's box of anxieties and threats to the fundamental components of British national identity. Moreover, having raised profound apprehensions, the *Express* placed its answer to the Common Market question in the certainties of who 'we' were, who 'we' are and who 'we' might become. Chained or not, Beaverbrook's Crusader raised significant questions about the relationship between integration and national identity, which, as we shall see in Chapter 5, the Macmillan Government ignored at its peril.

3

Pundits

As Beaverbrook's campaigners discovered, prominent anti-Market 'experts' were scarce and some were in any case reluctant to align themselves with his crusading practices. Some pundits feared compromising their independent voices. For others, Common Market opposition was less a principled certainty than an evolution towards dissent based upon the terms emerging from the negotiation process. Those who joined the debate faced analytical obstacles. Economic and political comparisons, in particular, were complicated by the absence of fixed terms of entry, an embryonic agricultural policy and the relative youth of the Common Market. 'The calculation of gains and losses is difficult', E. J. Mishan wrote. 'In any event there must be plenty of guesswork about the new pattern of trade.'[1] Punditry was also an exercise bound by the constraints of public expectation and journalistic demand, whereby commentators restricted their judgements to a particular realm of expertise. Given both the uncertain and expansive implications of Common Market membership, this was no easy task.

Nonetheless, as this chapter will show, a prominent group of historians, economists and political scientists embraced the anti-Market position. Irrespective of their academic disciplines, analysis inexorably led pundits to emphasise the political rather than the economic goals of the Treaty of Rome. The political angles in turn accentuated considerations of history and national identity, through a preponderance of 'us' and 'them' comparisons. The more the Common Market was treated as a political entity the more patriotic and vehement was the technical opposition to British entry. But this tendency was more than an analytic convenience. Rather, it was a reflection of banal nationalist assumptions about British uniqueness. That tendency was by no means a guarantee of

---

[1] E. J. Mishan, 'The Economic Case Against Joining the Common Market', *Listener*, 14 September 1961, p. 372.

consensus, however. Indeed, expert opinion diverged precisely because it was formulated through varying interpretations of Britain's historic development and future role.

Historians

More than most, committed anti-Market historians played upon the imagined nation and the banal components of belonging. In each case, the fundamental nature of Britishness and the defining elements of British national interest were thought to be at stake. The anti-Market conclusions were constructed through contrasting interpretative assumptions. In part this was a matter of political inclinations but the manner in which the pundits joined and pursued the debate also played a role. Above all, it was a function of defining the essence of the nation's unique historic evolution.

C. E. Carrington

Tributes to an imperial past and assessment of the Common Market application as a strategic mistake placed the historian C. E. Carrington within the broad discourse of anti-Market sentiment. For Carrington the Commonwealth was a distinguished and uniquely British construct, 'an association rarely understood by outsiders'.[2] On the basis of its continued association, he declared 'Britain is still much more than an island in the North Atlantic'.[3]

As was the case with many others who objected to British membership, Carrington's Commonwealth enthusiasm was informed by personal experience. The son of a clergyman, Carrington was born in West Bromwich in 1897. When he was five years old the family moved to New Zealand, where he remained through his schooling, at Christ's College. Distinguished service in both World Wars followed, as well as a scholarly pursuit of Commonwealth interests. In 1954 Carrington became Chair of Commonwealth Relations at the Royal Institute of International Affairs, a post he held at the time of Britain's first application. His written work addressed a variety of Commonwealth themes and included the authorised biography of Rudyard Kipling and partial editorship of the *Cambridge History of the British Empire*.[4] Carrington never denied the

---

[2] C. E. Carrington, 'Commonwealth or Common Market', *Statist*, 15 December 1961, p. 1205.
[3] C. E. Carrington, *The Liquidation of the British Empire* (London, 1961), p. 68.
[4] L. E. Benians, Sir J. Butler and C. E. Carrington (eds), *The Cambridge History of the British Empire: Vol. 3, The Empire – Commonwealth 1870–1919* (Cambridge, 1959).

Victorian foundations of his views[5] and identified Gordon, Cromer, Kitchener, Lawrence and Allenby as 'shining' if unfashionable British heroes.[6] Nor did his romantic streak lead him to underestimate the unifying force of shared identity, kinship and culture, 'the immaterial bonds of the Commonwealth, "lighter than air but stronger than steel"'.[7]

Carrington's rendering of a 'Commonwealth before Common Market' imperative was distinctive both in its presentational methods and, more importantly, in the assumptions of its supporting logic. With the exception of one article printed in the ACML collection *Britain Not Europe*,[8] his written efforts remained aloof from pressure group affiliation.[9] A tenor of scholarly authority paralleled the independent standing. He appreciated the reality of sentimental connections but his Common Market arguments largely 'eschewed the introduction of emotional factors'.[10]

Carrington's detachment from Beaverbrookian imperial glorification was a matter of conviction rather than academic method. Essentially, his Common Market views derived from a wider devotion to free trade as the historic determinant of both British uniqueness and Commonwealth viability. The European question, he argued, amounted to more than the choice implied by Commonwealth versus Common Market rhetoric.

> What we are to decide is whether the liberal, world wide, Commonwealth tradition is still to provide the first principle of British policy or whether this is now to take second place while we commit ourselves to a regional bloc sheltered behind a tariff wall and engaged in a project of federal union.[11]

In the wider debate those convictions occupied a minority position. Carrington asked, 'Are there no liberals (with a small initial letter) left in Britain?'[12]

As the title of his *The British Overseas: Exploits of a Nation of Shopkeepers*[13] revealed, Carrington placed national uniqueness within a commercial and expansive definition of the Commonwealth experience.

---

[5] *The Times*, 25 June 1990, p. 14.
[6] Carrington, *The Liquidation*, p. 70.
[7] *Ibid.*, p. 85.
[8] C. E. Carrington, 'Commonwealth or Common Market?', in R. H. Corbet (ed.), *Britain Not Europe. Commonwealth Before Common Market* (London, 1962), pp. 39–40.
[9] C. E. Carrington, 'Commonwealth or Common Market?', *Statist*, 15 December 1961, pp. 1204–5; 'Between the Commonwealth and Europe', *International Affairs*, 38:4 (October 1962), pp. 449–59; letters to *The Times* 17, 25 July 1961, 14 July 1962 and 6 February 1963.
[10] Carrington, 'Between the Commonwealth and Europe', p. 457.
[11] Carrington, 'Commonwealth or Common Market?', in *Britain Not Europe*, p. 37.
[12] Carrington, letter to *The Times*, 17 July 1961.
[13] C. E. Carrington, *The British Overseas: Exploits of a Nation of Shopkeepers* (Cambridge, 1968).

Frequent devotionals to Adam Smith linked Carrington to the older liberal approach to Empire.[14] 'No country other than Britain', he wrote, 'has yet learned the simple lesson that a liberal import policy promotes exports'.[15] Despite reservations about the merits of decolonisation in some individual cases, he embraced the emergence of independent Commonwealth states as a notable achievement.[16] The transition, he argued, was a shift away from the theories of 'Chamberlain, Milner and the Round Table group, and towards the decentralised system of Laurier and Smuts'.[17] The corollary of the free trade embrace was a denial of a closed imperial system. In a paraphrase of Adam Smith he warned that 'it was not only bad policy, it was bad business and unworthy of "the nation of shopkeepers"'.[18] Where Beaverbrook lamented unfulfilled possibilities in the Ottawa Conference of 1932, Carrington found wisdom in Baldwin's response to protectionist agitation.[19]

Carrington's patriotic instincts were neither flagrantly anti-European nor based upon the absolutes of national sovereignty. In fact, he thought European negotiations offered a belated opportunity for enhanced 'cultural co-operation'.[20] He was reconciled to the eventualities of internationalism and world government.[21] Nonetheless, his recognition of global forces stopped short of an acceptance of internationalism on any terms. Carrington objected to the Government's application because he believed in the merits of a British model for international economic and political relations. 'We in the Commonwealth have found a better way. Our economy has prospered precisely because it never became or attempted to become, a closed market.'[22]

The essence of the Common Market threat thus lay in its denial of the proven principles of the 'Commonwealth way'. Carrington criticised the project's violation of economic pragmatism. He contrasted extremes, offering 600 million Commonwealth consumers against 200 million Europeans and 40 per cent of trade against 14 per cent.[23] He extended the case to invisible exports and warned that services amounting to 7s for every 20s of goods sold abroad risked falling into European hands.[24]

---

[14] For an abbreviated discussion of radical and Cobdenite attitudes to Empire see P. K. O'Brien, 'The Costs and Benefits of British Imperialism 1846–1914', *Past and Present*, 120 (August 1988), pp. 161–6, 195–200.

[15] Carrington, 'Between the Commonwealth and Europe', p. 452.

[16] Carrington, *The Liquidation*, pp. 44, 68, 87.

[17] Carrington, 'Between the Commonwealth and Europe', p. 452.

[18] Carrington, *The Liquidation*, p. 83.

[19] Carrington, 'Between the Commonwealth and Europe', pp. 449, 456; letter to *The Times*, 6 February 1963.

[20] *Ibid.*, p. 459.

[21] *Ibid.*, p. 455.

[22] Carrington, 'Commonwealth or Common Market?', in *Britain Not Europe*, p. 39.

[23] *Ibid.*, p. 37.

[24] Carrington, 'Between the Commonwealth and Europe', pp. 450–1.

More importantly, Carrington's advocacy of free trade suggested the presence of a moral subtext, 'a right' and a 'historic principle' before which Common Market protectionism stood as a 'gross breach of faith'.[25] Virtuous free trade projected an international 'duty' to secure higher standards of living for the developing nations.[26] Finally, Carrington found the Common Market a contravention of sound international relations. The transition from Empire to Commonwealth offered a proto-type for the treatment of national sovereignty issues. The 'genius of the Commonwealth', he argued, was its gradual 'substitution of functional co-operation for imperial sovereignty', whereas the binding Treaty of Rome offered only a 'reactionary' and 'retrograde' approach.[27]

A. J. P. Taylor

The relative detachment of Carrington's anti-Market pursuits con-trasted with the Beaverbrook-inspired protests of the Oxford historian A. J. P. Taylor. No stranger to the press world,[28] Taylor wrote for the *Sunday Express* under annual contract from 1956 to 1982. However, the juxtaposition of his socialist allegiances and academic credentials with the capitalist populism of the *Sunday Express* invited controversy. Critics accused Taylor of selling out, a charge which gathered momentum after the publication of his biography of Beaverbrook.[29] Speculation surrounded the question of whether Taylor owed his *Sunday Express* contract to direct Beaverbrook 'patronage'.[30] For his part, Taylor contended that his *Sunday Express* work began before he met Beaverbrook.[31]

A cynical explanation for Taylor's participation in the anti-Market campaign would characterise his work as little more than deference. Beaverbrook was both a 'patron' and an object of devotion. Taylor confessed that 'Max Beaverbrook well knew how to steal the hearts of men. He certainly stole mine.'[32] The reality, however, was more complex. Taylor's affinity with the Beaverbrook ethos and Common Market posi-tion was the product of intense friendship and professional responsibility,

---

[25] *Ibid.*, p. 449.

[26] Letter to *The Times*, 17 July 1962.

[27] Carrington, 'Between the Commonwealth and Europe', p. 455.

[28] Taylor's previous forums included the *Manchester Guardian*, *New Statesman* and the *Observer*.

[29] A. Sisman, *A. J. P. Taylor: A Biography* (London, 1994), p. 355.

[30] R. Cole, *A. J. P. Taylor: The Traitor Within the Gates* (London, 1993), p. 207; Sisman, *A. J. P. Taylor*, p. 262.

[31] Taylor, *A Personal History*, p. 214.

[32] Taylor, *A Personal History*, p. 221. For similar sentiments see also *A Personal History*, p. 252; *Beaverbrook*, p. 632; *English History*, p. vii; Taylor to Beaverbrook, 25 April 1963, BBK C/305.

mutually admired styles of political opposition and compatible British patriotic instincts.

Shared advantage and admiration typified the relationship between Taylor and Beaverbrook. There is no reason to doubt the presence of genuine friendship but, as the critics understood, it was also a marriage of convenience. Taylor provided the *Express* with accredited punditry. But he was also in a position to satisfy Beaverbrook's craving for respect as both a historian and a historic figure. Apart from the *Sunday Express* salary, Taylor benefited from Beaverbrook's largesse in the form of cigars, cheese and claret, as well as invitations to the legendary dinners at Cherkeley.[33] Taylor's association with the *Sunday Express* also coincided with a downturn in his fortunes at Oxford. Frustration at losing out to Hugh Trevor-Roper in the appointment to the Regius Chair of History in 1957 was tempered by an emerging professional identity as a populist historian. Taylor conceded, 'In the years after 1956 I ceased to count in the academic world but I had more fun'.[34]

Socialist principles, devotion to the CND and objections to Suez placed Taylor at odds with central elements of the late 1950s *Express* perspective. But as we have seen, radical politics rarely stood in the way of Beaverbrook's friendships or employment policies. Michael Foot complained that 'people just didn't understand Beaverbrook's radicalism'.[35] It was a sentiment echoed by Taylor. In Beaverbrook, such men found a manner of political opposition that transcended party categorisation.

The affiliation between Beaverbrook and Taylor is best understood as a union of patriotic intuitions. The most significant affinity centred upon the patriotic value of political opposition. *The Trouble Makers*, a 1957 published version of Taylor's Ford lectures, defined idealistic resistance to English foreign policy in terms of radicalism between the late eighteenth century and World War II. Accordingly, dissent was a patriotic anti-authoritarian act of perceived moral or intellectual righteousness. Far from betraying the national interest, Taylor argued, dissenters were invariably 'deeply English in blood and temperament, often more so than their respectable critics'.[36] Foreign policy protest was likewise indicative of a national character trait, 'a quality peculiar to English speaking peoples'.[37]

As Taylor's histories and Beaverbrook's life demonstrated, both revelled in the status of gadfly. Taylor viewed Beaverbrook, in the

---

[33] Correspondence in BBK C/305. Kathleen Burk makes note of such points but concludes that their relationship was 'unfathomable'. K. Burk, *Troublemaker: The Life and History of A. J. P. Taylor* (London, 2000), pp. 315–16.

[34] Taylor, *Personal History*, pp. 216–17.

[35] Interview with Michael Foot, 27 October 1998.

[36] A. J. P. Taylor, *The Trouble Makers: Dissent Over Foreign Policy 1792–1939* (London, 1957), p. 14.

[37] *Ibid.*, p. 13.

heroic mould of his *Trouble Makers*, as 'a great disturbing element ... who never took things for granted'.[38] Beaverbrook reciprocated with a *Sunday Express* devotional to Taylor, 'The Man Who Likes to Stir Things Up'.[39] Taylor's *Sunday Express* contract allowed him to bring 'history to ordinary people'[40] as a populist dissenter, a role that implicitly clashed with the pretensions of academia. In his first Ford lecture he explained, 'Conformity may give you the quiet life; it may even bring you a University Chair. But all change in history, all advance, comes from the nonconformists.'[41] The recipe for Taylor's *Sunday Express* articles thus included a desire to please Beaverbrook, explore populist rhetoric and pursue the patriotic tradition of his heroes.

Compatible patriotic intuition also accounted for Taylor's success in mimicking the style and themes of the anti-Market campaign of the *Express*. Despite his sensitivity to flawed generalities,[42] Taylor was a national historian and approached comparative analysis with a regard for the importance of typologies. In 1945 he wrote:

> A political community has a way of life like a school or a trade union; and the individuals, so far as they are members of that community, are shaped by that way of life, even while they are helping to change it. 'National character' is the shorthand which the historian must use to express the effect on a community of geographical, political and social surroundings.[43]

Upon this basis Taylor's post-war historicism offered condemnations of European excesses and celebrations of British virtues. *The Struggle for Mastery of Europe*, for instance, excluded the Italians from a discussion of 'moral codes' in the conduct of European diplomacy. 'It becomes wearisome', he noted, 'to add "except the Italians" to every generalisation. Henceforth it may be assumed.'[44] German history, he argued, lacked evidence of pragmatism and was consistent only in its propensity for violent upheaval.[45] Of the German people, he wrote 'There were, and I dare say, are millions of well-meaning kindly Germans; but what have they added up to?'[46] Like Beaverbrook, he typically defended Russian

---

[38] A. J. P. Taylor, 'Why Do I Write for This "Awful Newspaper"?', *Sunday Express*, 27 May 1962.

[39] Beaverbrook, 'The Man Who Likes to Stir Things Up', *Sunday Express*, 21 October 1963.

[40] Taylor, *Personal History*, p. 220.

[41] Taylor, *The Trouble Makers*, p. 14.

[42] A. J. P. Taylor, *The Struggle for Mastery of Europe 1848–1918* (Oxford, 1954), pp. xxi–xxii.

[43] A. J. P. Taylor, *The Course of German History* (London, 1945), p. 14.

[44] Taylor, *The Struggle for Mastery*, footnote 4, p. xxiii.

[45] Taylor, *The Course of German History*, p. 13.

[46] *Ibid.*, p. 8.

fears of German ambitions[47] and abhorred plans for German rearmament in the Cold War scenario.

Assumptions about the virtues of dissent facilitated Taylor's entry
to the nationalist spirit of Beaverbrookian logic on both banal and
cultivated levels. However, whereas the style and approach to national
typologies was harmonious, the approach diverged over the precise
details of Britishness. Crucial differences were highlighted in the first
and last pages of *English History 1914–1945*. Taylor, for instance, placed
greater emphasis upon England in the British equation. 'England' was
both the literal and the patriotic focus, with the provocatively labelled
'lesser breeds' of Scotland, Wales and Ireland allowed entry only in
moments of obvious relevance. Taylor's tribute to Britishness amounted
to a eulogy for the virtues of civility, tolerance, patience and generosity
rather than an exhortation to the expansive possibilities of Commonwealth kinship. The first footnote on the last page of *English History*
concluded that 'British here means, perhaps for the last time, the peoples
of the Dominions and the Empire as well as the United Kingdom'.[48] In
fact, the issue of Empire Free Trade formed the greatest chasm between
the two men. Taylor admired the idealism in Beaverbrook's imperial
devotion, but rated Empire Free Trade a 'fantasy' and a 'dead cause',[49] a
construct of 'pure sentiment' devoid of a functional plan.[50]

Of course, mounting the *Express* soapbox required submission to
the usual Beaverbrook expectations. 'I was not in his power', Taylor protested,[51] but the topics for the *Sunday Express* pieces were set by John
Junor,[52] one of Beaverbrook's most reliable accomplices. It is unclear how
much effort Taylor put into these articles. In certain company he downplayed his work, dubbed Junor 'a blockhead' and rapidly composed the
pieces in the very language of Junor's telephoned instructions.[53] Work
for Beaverbrook also invoked thematic limits. Taylor defended his work
as 'radical articles – not of course socialist ones and certainly not any
against the Empire'.[54]

In essence, the anti-Market *Sunday Express* articles were vintage
Beaverbrook in a bottle labelled 'Taylor'. The radicalism in Taylor's
work bore closer resemblance to Beaverbrook's style of dissent than
to leftist political values. Ventures into socialist territory carried an
obvious regard for *Express* sensibilities and those of 'the Principal

---

[47] A. J. P. Taylor, 'Are We Being Fair to the Russians?', *Sunday Express*, 19 November
1961.
[48] Taylor, *English History*, p. 600.
[49] *Ibid.*, p. 228.
[50] Taylor, *Beaverbrook*, pp. xiv, 168, 263–4, 274, 276–7.
[51] Taylor, *Personal History*, p. 221.
[52] A. J. P. Taylor to Beaverbrook, 5 June 1962, BBK C/305.
[53] Sisman, *A. J. P. Taylor*, p. 261; Junor, *Home Truths*, p. 113.
[54] Taylor, *Personal History*, p. 214.

Reader' in particular. For instance, proud admission of his 'Labour left' credentials was accompanied by opposition to the Labour Party's UN line as well as assurances to Conservative readers that leftists were a small minority within Gaitskell's anti-Market group.[55] Taylor likewise addressed unemployment by pointing to a burgeoning 'two nations', with a north–south divide, but pegged the blame for its emergence on the Government's uncertain approach to Common Market policy. He linked Common Market entry with predictions of additional northern hardships caused by the anonymous and bureaucratic version of European planning. 'The Common Market puts plans before the people', he wrote. 'It lays the axe to the root of the welfare state.'[56]

An element of indecision lurked behind Taylor's initial treatment of Common Market. In July 1961, he declared himself open to the arguments but denounced the Government's failure to present a case. Of Macmillan's Common Market policy he wrote: 'Either it means what it says in which case it is full of dangers. Or it does not, in which case it is a swindle.'[57] In early December 1961, he leaned against membership on the basis of its threat to high-wage and full-employment policy. But by the end of the month all caution vanished as Taylor expounded the full *Express* version of a Common Market apocalypse:

> It means the end of the Empire, the end of the British Commonwealth. We shall cease to be an independent country.... We shall be back where we started, when Britain was a province of the Roman Empire.[58]

This article, from late December 1961, set the template for the remainder of Taylor's Common Market pieces.

The endangered Commonwealth, when not an overt topic, provided the anti-Market subtext. Selection of the terms 'Britain' or 'Great Britain' rather than 'England' suggested a sensitivity for the *Express* outlook or, perhaps, editorial intervention. While Taylor's arguments excluded an Empire Crusade endorsement, they nonetheless exploited the patriotism of Commonwealth unity as grounds for dissent and celebration of British uniqueness. He defended Beaverbrook and justified *Express* Britishness before charges of imperial sentimentality. Only the Commonwealth, he argued, had participated in both World Wars from beginning to end. 'All others came in late or went out early. This is not romance or

---

[55] A. J. P. Taylor, 'Why Don't These "Top People" Think for Themselves?', *Sunday Express*, 21 October 1962.

[56] A. J. P. Taylor, 'The Bitter Truth About Britain's Unemployed', *Sunday Express*, 2 December 1962.

[57] A. J. P. Taylor, 'Are We Being Told the Whole Truth?', *Sunday Express*, 2 July 1961.

[58] A. J. P. Taylor, 'Must We Always Take Orders From America?', *Sunday Express*, 31 December 1961.

fancy. It is fact, one of the few certain facts of our time.'[59] Similar argu-
ments urged the Dominion Prime Ministers, Bob Menzies of Australia,
Keith Holyoake of New Zealand and John Diefenbaker of Canada, to
'speak for Britain' in the same way that Labour's trouble-making
Arthur Greenwood had spoken for England and against appeasement
in 1939.[60] Taylor's submission to Beaverbrookian instincts even cited
Joseph Chamberlain's unfulfilled dream as proof of Britain's inadequate
Commonwealth trade leadership.[61]

Emphasis upon the historic sanctity and virtues of British independence supplemented homage to the Commonwealth. The fountainhead
of British greatness, Taylor argued, superseded the quantitative comparisons of population or industrial capacity. Instead, Britain owed its
pre-eminence to a tradition of 'free institutions and our independence
of spirit'.[62] His observations celebrated England's detachment from
Hitlerian or Napoleonic subjugation and gelled with the triumphal
Express line on Europe. 'No European country', he wrote, 'has our past
record of constitutional freedom'.[63]

Extrapolation of the isolationist past incorporated the perpetual risks
of association with the Continental 'other'. *Express* bravado accentuated
Taylor's usual distaste for German history. His cautionary tale of commercial and military ambition located the model for Common Market
advance in the *Zollverein*'s elimination of individual German states. The
inescapable conclusion suggested a revived German bid for supremacy
by Common Market means. 'If history be any guide', he told *Express*
readers, 'it is a way of ensuring that Hitler will win after all. Long Live
the New Order in Europe!'[64] Converse fears resonated in treatments of
democratic weakness in other European states. In France, for example,
Taylor located the seeds of a fascist threat from the Organisation de
l'armée secrete, despite de Gaulle's patriotic standing. Assuming economic integration led to political integration, Britain risked being linked
with de Gaulle's Algerian difficulties. Europe, Taylor concluded, was less
a matter of Common Market than 'common ruin'.[65]

---

[59] Taylor, 'Why Do I Write For This "Awful Newspaper"?'
[60] Taylor, 'Will Menzies Speak for Britain?', *Sunday Express*, 9 September 1962. As
deputy leader of the Labour Party, Greenwood was a vocal critic of Chamberlain and
appeasement. Taylor clearly regarded Greenwood's 2 September 1939 speech to the
Commons as a particularly poignant patriotic moment. It featured on the last page
of *The Trouble Makers* as well as in his anti-Market *Sunday Express* articles of 13
May and 9 September 1962.
[61] A. J. P. Taylor, 'Why Do We Stir Up Trouble in the Family?', *Sunday Express*, 3
December 1961.
[62] Taylor, 'Will Menzies Speak for Britain?'.
[63] Taylor, 'Why Don't These "Top People" Think for Themselves?'.
[64] Taylor, 'Are We Being Told the Whole Truth?'
[65] A. J. P. Taylor, 'Must de Gaulle's Enemies Drag Us Down Too?', *Sunday Express*, 11
February 1962.

Questions of national independence also revealed concerns about British significance in the comparative 'great powers' scenario. In particular, Taylor depicted the Common Market application as symptomatic of a wider surrender to US foreign policy. While avoiding the complete list of *Express* grievances, and therefore the inconvenience of his stance on Suez, Taylor nonetheless spoke generally of Washington's two decades of dominance over British decision making. He pointed to the 1946 loan as a seminal mistake, heralding Britain's 'retreat from greatness'. Only 'independence' rather than 'subservience', he counselled, offered Britain a sustained voice in world affairs.[66] Taylor also accused Ormsby-Gore, the British Ambassador, of failing to press the British case in Washington. Accordingly, friendship with Kennedy, family ties and even Lady Ormsby-Gore's Catholicism all compromised the strength of Britain's independent voice. Taylor recommended the appointment of a Canadian, Australian or New Zealander capable of pushing British interests with greater vigour.[67]

The domestic counterpart to entanglement-free foreign policy was a plea for democratic treatment of the Common Market application. Taylor's critique of the pro-Market spirit mocked the fashionable intellectual conformity of the pro-European position.[68] He repeatedly chastised the Government for its failure to engage the public in an honest dialogue of pros and cons. His appeal for freedom from obfuscation and duplicity warned that 'Our future is being mortgaged in darkness. Without our consent. Without our knowledge. Our great days are ending.'[69] In the aftermath of the veto, Taylor reckoned only an election could clear the decks and liberate Britain's fortunes.[70]

Sir Arthur Bryant

At the apogee of nationalist historicism in anti-Market guise stood Sir Arthur Bryant. In retrospect, Bryant's histories enjoyed less academic cachet and rather more popularity than the efforts of Carrington and Taylor. A recent Thatcherite critique described his work as 'chocolate box history', delivering '"Alfred-and-the-cakes"' sermons on English greatness.[71]

---

[66] Taylor, 'Must We Always Take Orders From America?'

[67] A. J. P. Taylor, 'I Say Ormsby-Gore Should Be Recalled', *Sunday Express*, 13 May 1962.

[68] Taylor, 'Why Don't These "Top People" Think For Themselves?'.

[69] A. J. P. Taylor, 'Macmillan Has Not Found the Answer Yet', *Sunday Express*, 15 July 1962.

[70] A. J. P. Taylor, 'Why Don't We Have an Election Now?', *Sunday Express*, 27 January 1963. This was entirely consistent with the line pushed by John Gordon and John Junor in their *Sunday Express* columns.

[71] Andrew Roberts, 'Patriotism: The Last Refuge of Sir Arthur Bryant', in *Eminent Chuchillians* (London, 1994), pp. 290, 319.

A. L. Rowse thought Bryant 'intellectually second rate' but more importantly considered him 'the most popular historian of his time'.[72]

Whatever his reputation, Bryant was ideally placed in the early 1960s to pursue the Common Market topic in the style and format he knew best. With established patriotic credentials, Bryant emerged as the most prolific of the anti-Market movement's historian pundits. Once engaged, he immersed himself in the cause. He exchanged letters with many other prominent opponents[73] and his convictions carried him to greater levels of activism in the subsequent debates leading up to the 1975 referendum on Britain's continued membership of the EEC.[74] As we shall see, the impetus for Bryant's participation was twofold. In part, his opposition derived its momentum from Beaverbrook's overtures, from which he remained aloof but nonetheless drew inspiration. To a far greater extent, however, Bryant's anti-Market stance was an application of his previously developed views on the nature of historic change and national identity.

Taylor's presence in the Beaverbrook lair did not preclude the latter making overtures to other historians. In May 1962 the shadows of the *Express* campaign reached Bryant with a request of support from Garfield Weston, Beaverbrook's freelance campaign recruiter. Weston, Bryant and Beaverbrook subsequently met in early June but the enticement of an *Express* rostrum failed to draw Bryant into the fold. While flattered, he appeared wary of alignment with the Beaverbrook machine.[75]

A mix of personal and professional instincts contributed to Bryant's caution. With his *Sunday Times* contract up for renewal in 1962, he feared compromising a twenty-one-year relationship.[76] Suspicions may also have been wrought by *Express* treatment of his earlier work. Bob Pitman, who later became one of Bryant's dear friends, had savaged Bryant's *The Turn of the Tide* in 1957 for its depiction of Churchill.[77] Furthermore, Bryant reckoned his anti-Market impact was maximised by maintaining the 'independent' reputation of his *Sunday Times* and

---

[72] A. L. Rowse, *Historians I Have Known* (London, 1995), pp. 30, 33. Rowse assisted with the proof-reading of Arthur Bryant's *The Story of England: Makers of the Realm* (London, 1954) and featured in the dedication of his *The Years of Endurance: 1793–1802* (London, 1942).

[73] This group included Beaverbrook, Lord Salisbury, Leo Russell, Henry Drummond-Wolff, Anthony Eden, Piers Debenham, Viscount Hinchingbrooke and Viscount Montgomery. John Paul of the ACML, R. F. Wright of Commonwealth Fellowship and Richard Briginshaw of the FBM also contacted him. See AB Papers H/4, H/5, H/6, F/21.

[74] In the early 1970s Bryant served as President of the Common Market Safeguards Campaign and Chairman of the National Common Market Petition Council. See AB Papers H/6 and H/7.

[75] AB Papers H/4.

[76] A. Bryant to C. D. Hamilton, 11 June 1962, AB Papers H/4.

[77] Pamela Street, *Arthur Bryant: Portrait of a Historian* (London, 1979), pp. 153–4.

Illustrated London News forums.[78] By declining the offer of a dedication in Bryant's *A Choice for Destiny* in 1962, Beaverbrook appeared to
concur. He confessed, 'It would be a mistake to dedicate it to me as I am
"suspect" by all those politicians who support the Common Market'.[79]

Most importantly, Bryant was circumspect about a historian's campaign role and capacity to shape public opinion. He admitted to Weston,
'Twice in my life I've thrown my hat over the moon for what I believed
in and merely damaged myself and my capacity for further usefulness
without achieving anything for the cause I was trying to help.'[80] In particular, Bryant referred to a controversial treatment of Germany and
appeasement that left him, as he admitted, 'almost in disgrace'.[81]

Beaverbrook's appeasement record also courted embarrassment, as it
included extensive correspondence with Ribbentrop and an isolationist
refusal to contemplate the possibility of war. The *Express* response to the
Munich Agreement, for instance, printed the headline 'PEACE' in the
largest typeface Fleet Street had ever seen.[82] Beaverbrook was famously
stung when Noel Coward's 1942 film *In Which We Serve* featured a
'No War This Year' copy of the *Express* floating on the sea following
the sinking of a British destroyer. In fact, Beaverbrook's escape from
the *Guilty Men* diatribe was undoubtedly a product of his subsequent
contributions to the war effort and his relationship to its authors.[83]

Bryant's approach to the German question was compromised by
a series of poor judgements. Under his editorship, the National Book
Association[84] made *Mein Kampf* its selection for January 1939. He
accepted an invitation to visit Nazi authorities in the summer of 1939
and in early 1940 published *Unfinished Victory*, a sympathetic account
of the German cause.[85] Written with the intention of preventing war,
though in fact published too late to do so, Bryant's introduction claimed

---

[78] A. Bryant to Beaverbrook, 9 June and 8 July 1962, BBK C/76.
[79] Beaverbrook to A. Bryant, 16 June 1962, BBK C/76.
[80] A. Bryant to G. Weston, 1 June 1962, AB Papers H/4.
[81] Bryant quoted in Street, *Arthur Bryant*, p. 112.
[82] Chislom and Davie, *Beaverbrook*, p. 354.
[83] Cato, the author of *Guilty Men*, was in fact a syndicate of three writers, Michael
Foot, Frank Owen and Peter Howard, all of whom were Beaverbrook employees.
[84] According to Philip Williamson, Stanley Baldwin agreed to serve as first President
of the National Book Association if it retained a cross-party appeal. Under Bryant's
leadership, however, the Association lurched to the right, with consequences for
Baldwin's political reputation. P. Williamson, *Stanley Baldwin: Conservative Leadership and National Values* (Cambridge, 1999), pp. 323–4. For more on Bryant's
inter-war activities and role with the National Book Association see E. H. H. Green,
'The Battle of Books: Book Clubs and Conservatism in the 1930s', in *Ideologies of
Conservatism* (Oxford, 2002), pp. 135–56.
[85] For a politicised indictment of Bryant's handling of the German issues, see Roberts,
'Patriotism', especially pp. 291–315. See also Rowse, *Historians I Have Known*, p. 33;
and Street, *Arthur Bryant*, pp. 105–12.

'I and those who thought like me were men running downhill after a steamroller hoping to stay its course by propping matches against it'.[86] Ultimately, *Unfinished Victory* ignited only controversy in its treatment of the rise of the Third Reich and Jewish 'aliens of cosmopolitan taste'.[87]

Under the circumstances, wartime patriotism offered redemption. Bryant, like the *Express*, quickly retooled and joined in the nationalist propaganda. In *English Saga*, published in September 1940, Bryant concealed his own errors within the national fate:

> Nations like men must reap what they sow.... Man may learn from his mistakes and, when he has made atonement, raise his stature by self-regeneration. Here also, he learns and acts not as an isolated individual but as a member of a continuing society in which his own birth and death are but a seasonal part. A great nation is a society that learns from its prior follies and in learning recreates itself.[88]

It was typical of Bryant's work that his own fortunes should be so intertwined with the lessons of the national past.

The doubts in Bryant's contemplation of an anti-Market position vanished in mid-1962. His patriotic instincts, manifest weekly in the 'Our Notebook' *Illustrated London News* column,[89] all leaned against membership. It seems reasonable to conclude that Bryant craved an activist position in the debate, but one secured on his own terms. Beaverbrook's overture provided a spur.

Within a fortnight of meeting Beaverbrook and Weston, Bryant secured space in the *Sunday Times* for his own anti-Market piece.[90] To its editor, C. D. Hamilton, he was effusive in thanks and zealous in spirit:

> For it would have been wrong for me to remain silent in a matter in which I feel so deeply – for more than I have ever felt about any public issue. It isn't that I don't see the arguments for our joining the Common Market, but I am convinced that to do so would be morally wrong and ultimately disastrous. We are a global and maritime, not a continental people, and every attempt in our history to behave otherwise has ended tragically and forced us back on our true destiny.[91]

Bryant followed the article with a letter to *The Times* three weeks later proclaiming the step leading to Europe 'the most momentous in our history'.[92]

---

[86] A. Bryant, *Unfinished Victory* (London, 1940), p. x.
[87] For examples of Bryant's treatment of the Jews see *Unfinished Victory*, pp. 136–52.
[88] A. Bryant, *English Saga: 1840–1940* (London, 1940), p. 377.
[89] Bryant succeeded G. K. Chesterton as author of the 'Our Notebook' column in 1936.
[90] A. Bryant, 'The British Nations and Their Heritage', *Sunday Times*, 24 June 1962.
[91] A. Bryant to C. D. Hamilton, 16 June 1962, AB Papers H/4.
[92] Letter to *The Times*, 13 July 1962.

Beaverbrook provided the idea and inspiration for *A Choice for Destiny*, a selection of Bryant's *Illustrated London News* articles written between June 1961 and July 1962.[93] Nor is there any doubt who influenced the subsequent *Express* reviews. 'You can almost smell the roast beef of Old England as it sizzles on the spit', claimed the *Express* Literary Editor, who also suggested that 'every word is based in fact'.[94] Bob Pitman's *Sunday Express* review added, 'The Church of England has been described as the Tory Party at prayer. Sir Arthur Bryant could almost be called the Tory Party at thought.'[95] Mutual flattery typified correspondence between Bryant and Beaverbrook in the summer of 1962, the latter paying tribute to the movement's 'most powerful exponent of the written word' and the former pledging to fight the Common Market to the end by all means at his disposal.[96]

A Choice for Destiny sold 10,000 copies before publication. Indeed, the agreement with Collins to publish 50,000 copies appeared to fall short of demand.[97] The book had been reprinted three times by mid-September and emerged as a propaganda tool, with copies sent to politicians and anti-Marketeers alike. Bob Menzies, Hugh Gaitskell, Lord Salisbury, Lord Woolton, Lord Goddard, Keith Holyoake, Sir Harold Caccia, Lord Lambton, Maurice Petherick and Charles de Gaulle all acknowledged receipt of the book.[98] Gaitskell replied with words of encouragement, urging Bryant to push the Conservative Party to maintain its Commonwealth pledges. 'It is likely to be more effective than anything we can do from our side.'[99]

Bryant's anti-Market approach was embedded in previous tributes to the primacy of national history and national identity.[100] In his world-view the two elements coalesced in a mutually exclusive bond. If, as we have seen, Taylor regarded national character as historical 'short hand', Bryant treated it as both a foundation and a manifestation of the national experience. His 1934 book *The National Character* drew upon its subject as a priceless 'asset' historically determined by ethnic distinctiveness, geography and even climate.[101] Similar sentiments flowed six years later

---

[93] A. Bryant to Beaverbrook, 16 August 1962, BBK C/76.

[94] P. Grosvenor, 'This Gamble That Threatens Our Heritage', *Daily Express*, 17 August 1962.

[95] *Sunday Express*, 19 August 1962.

[96] Beaverbrook to A. Bryant, 13 July 1962, AB Papers H/4; Bryant to Beaverbrook, 31 July 1962, BBK C/76.

[97] A. Bryant to Beaverbrook, 23 August 1962, BBK C/76.

[98] AB Papers H/4. Excerpts were also reprinted in the Forward Britain Movement *Bulletin*, no. 19 (August 1962), p. 6.

[99] H. Gaitskell to A. Bryant, 20 September 1962, AB Papers H/4.

[100] In particular, Bryant singled out *English Saga*, *The Spirit of Conservatism* (London, 1929) and *The Story of England* as being especially relevant. Bryant to C. D. Hamilton, 16 June 1962, AB Papers H/4.

[101] Arthur Bryant, *The National Character* (London, 1934). For original manuscript see AB Papers M/17.

from *English Saga*. His celebration of the national inheritance claimed 'we cannot recreate the past but we cannot escape it. It is in our blood and bone. To understand the temperament of a people, a statesman must first understand its history.'[102]

Despite claims for the elusive or deterministic nature of history, Bryant's work betrayed a process of recreation and escape in equal measure. Romantic mysticism coloured much of his vision. A self-described 'very late Victorian',[103] his utopian tendencies engendered a nineteenth-century Mazzinian spirit. In contrast to the self-aware or manipulated patriotism of Beaverbrook and Taylor, Bryant engaged national questions with a literal earnestness born of faith in historical certainty. His narratives invariably concluded with populist tributes to the native genius and virtues.[104] His histories likewise betrayed escapist instincts. Before the pressures of work, history provided a brief 'holiday taken not in space, but in time. I leave England not for the Continent, but 1950 for some other year or period.'[105] Escape was also a larger national prerogative, reconciling national virtues with the less attractive aspects of contemporary existence. Within every Englishman's heart, he wrote, 'there is a treasured England of his dreams'.[106]

Political instincts, both conservative by nature and Conservative by party, also conditioned Bryant's patriotism. His steadfast support of the Tory Party included advisory work for Conservative Central Office (CCO), authorship of his first book, *The Spirit of Conservatism* for the 1929 general election and, later, chairmanship of the party's Bonar Law College at Ashridge. These tributes to Conservatism emphasised pragmatism over theory and relied heavily upon Disraeli as a unifying link between the Tory ancients, the spirit of Burke and the contemporary message of Baldwin. Above all, it was a Tory paternalist world-view trumpeting the merits of a controlled historic evolution.

High-Tory sympathies and mystical tendencies had particular consequences for Bryant's exposition of national identity and objections to membership of the Common Market. The centrality of Disraeli's Englishness meant that institutions assumed paramount importance as guarantors of rights and liberties. Bryant linked the monarchy, Lords, Church, Commons, law courts and local government with the more recently developed joint stock and manufacturing companies, the press and trade unions. Since Disraeli's 'national greatness' quotient also measured the fondness of citizens for their institutions, Conservatives

---

[102] Bryant, *English Saga*, p. 9.
[103] Bryant quoted in Street, *Arthur Bryant*, p. 26.
[104] For example see Prelude to *The Story of England*, pp. 11–26.
[105] Bryant quoted in Street, *Arthur Bryant*, p. 205.
[106] Bryant, *National Character*, p. 20.

were obliged to balance change with institutional preservation.[107] An organic, romanticised view of the past also led Bryant to locate his lost Eden in a pre-industrial, agrarian age. Conscious amplification of Baldwin's 'On England'[108] and *English Saga*'s exposition of historically 'English types'[109] lent a sense of loss. Bryant asserted that 'Our culture – to use a terrifying and much misused word – is a country culture', one unsurpassed by modern encroachments.[110] Above all, Bryant's world-view embraced an 'inevitability of gradualness'[111] paradigm for the construction of history, national character and therefore patriotism. It was through such forces that Bryant traced the development of England as the progeny of Europe and, subsequently, the mother of Great Britain, the Empire and latterly the Commonwealth. And it was precisely by this model that Bryant's Anglo-centric identity incorporated the British as the 'English speaking peoples'.

Bryant's anti-Market writings featured those distinctive patriotic themes in microcosm. He situated Britain's dilemma within the soothing certainties of a historical national identity, the story of 'what we are and how we came to be'.[112] The perils of Common Market membership, he wrote, 'All ... arise out of our history'.[113] No theme, however, loomed larger than the organic evolution of history. As the first sentence of 'The British Nations and Their Heritage' reminded readers, 'A nation is the product of its history – a living organism for evoking and transmitting virtues without which no community can endure'.

Before considering Bryant's attack on the dual sacrifice demanded by membership of the Common Market, two other contextual aspects deserve comment. First, Bryant's celebrations of the past occasionally exposed wider fears of loss. In this instance, traditional regard for the physical welfare of the countryside was displaced by a wider philosophic concern for the validity of controlled evolution and the vitality of Tory paternalism. Consternation over the European application was compounded by Conservative allowances for unfettered capitalism and decolonisation during the previous decade. For Bryant,

---

[107] Bryant, *The Spirit of Conservatism*, pp. 33–5, 74–5.

[108] Baldwin's speech 'On England and the West' was originally delivered to the Royal Society of St George, 6 March 1924. The speech celebrated the Englishman's characteristic 'kindness', 'individuality' and 'staying power', as well as a national love of 'justice', 'truth', 'humanity', 'home' and countryside. Bryant quoted from it in *The Spirit of Conservatism*. See S. Baldwin, *On England and Other Addresses* (London, 1926), pp. 1–9.

[109] Chapter titles included 'The Country Gentleman', 'The Yeoman Farmer', 'The Parson' and the 'Housewife'.

[110] Bryant, *English Saga*, p. 25.

[111] *Ibid.*, p. 370.

[112] Bryant, 'The British Nations'.

[113] Bryant, *A Choice for Destiny*, p. 46.

these developments betrayed essential ideals for the preservation of national institutions and attitudes.[114] Subsequent frustration may have contributed to Bryant casting Gaitskell as a pragmatic English patriot, a latter-day Salisbury, Asquith or Baldwin.[115] Likewise, Bryant eulogised British national greatness while offering combative and escapist remedies. Surprisingly, he agreed with Dean Acheson's assessment of Britain's lost imperial role. His protest against the permanence of any lost prestige, however, affirmed a faith in regenerative native virtues: 'The race – or, is it, the island air? – is as fertile in human genius as it ever was'.[116]

Second, Bryant's treatment of identity in the European context avoided the more extreme manifestations of the 'us' versus 'them' dichotomy. Belief in enduring national greatness contributed to a tolerance of European 'others'. An English and subsequently British identity imagined as ancient and independently evolved thus required little negative reinforcement. Bryant's approach was also a product of gradualist nationalism. An emphasis upon evolution in Britain's teleology accepted the 'English speaking peoples' as descendants of a European legacy.[117] He likewise regarded the Commonwealth as Britain's contribution to the 'European heritage'.[118] European nations were also acknowledged to be products of a gradualist process, one yielding diverse national characters and the historic legitimisation for greater unity.[119] In expansive moments Bryant appeared to contemplate Common Market entry, provided membership included the Commonwealth and abandoned utopian plans for the abolition of national identities.

Acknowledgements of past European connections were, however, highly qualified. Bryant resented Macmillan's description of the British as 'offshore islanders'. In fact, Bryant's Common Market objections incorporated British uniqueness in a succession of unbreakable connective chains. Those connections incorporated a paradoxical lineage of Britishness as both an insular and an outward-looking phenomenon. Accordingly, from the bedrock of a distinctive national history emerged a correspondingly unique imagined community. England's historic isolation from Continental influences and instability gave rise to an unusual 'common identity':

> It made us a 'peculiar' people with the insular attribute – an insularity, spiritual as well as geographical – that was expressed, not without

---

[114] *Illustrated London News*, 4 August 1962, p. 164.
[115] *Illustrated London News*, 1 December 1962, p. 870. For additional examples of Bryant's views on Gaitskell see *Illustrated London News*, 2 February 1963.
[116] *Illustrated London News*, 29 December 1962, p. 1040.
[117] Bryant, *A Choice for Destiny*, pp. 14–15.
[118] *Ibid.*, p. 11.
[119] Bryant, 'The British Nations'; and *Illustrated London News*, 14 July 1962, p. 46.

arrogance in Milton's famous phrase about 'God's Englishman' and Gilbert's comic song from Pinafore.[120]

Insularity, he argued, was the nation's 'lifeblood', the well-spring of national feeling and achievement.[121] But Bryant also depicted isolation as the evolutionary transitional instinct whereby the English looked outward. Adventurism and colonisation, the fruits of seclusion, thus provided the historic leap from England to Great Britain to Empire and Commonwealth. A collective identity followed as connective realities of ethnicity, language, political and legal institutions and instinctive character were transported overseas.

The Common Market proposition was fundamentally incompatible with Bryant's imagined Britishness precisely because it breached the organic evolution of national character and history in two primary realms. On the one hand, the derogation of national sovereignty implicitly denied the institutional achievements of the insular English tradition. Predictably, Bryant retrieved sovereignty through mystical progression rather than constitutional technicality and conceptualised it as both root and branch of national greatness and institutional stability. Europe, by way of contrast, offered only traditions of inflexibility, leading to revolution and, in the Treaty of Rome in particular, 'binding', 'rigid', 'inelastic' excesses.[122] Britain, he argued, risked being outnumbered three to one by the 'majority control of Latins and Teutons' and their differing 'ways of thought and habit and political practice and ideology'.[123]

On the other hand, the Common Market also struck at the Commonwealth, itself a manifestation of the outward-looking impulse within the British character. Like Beaverbrook, Bryant's analysis favoured the Tory Democracy of Joseph Chamberlain as well as the spirit of Rhodes and Disraeli, though he acknowledged the viability of free trade within a maintained structure of co-operation between Britain and its dependencies.[124] More emphatically, Bryant's logic sought refuge in the emotive issues of British identity and Commonwealth kinship. Thus, if the counterpart of English insularity was an outward-looking trade network, the pre-condition for its realisation as an identity rested with the spread of a collectively imagined British populace. By this reckoning Canada, Australia and New Zealand were 'fellow British nations'[125] or 'new Britains', their 30 million residents were Burke's '"sons of Britain"',[126]

---

[120] Bryant, *A Choice for Destiny*, p. 13.
[121] Bryant, *Illustrated London News*, 8 September 1962, p. 348.
[122] For examples of this line see Bryant, *A Choice for Destiny*, pp. 40–3; letter to *The Times*, 13 July 1962.
[123] A. Bryant, 'An Historian Protests', *The Director*, January 1963, p. 79.
[124] Bryant, *A Choice for Destiny*, pp. 10, 19, 61.
[125] Bryant, 'An Historian Protests', p. 79.
[126] Bryant, 'The British Nations'.

or more commonly 'the English speaking peoples'. Bryant denied invoking a 'colour bar'[127] and occasionally wrote of the '600 multiracial millions' still learning the ways of British democracy.[128] To all intents and purposes, however, ethnicity prevailed, restricting shared identity to the Dominions and white inhabitants of Africa. It was in this spirit that he labelled Common Market entry 'tantamount to a permanent and arbitrary division of the English race'[129] or, in more dramatic mode, 'an act of fratricide, and, I believe, in the long run suicide'.[130]

Economists and political scientists

The Common Market question allowed historian pundits to include sentimental or objectified versions of the past. Patterns of international trade and the constitutional aspects of the Rome Treaty, however, also demanded conjectural answers from economists and political scientists. A largely dispassionate approach reflected the academic standing of the participants, the intricacies of cost–benefit analysis and the use of less populist forums. As contemporary observers recognised, technical treatments of political economy largely resisted the temptations of patriotic romanticism. *The Times'* review of work by James Meade and William Pickles, for example, lauded the presentation of 'reasoned cases without the usual emotional overtones'.[131]

To a far greater extent, however, their attitudes were shaped by realistic assessments of Britain's international standing. Professor James Meade's call for the revision of great power illusions suggested 'We … must forget our romantic dreams of grandeur. Moreover, we must fight against our tiresome fault of self-satisfied priggishness.'[132] In general, anti-Market economists and political scientists were reconciled to the decreasing sanctity of nation state independence. William Pickles, a defender of legal sovereignty, conceded that 'the era of small and wholly sovereign nation states is over'.[133] Their objections to Europe were none-theless grounded in assumptions about the continuing significance of a British contribution to the international system. Most analysts offered British models for emerging internationalism, ones that accounted for

[127] Bryant, *A Choice for Destiny*, p. 62.
[128] Bryant, 'An Historian Protests', p. 79.
[129] *Illustrated London News*, 14 July 1962.
[130] Bryant, *A Choice for Destiny*, p. 49.
[131] *The Times*, 2 April 1962, p. 14.
[132] J. Meade, *UK, Commonwealth and Common Market*, Hobart Paper No. 17, 1st edn (London, 1962), p. 9.
[133] W. Pickles, *Not With Europe: The Political Case for Staying Out*, Fabian Tract No. 336 (London, April 1962), p. 12.

the needs of developing nations, preserved elements of national sovereignty and transcended the narrow confines of the Common Market.

James Meade

James Meade, Professor of Political Economy at Cambridge and former Director of the Cabinet Economic Section,[134] exemplified the 'wait and see' position. His embrace of internationalism was the fulcrum for both Common Market hopes and fears. He believed in the bonded fortunes of the developed and developing worlds. 'The sooner we start to consider the question in this wider setting, the greater the chance of ultimate success.'[135] In an ideal form he thought the Common Market could enhance the development of 'One World which ... must necessarily be our main political objective'.[136] Meade's final verdict, however, depended upon whether the terms of entry obstructed or facilitated larger internationalist priorities. His eventual doubts thus grew from dissatisfaction with the detailed form rather than the idealistic aspirations of the Common Market project. Liberal trade policy was the vehicle for Meade's vision of global unity. Regional trade blocs were, at best, a step towards larger objectives.

While he was open to membership,[137] Meade's conditions for British entry blended with the growing tide of scepticism. In 1962, the first edition of *UK, Commonwealth and Common Market* dismissed the economic benefit projections of the pro-entry lobby as well as the premise that only the Common Market could provide British industry with a required dose of competition. Meade focused on Commonwealth trade, since the issue provided contextual links to the fate of the developing world. He concluded:

> The general moral is clear. The UK could and should join the EEC if it has real promise of becoming a liberal, outward looking institution. But she should not join if it is designed as a tight parochial European bloc. For the UK treatment of the Commonwealth and of the Sterling Area must be the test.[138]

---

[134] For a short biographical summary see R. M. Solow, 'James Meade at Eighty', *Economic Journal*, 97:388 (December 1987), pp. 986–8.

[135] Meade, letter to *The Times*, 9 January 1962.

[136] Meade, *UK, Commonwealth*, p. 10.

[137] Meade joined a large group of fellow academics, politicians and business leaders in signing a letter drafted by Common Market Campaign. The statement supported British entry in 'principle' if consultation with the Commonwealth and EFTA did not produce insurmountable obstacles. Press statement, Common Market Campaign, 25 May 1961.

[138] Meade, *UK, Commonwealth*, p. 50.

National identity rarely materialised as a direct topic of Meade's work. Yet, the banal politico-historic trappings of free trade British-ness underscored his Commonwealth test. Despite its economic focus *UK, Commonwealth and Common Market* accepted the primacy of political questions. Britain, he argued, offered Europe the 'Gladstonian virtues' of 'Habeas Corpus, parliamentary democracy, one-man-one-vote and freedom of speech'. Looking outward, he added was a British 'habit ... which is less ingrained in most Europeans'.[139] For Meade, like Carrington, the free trade achievement of Commonwealth unity before the diversity of race, geography and economic development verified the presence of external instincts.

Meade's response to the emerging negotiated terms and his suggested alternatives further exposed a belief in the wisdom of British free trade traditions. A prologue to the second edition of *UK, Commonwealth and Common Market*, published in November 1962, stated that the final terms on offer were likely to 'fall far short' of the essay's aims. Meade advocated the unilateral elimination of British import restrictions, in concert with multilateral negotiations for tariff reductions. The risks, he argued, could be managed through a wages policy and fluctuation of sterling's exchange rate. Creation of a North Atlantic free trade com-munity remained the overriding goal.[140]

Meade's alternative path to liberal internationalism was inspired by the particulars of national experience. Britain, he conceded, no longer carried 'great power' distinctions in political or military terms. None-theless, it retained a capacity to lead by 'example'. Britain offered the world

> a great tradition of innovation and experiment in social, political and economic institutions; and history has given us contacts with many dif-ferent countries. If only we could throw off our present self-satisfied sloth, we might still be able to play an important role in combining the pro-gressive economic policies at home with the building of a great liberal North Atlantic free-trade community.[141]

De Gaulle's veto confirmed Meade's fears and prompted a thematic mix of politics, economics, internationalism and national regeneration. Exclusion of the world's English-speakers raised the 'fearful political implications of a tight European block from the Urals to the Atlantic'

---

[139] Meade, *UK, Commonwealth*, p. 10.
[140] J. Meade, 'The Common Market. Is There an Alternative?', Prologue to 2nd edn of *UK, Commonwealth and Common Market*, Supplement to Hobart Paper No. 17 (London, 1962), p. 7. Also published in Susan Howson (ed.), *The Collected Papers of James Meade: Vol. 3, International Economics* (London, 1988), pp. 274–84. See also *The Times*, 23 November 1962, p. 22.
[141] Meade, 'The Common Market', p. 20.

and amounted to a 'rich man's club with 100 per cent discrimination against outside poor countries'.[142] He advocated a British–EFTA overture to the EEC for the creation of a wider European free trade area. Bolder measures again envisaged unilateral tariff reductions as encouragement for the liberal trade directions of the Kennedy administration. British greatness remained wed to the fortunes of the outside world and begged the courage of national will and the traditions of liberal trade. Meade asked, 'Can we regain our sense of national purpose and find the political leadership necessary for these great ends?'[143]

Sir Roy Harrod

The early Common Market stance of Roy Harrod, Nuffield Professor of International Economics at Oxford,[144] paralleled Meade's 'wait and see' doubts. But his eventual shift towards the anti-Market position was a transition made all the more profound by an earlier pro-Europe outlook. In a 1962 letter to the Prime Minister, Harrod highlighted his previous work for the European Movement, attendance at the Hague meetings in 1948 and support for Maudling's Free Trade Area quest. 'But', he wrote, 'I detest the Treaty of Rome'.[145]

In a January 1962 article entitled 'Britain, the Free World and the Six', Harrod outlined his provisional stance by linking the European issue to international trade concerns. 'We are all members of one another', he wrote. 'Trade not Aid' provided increased export revenues for developing countries and thus accorded with the interests of Britain and the free world. The Commonwealth model, he argued, provided an example and ethos for world trade. Any shift in purchasing patterns from the poorer to richer nations inspired by the Common Market thus amounted to a 'retrograde step' in British and world affairs.[146]

Though noncommittal in its ultimate verdict, 'Britain the Free World and the Six' foreshadowed Harrod's subsequent conversion to the anti-Market side. His darker scenarios envisioned vast Common Market agricultural surpluses and Communist advances in poorer nations. His concern about a pro-entry 'bandwagon effect' was based on his view that 'When a cause becomes fashionable, arguments become nebulous'.

---

[142] J. Meade, 'A Time to Be Radical', letter to *The Times*, 1 February 1963.

[143] *Ibid.*

[144] For a summary of Harrod's life and work see H. Phelps Brown, 'Sir Roy Harrod: A Biographical Memoir', *Economic Journal*, 90:357 (March 1980), pp. 1–33.

[145] R. Harrod to H. Macmillan, 8 August 1962, PRO, PREM 11/3742.

[146] Sir Roy Harrod, 'Britain, the Free World and the Six', *The Times*, 2 January 1962. For the consistency of this view, see also R. Harrod, 'The Case Against Signing the Treaty of Rome', *The Director*, 15:6 (December 1962), pp. 444–5.

Other audiences took note of Harrod's positions. James Meade[147] endorsed the implications of a rich and poor divide while Leo Russell appreciated its contrast with the 'woolly and wishful thinking' of Common Market advocates.[148] Douglas Jay 'wholeheartedly' agreed with Harrod's trade line, while William Pickles praised its 'plain common sense'.[149] Opposition groups tendered requests for his support. Harrod remained independent but 'Britain the Free World and the Six' was reprinted for an ACML collection of essays.[150] He also attended a debate conference sponsored by the FBM in July 1962. Though neutral on British membership, he publicly predicted that the negotiated terms would force him into the opposition camp.[151]

Harrod's most important audience was in Number 10 Downing Street. To the discomfort of economic advisors, Macmillan's regard for Harrod's Keynesian advice made concern about deflation a fixture of internal discussions during the late 1950s.[152] Harrod, who had been one of Macmillan's tutors at Oxford, was still offering lessons in political economy in 1961 and 1962. Unlike Meade's, Harrod's long-term free trade goals were qualified by an initial dose of protectionism. Sceptical of using wage policy to control demand, he advocated a growth policy combined with £300 million of cuts in non-essential, non-Commonwealth imports. His political assessment hinted at a lack of positive leadership and he predicted by-election woes. Harrod argued:

> it is this feeling that the British don't know what to do to get out of their difficulties that is so bad for confidence – as it was in 1931 and 1949....
> The grand people may afford to be Olympian. But the middling and small people, finding that business is rotten, will incline towards a change in Government.[153]

Harrod's advice was particularly unwelcome in the corridors of the Treasury and the Board of Trade. Tim Bligh, Macmillan's personal secretary, complained 'I am afraid Sir Roy Harrod is obsessed with the idea of import restrictions and is becoming rather boring'. Of a postponed

---

[147] For the exchange of ideas between Harrod and Meade in the 1930s, the 'Trade Cycle Group' and later development of the 'growth research programme', see W. Young, *Harrod and His Trade Cycle Group* (New York, 1989), pp. 51–7, 173–201.

[148] Letters to *The Times*, 9 January 1962.

[149] Letters to *The Times*, 5 January 1962.

[150] R. Harrod, 'Britain the Free World and the Six', in R. H. Corbet (ed.), *Britain Not Europe* (London, 1962), pp. 33–5.

[151] *The Times*, 17 July 1962.

[152] In his memoirs, Macmillan referred to Harrod as 'a friend on whose judgement I placed great reliance'. Macmillan, *At the End of the Day*, p. 85.

[153] R. Harrod to H. Macmillan, 14 January 1962, PRO, PREM 11/3742. See also R. Harrod, 'Debate on Sterling. The Case Against Devaluation', *Statist*, 8 December 1961, pp. 1122–4.

meeting between Harrod and the Prime Minister, he wrote 'The ways of Providence are truly inscrutable'.[154]

Macmillan, according to Alistair Horne, was increasingly disillusioned with Harrod's economic advice and disappointed by his anti-Market stance in 1962.[155] But whatever his frustrations, the archives reveal that the Prime Minister remained attentive to Harrod. In December 1962, for instance, Macmillan passed a letter from Harrod to the Chancellor of the Exchequer and confided:

> As you know, I regard him very highly as a man of considerable genius. He is often wrong, but then he is often right.... Of course Roy has completely changed his views on the Common Market, but I always think his opinions are worth taking account of. Do not pass this on to your Department, who have a great dislike of Roy, but send it back to me when you have finished.[156]

Harrod's decision to attend the July 1962 FBM conference reinforced Whitehall's frustrations at his continuing influence at Downing Street. The Foreign Office (FO) and Admiralty House actively conspired to discourage his participation. Harrod was warned of the FBM leader's previous links to the Communist Party and the likely anti-Market temper of the gathering. Harrod was unmoved and regarded the aims of the conference as both 'reasonable' and 'sensible', especially after discussions with Douglas Jay, a fellow attendee.[157] 'I tried to stop Sir Roy attending it. I did my best',[158] confessed the Admiralty official. By accident or design, the same official encountered Harrod at the Beefsteak Club following his conference address and secured a copy of the speech notes. Harrod's text, combined with earlier assurances, confirmed a 'wait and see' judgement. But reservations were equally apparent, as Harrod warned that official:

> I have a horrible feeling that what we can get is unlikely to be good enough. In my heart of hearts I wish that the whole thing could come to an end and that we should start again in much more favourable circumstances.[159]

In contrast to the measured tone of his public economic verdicts, Harrod's patriotic instincts were fully realised in his private assessment

---

[154] T. Bligh to Prime Minister, T. Bligh to P. W. Carey, 25 January 1962, PRO, PREM 11/3742.

[155] Horne, *Macmillan*, pp. 339, 357.

[156] H. Macmillan to Chancellor of the Exchequer, 9 December 1962, PRO, PREM 11/3742.

[157] Correspondence between R. T. Higgins and J. Wyndham, 10 and 13 July 1962, PRO, PREM 11/3823.

[158] J. Wyndham to R. T. Higgins with copy of Harrod speech notes, 16 July 1962, PRO, PREM 11/3823.

[159] R. Harrod to J. Wyndham, 13 July 1962, PRO, PREM 11/3823.

of the political implications. His enthusiasm for global interconnection contrasted with an attachment to the continuing integrity of a British nation state. In his correspondence with Macmillan those allegiances were manifest in the recurring language of anti-Market populism. For example:

> If the political bondage involved in membership of the E.E.C. is formal only, as, I suppose, de Gaulle wishes, then there is clearly *no* 'political' advantage in our joining to be set against the grave economic loss, which, in my judgement, this country must suffer if it joins. But if the bondage is real, then it is the final quietus of Britain. It will be the end of a country which has played its part in the world since 1066, bad as well as good, but we like to believe the good has predominated. We shall have to think up a suitable epitaph.[160]

An early academic grounding in philosophy and modern history undoubtedly informed Harrod's world-view. While that was perceived as a weakness by fellow economists, it may well have appealed to Macmillan's own historic sensitivities.[161]

Harrod posited a conspiracy behind this doomsday scenario, one which incorporated both America's 'emotive' urge and Kennedy's 'Irish desire'. The US, Harrod warned, sought a logical conclusion to its War of Independence by eliminating 'former masters' from the world map.[162] He appealed to Macmillan's sense of duty and history. The 1962 Commonwealth Conference, he suggested, offered a moment for Disraelian opportunism. By announcing a withdrawal of Britain's application, Macmillan could enhance his 'personal reputation and retrieve the greatness of the party'.[163] To his doubts about the supposed benefits of membership Harrod added fears for the balance of payments. Membership, he claimed, would lead to significant economic loss as Britain bought 'dear what she formerly bought cheap from the Commonwealth'.[164] His proposals for an alternative policy and methods for dealing with Kennedy were equally forthright. The Americans, he counselled, should be told of the futility of the negotiations and advised that the Organisation for Economic Co-operation and Development (OECD) held far greater potential as an international forum for growth and tariff revision.[165]

---

[160] R. Harrod to H. Macmillan, 8 August 1962, PRO, PREM 11/3742.
[161] Phelps Brown, 'Sir Roy Harrod', p. 30.
[162] R. Harrod to H. Macmillan, 8 August and 5 November 1962, PRO, PREM 11/3742.
[163] R. Harrod to H. Macmillan, 9 and 13 September 1962, PRO, PREM 11/3742.
[164] R. Harrod to H. Macmillan, 13 September 1962, PRO, PREM 11/3742.
[165] R. Harrod to H. Macmillan, 5 November 1962, PRO, PREM 11/3742.

Publicly, Harrod's assault on the British application continued in a more detached vein. In October he secured the support of fellow economists R. F. Kahn, Nicholas Kaldor and H. D. Dickinson. In a co-signed letter to *The Times* the group warned of diversions away from Commonwealth trade and denied the claims of economic gain from membership of the Common Market.[166] A December article in *The Director* added more detailed economic objections. On this occasion Harrod, like Meade, offered his support for EFTA expansion. Harrod was far more prescient in recognising Europe's desire to harmonise indirect taxation and welfare provisions. In fact, he was one of the only pundits to envision economic union leading to monetary union. The pound would have to remain separate, he warned. Europe would be unwilling to pay off £3,500 million in sterling liabilities and balance of payment difficulties would prohibit their being paid off in stages. All Harrod's assessments pointed to the same conclusion. Potential economic growth in developing countries meant that Britain's moral responsibility and future prosperity depended upon a continuing maintenance of connections with the wider world.[167]

E. J. Mishan

Meanwhile, at the London School of Economics, Dr Edward Mishan and Dr William Pickles (discussed below) abandoned the cautious restraint of the 'wait and see' position. In fact, the tandem's initial public objections anticipated Macmillan's announcement to Parliament by almost two months. Economic issues fell to Mishan, whose opinions were largely engaged in a refutation of presumed benefits of the Common Market. He shared Harrod's balance of payment concerns. Accordingly, entry into an expanding market in no way guaranteed balance of payments surpluses. If anything, Britain's higher prices would aggravate the situation, by creating surpluses on the side of imports.[168] Nor did exposure to Common Market competition offer a panacea for efficiency at home. The supposed benefits of large-scale and increasingly specialised production, he argued, were overstated. Too much inter-European trade was based upon exchanges of similar manufactured goods at prices higher than those offered by the Commonwealth or the United States. Moreover, expectations of sharing in Europe's higher growth rates ignored the fact that its most dramatic increases had preceded the formation of the Common Market.[169]

---

[166] Letter to *The Times*, 15 October 1962.

[167] Harrod, 'The Case Against', p. 445.

[168] K. Klapholz and E. J. Mishan, letter to *The Times*, 21 August 1961.

[169] 'Against the Market', *Third Programme*, 7 December 1961, BBC WAC, Film T 343; E. J. Mishan, 'The Economic Case', pp. 371–3. Mishan remained wed to these views, which appeared in near identical form later in the decade. See E. J. Mishan, *Twenty-One Popular Economic Fallacies* (London, 1969), pp. 171–80.

Mishan's critique paid less homage to the forces of liberal trade internationalism. True, he criticised the Common Market for sheltering cartels.[170] But, in a departure from the premise of free trade determinism, he suggested that 'There is no historical evidence that an extension of the area of free trade promotes growth'.[171] His defence of the domestic economy likewise appeared to suggest the transcendence of emotive national instincts over market forces. The notion that British agriculture must necessarily contract before Common Market competition failed to account for its social value. Britons, on their 'overcrowded island', he contended, 'may prefer more farmland to factory sites, more fresh air to factory smoke, more green space to more towns and cities'.[172]

Those hints were symptomatic of broader intentions. For Mishan, cost–benefit details paled before the penultimate question of autonomy. De Gaulle's veto thus exposed the 'tedious bickerings at Brussels over pigmeat and the like as an irrelevant charade'.[173] Elimination of an economic rationale for entry left Mishan free to prosecute the Government's 'tacit conspiracy to evade the chief issue ... namely, political sovereignty'.[174]

Mishan's bid for objectivity contrasted the 'stirring noises' of Government bandwagons with the 'conclusions of detached economic analysis'.[175] His counterpoint defence of sovereignty, however, was itself prone to the 'stirring noises' of national uniqueness. He parted company with other pundits by avoiding a celebration of liberal internationalism or Commonwealth heritage. Instead, he fused questions of national sacrifice and comparative political traditions. His letter to *The Times* of 2 June 1961 warned of the dangers to a 'rare heritage of social maturity and political stability'. Britain's existence, he warned, was under threat. The debate was not a question of 'missing the bus', but rather of 'giving up our birthright for a marriage of European pottage'.[176]

William Pickles

The endorsement of political over economic considerations found its most ardent champion in William Pickles, Senior Lecturer in Political Science at the London School of Economics. The EEC founders, Pickles maintained, had always intended economics as means to a political

---

[170] Mishan, letter to *The Times*, 2 October 1962.
[171] Mishan, 'The Economic Case', p. 373.
[172] *Third Programme*, 7 September 1961, BBC WAC, Film T343.
[173] Mishan, letter to *The Times*, 25 January 1963.
[174] Mishan, letter to *The Times*, 2 June 1961.
[175] Mishan, letter to *The Times*, 2 October 1962.
[176] In this context the use of the terms 'birthright' and 'pottage' allude to the Old Testament story of Esau (Genesis 25: 29–34).

end.[177] He joined Mishan in *The Times* with an opening attack on the duplicities of pro-entry economics. 'The impression grows that someone is trying to sell us a political pig in an economic poke.' It was time, he suggested, to take 'a long and careful look at the pig'.[178]

Pickles' effort was emblematic of anti-Market punditry in its relative isolation. Few legal experts shared his fears for technical violations of sovereignty.[179] Sir Edwin Herbert, President of the Law Society, foresaw changes but thought a decision to accede to the Treaty of Rome was itself an act of sovereignty.[180] In a *Daily Telegraph* survey of 'academic lawyers', only Pickles prophesied dire threats to British sovereignty.[181]

Pickles was also typical in his propensity for combining sophisticated arguments with conspiracy theory and banal appeals to national identity. Longer analytical articles exploring precise constitutional details[182] were counterbalanced by emotive depictions of a nation under threat. Common Market membership, he suggested, raised the possibility that Britain would 'disappear' in a federated Europe.[183] It represented an 'inglorious revolution to destroy the work of seven centuries'.[184] He was attuned to the concerns of 'the common man' and the need for a consultation of the electorate.[185] It was a powerful mix, one that led the *Sunday Express* to herald him as a 'distinguished political scholar'[186] and forced BBC programmers to include his views with caution. In its pursuit of balance, the Corporation needed Pickles' 'valid and sensible arguments'. However, his 'sinister allusions' to the influence of City of London finance over pro-Common Market campaigns and BBC coverage were deemed unsuitable for broadcast.[187]

---

[177] For example, see W. Pickles, 'Keep Out of Europe.... The Political Case', *Statist*, 17 November 1961, p. 882.

[178] Letter to *The Times*, 2 June 1961.

[179] One exception was Sir Henry Slessor, a former Justice of Appeal, who emphasised the inflexibility of Roman Law traditions. He estimated that accession to Europe would require the amendment or repeal of eighty tracts of English law. See Sir Henry Slessor, 'The Common Market and the Common Law', *Listener*, 23 August 1962, pp. 267–9.

[180] *Britain on the Brink*, broadcast 24 September 1962, BBC WAC, Film 17/18.

[181] T. E. Utley, 'Will Parliament Lose Its Sovereignty?', *Daily Telegraph*, 30 September 1962. Experts surveyed included Lord Dilhorne, Sir H. Waldcock, Professor Emlyn Wade, Sir Arthur Goodhart, Professor H. W. R. Wade and William Pickles.

[182] See in particular Pickles, *Not With Europe*; and 'Political Power in the EEC', *Journal of Common Market Studies*, 2 (1963), pp. 63–84.

[183] Letter to the *Sunday Times*, 24 June 1962.

[184] W. Pickles, 'The Inglorious Revolution', *Daily Express*, 13 November 1961. See also W. Pickles, 'Stuck – in Plaster of Paris', *Daily Express*, 1 January 1962.

[185] *Britain on the Brink*; letter to *The Times*, 15 October 1962.

[186] *Sunday Express*, 1 April 1962.

[187] Head to Talks and Current Affairs to Mr Grisewood, 31 October 1962, BBC WAC, R/51/793/1 File I – 64.

In a debate characterised by vague treatments of sovereignty, Pickles' differentiation of political and legal concepts was unique. He defined political sovereignty as 'a nation's right to do what it wants on its own territory'. This concept, he conceded, had already been eroded and was no longer plausible in absolute terms. For small nations in particular, a partial derogation of powers to bodies like the North Atlantic Treaty Organisation (NATO) and the UN was a desirable national response to international needs.[188] On this point and others, Pickles' outlook blended with elements of pro-entry internationalism. In BBC debates, he agreed with Uwe Kitzinger's assessment of pressing world issues. Both acknowledged the inevitable erosion of sovereignties, the widening gap between nations rich and poor and the need for extensions of free trade. Opinions diverged, however, over the sacrifices demanded by the Treaty of Rome. Kitzinger viewed the EEC as a vehicle for transcending the dangers of nationalism. Pickles strenuously objected to a breach of national prerogatives.[189]

Pickles' objections hinged upon the delineation of an inviolable legal sovereignty, one defined with reference to parliamentary traditions. Accordingly, the sovereignty of Parliament was

> a vital part of the British concept of democracy, hard won in centuries of struggle against arbitrary rule, from Magna Carta to Act of Settlement. Stated in its briefest form, it is the right of Parliament – Queens, Lords and Commons – to say what shall be law in this country. Today no other right is superior to that.[190]

His emphasis upon Parliament was instructive in two important ways. First, it revealed an attachment to the value of nation states. Legal sovereignty thus remained a national domain in an age characterised by rising interdependence. Second, references to parliamentary democracy invited a regard for the British system, with all its attendant distinctions. As a result, Pickles' analysis was drawn towards 'us' and 'them' disparities.

Despite offering a narrowed conceptual definition, Pickles, like most pundits, used sovereignty as a conduit for a variety of political objections. He was unequivocal in his dislike of Britain's proposed membership. 'I don't like the Treaty of Rome and I don't like anything like the Treaty of Rome', he told the BBC.[191] Socialist principles accentuated Pickles' protests, nowhere more so than in the Fabian pamphlet *Not With Europe*. The Treaty of Rome was intrinsically flawed, he suggested, because it

---

[188] Pickles, *Not With Europe*, p. 12.
[189] *Britain On the Brink*; *In or Out*, 17 November 1962, BBC WAC, Film 17/18.
[190] Pickles, *Not With Europe*, p. 13.
[191] *Tonight* programme, 2 April 1962, BBC WAC, Film 47/48.

aspired to federalist political goals through entirely outdated laissez-faire ideology. Governmental control of planning powers was a casualty of the process. An unlikely alliance of federalists and Adam Smith disciples, he argued, planned integration in the service of an exploitative economic system. He wrote: 'This is planning only in order to prevent planning. It is trying to use modern knowledge and techniques to adapt the world to the economic superstitions of the eighteenth century.'[192] Membership would force the overturn of parliamentary legislation governing the location of industry, areas for development, transport routes and provisions for the operation of agriculture, iron and steel. Control over strategic, employment, welfare and balance of payment matters would likewise be compromised in varying degrees.[193]

Pickles' objections to the Treaty reflected not merely socialist values, but those of British socialism in particular. Here he walked a fine line. Many European socialists had ardently supported the Common Market project but failed to convert their British counterparts. With hindsight, Pickles regarded the gap as irrelevant. Continental socialists, he alleged, had lacked the practical strength needed to secure planning provisions for the Treaty of Rome. Practicalities, however, obscured a latent differentiation of principles in Pickles' arguments. British Labour, he contended, had wisely objected to federalism as 'anti-Socialist'.[194] He insinuated that the rigid Common Market project was anathema to the spirit and tenor of British socialism:

> No Socialist objects to innovation and experiment; indeed, we all want them. But one can be both cautious and leave room for adaptation and change, as unexpected realities reveal themselves. The more we believe in the need for change, the stronger the case for elasticity, precisely because we want to give our experiments a chance to succeed.[195]

Thus, Labour, by virtue of its particular socialist approach, had quite properly settled on its 'wait and see' policy.[196]

Pickles' critique also raised legitimate and detailed questions about the structural shortcomings of Common Market institutions. More often than not, those flaws were coupled with emotive references to a European, and frequently French, historic context. 'The machinery', he claimed, 'provides for a mixture of bureaucracy and anarchy'.[197] The Treaty of Rome was a schizophrenic one, he suggested, whose designs for unity were built on mantles of historic distrust. He depicted Europe

---

[192] Pickles, *Not With Europe*, p. 16.
[193] Pickles, 'Keep Out of Europe', p. 882.
[194] Pickles, *Not With Europe*, pp. 6, 28.
[195] *Ibid.*, p. 5.
[196] *Ibid.*, p. 40.
[197] Pickles, 'Keep Out of Europe', p. 882.

as divided on a scale not seen since the age of Napoleon. Arguments between advocates of federal and confederal ambitions fractured progress on agricultural, trade, gender, exchange rate and colonial issues.[198] *Not With Europe* detailed a litany of undemocratic defects in the EEC's structure. The Council, he complained, lacked accountability and its qualified majority voting led to a proliferation of 'horse trading alliances' as small groups blocked initiatives. The procedures of the European Court were 'wholly Continental'. So too were those of the European Parliament. According to Pickles, its powers had been circumscribed so fully that it bore little resemblance to a parliamentary body at all. The Commission was 'antidemocratic' and its monopolistic rights of initiative and decision found historic equivalent only in the constitutions created by Sieyès for Napoleon I. Worst of all the Treaty placed Britain's traditional methods at odds with a written constitution. In Pickles' view, the Common Market created codified rigidity where Britain preferred flexibility. European rules could not be applied to Britain with any guarantee of permanence. In the absence of a formal constitution Britain could implement European laws only through Acts of Parliament, ones which subsequent Parliaments could simply amend or overturn.[199]

For Pickles, gaps between the principles and political structures of Britain and Europe affirmed a fundamental incompatibility. His 'us' and 'them' distinctions tended towards qualitative rather than moralistic judgements. In sum, however, they pointed to the same banal conclusion. He told BBC listeners, 'I think that Europeans run their own affairs their way and us in our way. I think the trouble is they, perhaps, don't mix.'[200] Europe's politics, based on the assumptions of Rousseau and 'Napoleonic adaptations of Roman law', were completely foreign to 'pragmatic Britons'.[201] Federalism, he predicted, would founder before the sentiments of nations. Expansion of the Six would merely aggravate splits between 'temperaments' of the Latin–German nations and those of a Dutch–British–Scandinavian group.[202] Pickles located Britain's rightful place with the Commonwealth, NATO and the old Organisation for European Economic Co-operation (OEEC). Inside the Common Market, he wrote, 'we shall perish as we tear each other's guts out and shout "unity" in a dozen different languages'.[203]

---

[198] Pickles, letter to *The Times*, 27 July 1961; W. Pickles, 'Will the Common Market Ever Work?', *Sunday Express*, 6 August 1961.
[199] Pickles, *Not With Europe*, pp. 13–15, 20, 21. See also 'Keep Out of Europe', p. 883; and letter to *The Times*, 24 June 1962.
[200] *In or Out*.
[201] Pickles, *Not With Europe*, p. 8.
[202] *Third Programme*, 20 November 1962, BBC WAC, Film 204.
[203] Pickles, 'Will the Common Market Ever Work?'

Conclusion

As an intellectual exercise, anti-Market punditry sought to evaluate and reconcile disparate concepts and forces. Experts clarified the relative importance of politics and economics. They harmonised the paradox of Britain's insular character with the impulses leading to Empire and Commonwealth. They fused a glorious past to the demands of the future. Some aligned academic analysis with the populist needs of a political debate. All of this, however, was subtext to one overriding issue. Intentionally or unintentionally, directly or indirectly, all pundits were attempting to reconcile Britain's independent existence with a trend towards international interdependence.

Despite yielding elements of consensus, the process was typified by an absence of co-ordinated opposition. There were exceptions of course. In all probability, James Meade and Roy Harrod exchanged opinions. William Pickles and E. J. Mishan clearly colluded at the London School of Economics. Taylor was contracted to the Beaverbrook campaign. Overall, though, dissent was a solitary exercise. Bryant and Harrod largely resisted the overtures of organised anti-Market forces and preserved independent voices. James Meade was frustrated when groups on both sides of the debate used his opinions to serve their own purposes.[204] Carrington, as we have seen, was distressed by the lack of an anti-Market liberal fellowship. An alliance of populist historians never materialised. Taylor had dismissed Bryant's work as 'scissors-and-paste'[205] and there is no evidence of correspondence between the two before 1970.[206] Timing and the conditional nature of the British application also played a role. Unlike the outright opponents, economists and 'wait and see' advocates were hostage to the disclosure of negotiated terms.

On economic topics, most pundits catalogued a similar list of anxieties and prevailing trends. They unanimously condemned the pro-entry economic case as inflated. Most argued for a reduction of global trade barriers, lamented the disparities of wealth between rich and poor nations, and championed the cause of Commonwealth trade.

But the prospects for an economic consensus foundered on the diagnosis of Britain's plight. Mishan and Harrod feared for balance of payments. Meade and Harrod split over the merits of a wages policy. For Bryant the Common Market inflamed suspicions of international finance.

---

[204] Meade claimed this was one reason why he clarified his opinions in a second edition of *UK, Commonwealth and Common Market* (see p. 5). For an example of the treatment of his views see *Sunday Express*, 1 April 1962.

[205] A. J. P. Taylor quoted by Rowse, *Historians I Have Known*, p. 36.

[206] Bryant's first correspondence with Taylor made mention of past criticism. See A. Bryant to A. J. P. Taylor, 15 February 1970, AB Papers E/3 (57/2).

Opinion splintered most dramatically over the merits of free trade policy. For Carrington, the old liberal *Wealth of Nations* creed defined a 'British way' and provided the historic basis of the Commonwealth achievement. Taylor acceded to the quirks of the perpetual Empire Free Trade Crusade. Meade promoted worldwide free trade as the penultimate goal. Harrod wanted free trade but advocated a short-term dose of protection. Mishan and Pickles wanted freer trade but only if the cost to British interests was not too great. Suggestions for free trade alternatives generally lacked depth and sophistication. Most pundits advocated the extension of EFTA. But those proposals ignored the extent to which this had failed as a British policy priority in the late 1950s.

A genuine anti-Market consensus, irrespective of academic approach, identified the Treaty of Rome with political rather than economic ends. It was a crucial distinction because it led analysis towards the identity issues of national uniqueness. In retrospect it was also inevitable. The tendency of experts to champion their alternative policies as acts of national regeneration exposed an assumption that Britain's fortunes had gone awry. This reinforced a predilection for juxtaposing current troubles against an idealised past. It also fed a Whiggish desire to restore the evolutionary balance of a historic British path. The case was similarly fortified by distinctions drawn between economic and political relationships. Within certain limits, pundits accepted economic interdependence as a feature of expanding commerce. It was a reality highlighted by nods to the Commonwealth experience and betrayed by fears about the costs of membership to consumers, farmers and poor nations. But economic relations leading to political integration raised a more alarming set of issues. The stakes thus rose, or were pushed, from issues of trade balance to the long-term survival of a sovereign British nation state. As a result, the political, institutional and temperamental manifestations of unique Britishness became the bedrock of anti-Market analysis.

4

Pressure groups

For all its vocal populism, the anti-Market campaign lacked a unified crusade structure. The *Express* supplied flags and slogans but did so on its own terms, with its own agenda. Pundits fed rather than led the cause, generally preferring forums of political expression to organisations for political pressure. Conservative anti-Market MPs avoided formal affiliation with extra-parliamentary groups devoted to overturning Government policy. Meanwhile Labour MPs organised their own protest body for the purpose of converting fellow members of the parliamentary party. Hence, grassroots activism was left to its own devices.

In the absence of a dominant organisational structure, anti-Market sentiment dispersed among pressure groups representing every shade of political and patriotic instinct. Not surprisingly, 'promotional' protest groups have been characterised as the fringe of the European debate.[1] Henry Fairlie, a contemporary critic, disparaged the organisations as purveyors of xenophobia and hysteria. 'One would hardly believe that people could form bodies with such titles if they were not there.... I do not think it adds up to a serious political movement at all.'[2]

Analysis of pressure groups most often highlights the role of 'peak' or 'sectional'[3] organisations, such as the TUC or FBI, and seeks conclusions relating to either cumulative political impact or influence on policy-making processes.[4] The primary vehicles of anti-Market pressure,

---

[1] R. Lieber, *British Politics*, pp. 309–10; Tratt, *The Macmillan Government and Europe*, p. 106.

[2] Fairlie, 'The Earl of Sandwich's Crew', p. 296.

[3] Lieber, *British Politics*, pp. 6–8.

[4] Lieber, *British Politics*, is but one example. See also the chapters by B. Rosamund, 'The Integration of Labour? British Trade Union Attitudes to European Integration', and J. Greenwood and L. Stancich, 'British Business: Managing Complexity', in D. Baker and D. Seawright (eds), *Britain For and Against Europe* (Oxford, 1998), pp. 130–47 and 148–64; and A. Butt Philip, 'British Pressure Groups and the

however, were 'promotional' or issue groups designed to propagate particular viewpoints rather than to broker with the Government on behalf of organised labour or business interests. The diversity of anti-Market groups and their separation from the corridors of power makes their precise influence difficult to assess. Despite the predominant language of national belonging, dissenting bodies never constructed a unified protest. Moreover, pressure group ambitions were compromised to varying extents by fixed political orientations as well as an inability to obtain high-profile leadership, funding or party validation. An 'amateur' spirit prevailed, even among those groups with superior organisational structures.[5]

Yet, irrespective of their political impact, anti-Market pressure groups demand analysis precisely because they applied pressure from outside the traditional avenues of political influence. Without an organisational or partisan structure imposed from above, the associations facilitated the expression of hardened populist opposition. One study of pressure politics concluded that anti-Market groups were 'distinctly one-party extremist, lacking access, aiming to become mass movements'.[6] More elaboration is necessary, however. It should be noted that pressure group opposition arose and was expressed through a complex set of impulses. The most obvious allusions to national identity set British interests against those of European 'others'. But for single-issue groups in particular, a Common Market *raison d'être* gave rise to all manner of comparative distinctions and prejudices. Furthermore, as the tendency of groups to form along one-party lines suggested, Common Market dissent set questions of a British 'us' in a political context. It also betrayed underlying discontent, whereby Common Market opposition functioned as a complete or partial expression of wider frustrations. Pressure groups were thus defined both by allegiance as well as opposition to the respective political traditions they claimed to represent. In this dynamic, pressure groups were frequently opposed to their chosen party's policy while claiming to retrieve particular aspects of that party's political values.

Recourse to nationalism was the natural outcome and two overlapping lines of dissent linked assertions of Britishness and 'otherness'. First, tactical considerations meant that patriotism was manipulated for the sake of wider representation and influence. Groups 'lacking access', protecting particular policies, myths or symbols and seeking 'mass' appeal thus sought refuge in the language of patriotism. Second, and more commonly, banal discourses provided the only unifying language

---

European Community', in S. George (ed.), *Britain and the European Community: The Politics of Semi-Detachment* (Oxford, 1992), pp. 149–71.

[5] Windlesham, *Communication and Political Power*, p. 173.

[6] *Ibid.*, p. 171.

available within particular constructions of Britishness. Indeed, opposition was characterised by an emotive allegiance to the vague abstractions of a national idea rather than to a quantifiable calculus of political or economic loss or gain. The pluralities manifest in anti-Market dissent were thus a partial function of competing visions of national identity.

Single-issue pressure groups

Anti-Market groups were neither at cross-purposes nor politically exclusive in all cases. There were instances of collaboration, most often typified by shared platforms at public meetings.[7] Nevertheless, attempts to secure a unified front met with limited success. In one such example, the AntiCommon Market Union, led by Norman Smythe,[8] devoted itself to organising Albert Hall rallies in the summer of 1962. Its letterhead listed the AntiCommon Market League, Keep Britain Out, the British Housewives' League and Scottish Housewives' Association as formal members, but organisational meetings also included representatives from the FBM, the League of Empire Loyalists, the True Tories and individuals such as William Pickles. The Union failed to secure an endorsement from Beaverbrook, who declined a speaking invitation on account of age and gout. But the actual reasoning emerged in an internal *Express* memo. 'Lord Beaverbrook', it revealed, 'says he cannot work with the League of Empire Loyalists'.[9] Beaverbrook's reservations were an omen. While the 26 August 1962 rally drew a crowd of 3,000, the proceedings were repeatedly challenged by dissonant voices. Viscount Hinchingbrooke was baited by liberals while others mocked Norman Smythe's 'trans-Atlantic' accent. Major-General Richard Hilton, leader of the True Tories, suffered double humiliation when his speech was heckled by Empire Loyalists and cut short by the chairman of the meeting.[10]

The absence of effective unity propelled Leo Russell's attempt to establish an extra-parliamentary, non-partisan challenge to pro-entry organisations. The resulting AntiCommon Market Council, founded in late 1962, conceded that opposition efforts had been 'too amateur – to counter and counter-attack' with factual arguments or thoughtful

---

[7] This often led to unlikely combinations. To cite but one example, a meeting at Caxton Hall in London on 28 September 1961 was planned to include the Forward Britain Movement, League of Empire Loyalists, Patriotic Front, Commonwealth Industries Association and the Council for the Reduction of Taxes.

[8] According to Robert Lieber, Smythe had previously served as an activist for Henry Wallace in the United States. R. Lieber, *British Politics*, p. 209.

[9] Beaverbrook to J. Macmillan, 5 July 1962. See also Beaverbrook correspondence with Norman Smythe and J. Macmillan, 20, 22 June and 4 July 1962, BBK H/220.

[10] *The Times*, 27 August 1962. The tone of *The Times* account suggests that its correspondent was amused rather than impressed by the proceedings.

alternatives.[11] The Council's first meeting, at the Brooks Club in London, included Lord Strang, former Head of the Foreign Office, Lord Wilmot, a former Labour minister, Sir Edward Speers, chair of the Institute of Directors, A. J. F. MacDonald of the Liberal Council, Sir Arthur Bryant, Lord Sandwich, Piers Debenham and the ubiquitous William Pickles. The group achieved a unity of purpose[12] but its goals were overtaken by events as de Gaulle vetoed Britain's application.

AntiCommon Market League (ACML)

An effort to mobilise Conservative activists against the Common Market application commenced during the summer of 1961 with a series of organisational meetings at the home of John Paul, a director of the Mobil Corporation. 'It is our aim', the group declared, 'to influence public and parliamentary opinion in every possible way to achieve a reversal of the disastrous decision announced on August 2nd'.[13] The ACML was publicly launched at a 4 October 1961 meeting with Derek Walker-Smith MP as the featured speaker. From the beginning, the League presented its audience with an explicit choice between Commonwealth and Common Market, warning 'You cannot have both'.[14]

While it eventually achieved a degree of cross-party membership, the ACML is best understood in the context of its dissenting relationship with the Conservative Party. Its initial membership[15] and entire leadership were drawn from Conservative ranks. The founder and chairman, John Paul, had been a minor but active figure in Conservative politics following wartime service as a Bomber Command squadron leader. In both 1950 and 1951 Paul stood unsuccessfully as a Conservative parliamentary candidate, losing out on the first occasion to Clement Attlee at Walthamstow West.[16] He served on the Executive Committee of the National Union of Conservative Associations and chaired the South Kensington Conservative Association until March 1961. An honorary secretary of the Society for Individual Freedom, Paul was also chair of the General Purposes Committee at the Primrose League, a position that allowed him access to the platform at the 1962 Conservative Party

---

[11] Correspondence between Leo Russell and A. Bryant, 21 November 1962, AB Papers H/4.

[12] A. Bryant to G. Weston, 20 September 1962, AB Papers H/4.

[13] AntiCommon Market League statement and membership form, September 1961.

[14] AntiCommon Market League, 'Conservatives and the Common Market', 12 October 1961.

[15] J. Paul to Beaverbrook, 5 October 1961, BBK C/269.

[16] Paul was a distant second, polling 8,988 votes compared with Attlee's 21,095. Paul came closer at Southampton in 1951, losing to the Labour candidate, Dr H. M. King, by a mere 495 votes. Statistics from F. W. S. Craig, *British Parliamentary Election Results, 1950–1970* (Chichester, 1971).

conference.[17] David Clarke, the League's honorary Treasurer, was a Hayes and Harlington Urban District Councillor and an activist in the Home Counties North branch of the Young Conservatives. Michael Shay, the honorary Secretary, was chair of the Feltham Young Conservatives.[18] Paul's wife, Diana, though she was not listed as an officer, played an active role in League affairs. A Kensington Borough town councillor and vice-chair of its Housing and Town Planning Committee, she proved an enthusiastic chair and speaker at the League's public meetings.

Despite its ostensible affiliation with Conservative politics, the League's leadership was galvanised by dissatisfaction with the trends of Government policy. Diana Paul, for instance, charged the London Area Women's Conference with 'brain-washing'[19] its members on Common Market issues. The Prime Minister, John Paul contended, was in the thrall of a 'left wing, quasi-liberal bias'.[20] He wrote to Beaverbrook, 'You once said to me "no one really hates these days"; they do – anti-Common Market folk hate Harold Macmillan, and the vanity of the man is such that it would be good for him to know it.'[21] In addition to the League, David Clarke and Michael Shay were active members of the Sixty-One Group, a clutch of Young Conservatives that espoused a right-wing agenda. Shay labelled Macmillan a leftist, Cabinet minister Peter Thorneycroft a free trade Liberal with an Italian wife and back-bench Conservatives as both '"pink"' and '"faceless"'. A merchant banking community rife with recent European immigrants, he contended, influenced the affairs of pro-entry pressure groups.[22]

The passion behind the League's rhetoric gave pause to prospective patrons and supporters. Beaverbrook held his ground. It was the Common Market application, he argued, not Harold Macmillan, which the *Express* wanted to 'destroy'.[23] Sir Roy Welensky described Paul as 'fairly balanced' but was suspicious of his 'rabid anti-Marketeer' tendencies.[24] Paul eventually lost his job when Mobil Oil judged his political

---

[17] John Paul leaflet, 30 November 1963. The Primrose League complained that Paul's speech failed to represent their views. Sir H. Kerr, Chancellor of the Primrose League to Conservative Central Office, 9 November 1962, Department of Special Collections and Western Manuscripts, Bodleian Library, Oxford, Conservative Party Archives, Conservative Central Office files (hereafter cited as CPA, CCO) 3/6/139.

[18] Windlesham, *Communication and Political Power*, pp. 172–3.

[19] D. Paul to B. Pemberton, 30 November 1961, CPA, CCO 3/6/65.

[20] J. Paul to Sir Roy Welensky, 30 March 1963, Bodleian Library of Commonwealth and Africa Studies at Rhodes House, Oxford, Sir Roy Welensky Papers (hereafter cited as MSS Welensky) 654/1.

[21] J. Paul to Beaverbrook, 10 February 1962, BBK C/269.

[22] M. Shay, 'The Conservative Europeans', in R. H. Corbet (ed.), *Britain Not Europe. Commonwealth Before Common Market* (London, 1962), pp. 25–7.

[23] Beaverbrook to J. Paul, undated but February 1962, BBK C/269.

[24] R. Welensky to B. M. de Quehen, 16 and 21 June 1965, MSS Welensky 743/3.

activities 'incompatible' with directorship of an American subsidiary and forced him to resign in August 1962.[25]

A similar wariness was evident in the disposition of anti-Market MPs. Derek Walker-Smith, Robin Turton, Anthony Fell, John Biggs-Davison, Paul Williams and Peter Walker all spoke at League-sponsored events. They avoided formal affiliation, however, and the ACML relationship with back-bench MPs ought not be overstated.[26] On the platform and in print, MPs were referred to as either 'guests' or 'guest speakers'. League activists at the South Dorset by-election were ordered to refrain from putting candidate names on any of their literature or pamphlets.[27] Publicly at least, Viscount Hinchingbrooke maintained his independence from the League right up until assuming its presidency at the end of 1962. Privately, Paul complained that MPs were 'a spiritless lot, afraid of the whip'.[28]

The Conservative Party showed no inclination to provide Paul's views with public airing and refused his calls to address its 1961 conference. Paul responded by distributing 2,000 anti-Market leaflets to delegates, though, as he admitted, this 'had little effect on the result'.[29] Paul's requests to Beaverbrook Newspapers for press coverage and deposit money to finance his parliamentary candidacies were turned down. Proposed candidacies at Orpington and Oswestry and West Derbyshire brought objections from Max Aitken, who complained 'He has been carpetbagging for an official Conservative candidature lately and I think this would be brought out in any campaign. Loss of a deposit would be a disaster for the *Daily Express* campaign against the CM [Common Market] which is going so well.'[30]

The League's precarious finances compounded Paul's frustrations. The distribution of a single circular to all those on the League's mailing list alone cost £500.[31] Paul provided the bulk of the organisation's funding,[32] estimated at £10,000, and received additional donations of £4,000 from Garfield Weston and £5,000 from an anonymous 'friend'.[33] Entreaties to

---

[25] *Daily Telegraph*, 5 September 1962.

[26] Michael Kandiah correctly highlights the linkage but somewhat overstates the depth of ACML influence with parliamentarians. M. Kandiah, 'British Domestic Politics: Conservatives and Foreign Policy', in W. Kaiser and G. Staerck (eds), *British Foreign Policy, 1955–64: Contracting Options* (London, 2000), p. 78.

[27] AntiCommon Market League circular, November 1962.

[28] J. Paul to R. Welensky, 30 March 1963, MSS Welensky 654/1.

[29] J. Paul to Beaverbrook, 15 October 1961, BBK C/269.

[30] M. Aitken to Beaverbrook, 30 April 1962, BBK H/221.

[31] *Anti-Common Market Newsletter*, 9 February 1963.

[32] J. Paul to R. Welensky, 24 April 1964, MSS Welensky 708/3. One early theory circulating at Conservative Central Office suggested that Mobil Oil was providing Paul with funding to push its own anti-Market agenda. A. A. Hammond to Chief Organisation Officer (COO), 1 September 1961, CPA, CCO 500/31/3.

[33] J. Paul to Beaverbrook, 11 January 1963, BBK C/269.

Beaverbrook for a further £10,000 were made in vain.[34] Publicly, however, the organisation wore its financial difficulties as a badge of integrity and thereby accentuated its critique of international finance. Accordingly, the pro-entry movement was tainted by '"Big Money" ... much of it of foreign origin'.[35] Conservative Central Office, the Liberal Party and the European Community Information Service, it was alleged, had received £1 million from industrial and financial concerns since the war. The League, by way of contrast, found its 'strength' and security from the modest donations of 'ordinary private individuals'.[36]

The ACML made the most of its resources, however, and claimed 30,000 members by January 1963.[37] During 1962 alone it provided speakers for 240 public meetings. Those events were geographically diverse and included presentations at thirty-five public debates, thirty-five 'educational' establishments, thirty-four Rotary Clubs or round tables, twenty NFU branch meetings and the remainder at women's organisations and other gatherings.[38] Attendance at League events was subject to considerable variation. Infrequent large rallies, such as that at Westminster Central Hall in September 1962, drew as many as 2,000 people. More typical, however, were smaller gatherings, of between 50 and 100 listeners. One visitor to a meeting near Folkestone lamented the League's failure to draw more than 120 from a regional population of 80,000. 'And the night', he reported, 'was not cold, as the chairman diplomatically stated'.[39]

The League's production of written propaganda exceeded its dedication to public events. During the course of its 1961–63 pamphleteering campaign, its distribution matched that of Conservative Central Office, with nearly 2 million pieces.[40] One million of those were in the form of a 'Common Market Quiz', which set the threat to Britain in question-and-answer format. League members received monthly doses of propaganda, updates on Common Market news and attacks on the Government in the *AntiCommon Market League Newsletter*. In addition, a series of eight pamphlets was produced, each addressing a different Common Market theme.[41] The League's most ambitious publication, *Britain Not Europe*, contained seventy-two pages of articles by anti-Market pundits and MPs as well as former members of the military and civil service. Emphasising

---

[34] There is no indication that Beaverbrook exceeded his 1963 donation of £1,000. J. Paul to Beaverbrook, 3 June 1963, BBK C/269.

[35] *AntiCommon Market League Newsletter*, January 1962.

[36] AntiCommon Market League, *Press Information*, 1962.

[37] AntiCommon Market League, *Press Information*, November 1963.

[38] AntiCommon Market League, *New Year Newsletter*, 31 December 1962.

[39] N. Easton to Beaverbrook, 19 December 1962, BBK F/4.

[40] Windlesham, *Communication and Political Power*, p. 178.

[41] Titles included *Britain's Sovereignty and the Common Market*, *Britain's Offer of Free Trade to Canada* and *The Common Market and British Law*.

Commonwealth and federalist themes, *Britain Not Europe* eventually sold 38,000 copies at one shilling apiece. Pamphlets were in turn complemented by an indeterminate number of posters, car stickers and stamps, all bearing a 'Commonwealth Before Common Market' slogan.

National identity in the League's approach to the Common Market was indelibly marked by the attraction–repulsion mechanism in its relationship with Conservatism. Throughout, tensions arose between a 'country before party' transcendence of politics and a desire for the recovery of Conservative cultural values and symbols. Diana Paul's description of the League as a 'British institution'[42] suggested that, as a structural entity, it aspired to a patriotic high ground of the sort normally reserved for the Conservative Party. At the same time, however, national symbols were appropriated in an overtly political context. A sacrifice of national independence, Commonwealth and agriculture was thus not merely an affront to national sentiment: it was a contravention of the 'basic, long cherished values of Conservative policy'.[43]

ACML Britishness resonated with the claims of Conservative fellow travellers. John Paul imagined himself as an Empire man in the Beaverbrook mould, a fellow Crusader devoted to keeping Commonwealth issues in the public eye.[44] The League's regard for the tides of history pointed up the evolutionary impulses so prominent in Sir Arthur Bryant's work (see Chapter 3). 'The history of Britain', it claimed, 'has been insular and imperial'.[45] As the title *Britain Not Europe* and the slogan 'Commonwealth Before Common Market' suggested, Britons faced an inescapable choice between national greatness and irretrievable loss. The EEC application was a tacit admission of weakness, of having accepted the status of a 'fifth rate power'. Joining Europe meant a diminution of national voice, a one-seventh stake in the pool of recently defeated and liberated European nations.[46]

Whatever its distaste for Harold Macmillan, the League underscored the threat to British independence by blaming outside, specifically American influences. At League meetings, Viscount Hinchingbrooke thought US pressure the only plausible explanation for Macmillan's European policy.[47] The US President was demonised as the 'true son' of

---

[42] Diana Paul, speech in Cardiff, 7 November 1962, quoted by H. Davies in report to COO, 15 November 1962, CPA, CCO 500/31/3.
[43] AntiCommon Market League leaflet, *Conservatives and the Common Market*, 12 October 1961.
[44] J. Paul to Beaverbrook, 30 June 1961, BBK C/269.
[45] AntiCommon Market League, *British Sovereignty and the Common Market*, Pamphlet No. 2.
[46] AntiCommon Market League, Statement and Membership Form, September 1961.
[47] See Hinchingbrooke speech at Barnes, quoted in the *Daily Express*, 19 January 1962. See also report on Hinchingbrooke speech at Cardiff in H. Davies to COO, 15 November 1962, CPA, CCO 500/31/3.

the anti-British Joseph Kennedy.[48] Blind anti-Communism, *Britain Not Europe* argued, put European entry ahead of national identity:

> It disregards the facts of life, the facts of national pride. Out of patriotism people have sacrificed all for their country. By destroying national pride and putting in its place a soulless, technocratic 'community', defence against Communism could go by default. To subjugate all … is to ultimately substitute State for Nation…. Britain's voice and influence in the affairs of men would be lost in the cacophony of an ill-assorted United States of Europe.[49]

The Government, it was believed, was capitulating to external pressures and demonstrating an insufficient regard for British greatness.

In the League's hierarchy of national interests British farming occupied less hallowed ground than sovereignty or the Commonwealth. Though Robin Turton used an ACML forum to proclaim small farmers 'the backbone of England',[50] farming generally featured as part of a more banal exposition of producer and consumer interests. Accordingly, farming was a precarious vocation whose welfare, and therefore that of British consumers, hinged upon the British system of price guarantees. Exposure to European competition via the CAP, it was thought, would destroy British horticulture and British consumers would bear witness to a farming depression reminiscent of the inter-war years.[51]

The ACML also used agriculture to facilitate tributes to the merits of imperial preference. While that line set the League at odds with the historicism of Carrington, it echoed the imperial crusading of the *Express*. Paul's alignment with the Commonwealth trade cause was more than an attempt to curry favour with Beaverbrook. In the ACML's imagination of Commonwealth, preferences performed a dual function by guaranteeing overall unity while satisfying the mutual trade interests of individual nation states. It was an under-appreciated historic process, whose virtues, Paul argued, '"Europeans" and free traders always chose to ignore'.[52] Anglo-Canadian trade, it was claimed, had shown free trade liberalism to be 'anachronistic'.[53] The League, like all Commonwealth devotees, celebrated trade potential and the Ottawa Agreements by simplistically highlighting the disparity between 170 million European

---

[48] AntiCommon Market League, *New Year Newsletter*, 31 December 1962.

[49] Sir Clifford Heathcote-Smith, 'American Influence in European Union', in R. H. Corbet (ed.), *Britain Not Europe. Commonwealth Before Common Market* (London, 1962), p. 18.

[50] R. Turton, 'Agriculture: The Vital Issues', in R. H. Corbet (ed.), *Britain Not Europe. Commonwealth Before Common Market* (London, 1962), p. 65.

[51] AntiCommon Market League, 'Statement', September 1961; and *Conservatives and the Common Market*, October 1961.

[52] Copy of draft letter to *The Director*, undated, probably August 1961, BBK C/269.

[53] AntiCommon Market League, *Britain's Offer of Free Trade to Canada*, Pamphlet No. 6.

consumers and 650 million in the Commonwealth. The choice, then, was not between the bleak determinism of '"Europe or Poverty"' but rather between '"Europe or Prosperity"'.[54]

Allusions to unity and consumer millions apart, the Commonwealth actually served narrower meditations on British greatness. Thus, the 'largest political and economic union in the history of mankind' was a matter of 'national destiny', one which allowed Britain to continue as 'a dominant partner in the Western Alliance'.[55] A national focus was augmented by references to the 'British Commonwealth' and accompanying devotionals to the sanctity of the Dominion family. In bold typeface the League *Newsletter* asked rhetorically, 'What kind of British Government is this, that jeopardises the friendship, loyalty and dependability of Australia, Canada and New Zealand for the favours of Italy?'[56]

The League's 'Commonwealth Before Common Market' identity was shaped by relationships with the outside world and a Beaverbrookian interpretation of trade, Empire and international standing. National sovereignty was its 'insular' counterpart. In its technical approach to Common Market legalities, the ACML relied upon the legal pronouncements of William Pickles and Sir Henry Slessor to set unwritten against written constitutions, flexibility against codified stasis and the supremacy of Parliament against binding treaties.[57] In total, however, sovereignty was immersed in the wider banalities of institutional differentiation.

Reliance upon the institutional manifestations of Britishness was facilitated in part by a regard for the Common Market as a political rather than an economic grouping. It also grew out of a definition of sovereignty that equated the decision-making bodies of parliamentary democracy with expressions of national will. Accordingly, sovereignty embodied 'the right of a nation to decide its own policies in every field of politics, from internal national matters to international decisions'.[58] The structures of national independence were, moreover, infused with the Conservative instincts and evolutionary historicism that typified Bryant's work. By joining Europe, Britain was 'forsaking forever her identity and sovereignty, her institutions – *the toil of her forefathers through five hundred years of history*"'.[59] The League compilation of fundamental principles, derived from the spirit of Disraeli and Dicey,[60]

---

[54] AntiCommon Market League, 'Statement', September 1961.
[55] *Ibid.*
[56] AntiCommon Marlet League, *Newsletter*, 4 June 1962. See also *Conservatives and the Common Market.*
[57] AntiCommon Market League, *The Common Market and British Law.*
[58] AntiCommon Market League, *British Sovereignty and the Common Market.*
[59] *Ibid.*
[60] Major General Sir E. Spears, 'Britain the Loser', and D. Walker-Smith, 'British Sovereignty and the Common Market', in R. H. Corbet (ed.), *Britain Not Europe. Commonwealth Before Common Market* (London, 1962), pp. 8–11, 13–15.

appeared to embody elements of a national character. British democracy, it was argued, had evolved to include the virtues of 'independence', 'self-reliance', 'tolerance' and 'willingness to compromise'. By comparison, Europe's democracies were portrayed as underdeveloped and tainted by the subversive, destabilising forces of Catholic history and, latterly, Communist infiltration. The chief nations of the Common Market, it was pointed out, had all been part of the Holy Roman Empire. 'For them, political union is merely a reunion; they will join an old system which was allowed to disintegrate and is now being rebuilt.'[61]

Keep Britain Out (KBO) campaign

The Liberal counterpart to League pressure developed on a much smaller scale, in August 1961. As its name implied, opposition to Britain's application dictated KBO's immediate mission. Its lines of development, however, again derived from a set of antipathetic impulses that, in this case, set an interpretation of liberal philosophy against Liberal Party policy.

For its founder and chairman, Oliver Smedley, the KBO campaign was but one instance of extra-parliamentary agitation in a lifetime devoted to the values of free trade. A decorated veteran[62] and successful chartered accountant, Smedley began organising pressure groups in the early 1950s. These eventually included the Farmers and Smallholders Alliance, the Cheap Food League and the Council for the Reduction of Taxes. He helped found the Institute of Economic Affairs and, along with S. W. Alexander and J. S. Harding, became a leader of the Free Trade Union in 1958. In 1964 he contested the BBC monopoly by launching Radio Atlanta, an offshore 'pirate' station subsequently known as Radio Caroline. Smedley's controversial enterprise gained further notoriety in 1966 when Reg Calvert, a fellow radio pirate, attacked him in his Essex home. Smedley shot and killed Calvert but all charges were subsequently dismissed by a jury.

S. W. Alexander shared a devotion to free trade and assisted Smedley in many of these ventures.[63] Ironically, Alexander's professional career had been dominated by service to the great protectionist Lord Beaverbrook. During World War I he performed secretarial duties for Beaverbrook at both the Canadian War Records Office and the Ministry of Information. Alexander was awarded an MBE in 1918 and went on to become the City Editor of the *Daily Express*, the *Sunday Express* and the *Evening Standard*. Alexander's principles were undoubtedly bolstered by acquaintance with Beaverbrook, a man he regarded as fundamentally

---

[61] AntiCommon Market League, *British Sovereignty and the Common Market*.
[62] Smedley joined the Honourable Artillery Company in 1939 and, after being wounded on three occasions, was awarded the Military Cross.
[63] For Alexander's obituary see *The Times*, 25 March 1980.

'evil'.[64] He left Beaverbrook Newspapers to become proprietor and Chief Editor of the moribund *City Press*. With Smedley as Deputy Editor, *City Press* became a mouthpiece for free trade liberalism. In addition, Alexander co-founded the Society of Individualists, with Sir Ernest Benn, founded the City of London Free Trade Club, served as a President of the Free Trade League and Cobden Club and was an honorary Treasurer of the Anti-Dear Food Campaign.

Alexander and Smedley had a tenuous relationship with party politics. Alexander ran as an independent candidate for the City of London in 1945 and North Ilford in 1950 but failed on both occasions. During his lifetime, and as late as 1987, Smedley stood for Parliament on eighteen occasions, most often as an independent. In the 1950s he had joined the Liberal Party and ascended to the position of Vice President but the Party's embrace of the Common Market application proved a step too far. Smedley's views were never likely to gain favour in a party thoroughly committed to Common Market membership. The main pro-entry resolution at the 1961 Liberal Party conference predicted benefits for agriculture, pledged its vigilance against the development of a fortress Europe and was passed by the 1,300-strong delegation with only five dissenting votes.[65] Smedley's conference speech elicited cries of dissent and slow hand clapping from the delegates. 'By abandoning the policy on non-discrimination in foreign trade', he warned, 'the Liberal Party is destroying itself. You will be forced into the position of having to defend Mr. Macmillan.'[66] Smedley focused his attack on Lady Violet Bonham-Carter, her son Mark and her son-in-law, the Liberal leader Jo Grimond, all of whom were seated behind him on the dais. Party policy, he claimed, was advanced by 'the baleful influence of our mother figure, or is it grandmother figure or mother-in-law figure. I don't know which it is.'[67] By the following year's conference Smedley had resigned from the party.

Lacking both funding and a sizeable membership, KBO took on the appearance of a highly personal crusade. With the assistance of a small committee,[68] Smedley and Alexander printed and distributed thousands of leaflets, spread propaganda through the *City Press* and, where possible, provided speakers. Smedley regarded a 26 August 1962 rally at the

---

[64] S. W. Alexander, *Save the Pound – Save the People: Montagu Norman versus Beaverbrook, Keynes, Boothby, and the Political Pygmies* (London, 1978), p. 22.

[65] *The Times*, 23 September 1961. An amendment requesting assurances for Commonwealth producers and underdeveloped nations received only thirty votes.

[66] Smedley speech quoted in *The Times*, 23 September 1961. See also *Daily Express*, 23 September 1961.

[67] Smedley quoted on the *Ten O'Clock* programme, 22 September 1961, BBC WAC, T537/538.

[68] The 'provisional committee' for 1962 was listed as Smedley, Alexander, Christopher Frere-Smith, W. A. Newton Jones, Simon Knott and George Winder.

Albert Hall as the 'climax' of KBO's first campaign.[69] It was, however, a group affair shared with speakers from other organisations. The same was true of its sponsorship of a Trafalgar Square rally three weeks later. Among the assembled crowd were large numbers of CND supporters, who would have been drawn by the presence of Will Griffth, MP, and Ron Leighton, a leader of the FBM.[70]

Smedley's defection from the Liberal Party was virtually pre-ordained. He was an early anti-Marketeer and in July 1961 predicted the application would fail under the weight of Government pledges to protect the interests of British agriculture, EFTA and the Common-wealth.[71] He had, moreover, signalled his intentions with the formation of KBO in the month before the 1961 Liberal Party conference.[72] The circumstances surrounding the formation of KBO demonstrate just how far its antipathy to the Common Market and Liberal politics was a matter of principle. In 1961, Smedley was chair of the Free Trade Union, an organisation established in 1903 by exponents of free trade and enemies of Joseph Chamberlain. Its first public debate on the Common Market, in the summer of 1961, occasioned splits between what Smedley called 'wishy-washy liberals' loyal to party policy and the 'true free traders', who viewed the Common Market as naked protectionism. With pro-Europeans in the ascendant, Smedley formed KBO to prevent resignations from the Free Trade Union.[73]

In the age of 'Butskell', Smedley and Alexander's organisations were vestigial outposts of Cobdenite free trade. But, small though they were, those groups were notable because they provided a narrow bridge to the broad nineteenth-century values of Manchester School liberalism. What is more, features of the Cobdenite tradition that they upheld subsequently appeared within libertarian Conservatism in the last quarter of the twentieth century.[74] KBO's anti-Market campaign, like the *Express* crusade, was entrenched in resurrected 'dear food' battles of the past. But a shared antipathy for European entanglement was predicated on two divergent conceptions of political economy. Ironically, Smedley and Alexander played Cobden and Bright to Beaverbrook's Chamberlain in the subtext of anti-Market dissent.[75]

---

[69] O. Smedley, *Out! UK in EEC Spells Disaster* (London, 1986), p. 17.

[70] For a report on the rally see *The Times*, 17 September 1962.

[71] O. Smedley, letter to *The Times*, 13 July 1961. At this time Smedley was offering his opinions as chair of the Free Trade Union and Cobden Club.

[72] *Daily Express*, 23 August 1961.

[73] Smedley, *Out!*, pp. 15–16.

[74] A. Howe, *Free Trade and Liberal England, 1846–1946* (Oxford, 1997), pp. 274–5. See also A. Butt Philip, 'The Liberals and Europe' in V. Bogdanor (ed.), *Liberal Party Politics* (Oxford, 1983), pp. 217–40; A. Gamble, 'Liberals and the Economy', in Bogdanor (ed.), *Liberal Party Politics* (Oxford, 1983), pp. 199–201.

[75] Despite his allegiance to Cobdenite free trade, Smedley wrote an anti-Market

KBO's endorsement of Cobdenism addressed questions of fiscal management and, in keeping with Smedley's accounting background, included a commitment to sound finance. Smedley was troubled by British economic performance and he feared an 'incipient economic crisis' and a devaluation of sterling in the summer of 1961. He called for an end to the issue of new paper money through an alternative programme of spending cuts, a floating pound and unilateral tariff reductions via the 'British expedient' of 'most favoured nation' clauses.[76]

Existing economic difficulties aside, Smedley rejected Common Market membership because it transgressed the central tenets of free trade and, by extension, the sources of British greatness. The most basic of those assumptions was the idea that British prosperity through the ages had been dependent upon the procurement of food and raw materials from the least expensive sources. Smedley defended 'the tradition of "buying cheap"' as a national right. Accordingly, food and raw materials obtained at free market prices allowed workers to obtain the highest possible standard of living, reduced production costs and thereby maximised exports. The 'dear food' CAP, by contrast, would damage Britain's competitive advantage by artificially raising the cost of living and wages.[77]

Tariff and prosperity issues also summoned Cobdenite interpretations of Britain's imperial heritage. Free traders, Alexander claimed, were better Empire managers than protectionists by virtue of a devotion to invisible exports. Insurance, banking, finance and shipping, it was argued, had flourished under the guidance of British business practices and principles. 'They are our most valuable exports. And they depend on integrity, sound money, the honesty of merchants and bankers for which this country was famed and is still famed, and above all to free trade and free markets.'[78]

As the issues of consumer interest and imperial management suggested, fiscal affairs were merely the leading edge of a Cobdenite orientation that clashed with Common Market entry. In fact, free trade was upheld as a vehicle of moral virtue. It was no accident that during the course of the KBO campaign the *City Press* and Free Trade League pledged sympathy with the evolving views of James Meade and reprinted a 1935 pamphlet entitled *The Moral Case for Free Trade*. The pamphlet preached free trade as an 'essential condition' to international 'peace and goodwill', 'personal liberty', 'democracy' and 'purity of government', among others.[79] Along

---

piece for the *Express*. See 'Our Freedom Is What They Want to End', *Sunday Express*, 25 February 1962.

[76] Smedley, letter to *The Times*, 21 July 1961.

[77] Smedley, *Out!*, pp. 19–50.

[78] Alexander, *Save the Pound*, pp. 13–15.

[79] *City Press* and Free Trade League, *The Common Market – The Alternative*. An undated (probably 1962), reprint of C. T. Brock, *The Moral Case for Free Trade* (1935), p. 3.

with previous pronouncements by Alexander and Smedley, the argument affirmed a belief in the existence of a natural design.

The notion that free trade offered the best prospects for peace between nations was a hallmark of the Cobdenite legacy, one that reached back to the 1840s.[80] These views sprang from an evangelical and anthropomorphic spirit that transposed morality and genius from the discourse of individuals to the geopolitics of individual states. Accordingly, free trade facilitated the peaceful interaction between nations in a world of nation states. Protectionism, by comparison, was devoid of morality because it offered artificial barriers to the designs of nature, the course of justice and the equilibrium achieved by the laws of supply and demand.[81]

The immorality of protectionism in turn led to distinctions between nationalism and patriotism. 'Tariffs are war and breed wars', Alexander had argued in a 1947 debate with Robert Boothby.[82] Brock had likewise written 'Protection is the outcome not of true patriotism, but of its caricature, narrow and selfish nationalism.... Protection and war are branches of the same tree.'[83] While nationalism born of protection was intrinsically evil, a distinct form of patriotism was nonetheless laudable. In a paraphrase of Dr Johnson, Smedley suggested that patriotism was neither '"the last refuge of the scoundrel"' nor 'the last refuge of the patriot'.[84] This was a crucial distinction because it legitimised a belief that virtuous patriotism was the rational response to national greatness, one that superseded emotional attachments to homeland. It also suggested that Smedley was sensitive to charges of xenophobia. At one of its rallies he claimed that KBO was not '"anti-European"' but it was 'old fashioned enough to be pro-British'.[85]

Having identified himself with the 'sound' realm of patriotism Smedley nonetheless lionised Britain's greatness in robust terms. His historical judgements combined A. J. P. Taylor's Whiggish fondness for radical traditions and Arthur Bryant's regard for evolved organic institutions (see Chapter 3) with the banalities of patriotism. Individualism was paramount and featured in his selection of three particular points of national pride. The first of these was the 'invention of the concept of "freedom of the individual" ... a uniquely British contribution to our civilisation'. It was, he claimed, an intellectual construct developed and refined by Bacon, Hobbes, Milton, Locke, Berkeley, Hume, Petty, Smith and Mill. But it was also a function of the Protestant spirituality that separated Britain

---

[80] Howe, *Free Trade and Liberal England*, pp. 295–306. As Howe also notes, the Cobden Club used the phrase 'Free trade, peace and good will' as its slogan.

[81] Brock, *The Moral Case*, p. 12.

[82] Alexander, *Save the Pound*, p. 17.

[83] Brock, *The Moral Case*, p. 3.

[84] Smedley, *Out!*, p. 8.

[85] *The Times*, 17 September 1962.

from Roman Catholicism. Geography played its part, too, and insularity was credited with breeding unique patterns of instinct and behaviour. 'The particular qualities Islanders have to offer are constantly needed as leaven by Continental populations whose ambitions tend toward a species of homogeneity which is reformable only by revolution or civil war.'[86] Two other benchmarks of British pride, parliamentary democracy and the common law tradition, were presented as the products of historic evolution. These had sanctified the sovereignty of Britain's thousand years of history and charged its people with a singular obligation: 'We, and no other people on earth, are the true inheritors and testators of God's ultimate gift to the human race, the gift of personal freedom'.[87]

Predicated though it was on the evils of protectionism, KBO's anti-Market literature went beyond the rhetoric of Cobdenism. Free trade allegiance, celebration of national genius and regard for organic historic evolution were largely incorporated under the banner of sovereignty. This was partly because, as Smedley's *Sunday Express* article claimed, the British electorate itself was sovereign and subject to no higher authority. It was enshrined by the assumption that sovereignty and economy were inseparable topics.[88] It may also have reflected a desire to provide a rallying point for Britons whose patriotic instincts did not extend to an orthodox embrace of free trade. Article 189 of the Treaty of Rome,[89] described as the 'most disgraceful proposal ever put before the British people',[90] thus became a focal point for the group's attack. Entanglement with Europe meant the removal of the right of Parliament and the people to determine its most important policy priorities.[91] The thousand years of history and the evolved system of constitutional monarchy and democratic politics were imperilled by surrender to European bureaucracy. Parliament would become a 'county council' and the Queen a figure on par with Princess Grace.[92] A call to action asked British patriots, 'Are you going to let this disgraceful betrayal go by default? Don't let 'em do it! Keep Britain Out! Keep Britain Out! Keep Britain Out!'[93]

---

[86] Smedley, *Out!*, pp. 9–10, 13–15.

[87] *Ibid.*, p. 14. See also pp. 51–66.

[88] Smedley, 'Our Freedom'.

[89] Article 189 alluded to the decision-making powers of Common Market institutions and the extent to which these were binding upon member states.

[90] Keep Britain Out, poster reprinted from the *City Press*, 'Don't Let 'em do it!', undated.

[91] Keep Britain Out, open letter, 'Who Governs Britain', 16 January 1962. This letter was part of a mass mailing and its enclosures also included Roy Harrod, 'Britain, Free World and the Six', *The Times*, 2 January 1962; 'Propaganda Victims', *City Press*, 15 December 1961; D. Jay, 'The Common Market Mirage', *New Statesman and Nation*, undated. For a copy of this mailing see Modern Manuscripts Collection, Wren Library, Trinity College, Cambridge, R. A. Butler Papers F/124.

[92] Smedley, 'Our Freedom'.

[93] Keep Britain Out poster, 'Don't let 'em do it!'

Forward Britain Movement (FBM)

The objections of leftists and trade unionists to Britain's application found an early home with the creation of the FBM in May 1961. Its influence on the political landscape was no greater than that of its ACML and KBO counterparts; nor did its methods depart from the typical patterns of promotional pressure. Its founder and leader, Richard W. Briginshaw, described the Movement as 'patriotic in the best sense, obviously and intentionally political, but strictly non-party'.[94]

However ecumenical its appeal, Forward Britain was notable for mixing patriotism with the values of trade unionism and the Labour left. At its first press conference, the FBM presented a list of objectives that stretched well beyond the Common Market. These included opposition to international finance, preservation of national sovereignty, the development of higher living standards, expansion of the British market, investment in industry, respect for workers, reductions in defence spending and a doubling of investment in Britain's education system.[95] The FBM was by no means the lone voice of socialist opposition. As we shall see in Chapter 5, a body of Labour MPs pressed similar anti-Market agendas. But it was an extra-parliamentary protest given added significance by political circumstances. At a time when the TUC and the Labour Party were noncommittal on the Common Market issue, Briginshaw and the FBM tapped a small but vocal constituency of union dissent.

Robert Lieber's contention that objections by TUC leftists were essentially political or personal[96] needs some refinement. While accession to the Treaty of Rome was regarded as a political act, its provisions were understood to include profound economic consequences for Britain. A July 1961 letter to *The Times*, signed by nineteen trade union officers, including Briginshaw, articulated anxieties that the Rome Treaty would undermine wage levels and expose weaker industries to unrestricted European competition.[97] At the 1961 TUC conference J. E. Mortimer of the Draughtsmen's and Allied Technicians' Association argued that the Common Market was a reversion to the values of nineteenth-century liberalism that had created cyclical depressions and recessions. Briginshaw and A. K. Milner of the Association of Supervisory Staffs, Executives and Technicians joined Mortimer in support of a motion that declared the Rome Treaty harmful to British national interests. But theirs was a minority view. Having already approved the General

---

[94] Briginshaw statement to the press, 8 June 1961, quoted in Forward Britain Movement advertisement. Undated, probably 1962.
[95] *Ibid.*
[96] Lieber, *British Politics*, pp. 111–12.
[97] Letter to *The Times*, 21 July 1961.

Council's statement that favoured negotiations and offered conditions for entry, delegates overwhelmingly rejected the anti-Market motion.[98]

Forward Britain's campaign methods mirrored those employed by the other pressure groups. The *Forward Britain Movement Bulletin*, though primitive in appearance, was published at least once per month and, bolstered by quotes from other sources, stretched up to twelve pages in length. A pamphlet, *Common Market Realities*,[99] was published and distributed to all MPs in April 1962. Other pamphlets, fliers and posters were issued, as were car stickers, envelope stamps and badges carrying a 'Britain Yes Common Market No' slogan.

The FBM provided speakers for approximately 200 public meetings[100] and sponsored larger rallies in London. Its first substantial public meeting drew a crowd of 500 to the Caxton Hall on 15 September 1961. A splinter group of 100 attendees, invigorated by the speeches of Viscount Hinchingbrooke and Sidney Silverman among others, marched in protest up Whitehall to the Prime Minister's temporary lodgings in Admiralty House while singing 'Rule Britannia'.[101] Briginshaw organised conferences, including a three-day 'Britain–Commonwealth–EFTA conference' in the House of Commons committee rooms in July 1962[102] that the FBM called the 'historic milestone of our campaign'.[103] From the premise that Britain faced an inevitable choice between Commonwealth and Common Market, the conference explored alternative policies. Particular emphasis was placed upon finding ways to link a renewed Ottawa preference system with the provisions of EFTA.[104] Delegates included Sir Roy Harrod, Douglas Jay, William Pickles, Jennie Lee, Barbara Castle and Oliver Smedley. In other events leading up to the 1962 Commonwealth Prime Ministers' Conference, Forward Britain joined the AntiCommon Market Union rally in the Albert Hall. It also sponsored a march from the Imperial War Museum that preceded the

---

[98] *The Times*, 6 September 1961. Officers of the Amalgamated Engineering Union, Transport and General Workers, Chemical Workers, Amalgamated Society of Woodworkers as well as Sir Alan Birch of the General Council all spoke out against the anti-Market motion. Three weeks later Briginshaw criticised the TUC for failing to adequately represent the interests of the labour movement. See Briginshaw, letter to *The Times*, 26 September 1961.

[99] Forward Britain Movement, *Common Market Realities* (London, April 1962).

[100] R. Leighton, *What Next for Britain?* (London, 1963), p. 1.

[101] *Daily Express*, 16 September 1961.

[102] The FBM had also organised an earlier conference (11–15 March) entitled 'Towards a World Conference on Trade and Development'. R. Briginshaw to A. Bryant, 2 January 1962, AB Papers H/4.

[103] *Forward Britain Movement Bulletin*, No. 18, 25 July 1962. For the published conference details see Forward Britain Movement, *Britain Should Stay Out. Report of the Proceedings of the Britain–Commonwealth–EFTA Conference* (London, 1962).

[104] Draft notes on the Britain–Commonwealth–EFTA conference, A. A. Percival to Beaverbrook, 8 July 1962, BBK F/3.

9 September Trafalgar Square rally. In an attempt to broaden its patriotic base, Commonwealth citizens as well as ex-service men and women were urged to add their flags and decorations to a march led by a band and massed Union Jacks.[105]

FBM fervour hinted at possibilities for political involvement and direct action. Briginshaw, like John Paul, broached plans for a by-election stand as an anti-Market candidate.[106] The *Bulletin* encouraged its readers to graffiti walls and streets with the 'Britain Yes! Common Market No!' slogan.[107] A. A. Percival, a member of the FBM's national committee, pledged his willingness to use violent means in the spirit of 'Carson and "the Curragh"'.[108] In practice, however, the Movement's protests remained both conventional and legal.

Like all anti-Market groups, the FBM laboured under financial constraints. By the end of August 1962 it had collected a total of £5,000, including small donations from the *Express*, but carried more than £1,400 in outstanding debts.[109] Its recruitment drive was more successful. Prospective members signed a pledge 'to support the struggle for the Independence and Sovereignty of Britain and the British people', with an added proviso that revoked membership in the event of wavering loyalties.[110] In August 1962 the FBM estimated its membership at 7,000[111] and by October, it was claimed, 10,000 had joined. If applications were arriving at a rate of 100 per week,[112] that figure was, in all likelihood, overstated. Nonetheless, confidence was such that in the autumn of 1962 a designated committee was charged with the creation of FBM Youth Groups.

Forward Britain was most distinctive in its promotion of a national identity derived partly from obligations to the values of trade unionism and the Labour left. Employee interests, for instance, featured in an elevation of material over mystical patriotism. Briginshaw praised Beaverbrook's crusade but thought '"God, Queen and Empire"' an inaccurate reading of the stakes. It was, he wrote in the *NATSOPA Journal*, a question of 'Britain, bread and butter and our people'.[113] Progressive instincts also determined the selection of heroes and historic precedents. Thus,

---

[105] *Forward Britain Movement Bulletin*, No. 19, 23 August 1962.
[106] *Daily Express*, 24 August 1961. Briginshaw did not subsequently run in the by-election at Moss Side Manchester.
[107] *Forward Britain Movement Bulletin*, No. 20, 18 September 1962.
[108] A. A. Percival to Beaverbrook, 3 June 1962, BBK F/3.
[109] Blackburn to Beaverbrook, 30 and 31 August 1962, BBK H/224. Cheques from the *Express* totalled £500, with a further £500 provided in the form of advertising.
[110] Forward Britain Movement, membership application.
[111] Briginshaw interviewed in *Daily Express*, 24 August 1962.
[112] *Forward Britain Movement Bulletin*, Nos 20 and 21, 18 September and 17 October 1962.
[113] Briginshaw quoted in the *Daily Express*, 30 June 1962.

Magna Carta, Cromwell and the Glorious Revolution were joined by the Reform Bills, the Chartists and suffragettes.[114]

FBM patriotism was also invoked as a form of protest against the status quo and prevailing visions of national identity. Change was regarded as an inevitable force that Britain needed to accommodate with greater dexterity. For Ron Leighton, the world was in the throes of a 'social, scientific and technological revolution' with which Britain and its institutions had failed to keep pace. The country, he argued, had shown signs of 'stagnation' and 'decay'[115] and he pleaded for liberation rather than Common Market entanglement. Leighton's solution to Britain's ills showed a striking regard for the centrality of patriotism and the fluidity of national identity. His logic presumed that if the world had changed, so too must Britain's imagination of itself. He wrote: 'we must evoke anew a sense of patriotism, meaning not empty flag waving, but concern for and love of one's country, and wanting the best for its people; putting the national interest before selfish private interest'.[116]

The FBM's reconstruction of national identity was also a search for harmony between the suppositions of socialist internationalism and the realities of national allegiance. It was partly manifest in claims for more sophisticated varieties of sentiment, ones dissociated from the extremes. 'We are not modern-day jingoists', one of its advertisements declared.[117] As if to emphasise the point, the FBM set itself as a sworn adversary of the fascist and pro-entry sympathies of Oswald Mosley's Union Movement.[118] Nazism and fascism were denounced as 'alien creeds' in a nation that revered decency, fair play and democracy.[119] FBM claims to moderation were supplemented by a willingness to bang the drum for Britain. Trade unionists, Briginshaw told the 1961 TUC conference, were not of a 'flag waving' disposition. But, he argued, patriotism was the 'essence' of the Common Market dilemma and the union movement could be counted upon as 'the most quietly patriotic one in the whole country'.[120]

---

[114] Forward Britain Movement, *Common Market Realities*.

[115] Leighton, *What Next for Britain?*, pp. 14–15.

[116] *Ibid.*, p. 16.

[117] Forward Britain Movement, leaflet with membership form, undated, probably 1962.

[118] Mosley's fascist organisation advocated a united Europe and championed the anti-immigrant cause in the 1950s and 1960s. Those latter sympathies were reflected in its decision to contest by-elections at North Kensington in 1959, Moss Side in 1961 and Middlesboro East in 1962. See N. Nugent and R. King, *The British Right: Conservative and Right Wing Politics in Britain* (Farnborough, 1977), pp. 185–6. For a personal recollection of the period, see the 'Epilogue' in N. Mosley, *Rules of the Game. Beyond the Pale: Memoirs of Sir Oswald Mosley and Family* (Elmwood Park, Illinois, 1991), pp. 564–76.

[119] *Forward Britain Movement Bulletin*, No. 19, 23 August 1962.

[120] *The Times*, 6 September 1961.

Forward Britain also sought middle ground by positing national independence as a precursor to 'genuine' internationalism. This was an essential component of leftist thinking, because sovereignty preserved economic planning as a national prerogative. Briginshaw favoured 'friendship among peoples', but regarded European integration as 'the reverse – a smelly cosmopolitanism so favoured in defeatist circles'.[121] Planning agendas were muted in the FBM discourse on national sovereignty because it was implicit but also because the group sought acceptance from a wider audience.[122] Ironically, its sovereignty arguments resembled those of liberal internationalists who shared the desire for increased international trade and development in poor nations but despised economic planning and state interventionism.[123]

The FBM's overarching concern for eroding British sovereignty was manifest in a protest dialogue that mixed the domestic and international, economic and political. Briginshaw began writing articles on these themes in the late 1950s but the Common Market provided a new urgency and a two-fold mission: 'Our task is to give impetus, firstly, to the efforts against British entry in the European Common Market and to get people moving along the whole front of resistance to the inroads into the independence and sovereignty of Britain'.[124]

The forces pushing Britain towards subjugation were identified through a mix of anti-establishment protest and paranoia. The conspiracy of high finance began at home, with warnings about 'parasites in our body politic', 'casinoism' and 'take over racketeering in high places'.[125] A theme revisited in nearly all the FBM's literature pointed to a pervasive spirit of surrender among British leaders. Macmillan was portrayed as the front for a pro-European syndicate of 'defeatists' and supra-nationalist financiers, 'merchant bankers and steel masters with Ruhr hopes'.[126] Those interests were charged with brainwashing the populace and discouraging debate. Briginshaw even accused the BBC of propagandising Common Market entry through *Woman's Hour* and the

---

[121] Briginshaw article in *NATSOPA Journal*, quoted in *The Times*, 2 June 1961.

[122] Michael Newman shares this view but overstates the extent to which the FBM abandoned a socialist outlook. M. Newman, *Socialism and European Unity* (London, 1983), footnote 107, p. 201.

[123] In 1947 Alexander had advocated free trade as 'the only answer' to state planning and claimed that Britain was becoming a 'totalitarian state'. Alexander, *Save the Pound*, pp. 12, 14.

[124] *Forward Britain Movement Bulletin and Digest*, July 1961. For an additional version of this see open letter from A. A. Skinner to British MPs, 16 April 1962. For a copy see Department of Special Collections and Western Manuscripts, Bodleian Library, Oxford, Conservative Party Archives, Conservative Research Department (hereafter cited as CPA, CRD) 2/43/1.

[125] Forward Britain Movement, advertisement, undated, probably 1962.

[126] *Forward Britain Movement Bulletin and Digest*, No. 20, 18 September 1962. For another example see No. 21, 17 October 1962.

statements of Dr Dale in the *Mrs Dale's Diary* radio programme. For its part, the BBC appeared nonplussed as its spokesman replied 'Dr Dale's opinions do not concern us. He is just a character in a radio series.'[127]

Subjugating pressures were also credited to external coercion and fit with an agenda that called for disarmament and the return of British soldiers from German soil. Vengeful Germans were described as intent on 'taking over Britain' and the Commonwealth markets through economic means.[128] America's push for British entry exposed a larger nuclear and military agenda that undermined any pretence of a functioning 'special relationship'. The presence of US missiles on British bases and submarines, a lack of consultation during the Cuban crisis and sacrifices to NATO pointed to one conclusion: 'The decision of DEATH FOR BRITAIN was taken in Washington, USA'.[129]

The FBM believed that Britain's economy, already a source of national vulnerability, would face further trauma under the provisions of the Treaty of Rome. The European design for agriculture was branded 'insanity for Britain' because it would sustain Continental producers through artificial prices, inflate Britain's food import costs, strain balance of payments and cause more suffering for the poor.[130] The Common Market was also 'too inward' for Briginshaw's liking and struck at the trading relationship with the Commonwealth, which had been both a source of British greatness and a benefit to the developing world.[131] The Commonwealth offered an economic model for trade and a political, multiracial model for international discourse that 'enhanced' and 'extended' British influence. It was 'the embodiment of what is good in our heritage', a convenient asset with established formal connections and informal sentiments. It was a matter of kinship, of common legal and political language and a common culture, exemplified, for instance, by an ability to distinguish 'a no ball from a googly … a supplemental question from a point of order'.[132] It was, above all, an imperative of British destiny.

If anything, the FBM's argument suggested that the concept of sovereignty had become too banal. Britons, having taken independence for granted, had failed to defend it with sufficient vigilance. The Treaty of Rome amounted to a 'reversal of history' as it demanded sacrifices not to a world body, but to a 'Little Europe' bloc, 'a reconstituted Holy Roman Empire'.[133] Forward Britain called for a second Battle of Britain,

---

[127] *Daily Express*, 11 January 1962.

[128] See in particular *Forward Britain Movement Bulletin and Digest*, July 1961.

[129] FBM membership flyer, 'Britain Must Break Free', undated. See also, Leighton, *What Next for Britain?*, pp. 8–9.

[130] *Forward Britain Movement Bulletin and Digest*, No. 23, 29 November 1962.

[131] R. Briginshaw to A. Bryant, 2 January 1962, AB Papers H4.

[132] Leighton, *What Next for Britain?*, pp. 11–12.

[133] Forward Britain Movement, *Common Market Realities*.

a national renewal based upon strength through trade rather than arma-
ments. 'We believe we can be great', Ron Leighton wrote, '*but we can
only re-establish the greatness of Britain by restoring our independence.*
This is the essential basis for recovering our fortunes, self-respect and
influence in the world. The strength we need is economic strength.'[134]

Multi-issue pressure groups

As we have seen, the promotional groups formed in direct response
to Britain's application carried wider designs and patriotic assumptions. The obverse of this was the presence of pressure groups and small
political parties that were predisposed to anti-Market sentiments by
their existing agendas. Some groups, such as the British Housewives'
League and the League of Empire Loyalists (LEL), found places under
the AntiCommon Market Union umbrella. Most laboured at the fringes,
displaced both from the levers of influence and from subsequent
historical accounts. Yet, despite their marginality, the protests animated
larger motifs, relating to the nature and preservation of Britishness, and
revealed just how far the Common Market featured within the dialogues
of political discontent.

Women's concerns

The treatment of women's issues revealed a male dominance in the
composition of anti-Market patriotism.[135] Symbols transcended gender,
as in the depictions of Britannia and homage to the Queen. 'Common
man' orientations, moreover, venerated women as national institutions
but ones confined to and exploited as models of domesticity. Women
nevertheless provided valuable leadership to the anti-Market movement.
Diana Paul, for instance, played a central role in the activities of the
ACML. In the LEL, females comprised half the council of *Candour* (see
below) and stood in three of its four by-election candidacies between
1957 and 1964.[136] On the left, Labour's anti-Market wing included the
likes of Barbara Castle, Jennie Lee and Shirley Williams.

As Ina Zweineger-Bargielowska has shown, the Conservative Party
organisation secured female support at the ballot box in the 1950s by

---

[134] Leighton, *What Next for Britain?*, p. 10.
[135] For a contemporary critique of male dominance in politics see 'Still a Man's
World for Women Politicians', *The Times*, 28 May 1962.
[136] Those on the *Candour* council included Lady Freeman, MBE, a barrister, Miss
Alice Raven, and Miss L. M. C. Greene and Miss N. A. Bonner, both MAs. *Candour*
publicity leaflet, 1959. Miss L. M. C. Greene stood as an LEL candidate at Lewisham
North in 1957 and Fife East in 1964. Miss R. M. de Bounevialle stood at Petersfield
in 1964.

acknowledging gender differences in its appeal.[137] A Conservative vote, however, was no guarantee of blind fealty. It is thus important to note that women with predominantly Tory sympathies secured representation and membership in both the AntiCommon Market Union and the FBM 'conference' through the efforts of the British Housewives' League (BHL) and Scottish Housewives' Association. While their opposition to the Government was manifestly a product of consumer interest and hearth-and-home Britishness, it was also an expression of political frustration and a protest against the directions of Macmillan's Commonwealth and European policies.

Formed by Irene Lovelock in 1945 to oppose rationing and austerity, the BHL defended the welfare of housewives and families. It criticised Government controls as misguided and incompatible with a 'happy homelife and the development of personality in accordance with Christian tradition'.[138] The Housewives, like Beaverbrook, made Baldwin a philosophic arch-enemy and claimed that 'the last vestige of Conservatism vanished with Mr. Bonar Law'.[139] Though its revolt against a post-war consensus peaked in 1947, the BHL was an unyielding middle-class supporter of Empire and opponent of the Common Market.[140] Similarly, the Scottish Housewives' Association had objected to EFTA in 1957 as a harbinger of Commonwealth betrayal and petitioned the Queen for intervention against Government policy.[141] Though reconciled to closer European ties and probable entry negotiations by 1960, it retained an unconditional allegiance to Commonwealth trade, advocated withdrawal from the GATT and protection for British farmers.[142] The Common Market application brought new realities, however, and a meeting of all branch presidents rejected membership, irrespective of terms.[143] In the following months the Scottish Housewives blasted

---

[137] I. Zweineger-Bargielowska, 'Explaining the Gender Gap: The Conservative Party and the Women's Vote, 1945–64', in M. Francis and I. Zweineger-Bargielowska (eds), *The Conservatives and British Society, 1880–1990* (Cardiff, 1996), pp. 194–223.

[138] The BHL mission statement featured on the back cover of *Housewives Today*, its membership newsletter.

[139] *Housewives Today*, No. 1, 1947, quoted in Beatrix Campbell, *The Iron Ladies: Why Do Women Vote Tory?* (London, 1987), p. 76.

[140] For an important analysis of this overlooked organisation during the 1940s and early 1950s see J. Hinton, 'Militant Housewives: The British Housewives' League and the Attlee Government', *History Workshop*, 38 (autumn 1994), pp. 129–56. Beatrix Campbell discusses the BHL in *Iron Ladies*, pp. 76–82, as does G. E. Maguire in *Conservative Women: A History of Women and the Conservative Party, 1874–1997* (London, 1998), pp. 144–6.

[141] Scottish Housewives' Association to the Queen, 19 March 1957. For a copy see House of Lords Records Office, London, John Biggs-Davison Papers (hereafter cited as BD Papers) 23.

[142] E. Patullo to J. Biggs-Davison, 30 September 1960, BD Papers 23.

[143] Scottish Housewives' Association to J. Biggs-Davison, 14 June 1961, BD Papers 23.

Macmillan's 'black betrayal' of national prestige and sovereignty and demanded his resignation.[144]

Religion

Secular but evangelical crusades and 'chosen people' uniqueness featured throughout the rhetoric of anti-Market Britishness. A xenophobic and literal spirituality, however, also lurked at the debate's edges. Protestant agitation was largely the preserve of local[145] or politicised sectarian movements and individual polemicists. But a thematic unity was evident in the reverence for the free and democratic Anglo-Saxon nation, its monarchy and its Empire.

Among conspiracy theorists, the Treaty of Rome evoked European decadence and 'sinister' plots of Catholic and, to a lesser extent, Zionist origins. The Church of the Nazarene called Europe a 'political and ecclesiastical Babylon'.[146] The editor of the *Recorder* railed against a Jewish plot to eliminate Catholicism and Protestantism alike.[147] Britain was driven into Europe, *Intelligence* claimed, by the godless, materialist cohorts of US finance and Communism.[148] The Protestant Truth Society, the Protestant Alliance and the Lord's Day Observance Society all saw the Treaty as a contravention of Protestant heritage hatched by an ambitious papacy. The Catholic EEC, it was argued, was 'diametrically opposed' to Protestantism and would destroy Britain's unique constitution, 'ideals' and 'way of life'.[149]

Ethno-religious versions of Protestant identity depicted an Anglo-Saxon Israelite tribe pursuing divinely ordained imperial and, latterly, Commonwealth missions. Entanglement with Europe therefore amounted to a transgression of both an ancient heritage and God's design. It was a philosophy expounded in purest form by the British Israel World Foundation, led by Commander D. H. Macmillan and the pages of *The Kingdom Voice*. In both cases the Scriptures supplied designs for British

---

[144] Scottish Housewives' Association to J. Biggs-Davison, 24 October 1961, BD Papers 23. E. Pattullo, letter to the *Sunday Times*, 2 May 1962.

[145] An anti-Catholic, anti-Market petition that caught the attention of Conservative Central Office, for instance, was traced to a clutch of villages in East Anglia. See B. T. Powell to COO, 13 July 1962, CPA, CCO 500/31/13. Similarly, the Bristol and Clifton Protestant League owed what little notoriety it had to its President, Viscount Alexander of Hillsborough.

[146] Church of the Nazarene, *The Flame*, 27:2 (March–April 1962), p. 16.

[147] E. A. Luther to Beaverbrook, 9 October 1962, BBK F/3. The *Recorder* was part of the Free Press Society and therefore a propaganda vehicle for Edward Martell.

[148] D. Tozer, 'Real Meaning of the Common Market', *Intelligence*, 1:15 (June–July 1961), p. 7.

[149] Protestant Alliance and Lord's Day Observance Society, pamphlet, *The Common Market and the Common Man* (1962). For a brief summary of Protestant Truth Society views see *Bournemouth Evening Echo*, 25 May 1962.

uniqueness and resistance to the 'satanic' plans for federation. British Israel's allegiance to an Anglo-Saxon brotherhood was such that it created four branches in Australia, two in New Zealand and one each in the United States, South Africa, Kenya and the Netherlands.[150] *The Kingdom Voice*, which still used lantern slides at its public presentations, cited Britain as the 'Stone Kingdom' of Daniel 2[151] and the imperial realm predicted by Genesis 35:11. Revelation, proclaimed the 'text-book of Britain's Protestant Faith', was used to interpret the Papal See as the Scarlet Woman with global pretensions.[152]

Those arguments came unhinged under the weight of Book of Revelation fatalism and paranoia. Reverend John S. Bevan of the Bristol and Clifton Protestant League attributed a Rome–Moscow plot to the combined efforts of 'Jesuits and the Grand Orient Masonic World Power'.[153] A British Israel lecturer used the Bible to predict an outer space invasion for the year 1997.[154] In a Soviet plot subtext, *The Kingdom Voice* translated 'CCCP' to the Greek 'λάτεινοσ' and, by substituting numerical values for letters, arrived at the sum 666.[155]

Rants from the Protestant fringe could be dismissed entirely were it not for their relevance to the banalities of imagined Britishness. It is crucial, for instance, to note that explicit anti-Jewish prejudice was merely the rough edge of a subtler anti-Semitism. Anti-Marketeers, as we have seen, engaged in routine denunciations of 'cosmopolitanism', 'internationalists', 'bankers' and 'financiers'. Jews were the unmentioned but implied 'other'. Protestant extremism also exposed affinities with the earliest expressions of British national identity.[156] This was hardly

---

[150] At its 1961 congress assembly meeting, the British Israel World Foundation endorsed a manifesto opposing accession to the Treaty of Rome and the accompanying sacrifice of national sovereignty and imperial preference. British Israel World Foundation, 'Manifesto', June 1961. H. E. Stough to Prime Minister, 13 October 1961, CPA, CCO 3/6/40.

[151] *The Kingdom Voice*, 23:11 (November 1961). This edition was sent to all MPs and members of the Government. R. A. Bradbury to Beaverbrook, 4 June 1962, BBK F/4.

[152] *The Kingdom Voice*, 24:7 (July 1962). Other biblical references in the same issue included 'Lo, the people shall dwell alone, and shall not be reckoned among the nations' (Numbers 23:9); 'Say ye not, a confederacy, to all to whom this people shall say, a confederacy; neither fear ye their fear nor be afraid' (Isaiah 8:12); 'Come out of her, my people, that ye be not partakers of her sins, and that ye receive not her plagues' (Revelation 18:4).

[153] Draft letter to *The Times*, J. S. Bevan to Beaverbrook, 10 July 1962, BBK F/4. See also J. S. Bevan, leaflet, *The European Common Market and the Jesuit Menace* (Bristol, 1962).

[154] J. Jeavons 'The Origin and the Destiny of the Commonwealth', quoted in *Wolverhampton Chronicle*, 2 March 1962.

[155] *The Kingdom Voice*, 24:7 (July 1962).

[156] For more on Protestantism and British identity see Colley, *Britons*, pp. 11–54. Adrian Hastings takes things further, arguing that Ulster Protestant extremism

surprising given the fact that groups such as the Lord's Day Observance Society and the Protestant Alliance had been founded in the first half of the nineteenth century.[157] Papal plot theories were, moreover, an appropriation of 'us' versus 'them' Britishness that was comparatively banal in the sectarian rhetoric of Scotland and Northern Ireland.[158] It is hardly surprising, then, to find Ian Paisley and the Free Church of Scotland[159] exploiting the debate. Ian MacColl, editor of the Scottish *Daily Express*, was 'disturbed ... at the Common Market activities of our Free Kirk brethren', and Beaverbrook sent orders that no attacks on Catholicism were to appear in his paper.[160]

Irrespective of their implausibility, the religious arguments caught attention in high places. Reports from Conservative field agents of anti-Catholic fervour were circulated among the highest ranks of Central Office.[161] In response, the Conservative Research Department drew up a memo for MPs detailing appropriate responses. Among other things, MPs were reminded of Protestant majorities in Germany and the Netherlands and the continuing vitality of the Dutch Royal Family. The Treaty of Rome, it was asserted, contained no clauses relating to religion, nor did it pave the way to papal domination.[162]

---

and the politics of Paisley are the 'anachronistic survival of English nationalism in seventeenth century guise'. Hastings, *The Construction of Nationhood*, p. 92.

[157] The Lord's Day Observance Society, founded by Joseph and Daniel Wilson in 1831, devoted itself to preservation of the Sabbath. Protestant Alliance was founded by the Earl of Shaftesbury in 1845. Chris Cook, *Sources in British Political History, 1900–1951: Vol. 1, A Guide to the Archives of Selected Organisations and Societies* (London, 1975), pp. 158–9, 217. In Scotland, the Lord's Day Observance Society was founded in Edinburgh in 1839 and Protestant Alliance in 1851. Nigel M. de S. Cameron, *Dictionary of Scottish Church History and Theology* (Edinburgh, 1993), pp. 18, 738.

[158] Edward Moxon-Browne has shown that Northern Ireland's 'British', 'Ulster' and 'Irish' national identities are more complex than is often assumed. He also suggests that Loyalists have incorporated EEC issues for use in their wider campaigns. E. Moxon-Browne, *Nation, Class and Creed in Northern Ireland* (London, 1983), pp. 4, 156–7, 160–1.

[159] A Free Church of Scotland editorial suggested that accession to the Treaty of Rome would 'advance the pretensions of the Pope to temporal as well as ecclesiastical supremacy'. *Monthly Record*, March 1962, quoted in *The Times*, 3 March 1962. It also wrote to the Prime Minister arguing that entry would cause social changes, loss of sovereignty and the destruction of the Commonwealth. *Daily Express*, 21 March 1962.

[160] Correspondence between Beaverbrook and I. MacColl, 12 and 14 August 1962, BBK H/220. Beaverbrook's Presbyterian background and crusading reputation made him a frequent target of Protestant requests for support. For examples of letters see BBK F/3 and F/4.

[161] See Mr Horton to COO, 15 May 1962, and B. T. Powell to COO, 13 July 1962 in CPA, CCO 500/31/3.

[162] Conservative Research Department, memo to MPs, 23 July 1962, CPA, CRD 2/43/1.

Youth groups

The pro-European contention that Britain's application was a policy for the younger generation was vindicated by opinion polls.[163] But anti-Market, pro-Commonwealth advocacy was not the sole province of a 'Colonel Blimp' culture. In fact, more youthful protests emerged to challenge Government policy and, more importantly, the prevailing visions of national identity.

From the left came pleas for an altogether new concept of patriotism and international policy. Claiming an endorsement from Lord Russell, Edward Maugham attempted to develop a Commonwealth Republic Party in 1962. The Common Market, he argued, was a white man's club and an American dictate that entrapped Britain in nuclear politics. The 'tinsel crowns and paper titles', he contended, must give way to a multiracial Commonwealth Republic with its own parliament, the first step towards one-world government. 'Youth', it was claimed, 'wants its own political identity today as never before'.[164] As a manifestation of traditional nationalism, the Common Market offered either nuclear holocaust or political dictatorship. Commonwealth Republicanism claimed 'The old order is dying. BUT YOU NEED NOT DIE WITH IT THIS TIME.'[165]

The Labour Party faced a larger challenge from the fifteen- to twenty-five-year-olds in its official youth section. From its inception in 1960, the cohesion of the Young Socialists' 600 branches was undermined by splits along Marxist and Trotskyite lines.[166] The group's drift to the left was evident in the approval of resolutions at its 1962 conference calling for the withdrawal of all nuclear weapons from British soil, detachment from military alliances and the return of British troops from service overseas. A large majority also rejected a pro-entry resolution while passing an alternative plan for pan-European working-class solidarity.[167]

On the right wing, the younger generation was less concerned with ushering in new identities than with recovering traditional values. In 1961 some younger members of the Tory Party founded both the Monday Club and the Sixty-One Group to contest the Conservative leadership's philosophical drift and its failure to uphold imperial greatness. Both groups shared an aversion for the Bow Group and exhibited libertarian Conservative leanings in policy aims, which included the defence of

[163] Spence, 'Movements in the Public Mood', p. 23.
[164] E. Maugham to Beaverbrook, 1 November 1962, BBK F/3.
[165] Commonwealth Republic Party, leaflet, *A Call to Youth* (1962).
[166] P. Barberis, J. McHugh and M. Tyldesley, with H. Pendry, *Encyclopedia of British and Irish Political Organisations* (London, 2000), p. 1038. For more on the group's infighting and difficult relationship with the Labour Party see Z. Layton-Henry, 'Labour's Lost Youth', *Journal of Contemporary History*, 11 (1976), pp. 290–304.
[167] *The Times*, 23 April 1962.

individual liberties, revision of the tax structure, welfare reform and law and order.[168]

Empire, however, was the Monday Club's obsession and in 1961 it published *Winds of Change or Whirlwind*, an attack on the Government's policy of 'abdication and appeasement' in Africa.[169] Those sentiments, intended initially for Conservatives under the age of thirty-five, made Commonwealth development a priority and attracted the patronage of the Marquess of Salisbury[170] as well as Lord Boyd of Merton.[171] In this context, the Common Market was suspect because it was the policy of Government leaders and a threat to the Commonwealth. Monday Club opposition was flexible to the extent that it demanded 'adequate guarantees' for British and Commonwealth agriculture. But it also argued that, in the absence of an electoral mandate, the Government had 'no moral right' to surrender national sovereignty.[172]

The Sixty-One Group, a splinter of the Young Conservatives, also criticised the Government's disregard for 'fundamental principles of Conservative philosophy'.[173] Though more racially inclusive in its definition of the Commonwealth, the Sixty-One Group's vision of 'dynamic' Conservative philosophy used a nineteenth-century template. Its membership leaflet opened with an extended quote from Disraeli:

> The issue is not a mean one. It is whether you will be content to be a comfortable England, modelled and moulded upon Continental principles and meeting in due course an inevitable fate, or whether you will be a great country, an Imperial Country, a country where your sons, when they rise, rise to paramount positions and obtain not merely the esteem of their countrymen, but command the respect of the world.[174]

European membership struck at the essential bonds of Commonwealth and, by ceding sovereignty, removed the British way from political and

---

[168] A. S. Garner to COO, 27 September 1961, CPA, CCO 3/6/16. See also Monday Club, newsletter and membership application, 1961. Sixty-One Group, information leaflet and membership form, 1961. For more on the Monday Club, especially after 1964, see P. Seyd, 'Factionalism Within the Conservative Party: The Monday Club', *Government and Opposition*, 7:4 (autumn 1972), pp. 464–87.

[169] Monday Club, pamphlet, *Winds of Change or Whirlwind* (London, 1961).

[170] Upon becoming its patron Salisbury declared 'There never was a greater need for true Conservatism than there is today'. *Daily Telegraph*, 26 January 1962.

[171] *The Times*, 27 March 1962.

[172] Monday Club, leaflet, *Policy and Aims* (London, 1962).

[173] R. Moate to R. A. Butler, 31 August 1961, CPA, CCO 3/6/142.

[174] Benjamin Disraeli quoted in Sixty-One Group information and membership leaflet, 1961. The text is drawn from Disraeli's 'Crystal Palace speech' of 24 June 1872, in which he contrasted Conservative and Liberal principles. For a full text of the speech see T. E. Kebbel (ed.), *Selected Speeches of the Late Right Honourable the Earl of Beaconsfield, Vol. 2* (London, 1882), pp. 523–35.

economic decision making. It was, in effect, a surrender of the national mission.[175]

Neither organisation grew to significant size,[176] nor did they pose a serious threat to Party unity.[177] But the Sixty-One Group's ambiguous relationship with official politics, especially its claim to have formed 'within the party',[178] irritated Central Office. Its chair, John Squires, and the members of its committee were leading members of Young Conservative branches in the Home Counties North Area. Its formation, moreover, roughly coincided with a pro-Commonwealth letter to *The Times* signed by three past Presidents of the Young Conservatives as well its current chair and vice-chair.[179] Peter Walker denied rumours of his links with the Sixty-One Group and criticised its methods[180] but his fellow MP Derek Walker-Smith pledged support.[181] In response the Central Office Agent for London planted an informer within the Sixty-One Group under an assumed name[182] while Central Office instructed all of its agents to discourage membership of both organisations.[183]

The Commonwealth lobby

A kaleidoscope of pressure groups, most of them small and local, merged Common Market opposition with their pro-Commonwealth accounts. The Christian Democratic Union of Ireland, for instance, lobbied Irish workers in Britain to pressure Dublin on issues relating to free enterprise, bureaucracy and eventual repatriation. But its agenda also urged the Irish Government to join Britain in the Commonwealth rather than Common Market.[184] The British Legion passed resolutions opposing any surrender of sovereignty or of links to the Commonwealth.[185] The Social

---

[175] Sixty-One Group, information and membership leaflet, 1961.

[176] In early 1962 the Monday Club had fifty active members engaged in its research groups. *Daily Telegraph*, 24 January 1962. The Sixty-One Group claimed an initial enlistment of 200 but Conservative Central Office reckoned the figure was closer to seventy or eighty members.

[177] Paul Bristol, the Monday Club's leader, assured local party agents that his organisation intended to support the Conservatives at election time. Mr Torey to B. T. Slinn, 15 February 1962, CPA, CCO 3/6/16.

[178] COO to R. A. Butler's secretary, 1 September 1961, CPA, CCO 3/6/142.

[179] Letter to *The Times*, 14 July 1961. Signed by Peter Walker, Roger Bowden, Geoffrey Finsberg, Terence Wray and Nicholas Scott.

[180] A. A. Hammond, memo to COO, 30 August 1961, CPA, CCO3/6/142.

[181] *Daily Express*, 8 September 1961.

[182] A. S. Garner memo to COO, 5 September 1961, CPA, CCO 3/6/142.

[183] COO to Central Office Agents, 17 August 1961, CPA, CCO 3/6/142; COO to Central Office Agents, 4 December 1961, CPA, CCO 3/6/16.

[184] *Evening Standard*, 16 May 1962; S. Loftus to Beaverbrook, 21 June 1962, BBK F/3.

[185] *The Times*, 5 June 1962.

Credit Policy League suggested the creation of a Commonwealth settle-
ments bank as a 'practical alternative' to Europe.[186]

Other groups had formed for the express purpose of advocating
Commonwealth interests. The Commonwealth First Society, based
in Warrington, coupled Europhobia with standard-of-living topics to
underscore the loss of cheap food and export markets. Articles 48 and
118 of the Treaty of Rome,[187] it predicted, would bring floods of Sicilian
workers, affiliation with racist Germans and the deterioration of Britain's
'best in the world' social services. A referendum, it concluded, was
imperative.[188] Meanwhile, in Crowborough, Lt. Col. R. F. Wright founded
the Commonwealth Fellowship to espouse a pro-Commonwealth policy
in constituencies throughout the south-east.[189] Its non-partisan claims
belied links with the ACML and a Beaverbrookian approach to 'common
man' and Dominion causes. It championed the interests of small
industries, farmers and traders and decried the pro-European pressures
of City finance and large manufacturers. Citing kinship and a century of
trade preferences, it claimed the Dominions as integrated components
of British national greatness.[190] Accordingly, New Zealand was 'as much
part of the British economy as Devon and Cornwall'.[191]

By and large, extra-parliamentary attempts to flesh out the ubiquitous references to a 'Commonwealth alternative' failed to penetrate the
debate. An Alternative Policy Committee suggested that 'Britain must
re-educate Britain to her Commonwealth role' but offered no blueprint.[192]
C. E. Carrington chaired a Commonwealth Purpose Group, but its non-
party discussions were kept confidential and limited to private dinner
events.[193] Sir Clifford Heathcote-Smith, Robin Turton, MP, and Russell
Braddon, an Australian author, fronted a Commonwealth Unity Group on

---

[186] G. H. Moore to Beaverbrook, 25 January 1963, BBK F/4. Social Credit supporters
occasionally distributed leaflets at anti-Market meetings attacking the hegemony
of international finance and calling for an abolition of taxation. For an example see
pamphlet in CPA, CCO 500/31/3.

[187] Article 48 refers to the free movement of workers, while Article 118 promotes collaboration between member states on social issues relating to employment, labour
legislation, trade union law and social security, among others.

[188] Commonwealth First Society, pamphlet, *Common Market – What This Means to
You* (Warrington, 1962).

[189] J. Macmillan to Beaverbrook, 12 March 1962, BBK H/220.

[190] R. F. Wright to J. Biggs-Davison, 25 January and 3 March 1962, 3 January 1963,
BD Papers 25; Commonwealth Fellowship, *Newsletter*, No. 3, November 1962.

[191] Commonwealth Fellowship, brochure, *The Commonwealth Fellowship* (Crowborough, 1962).

[192] H. Corbett to J. Biggs-Davison, 17 December 1962, BD Papers 23.

[193] Commonwealth Purpose Group, Minutes of the First Meeting of the Steering
Committee, 6 November 1962; Report to Members of the Group, 12 February 1963,
BD Papers 25.

behalf of a multiracial Commonwealth destiny.[194] The Common Market, it warned, exposed Britain to the 'putrescent' nationalism of Europe and raised the contingency of national survival. 'Without the Commonwealth', it asserted, 'there can be no Great Britain. Without Great Britain there can be no Commonwealth.'[195] Their thesis was received and dismissed by the Prime Minister with a polite acknowledgement.[196] Henry Drummond-Wolff, a former MP and veteran of Beaverbrook's Empire Crusade, returned from his residence in the United States to fight the Common Market. Fearful that Australia, New Zealand and Canada would fall into US hands, he drafted a plan in late 1962 that included an extension of the OECD, tariff reductions, duty-free Commonwealth trade and respect for national sovereignties.[197] In January 1963, Arthur Bryant helped condense his plans into shorter form but found the process 'technically the most difficult ... I have ever tackled'.[198]

For all the British pressure group investment in the Commonwealth cause there was little evidence of reciprocal activity. Following overtures to Beaverbrook, Rex Testro, a Melbourne businessman, funded the reprint of a *Sunday Express* article that ran in 500 newspapers throughout Australia in August 1962.[199] That same month he sent a letter to all British MPs chastising the decision to 'dump' their Commonwealth kin.[200] The relationship of the *Express* with Testro ended, however, after an anonymous letter revealed that Testro Brothers Ltd was under investigation by the Australian authorities for running 'operations designed to part unwary investors from their money'.[201] Meanwhile,

---

[194] After meeting with Heathcote-Smith, however, Lord Salisbury was under the impression that it was focused on relations with the 'white Commonwealth'. Lord Salisbury to A. Eden, 23 November 1961, AP 23/60/84.

[195] Commonwealth Unity Group to H. Macmillan and Commonwealth PMs, 22 August and 16 November 1961, BD Papers 23. See also Clifford Heathcote-Smith letter to the *Daily Telegraph*, 1 October 1962, in which he called British entry a violation of 'human nature'.

[196] H. Macmillan to Commonwealth Unity Group, 5 September 1961. Copy in BD Papers 23. Heathcote-Smith had been British Consul in Alexandria from 1924 to 1943. For a copy of his obituary see *The Times*, 7 January 1963.

[197] H. Drummond-Wolff, *The Commonwealth* (London, 1962). The pamphlet had a limited printing and was circulated to a small group for comments. A Bryant memo dated 21 November 1962 suggests that Drummond-Wolff had also established contact with Prime Ministers Nehru and Diefenbaker, Lord Beaverbrook, Douglas Jay, Denis Healey and Hugh Gaitskell, AB Papers H/4.

[198] A. Bryant to Viscount Montgomery of Alamein, 23 December 1962, AB Papers H/4. For the revised plan see H. Drummond-Wolff, *The Commonwealth Priority* (London, 1963). Copy in AB Papers H/5.

[199] R. Testro to Beaverbrook, 8 August 1962. See also Testro to Beaverbrook, 13 June 1962, BBK F/3. In his opening letter Testro expressed fears for a 'partition of the Empire' and called for a second 'Dunkirk'.

[200] R. Testro to MPs, 20 August 1962. For a copy see BD Papers 23.

[201] Beaverbrook's secretary to Beaverbrook, 16 August 1962, BBK F/3.

the Australian League of Rights published brochures stressing the political consequences of British entry to Commonwealth interests.[202] Sovereignty and national identity, it predicted, would vanish in the surrender to a foreign bureaucracy. With the support of contributors from Australia and New Zealand, the League funded a tour to Britain by its National Director, Eric Butler, and D. J. Killen, a representative from Queensland. During their month-long visit in the summer of 1962, Butler and Killen met with prominent anti-Marketeers and addressed more than fifty public meetings. But, as the Commonwealth Industries Association *Monthly Bulletin* complained, the British press 'practically ignored their visit'.[203]

Right wing and left wing

The aforementioned groups were joined by an eclectic set of organised forces at the far right and far left of the spectrum. On the specifics of Common Market demonology, divergent philosophies and interpretations of patriotism separated the extremes. Radical anti-Market politics, however, were predicated upon perceptions of an external, and often conspiratorial, threat to the British nation state and its Commonwealth. What emerged then were variegated arguments on behalf of national independence.

Oswald Mosley's Union Movement notwithstanding, anti-Market politics gelled with the philosophies of right-wing pressure groups. This was partly because Britain's application fitted within prevailing critiques of diminished national greatness, failed leadership and internationalist conspiracies. The deployment of national identity in right-wing politics bore more than a passing resemblance to fascism and the proliferation of such groups in the early 1960s suggested a deepening well of patriotic discontent.

In the 1950s, the LEL provided an incubator for the themes and future leadership of right-wing extremism. A. K. Chesterton, cousin of the novelist G. K. Chesterton and a former member of the British Union of Fascists, founded *Candour*, 'the British Views letter', in 1953 and gave it structural form the following year by creating the LEL. In the interim he had joined the *Express* newspapers and served as ghost writer for Beaverbrook's autobiography,[204] published in 1954. Chesterton thought

---

[202] Australian League of Rights, *The Common Market Threat to the British Commonwealth* and *The Surpressed Truth About the Common Market* (Melbourne, 1962).
[203] Commonwealth Industries Association, *Monthly Bulletin*, 256 (August 1962), p. 6. The Association also appears to have provided the visitors with logistical support during their stay in Britain. They also met with Beaverbrook and John Paul.
[204] Lord Beaverbrook, *Don't Trust to Luck* (London, 1954). Chesterton was also author of Mosley's official biography.

Beaverbrook a 'genius' but when the links to *Candour* emerged he was sacked.[205]

Empire Loyalism was an avowedly imperial and racist creed employed to resist the dissolution of Empire and the 'conspiracy' against British 'heritage'. *Candour's* enemies included 'the leprous disease of Communism', Jews, blacks and the New York- and Washington-based 'Empire of International Finance'.[206] International agencies, it contended, were the organised face of anti-British plots and the precursors of world government.[207]

Common Market opposition suited the LEL's 'fortress Britain' outlook and its dissent commenced as early as 1957. In *Britain's Graveyard*, Chesterton argued that British affiliation with Europe via EFTA would lead to monopoly power in the European Commission and the eventual surrender of national sovereignty to the dictatorship of European and world Communism. Chesterton targeted the working classes with arguments tailored by xenophobia and scare tactics. He predicted the dumping of cheap foreign goods at the expense of Commonwealth products, bankruptcy for British manufacturers, millions of lost jobs, a diminished standard of living and, ultimately, a surrender of Britain to the interests of the foreigner. 'Why', he asked, 'should British workers be expected to impoverish themselves to increase the pay packets of the Greeks? Why should they condemn themselves and their families to unemployment to find work for Italians?'[208]

Empire Loyalist membership peaked at 3,000 in 1958 and included former colonial administrators and military men, upper-middle-class women, anti-Semites and right-wing Conservatives.[209] But by the time of Britain's application it was a shrinking voice. League funding had been provided by Robert Key Jeffrey, a Briton based in Santiago, who pledged his entire fortune to Chesterton's group. When Jeffrey died in 1961, however, the Bank of Chile tied up the bequest with a court challenge.[210] The League's radical elements, moreover, had resigned their

---

[205] D. Baker, *Ideology of Obsession: A. K. Chesterton and British Fascism* (London, 1996), pp. 196–7.

[206] A. K. Chesterton, open letter, July 1959. For a copy see MSS Welensky 522/2.

[207] For other manifestations of the conspiracy theory see A. K. Chesterton, *The Menace of World Government* (London, 1955), *Empire or Eclipse: Grim Realities of the Mid-Twentieth Century* (London, 1965) and *The New Unhappy Lords: An Exposure of Power Politics* (London, 1965).

[208] A. K. Chesterton, *Britain's Graveyard: Dangers of the Common Market* (London, 1957), p. 13.

[209] Barberis, McHugh and Tyldesley, *Encyclopaedia*, pp. 184–5.

[210] A. K. Chesterton to Beaverbrook, 8 February 1963, BBK F/4. According to an undocumented version of the story, Jeffrey had donated £70,000 to the League since its inception and pledged his estate of £250,000 to Chesterton in 1959. Only hours before his death, however, Jeffrey signed a new will with his thumbprint that left the money to his nurse, who also claimed to be his daughter. In 1964 the Chilean court

memberships only to re-emerge as leaders of rival pressure groups. In 1956 Colin Jordan departed to form the White Defence League, while John Bean and John Tyndall left the following year and founded the National Labour Party.

The National Labour Party and the White Defence League in turn combined to form the British National Party (BNP) in 1960. Self-appointed defenders of British civilisation, the BNP added the Common Market to a list of conspirators that included Jews, Communists, non-white immigrants and financiers. At the time, however, the BNP and its 500 members were in disarray. In 1962 John Tyndall split from the BNP to form the National Socialist Movement with Jordan[211] and Martin Webster and, later that year, was imprisoned for equipping the neo-Nazi group Spearhead with weaponry.[212]

The year 1960 also saw the creation of the New Conservative Party by John Dayton, a builder whose credits included the Chiswick flyover. Frustrated by the BBC's enlistment of 'some hopelessly drooling idiot'[213] whenever it needed a right-wing spokesman, Dayton stood at the Harrow West and Bolton East by-elections in 1960.[214] After renaming his party the Patriotic Front for Political Action, he contested Oswestry in 1961 as an anti-Market candidate. Dayton believed that middle-class Britons wanted their country to escape economic duress but abhorred the sacrifice of freedom demanded by the Common Market.[215] His rudimentary but colourful campaign employed a blue double-decker bus adorned with posters and loudspeakers broadcasting 'Rule Britannia', 'Land of Hope and Glory' and, when passing the local Conservative committee rooms, 'Colonel Bogey'. Opponents claimed his campaign was driving towards the year 1898 but Dayton was unapologetic in his use of patriotism. 'People lead aimless lives today', he said, 'and a reasonable nationalism can restore to them a sense of purpose'.[216] In any event, Dayton polled

---

decided in her favour. G. Thayer, *The British Political Fringe: A Profile* (London, 1965), p. 63.

[211] In 1962 Jordan also contracted an alliance with Nazi interests in the United States and was named 'World Fürher', leader of the World Union of National Socialists.

[212] Nugent and King, *The British Right*, pp. 166–7. See also *The Times*, 3–5, 9 and 16 October 1962.

[213] W. F. Nicholas to W. W. Parker, 10 March 1961. Letter in MSS Welensky 522/9. The same letter suggested that Dayton was developing a scheme to broadcast his views from offshore radio.

[214] In 1960 Dayton polled 4.7 per cent of the vote at Harrow West and 1.2 per cent at Bolton East. C. F. H. Gilliard, a New Conservative candidate, polled 0.6 per cent at Bedfordshire. At Oswestry in 1961, Dayton received 2.8 per cent of the vote. F. W. S. Craig (ed.), *Minor Parties at British Parliamentary Elections, 1885–1974* (London, 1975), p. 73.

[215] *The Times*, 24 August 1961.

[216] *The Times*, 30 October 1961. See also an article from the *Advertizer*, undated, in a letter from J. Paul to Beaverbrook, 15 October 1961, BBK C/269.

a mere 2.8 per cent of the vote and in 1962 he abandoned independent action and joined the Labour Party.[217]

The True Tories' campaign was yet another of the 1960 attempts to re-educate the Conservative Party on patriotic principles. Major-General Richard Hilton,[218] a former Empire Loyalist, led the True Tories' crusade with a martial rhetoric typified by the phrases 'surrender', 'invasion' and 'appeasement'. Britain and its natural party of patriotism, the group believed, had been in terminal decline since the 'finest hour' of 1940. With slogans such as 'Be British and Proud of It', True Toryism drew upon 'religious faith', 'moral standards' and a patriotism 'free from arrogance on the one hand or false modesty on the other'.[219] In practice this meant a racist approach to Commonwealth and immigration policy, freedom from all foreign entanglements and a domestic prescription for low taxes, capital punishment and resistance to trade union demands. Its assessment of Europe was simple and direct: 'Common Market means the end of British independence. Every patriot must demand a General Election immediately.'[220]

On the radical left, preoccupations with national independence focused upon questions of nationalisation rather than nationalism. Flag waving was restricted in part by an affinity for class over national consciousness. Thus, among 'fundamentalist' socialists, the comparatively faceless forces of capitalism and Cold War militarism were identified as intrinsic evils of the Common Market project.[221] Extra-parliamentary pressures were also muted somewhat by their relationship to politics, since 'fundamentalists' claimed more potent representation in Parliament than their right-wing counterparts. At the very least, leftists could derive some consolation from the fact that a Conservative Government had promulgated Britain's application.

On the other hand, a parliamentary voice and Labour neutrality on Europe held out the possibility for policy conversion and therefore encouraged radical input. Not only was 'wait and see' an insufficient palliative for hardened anti-Market opinion, it also provided ammunition for the critics of Gaitskell's leadership. Moreover, as Forward Britain had shown, leftist sympathies were by no means an absolute barrier to the rhetoric of patriotism. On the left, as elsewhere, external threats from individual nation states or trans-national forces prompted a defence of Britain's national independence.

---

[217] *The Times*, 12 February 1962.
[218] Major-General Richard Hilton (retired) served in the Indian Mountain Artillery between the wars, became Brigadier General Staff to Allied Liberation Forces in Norway during World War II and later served as military attaché to Moscow.
[219] True Tories, campaign leaflet, *1961 Manifesto*.
[220] True Tories, leaflet, undated, in CPA, CCO 500/31/3.
[221] L. J. Robins, *The Reluctant Party: Labour and the EEC, 1961–75* (Ormskirk, 1979), pp. 16–17.

At its Easter 1962 conference, the Co-operative Party endorsed Labour's approach but its debates and votes suggested a significant body of dissent. Thus, while 5,522,000 votes were cast against an anti-Market amendment, it received the support of 2,983,000. Lord Alexander of Hillsborough and John Stonehouse, leaders of the Labour anti-Marketeers in the House of Lords and House of Commons respectively, were among the attendees who denounced the Common Market as an exclusionary monument to 'super-capitalism'.[222] Victory for Socialism, whose 1,000 members included Michael Foot and Ian Mikardo, published a statement opposing Labour's policy of neutrality in January 1962. The EEC, it argued, was a puppet of American foreign policy and a political structure that would drive up the cost of living and prevent future Labour Governments from nationalising industries. It exhorted the Labour leadership to adopt a 'positive opposition' to the Government's application.[223]

Nuclear politics featured in leftist dissent as well and were fuelled by the unilateralist controversies of the 1960 and 1961 Labour conferences[224] as well as the Cuban crisis and Polaris deal of 1962. CND, for instance, opposed the Common Market but its membership was shrinking following its split with the Committee of 100 in 1960.[225] Forward Britain, moreover, had already provided disarmers with direct access to anti-Market politics, as the presence of CND badges and 'Ban the Bomb' placards at its rallies suggested. In fact, a 1962 *Peace News* pamphlet implored CND to make European integration a more salient feature of its policy debates.[226] Its author, April Carter, outlined the unilateralist position and voiced orthodox leftist objections to the Treaty of Rome. Inevitable political union, she claimed, strengthened the right-wing European governments, heightened NATO and Cold War pressures and thereby threatened proposals for national neutrality as well as unilateral disarmament. A striking feature of her argument, however, was its accommodation of the rights of individual nation states over the centripetal forces for world government:

---

[222] *The Times*, 23 April 1962.

[223] *The Times*, 19 January 1962.

[224] At the 1960 Labour conference a unilateralist motion from the Transport and General Workers was passed. Gaitskell pledged his opposition to the policy and it was overturned at the 1961 conference.

[225] For a brief synopsis of CND's early development see P. Byrne, *The Campaign for Nuclear Disarmament* (London, 1988), pp. 42–53. For an example of its policies at the time of Britain's application see CND pamphlet, *The Bomb and You* (London, 1962).

[226] A. Carter, *The Common Market – A Challenge to Unilateralists* (London, 1962), pp. 27–35. Carter was well versed in disarmament politics, having served as Secretary of the Direct Action Committee from 1958 to 1961 and as staff editor of *Peace News* in 1962.

> The kind of supra-nationalism which seeks to submerge national iden-
> tity in a supra-national organisation would be particularly dangerous if
> applied to any real attempt to work out a new neutral Europe. Its sheer
> impossibility would tend to destroy the total concept of co-operative and
> open European Community ... would lead to factional disputes round
> various dogmas.[227]

National independence, in other words, helped temper the competitive
economic and arms race impulses that flourished in power bloc global
politics.

The Communist Party of Great Britain, enjoying a slight resurgence
in the early 1960s,[228] joined the chorus of unconditional opponents. Its
militant anti-Market literature called for 'emergency action by the entire
working class'[229] and offered a pro-Soviet line depicting the Common
Market as an anti-socialist capitalist union and a tool of NATO. Since
identity was a function of class consciousness, the economic consequences of membership incorporated wages, employment conditions
and the standard of living for workers, small farmers and the developing
Commonwealth.

But, as Michael Newman noted, Communist opposition was more
attuned to the foreign policy aspects of Common Market membership.[230]
In this regard Communism was hardly unique. As we have seen, pressure
groups and pundits of all political shades were drawn to political over
economic considerations, though, given its materialist values, this was
perhaps more conspicuous in the Communist case. Having adopted a
foreign policy focus, Communists were freed to assess the relative value
of nation states in power bloc politics and the international system as
a whole. Its conclusions made national independence paramount. As
a consequence, Communist objections, though distinctive, trod some
of banal paths of their less radical anti-Market counterparts. David
Bowman's description of a Kennedy–Adenauer plot, for instance,
resorted to the habitual anti-German devices:

> The dream of the Nazis under Hitler was to bring all Europe under their
> rule and influence in the 'European New Order', to provide markets for
> the modern and powerful German industry. Adenauer's Government
> pursues the same aim and is backed by American big business....[231]

---

[227] *Ibid.*, p. 22.
[228] In 1963 the Communists issued party cards to 33,004 registrants, an increase of
2,549 from 1962. The Young Communist League issued 4,064 cards, an increase of
817. *The Times*, 9 February 1963.
[229] D. Bowman, *The Alternative to the Common Market* (London, 1961), p. 3.
[230] Newman, *Socialism and European Unity*, p. 178.
[231] Bowman, *The Alternative*, p. 4.

Indeed, national independence was cited as the primary rationale for opposing the Common Market. In socialist terms that meant conserving the right to plan the economy, maintain social services, support the developing world, subsidise industry, control trade and alleviate unemployment. But the Communist definition of 'independence', however radical in its applications, was little more than a restatement of the mundane concept of national sovereignty. According to Bowman, it amounted to the British Government's 'right to control its own affairs' and 'the right of the British people to decide their own affairs'.[232]

Conclusion

The 'oddments'[233] against British entry fronted hardened anti-Market opinion with a vast assemblage of views. Opinions that in many cases bore the hallmarks of mainstream politics took on more radical overtones when pushed to their logical and illogical extremes. There was evidence of alliance in the shared rallies, the AntiCommon Market Union and the FBM conference. Protest literature quoted freely from the pool of dissenters, irrespective of political orientation. In the most unlikely of cases, the Communists even cited a speech from Viscount Hinchingbrooke.[234] Practical unity, however, was elusive, because divergent interpretations of party allegiance, economic and foreign policy and national identity drove the protests.

What truly united the pressure groups were banal assumptions about the sanctity of national freedom and a common perception that Britain's independence and international status were increasingly vulnerable. The arguments reflected a pessimistic and contentious relationship with the outside world. Commonwealth excepted, Britain had few friends and lacked the defences to resist intrusive external forces. The nation, it was suggested, risked subservience to the conspiracies of outsiders, be they Communist or capitalist, nationalist or supra-nationalist, European or American. Widely diversified prescriptions demanded a renewal for both Britain and Britishness. But in each case the preservation of independence and greatness was discussed with reference to the distinctive attributes of the British nation.

A number of the pressure groups, including the ACML, the Communist Party and British Housewives' League, survived to fight subsequent battles over Europe in either altered or attenuated form. On the far right, Major-General Richard Hilton transformed the True

---

[232] *Ibid.*, pp. 9, 14.
[233] Mr Howarth to P. R. Horton, 16 September 1961, CPA, CCO 500/31/3.
[234] Bowman, *The Alternative*, p. 4.

Tories into the Patriotic Party,[235] which along with the LEL joined the newly formed National Front in 1967. Among the single-issue groups, the decline of ACML membership from 30,000 to 7,500 by 1964 left a disillusioned John Paul wondering 'whether I haven't wasted my time and beggared myself into the bargain'.[236] But shortly thereafter he stood for Parliament against Ted Heath at Bexley, where he drew 2.25 per cent of the poll. In 1965, he founded *Political Intelligence Weekly*, a publication devoted to 'standing up for Britain and the British overseas'.[237] Paul died in 1969 but the ACML continued under the successive leaderships of Hinchingbrooke, Sir Robin Williams and Sir Richard Body. Keep Britain Out was recast as Get Britain Out, a broader organisation composed to fight the 1975 referendum. Forward Britain meanwhile provided one of the templates for the Common Market Safeguards Campaign, formed by Douglas Jay and Ron Leighton in 1970. Its ranks included Labour MPs such as Michael Foot, Barbara Castle and Peter Shore, while Sir Arthur Bryant, Sir Roy Harrod and Nicholas Kaldor were featured in its list of patrons.[238] Longevity, however, was no guarantor of compatibility. Oliver Smedley, despite repeated attempts, failed to merge the three groups into a single anti-Market entity.[239]

---

[235] The Patriotic Party described itself as 'Not right wing. Not left. But pro-British.' See correspondence between R. Hilton and R. Welensky in MSS Welensky, 708/3.
[236] Hinchingbrooke to A. Bryant, 17 January 1964, AB Papers, H6; J. Paul to Beaverbrook, 17 April 1964, BBK C/269.
[237] J. Paul to R. Welensky, 21 January 1965, MSS Welensky, 765/3. File also contains additional correspondence and materials from Paul's election campaign.
[238] Barberis, McHugh and Tyldesley, *Encyclopaedia*, pp. 129, 132, 136.
[239] Smedley, *Out!*, p. 16.

5

Politicians

Though it was not his first politicised statement on the Common Market, Gaitskell's 'thousand years of history' speech at Labour's 1962 Brighton conference is acknowledged as the definitive partisan moment of the debate. But it was a milestone reached quite late. Up to that point, the Conservative and Labour leaderships had buffered their respective positions with conditional policy statements. A search for 'terms satisfactory to' the Commonwealth, EFTA and agriculture, Macmillan pledged, underscored the Government's negotiating stance.[1] Labour's reply pushed that logic further, with an independent foreign policy and national economic planning added to its conditions for entry.[2]

Yet abstention from partisan confrontation was itself a calculated political response to perceived threats of party indiscipline and public uncertainty. Anxieties were supplied in part by 'nation before party' sentiment, as manifested in the 'strange bedfellows'[3] phenomenon. But while those tendencies were exhibited on pressure group rostrums and even in the content of Commons speeches, Parliament's anti-Marketeers organised themselves within party boundaries.[4] Of greater concern for party leaders therefore was the potential for internal divisions. It was a peril complicated by the fact that, as contemporary observers noted, fissures did not appear along the predictable left–right fault lines.[5]

---

[1] *Parliamentary Debates*, Commons, 5th Series, vol. 645, 31 July 1961, cols 928–33.
[2] Labour Party National Executive Committee, *Labour and the Common Market*.
[3] The commonly used phrase appeared in Gaitskell's speech at Brighton. It was also the subject of a cartoon by Low that depicted Gaitskell sleepwalking past a bed shared by Shinwell, 'Hinwhich', Cousins, 'Max B.', 'Monty', Jay and the Communist Party. *Guardian*, 16 October 1962.
[4] Interview with Lord Walker of Worcester (Peter Walker), 25 February 1998.
[5] See McLaren, 'Anti-Market', pp. 13–14; R. Rose, 'Tensions in Conservative Philosophy', *Political Quarterly*, 32 (1961), pp. 279–80.

Questions related to the nexus of anti-Market politics and patriotism thus went well beyond Brighton. Who were the anti-Market politicians and what role did they play within and outside party debates? How did ideas about Britishness condition their arguments? What impact did this have upon Macmillan and, more importantly, the public face of the Government's Common Market policy?

The first part of this chapter argues that Gaitskell's speech was as significant for its patriotism as for its politics. It evoked a personal disposition but also functioned as the leading edge of national assumptions present in varying degrees throughout Labour's anti-Market lobby. The chapter shows how emergent factions forced Gaitskell onto the Common Market fence and how, once there, he dealt with nationalist themes. Indeed, a central motif throughout the section involves the confrontation between internationalist ideals and allegiance to the prerogatives of the nation state. Labour's response to that issue, as we shall see, clashed with the views of Continental socialists. The section concludes by examining Gaitskell's handling of the Common Market issue after the Brighton conference. The second part of the chapter reveals that Macmillan's anxieties about Tory dissent went deeper than his memoirs indicated. It evaluates the challenge posed by MPs whose political objectives and patriotic inclinations were in support of sovereignty and the Commonwealth in particular. The section also explores threats directed at the Government from outside the Commons. It shows that factors such as the political opinions of Tory grandees and by-election politics brought challenges of variable intensity and effectiveness. The third and final section analyses the politics of propaganda and provides evidence of how far the anti-Marketeers succeeded in determining the Government's public approach to Europe. It shows that the Government, fearful of an adverse domestic reaction, avoided discussing the implications of entry. This reticence allowed opponents to contour the domestic debate by exploiting nationalist sensibilities. As a result, Government propagandising in support of entry was a belated exercise devoted to countering apprehensions and misconceptions.

Nationalism and internationalism – Labour's evolving opposition

The 'thousand years of history'

The notion of Gaitskell's Brighton speech as an exceptional patriotic political event has much to do with the reactions it inspired within the Labour Party itself. The eighty-minute address received a 'rousing reception'[6] and a lengthy standing ovation. The *Guardian* called it 'powerful ... surpassing even his best during the defence controversy'. 'Entry into

---

[6] *10 O'Clock* programme, 3 October 1962, BBC WAC, T541/542.

Europe', it added, 'has become the main battleground of British poli-tics'.[7] For an earnest anti-Marketeer like Douglas Jay, the speech was 'devastating ... unique ... in a different class ... an intellectual massacre'.[8] It had united the left, claimed Peter Shore, with an 'astonishing power' and 'intellectual honesty'.[9] Indeed, according to the legend, Dora Gaitskell turned to Charles Pannell at the conclusion and exclaimed, 'But look Charlie ... all the wrong people are cheering!'[10]

Gaitskell's speech was a shrewd political exercise, intended to sug-gest a change of emphasis rather than a reorientation of policy. Its final remarks kept Labour on the fence, with the conclusion that the moment for 'final decisions' was not yet at hand. Gaitskell offered up Labour's conditions for entry as neither 'impossible' nor 'unreasonable' and added 'I profoundly hope that they can be met'.

Few observers were convinced of its neutrality, however, primarily because thematic policy continuity was accompanied by conclusions cast in negative terms. What is more, those reservations comprehen-sively reflected the points made by Labour opponents of the Common Market. The economic arguments, Gaitskell conceded, were balanced but provided 'no compelling' reason for entry. He downplayed European growth figures, cited the conclusions of Roy Harrod (see Chapter 3) and emphasised the benefits of Commonwealth preference to British consumers and exporters. Gaitskell refuted the terms of entry rather than the European project as a whole and applauded the idealism behind the move for greater Continental unity. But a true internationalism, he contended, needed to address the fundamental questions of the 'haves' and 'have nots' and the threat posed by the division of East and West. A restatement of Labour's 'five conditions' policy highlighted the consequences of failing to secure acceptable terms. The EFTA ques-tion extended beyond trade to include a 'special relationship' with the social democracies of Scandinavia and the neutrality politics of Austria, Switzerland and Sweden. For British agriculture, entry was not only a change of support systems, it was accession to 'one of the most deva-stating pieces of protectionism ever invented'.[11] Gaitskell 'left the door

[7] *Guardian*, 4 October 1962.

[8] D. Jay, *Change and Fortune: A Political Record* (London, 1980), p. 286.

[9] P. Shore, *Leading the Left* (London, 1993), p. 83. Shore emphatically denied the rumour that he was the author of the Brighton speech. He did, however, write the National Executive Committee policy statement *Labour and the Common Market*. P. Shore, *Separate Ways: The Heart of Europe* (London, 2000), p. 3.

[10] Although the incident is often misquoted, Roy Jenkins has vouched for its authen-ticity. Interview with Lord Jenkins of Hillhead, 18 November 1998. The *Guardian*'s report noted that several of Gaitskell's traditional political allies 'ostentatiously abstained' from joining the ovation. *Guardian*, 4 October 1962.

[11] Labour Party press release, Hugh Gaitskell speech, 3 October 1962.

only just ajar' said the *Guardian*, while *The Times* concluded that he was, 'for all practical purposes, lowering himself off the fence'.[12]

The lasting impression of departure from the noncommittal position was sustained by patriotic sentiments and achieved by elevating 'belonging' from a question of material consequences to a transcendent threat posed to Britishness. If membership meant inclusion in a federated 'political unit', then national existence was at stake:

> It means – I repeat it – that if we go into this we are no more [than] a state (as it were) in the United States of Europe such as Texas and California.... This is what it means: it does mean the end of Britain as an independent nation state. It may be a good or a bad thing but we must recognise that this is so. We must be clear about this: it does mean, if this is the idea, the end of Britain as an independent European state. I make no apology for repeating it. It means the end of a thousand years of history. You may say 'Let it end' but, my goodness, it is a decision that needs a little care and thought. And it does mean the end of the Commonwealth. How can one seriously suppose that if the mother country, the centre of the Commonwealth, is a province of Europe (which is what federation means) it could continue as the mother country of a series of independent nations? It is sheer nonsense.[13]

He went on to cite the differences of national history and in particular Britain's relationship with the outside world. 'Where would our influence in the world be without the Commonwealth?', he asked. He recognised the vitality of an enlarged, multiracial body and claimed it as a legacy of the 'historic decisions of the Labour Government'. But he also paid tribute to the Old Commonwealth ties, epitomised by the sacrifices at Vimy Ridge and Gallipoli.

The retrospective comments of Gaitskell's contemporaries suggest unease with the rhetoric of Brighton and imply that his personal biases appealed to inappropriate national instincts. Denis Healey, though sharing similar views on Europe and the Commonwealth, disavowed Gaitskell's 'romantic chauvinism'.[14] According to Harold Wilson, the Brighton remarks were entirely unexpected by others in the party leadership.[15] Roy Jenkins was shocked by some of the emotional phrasing and noted that Gaitskell tended to get carried away by his own arguments.[16]

---

[12] *Guardian*, 4 October 1962; *The Times*, 4 October 1962.
[13] Labour Party press release, Hugh Gaitskell speech, 3 October 1962.
[14] D. Healey, *The Time of My Life* (London, 1990), p. 211.
[15] Wilson quoted in Charlton, *The Price of Victory*, p. 276. On the night before the speech, Gaitskell denied George Brown's request for an advance copy. Brown was forced to reconstruct his winding-up speech on the day, an effort he described as 'one of the worst speeches I have ever made'. G. Brown, *In My Way* (London, 1971), pp. 218–19.
[16] Interview with Lord Jenkins, 18 November 1998; R. Jenkins, *A Life at the Centre* (London, 1991), p. 148.

Michael Foot was adamant that whatever their differences of approach, none of Labour's anti-Marketeers 'were taking that view on xenophobic grounds ... and in that sense we were different from Beaverbrook'.[17]

Foot's remark raises the question of how far Labour socialism was able to accommodate allegiance to the nation state and, by extension, how that loyalty should have been expressed. The answer is invariably determined by the manner in which nationalism is defined. If one assumes that distinctions can be made between 'good' and 'bad' nationalism,[18] then Gaitskell's remarks might be accepted at face value. Provided it is applied towards loftier internationalist goals, wrote a supporter, 'we need not be ashamed of a measure of nationalism and patriotism'.[19] If, however, nationalism is held to be a negative force, then one might conclude, like Tom Nairn, that it was a cynical tool of convenience, one deployed to overcome socialist divisions for the sake of party unity.[20]

The view of Labour nationalism as negative opportunism carries analytical limitations. Socialist opposition to the Common Market, Michael Newman noted, tended to 'degenerate' into patriotic themes. But he conceded that the emotive burdens attached to the term 'nationalism' prevented it from providing an accurate description of Labour's position.[21] Indeed, as this study has suggested throughout, the opponents of British entry mixed Billig's metaphor of 'waved' and 'unwaved' flags. True, Gaitskell manipulated sentiment but behind the Brighton moment was a more comprehensive world-view. The instance of 'hot' nationalist rhetoric was an overt manifestation of the banal assumptions that governed both Gaitskell and Labour's evolving anti-Market approach. In parallel with constructions of British identity, the politics of national interest were viewed through a prism of internal and external priorities. An outward-looking regard for Britain's Commonwealth experience was thus matched by a defence of national prerogatives in the formulation of planned economies, foreign policy and agricultural safeguards.

Factions and conditions

Labour's adoption of the 'wait and see' policy had put Gaitskell astride an issue in which he had little interest.[22] Personal opinions aside, however, a series of political realities militated against taking a stand until

---

[17] Interview with Michael Foot, 27 October 1998.

[18] S. Howe, 'Labour Patriotism, 1939–83', in R. Samuel (ed.), *Patriotism: The Making and Unmaking of British National Identity* (London, 1989), vol. 1, p. 137.

[19] F. Beswick to Gaitskell, 16 October 1962, Special Collections, University College London Library, Hugh Gaitskell Papers (hereafter cited as HG Papers) File C/256.5.

[20] T. Nairn, *The Left Against Europe?* (London, 1973), p. 40.

[21] Newman, *Socialism and European Unity*, pp. 194–5, 268–70.

[22] B. Brivati, *Hugh Gaitskell* (London, 1996), pp. 412–13; Williams, *Hugh Gaitskell*, p. 702.

the autumn of 1962. The bulk of the party centre, like the wider public, was largely uncommitted. It is estimated that PLP opinion for, against or undecided split roughly into thirds in the autumn of 1961.[23] The Conservatives, moreover, had shown little interest in making the Common Market an electoral issue. Indeed, with Government support for entry itself contingent upon ongoing negotiations, Gaitskell viewed the 'conditions' policy as the 'only possible' option.[24] Added to this were hopes that the application might be scuttled by outside forces. Labour leaders knew of French intransigence and the difficulties faced by British negotiators.[25] Furthermore, it was thought that if the terms proved unacceptable to the Commonwealth, its leaders could jettison the application. In a scenario outlined by Gaitskell, Labour would reap political rewards if Macmillan either failed to secure an agreement or collided with Commonwealth expectations. 'Our line', he wrote, 'would then be almost certainly that they have mishandled the negotiations and that somebody else should take over the job'.[26]

If there was little to gain from taking an immediate stand on Europe, there was potentially much to be lost. As Gaitskell confided to President Kennedy, a focus on the terms of entry was propelled by necessities of party unity.[27] It was Labour's good fortune that hardening opinions did not strictly divide along the party's 'fundamentalist' and 'revisionist' fault.[28] Nonetheless, George Brown's claim that Labour avoided splits despite making a 'wonderful show of fighting'[29] rang hollow in the aftermath of fractious debates on Clause IV and disarmament. Gaitskell was in no mood to risk a divide on Common Market entry.[30] The intrinsic if paradoxical merit of the 'conditions' policy was that it allowed advocates

---

[23] Robins, *The Reluctant Party*, p. 33.

[24] H. Gaitskell to A. Calwell, 3 August 1962, HG Papers C/256.5.

[25] G. Brown to H. Gaitskell, 2 April 1962; T. Balogh to H. Gaitskell, undated but October 1962, HG Papers C/256.5. Of Heath's position Brown concluded 'I cannot help feeling that he still has prominently in his mind the idea that the Market *will* be wrecked by France and that some new association will then be formed'. See also conclusions of 'The Common Market Negotiations: Further Developments', RD 359, discussed in Home Policy Sub-Committee, November 1962, in Labour History Archive and Study Centre, National Museum of Labour History, Manchester, Labour Party Archives (hereafter cited as LPA), Commonwealth Department Files.

[26] H. Gaitskell to A. Calwell, 3 August 1962, HG Papers C256.5.

[27] H. Gaitskell to President Kennedy, 11 December 1962. Quoted in Williams, *Hugh Gaitskell*, p. 705.

[28] Robins, *The Reluctant Party*, pp. 16–18.

[29] G. Brown interviewed at the 1961 party conference, *10 O'Clock* programme, 5 October 1961, BBC WAC, Film T 539/540.

[30] Brivati, *Hugh Gaitskell*, p. 408; Williams, *Hugh Gaitskell*, pp. 704–5. *The Times* leader page observed 'He has – to use the description once applied to an American senator – to sit on the fence with both ears on the ground. So far as his party is concerned, the ground gives him only confused noises.' *The Times*, 10 September 1962.

and opponents of entry to agree upon the same policy while nurturing divergent expectations.[31]

A pro-European faction took early root and drew most notably from the right. Its membership included the Gaitskellites Roy Jenkins and George Brown as well as numerous members of the Campaign for Democratic Socialism (CDS).[32] Jenkins, who had resigned from the Labour front bench in July 1960 to focus on the case for entry, joined with Lord Gladwyn in forming the cross-party Common Market Campaign.[33] Along with John Diamond and Colin Beever, he also organised its party subdivision, the Labour Common Market Committee.[34] The proponents of entry championed the Common Market as a step in the direction of liberal internationalism as well as a spur to British trade, living standards and progressive forces on the Continent. Fears about the sacrifice of planning, free movement of labour and death of the Commonwealth were dismissed as narrow and overstated. Central to their mission was the idea that Europe offered a dynamic antidote for Britain's creeping malaise.[35] By May 1962, Diamond estimated that the pro-entry bloc commanded the support of eighty Labour MPs.[36]

Whatever their past links with Gaitskell, both Jenkins and the CDS feared an inexorable drift towards an anti-Market position. Jenkins pressed his concerns about the negative use of the 'conditions' policy and electoral consequences in May 1962, while the CDS executive lodged further complaints in September.[37] In both cases, however, Gaitskell responded as a hostage of political fortune and Commonwealth obligations.[38] To John Strachey he wrote 'No one regrets more than I do that

[31] Newman, *Socialism and European Unity*, p. 169.

[32] L. J. Robins noted the commonality between the groups as epitomised by the number of CDS supporters in the Common Market Committee. Robins, *The Reluctant Party*, p. 36.

[33] Details of the Common Market Campaign's policy agenda were presented in its newsletter, *Common Market Broadsheet*. See also its press release, 25 May 1961, a statement signed by a diverse list of academics, business people, diplomats and economists as well as thirty-two MPs, and a secondary press statement, letter from Lord Gladwyn to E. Heath, 7 June 1961. Copies of both are in R. A. Butler Papers F/124.

[34] For more see Jenkins, *A Life at the Centre*, pp. 104–5, 143–44; Pfaltzgraff, *Britain Faces Europe*, pp. 86–7.

[35] For Jenkins' articulation of these arguments see *Listeners Answer Back* programme, 13 July 1961, BBC WAC, T286; *Panorama* programme, 24 July 1961, BBC WAC, Film 31/32; R. Jenkins, 'From London to Rome', *Encounter*, 17:3 (September 1961), pp. 5–8.

[36] R. Jenkins to H. Gaitskell, 1 May 1962, HG Papers C/256.5.

[37] R. Jenkins to H. Gaitskell, 1 May 1962; F. Pickstock to H. Gaitskell, 19 September 1962; W. Rodgers to H. Gaitskell, 26 September 1962, HG Papers C/256.5.

[38] H. Gaitskell to R. Jenkins, 8 May 1962; H. Gaitskell to F. Pickstock, 20 September 1962, HG Papers C/256.5.

several close personal friends of mine should find themselves placed in a dilemma ... but the dilemma is not of my making'.[39]

The anti-Market bloc presented Gaitskell with a more complex problem, partly because of its growing numbers and partly because it drew both from the left and right edges of the party. In the autumn of 1961 Sir Lynn Ungoed-Thomas and William Blyton formed Britain and the Common Market[40] to organise anti-Market MPs and lobby their uncommitted counterparts. According to Richard Marsh's estimate, the anti-Market cause had grown to include between 100 and 115 Labour MPs by August 1962.[41] It was yet another instance of the 'strange bedfellows' phenomenon, one that aligned Denis Healey, Douglas Jay, Richard Marsh and Patrick Gordon-Walker with leftists like Barbara Castle, Konni Zilliacus and Manny Shinwell, as well as Michael Foot and Sidney Silverman, from whom the whip had been withdrawn.

The profile of their cause was enhanced when Lord Attlee started voicing doubts about entry in the summer of 1962. In a statement on 29 July dispatched to constituency parties by the Labour Committee on Britain and the Common Market, he rejected the terms of entry as detrimental to parliamentary powers, the Commonwealth relationship and, by extension, world peace and democracy.[42] Attlee's comments in the Lords the following week were offered with 'some hesitation' but provided greater detail. He was 'greatly disturbed' about a political link-up with unreliable democracies in Germany, France and Italy and described membership as a 'historic moment' but a 'step backward' from the internationalism implicit in the Commonwealth experience and the vision of world government. But, like other leftists, Attlee's internationalism was notably circumscribed by an allegiance to national prerogatives like planning. 'I may be merely insular', he told the Lords, 'but I have no prejudice in a Britain planned for the British by the British'.[43]

In the same speech Attlee confessed that some of his convictions had been rendered obsolete by old age. Indeed, these appeared more akin to personal reflections than political manoeuvres. On the primary issue of

---

[39] H. Gaitskell to J. Strachey, 27 September 1962, HG Papers C/256.5.
[40] The organisation has also used the label 'Labour and the Common Market'. Committee members listed in *The Times*, 31 July 1962, included W. Blyton, Edwin Gooch, John Stonehouse, Barbara Castle, Douglas Jay, Richard Marsh, J. Mendelson, E. J. Milne, John Norris, A. E. Oram, T. F. Peart, Norman Pentland, E. Shinwell and George Thomas.
[41] Richard Marsh, MP, interviewed on the *Gallery* programme, 2 August 1962, BBC WAC, Film 13/14. L. J. Robins estimates that in the autumn of 1962 there were as many as 155 Labour MPs against entry, 40 in favour and 40 undecided. Robins, *The Reluctant Party*, p. 33. The organisation undoubtedly overstated its support when it claimed that half the Labour Party opposed entry in the autumn of 1961. See article in the *Daily Express*, 17 November 1961.
[42] *The Times*, 31 July 1962.
[43] *Parliamentary Debates*, Lords, 5th Series, vol. 243, 2 August 1962, cols 426–32.

the Commonwealth, that approach had been foreshadowed in his 1960 Chichele lectures, which mixed the idealism of the multiracial Commonwealth with memories of Victoria's Jubilee, Kipling and the naive but 'intoxicating' boyhood vision of Empire on the schoolroom map.[44]

While those sentiments appeared to square him with much of the anti-Market movement, Attlee's eventual appearance in the Beaverbrook camp was by no means preordained. In June 1962 he declined invitations to write anti-Market pieces for the *Evening Standard* on the grounds that he had 'been so out of touch with things'.[45] A more plausible explanation dated from a row with Beaverbrook in Churchill's wartime Cabinet. Beaverbrook held Attlee responsible for his 1942 dismissal from the Ministry of Production and thought him a 'miserable little man'. For his part Attlee described Beaverbrook as 'the only evil man I ever met'.[46] Those animosities not withstanding, Attlee became a self-described 'strange bedfellow'.[47] In August, articles under his name began to appear. Most notable among these was 'I Say "Halt!"', a piece that was reproduced in the national press at *Express* expense as part of Beaverbrook's propaganda onslaught.

There was little thematic variation in Attlee's pronouncements on the Common Market, but his contributions to the *Express* were more emotive and, as a result, exposed unresolved if not unconscious tensions between internationalism and patriotism. The keystones of Attlee's case were thus served up as benchmarks of Britishness. In 'I Say "Halt!"' the Commonwealth was not merely a 'family' united by transcendent values, it was also 'characteristically British' and misunderstood by 'outsiders'. That outlook, moreover, contrasted with what he called a 'Continentalism' lacking the necessary validation of 'history' or a common 'way of life'.[48]

Though Attlee's patriotism was sufficiently developed for him to proclaim Britain the 'focal point of Western civilisation',[49] his articles were less reflective of chauvinism than of an affinity for the particularities of nationhood. In his defence of Commonwealth immigration, he described himself as a champion of 'internationalism but not of cosmopolitanism', which blurred national identities. He wrote:

> I do not believe in the fusion of all nations into one amorphous whole … I am opposed to destroying the individuality of nations. I believe that owing to history the Briton has developed over the centuries a national character of value to the world. So has the Frenchman, the Italian and the

[44] C. Attlee, *Empire Into Commonwealth* (London, 1961), see especially pp. 1–7.

[45] C. Attlee quoted in C. Wintour to Beaverbrook, 11 June 1962, BBK H/268.

[46] K. Harris, *Attlee* (London, 1982), p. 194.

[47] C. Attlee quoted in F. Beckett, *Clem Attlee* (London, 2000), p. 313.

[48] C. Attlee, 'I Say "Halt!"' Britain Must Not Become Merely a Part of Europe', *Sunday Express*, 12 August 1962.

[49] C. Attlee, 'I Say Britain Can Still Be Great', *Sunday Express*, 4 February 1963.

Dutchman. I do not want those characters to be blurred ... do not let us
attempt to put in place of age-long characteristics a vague Europeanism.[50]

Labour's anti-Marketeers, like their counterparts elsewhere, bound the
Commonwealth and federalist themes and thereby presented an inescapable choice between Europe and the wider world. In the opening Common
Market parliamentary debate, for example, Lynn Ungoed-Thomas argued
that merger with Europe would mean a loss of 'independence' and 'identity' for a British nation that derived 'tremendously important political
power' from its Commonwealth relationship.[51] Wilson famously added
that if Britain faced a choice, 'we are not entitled to sell our friends and
kinsmen down the river for a problematical and marginal advantage of
selling washing machines in Dusseldorf'.[52]

Those tendencies were most pronounced among leftist opponents.
The conception of the Common Market as a 'capitalist club', an enemy of
planning, a device of Cold War imperialism and a barrier to the UN was
pervasive. It was a position summed up by Michael Foot, who described
the Common Market's bureaucratic agents as enemies of 'democratic
socialism'. The project's failure to address international divisions
wrought by poverty and arms proliferation, he wrote, made it 'at best an
irrelevancy, at worst the creation of a new obstacle'.[53] Leftists dismissed
the argument that Britain needed exposure to the competitive pressures
of Europe. 'Competition', wrote Lynn Ungoed-Thomas, 'may cure only in
the sense that death cures – by obliteration'.[54]

Emphasising a choice between Common Market and Commonwealth
encouraged stark comparisons. As the FBM and the Communist Party
had demonstrated, the British left was not immune to xenophobic
tendencies.[55] At the time Michael Foot noted that 'A curious streak of
hysteria about Germany seems to be ineradicable in the orthodox British
mind'.[56] German rearmament, the Berlin Wall and the stationing of
German troops in Wales were woven into the debate by their resonance
with both East–West politics and the wartime memory. Europe was

---

[50] C. Attlee, 'Are We Barring the Right People from Britain?', *Sunday Express*,
4 November 1962. See also 'Yes, We're Still a First Class Power', *Daily Express*,
7 December 1962, and interview with the *Observer*, 7 October 1962.
[51] *Parliamentary Debates*, Commons, 5th Series, vol. 645, 3 August 1961, cols 1571,
1575.
[52] *Parliamentary Debates*, Commons, 5th Series, vol. 645, 3 August 1961, col. 1665.
[53] M. Foot, 'In My Opinion' column, *Daily Herald*, 25 September 1962, Labour
History Archive and Study Centre, National Museum of Labour History, Manchester,
Labour Party Archives, Michael Foot Papers (hereafter cited as LPA, MF Papers),
File P4, '*Daily Herald* Articles'.
[54] Sir Lynn Ungoed-Thomas, letter to *The Times*, 25 July 1961.
[55] Newman, *Socialism and European Unity*, pp. 18–20; Robins, *The Reluctant Party*,
pp. 193–4.
[56] M. Foot, 'As I See It' column, *Daily Herald*, 3 July 1962, LPA, MF Papers P4.

persistently represented as an unsuitable partner. In July 1961, for instance, a letter to *The Times* signed by seven leftist MPs chastised the advocates of entry for devaluing Britain's 'affluence' and 'influence'. Accordingly, European unity would force Britain into a 'speculative life-boat' shared with overpopulated Italy, unstable France, economically troubled Belgium and an ambitious West Germany 'preoccupied with thoughts of recovering lost territories'.[57]

Yet Miriam Camps' complaint that Labour policy was 'parochial' and coloured by an 'innate distrust of foreigners'[58] overstated the case. Publicly at least, parliamentarians were less likely than their pressure group counterparts to engage in Rhine-based conspiracy theories.[59] In fact, patriotic affinities with the wider anti-Market movement arose less from xenophobia than from the contradictions of a world-view that struggled to reconcile internationalist ambitions with the prerogatives and historic particularities of the nation state. The multiracial Commonwealth was thus symbolic both of global possibilities and of a political and economic relationship that was unique to the British experience. It was a view embodied in the notion of the Commonwealth as 'our window on the world'[60] and a sentiment that crystallised politically in the National Executive Committee's statement *Labour and the Common Market*. It concluded: 'the 700 million people of the Commonwealth, with whom history has linked us, form a truly international society, cutting across the deep and dangerous divisions of the modern world'.[61]

If anything, Labour sceptics were often wary of overplaying the national card and, as a result, largely avoided the term 'parliamentary sovereignty' in favour of 'national planning' or 'controls'. 'Sovereignty', Wilson suggested early in the debate, was an 'old world' term and incompatible with 'this modern age'. He added:

> The whole of political progress is a history of gradual abandonment of national sovereignty.... The question is not whether sovereignty remains absolute or not, but in what way one is prepared to sacrifice sovereignty, to whom and for what purpose. This is the real issue before us. The question is whether any proposed surrender of sovereignty will advance or retard our progress to the kind of world we all want to see.[62]

---

[57] Letter to *The Times* signed by E. Shinwell, J. Dugdale, L. Plummer, M. Foot, E. Smith, N. Pentland and A. Greenwood, 27 July 1961.

[58] Camps, *Britain and the European Community*, p. 448.

[59] In the June 1962 Common Market parliamentary debate, for instance, Harold Wilson praised speakers on both sides of the House for avoiding the 'xenophobic line we sometimes get'. *Parliamentary Debates*, Commons, 5th Series, vol. 661, 7 June 1962, col. 676.

[60] H. Wilson on the *Gallery* programme, 1 February 1962, BBC WAC, Film 13/14.

[61] Labour Party National Executive Committee, *Labour and the Common Market*.

[62] H. Wilson speech, *Parliamentary Debates*, Commons, 5th Series, vol. 645, 3 August 1961, cols 1667–8.

Choosing modernity, however, did not free Labour's conceptualisation of planning from the banal assumptions about national responsibilities. As a result, planning became emblematic of the broader desire to protect what Sidney Silverman described as the right to 'control our own affairs'.[63]

The notion that Gaitskell 'suddenly threw'[64] Labour into an anti-Market position ignores the fact that, despite its apparent impartiality, the 'conditions' policy was neither entirely neutral nor without leverage. In a 1961 assessment of party attitudes, the party's International Department described Labour's terms for entry as 'impossible' within the parameters of the Rome Treaty. On that score, it concluded, 'the policy is an anti-Common Market policy, and if the Party exerts heavy pressure on the Government on those lines it will make it considerably more difficult for the Government to negotiate British entry successfully'.[65]

While Gaitskell rode a noncommittal course until the latter half of 1962, both the mechanism for opposition and the banal nationalist assumptions upon which it was based were already in place. Taken as a whole, the 'five conditions' policy could be presented as an argument on behalf of socialist internationalism. The global challenge, argued *Labour and the Common Market*, was not the 'old rivalries' of Europe but the disparities between developed and underdeveloped nations and the splits between East and West. Europe's acceptance of Britain's conditions, it claimed, 'would mean a conscious decision to liberalise their commercial policy and to become an outward looking rather than an inward looking community'.[66] The underlying presumption, however, was that Britain's case was unique.

From the beginning, party researchers pitched negative assessments of British entry. Under David Ennals, the International Department issued a series of background papers on the vital questions in July 1961.[67] The reports offered tentative but wary conclusions about probable losses of economic planning controls, the end of imperial preferences, changes for British agriculture and 'considerable sacrifices' of national sovereignty. Irrespective of federal ends, Ennals argued, Britain faced

---

[63] Sidney Silverman speech, *Parliamentary Debates*, Commons, 5th Series, vol. 661, 7 June 1962, col. 771.

[64] Robins, *The Reluctant Party*, p. 1.

[65] International Department, 'Conservative and Labour Attitudes to the Common Market', p. 5, undated but probably late 1961, LPA, 'EEC Memoranda, Notes, etc. – 1963', Box 814. Sidney Silverman also described the conditions as 'unobtainable'. *Parliamentary Debates*, Commons, 5th Series, vol. 661, 7 June 1962, col. 762.

[66] Labour Party National Executive Committee, *Labour and the Common Market*, p. 2.

[67] International Department, Background Paper No. 1, 'The Common Market', Background Paper No. 2, 'The Political Implications of the Treaty of Rome', Background Paper No. 3, 'The Common Market – Commonwealth Economic Interests', July 1961, LPA, 'EEC Memoranda, Notes, etc – 1961'.

the immediate question of 'how far we are prepared to merge our identity with the Continent ... stressing in particular our determination to strengthen the Commonwealth as a bridge between the races and as a positive force in securing world peace'.[68]

Though Gaitskell would later play the federalist card against Britain's application, he clashed with Ennals in July 1961 over the imminence of European political unity. There was no existing institutional framework, Gaitskell's pragmatic argument suggested, to justify fears of federalism. Ennals, however, seized upon the 'emotive forces' driving integration. Institutions, he predicted, would follow from the political 'intent' demonstrated by European leaders at Bad Godesberg.[69]

Partly because of displeasure with Ennals, Gaitskell transferred the responsibility for Common Market policy studies to the Labour Research Department (LRD).[70] But with the LRD led by Peter Shore, a committed anti-Marketeer, the background reports continued in a negative vein. In March 1962, for instance, its advocacy of Commonwealth ties and worldwide free trade lauded Britain's 'unique' commercial position, a product of 'geographical accident' and 'historical choice'. Trade with underdeveloped nations, such as those in the Commonwealth, was an obligation for the industrialised West. But it was most poignant for Britain, a nation that through 'tradition and self interest ... should be taking a lead in this great free-trading experiment'.[71] Those lines echoed in August when the LRD response to the terms negotiated in Brussels predicted that entry would herald the disappearance of 'the identity of the Commonwealth as a separate trading system'. For the LRD the Commonwealth question was pre-eminent not only because of its centrality to Britain's international relationships but also because of its alignment with 'strong national sentiment'.[72]

Gaitskell and nationalism

Gaitskell's relationship with nationalism was more complex than the 'thousand years' rhetoric suggested. Much has been made of his personal convictions and the triumph of sentiment over rational argument.[73] Set

---

[68] International Department, Background Paper No. 2.

[69] Correspondence between H. Gaitskell and D. Ennals, 14 and 20 July 1961, LPA, International Department Files, 'EEC Correspondence – 1961'.

[70] Shore, *Leading the Left*, p. 80.

[71] Labour Research Department, 'The Common Market and the Commonwealth', RD 236/March 1962, pp. 1–2, LPA, Commonwealth Department Files (untitled file relating to first application).

[72] Labour Research Department, 'Commonwealth and Common Market – Notes on the Outline Agreement', RD 325/August 1962, pp. 1, 10, LPA, Commonwealth Department Files.

[73] Williams, *Hugh Gaitskell*, pp. 746–7; Brivati, *Hugh Gaitskell*, p. 413.

in the context of earlier statements, however, those patriotic tendencies appear less exceptional. In fact, Gaitskell's use of nationalism was, like Labour policy itself, a matter of 'sitting on the fence'.

Fervent appeals to Britishness in the autumn of 1962 appeared to herald a sea change partly because Gaitskell had previously dismissed those tactics. In the opening Common Market debate, he rebuffed 'extremists' on both sides for offering opinions inflamed by emotionalism rather than 'cool calculation'.[74] His April 1962 speech to the Fulham Labour Party denounced 'slogans and headlines, emotions and prejudices' in favour of 'cool, well-informed consideration'.[75] In a party political broadcast on 8 May he described as 'rubbish' the notion that British independence would be overwhelmed by 'a giant capitalist, Catholic conspiracy' inspired by Adenauer and de Gaulle. He charged those 'who just think of the past nostalgically' with failing to reconcile imperial images with the realities of the Commonwealth.[76]

Yet, while advocating detachment, Gaitskell laid a foundation for subsequent patriotic appeals in the same speech. He raised the spectre of federalism by warning that the negotiations could lead to binding political commitments. He validated national aspirations by arguing that, with or without the Common Market, Britain still had 'a part to play in the world'. He discussed the political and economic links to the Commonwealth as the 'nub of the whole question' but prefaced those remarks with a fulsome tribute to the 'British' peoples of Australia, New Zealand and Canada:

> They are part of the family – they came from here. They speak our language; they learn our literature. They have our traditions; they have our political institutions; they share our monarchy. And all of this surely means that we really cannot just turn around and say – well, we don't want to have anything more to do with you.[77]

Gaitskell's technique of dismissing and at the same time exercising nationalist sentiment became a feature of his speeches. His broadcast on 21 September 1962, the night after Macmillan's speech summarising the Commonwealth Prime Ministers' Conference, upheld an ideal form of European co-operation but offered the contrast of a doomsday federalist scenario. The Dominions were again described as 'British countries', the New Commonwealth a 'remarkable affair' born of colonial empire. If entry meant political unity, he concluded that Britain would be reduced

---

[74] *Parliamentary Debates*, Commons, 5th Series, vol. 645, 2 August 1961, cols 1495–6.
[75] H. Gaitskell, speech to the Fulham Labour Party, 14 April 1962, LPA, International Department File, 'Common Market – 1962'.
[76] H. Gaitskell, party political broadcast, 8 May 1962, LPA, International Department File, 'Common Market – 1962'.
[77] *Ibid.*

to a provincial status, 'no more than Texas or California in the United States of Europe. It means the end of a thousand years of history; it means the end of the Commonwealth.'[78]

Any doubts Gaitskell harboured about the patriotic viability of 'thousand years' rhetoric would have been erased by the popular response. His general correspondence files for September and October 1962 contained 916 letters from the public voicing near unanimous support for his 21 September broadcast.[79] Those letters bear a striking resemblance to correspondence in the Beaverbrook and Bryant files,[80] in part because so many were written by self-described 'life-long' Conservatives. One such writer urged him to continue speaking out on the grounds that 'this England of ours will lose its identity and its ties with the Commonwealth'.[81] Another 'dyed in the wool Tory' called the broadcast 'a speech the people of England have been awaiting for a long time'.[82] Peggy Longue, who claimed she had never written to an MP before, told Gaitskell to carry on the fight 'before we commit our country, lives, bodies and souls, not to mention blood ties with the Commonwealth'.[83]

Emboldened perhaps by the support of the anti-Market lobby, Gaitskell enlarged on the themes at Brighton. Once again, however, the speech opened with a disclaimer of nationalist intent. As if invoking a plea for the patriotic version of a middle way, he suggested that:

> There are certain ways in which we should *not* decide this issue. It is *not* a matter to be settled by attractive pictures of nice old German gentlemen drinking beer on the one hand or, on the other, by race or national hatred stimulated by past experiences. It should *not* be decided because on the one hand we like Italian girls, or on the other, we think we have been fleeced in Italian hotels. It should *not* be decided on the basis of whether we think French food is the best in the world, or because, as one of my correspondents put it, she was afraid Europe was out to poison us![84]

In a sense, Gaitskell was dismissing the subjective and mundane versions of national sentiment. The European question, this line suggested, was '*not*' about food, female beauty, holidays or cultural stereotypes.

---

[78] Labour Party press release, H. Gaitskell televised address, 21 September 1962. See also *The Times*, 22 September 1962.

[79] See HG Papers C/256.6. Almost all of the letters in files 1–5 pertain to the 21 September broadcast. One of the few dissenting notes was that of a young Labour supporter who complained 'Must the Labour Party always present such a static, middle-aged, backward-looking face to the country?' A. Daventry to H. Gaitskell, 24 September 1962.

[80] BBK F/3, F/4; AB Papers Box 69, F/21.

[81] H. C. Kimmins to H. Gaitskell, 21 September 1962, HG Papers C/256.6.

[82] H. Bowen Barnes to H. Gaitskell, 22 September 1962, HG Papers C/256.6.

[83] P. Longue to H. Gaitskell, 21 September 1962, HG Papers C/256.6.

[84] Labour Party press release, Hugh Gaitskell speech, 3 October 1962 at the party conference (original emphasis).

But, as later passages in the speech demonstrate, Gaitskell differentiated between the experiential identity of personal prejudices and what he depicted as the objective, if unpredictable, forces of history. His infamous 'thousand years' comments were thus preceded by a characterisation of Europe as Janus:

> for although, of course, Europe has had a great and glorious civilisation, although Europe can claim Goethe, and Leonardo, Voltaire and Picasso, there have been evil features in European history too – Hitler and Mussolini and today the attitude of some Europeans to the Congo problem, the attitude of at least one European Government to the United Nations. You cannot say what this Europe will be: it has its two faces and we do not know as yet which is the one which is to be dominant.[85]

Ironically, setting an unpredictable European destiny against the solidity of Britain's constitutional and Commonwealth traditions was itself an exercise in banal perceptions. Gaitskell tried to set himself above the fray, thinking perhaps that the dispassionate flags of history could be counted upon to wave themselves.

None of this was lost on Conservative observers who knew Gaitskell's rhetoric appealed across party lines. Perhaps out of fear that he might usurp the mantle of patriotic responsibility, efforts were made to link him with the nationalist extremes. At the Conservative Party conference R. A. Butler proclaimed 'For them a thousand years of history books. For us, the future!'[86] The *Spectator* accused Gaitskell of surrendering to a xenophobic left wing.[87] There was contempt for his balancing act. Central Office's *Notes on Current Politics* deplored the manipulation of 'prejudices'. 'He attacked and defended "reaction" in one breath',[88] it claimed.

Labour socialism versus Euro-socialism

It is crucial to note that Labour's 'fundamentalist' and 'revisionist' opponents of entry argued their case on what they believed to be valid socialist grounds.[89] Yet those arguments set them at odds with their counterparts on the Continent. Socialists of all hues evaluated the developing course of European unity in relation to the larger internationalist cause. On the

---

[85] *Ibid.*
[86] *The Times*, 12 October 1962.
[87] H. Fairlie, 'Mr. Gaitskell's Fatal Words', *Spectator*, 28 September 1962, p. 427. See also H. Fairlie, 'Mr. Gaitskell on the Rock', *Spectator*, 12 October 1962, p. 548.
[88] Conservative Central Office, *Notes on Current Politics*, No. 19, 8 October 1962, pp. 12–13.
[89] Interview with Michael Foot, 27 October 1998; Newman, *Socialism and European Unity*, p. 269.

issue of 'European Co-operation', the 1959 Socialist International advocated 'consolidation of existing European institutions' and 'functional agreements' towards economic growth and higher standards of living for workers. At the same time it stressed that Europe should become an agent for co-operative international relations rather than a closed coalition.[90] The following year, the European socialist parties' conference at Strasbourg recommended strengthening common institutions and centralised authority by replacing the separate agreements on Euratom, the ECSC and the EEC with a single treaty.[91] While those goals were sufficiently general to engender broad support, they were also vague enough to facilitate interpretations drawn from British perspectives. On that basis many concluded that what was good for Europe was not necessarily good for Britain.

By the spring of 1962 it became clear that Labour scepticism derived as much from a regard for the philosophy of British socialism as from policy details. Following a visit to Brussels, Barbara Castle wrote an article for the March 1962 issue of the *New Statesman* entitled 'The Anti-Socialist Community'. Subsequently reprinted as a Research Department document, Castle's piece stated:

> The most significant comment I heard in Brussels, made by one of the Commission's top men, was that the only thing Britain would be prevented from doing, once she joined, was to pursue a *politique unique*. In the context of the economic philosophy which inspires the Community, this means, in effect, that she would be debarred from pursuing even the cautious and experimental Socialist policy to which the whole of the Labour Party is committed.[92]

Fred Mulley, a member of the Common Market Committee, challenged Castle with pro-European views in the Home Policy Sub-Committee. He agreed that the Community was devoted to laissez-faire principles but believed the Treaty of Rome would still allow for planning at the national level.[93]

A subsequent report, issued in response to the dispute, revealed that Castle's views held sway in a Labour Research Department headed

---

[90] Comments on 'European Co-operation', General Resolution, Sixth Congress of the Socialist International, Hamburg, 14–17 July 1959. Copy in LPA, International Department Files, 'EEC Memoranda, Notes, etc – 1959'.

[91] Recommendations from the European socialist parties' conference, Strasbourg, 7–8 May 1960, LPA, International Department Files, 'EEC Memoranda and Notes, etc. – 1960'.

[92] B. Castle, 'Planning and the Common Market – The Anti-Socialist Community', RD 245/April 1962, LPA, Home Policy Sub-Committee minutes, 7 May 1962. It also appeared in *New Statesman and Nation*, 13 March 1962.

[93] F. W. Mulley, 'Planning and the Common Market', RD 252, LPA, Home Policy Sub-Committee Minutes, 7 May 1962.

by Peter Shore. The Treaty of Rome, the document 'Planning and the Common Market' concluded, was designed to supersede 'economic nationalism' and commanded the support of Europe's capitalists and socialist planners alike. It added:

> It is necessary to labour this point because while in all other European countries it is taken for granted, in Britain it is still met with persistent disbelief. Thus while socialists in the U.K. are asking the question 'How much U.K. planning will be possible if we join the Common Market', socialists in Europe are asking the entirely different question 'How much planning can be undertaken at the Community level'.[94]

European socialists were intent on federalist integration, the report concluded, and economic controls heretofore exercised by British Governments[95] would in future be undertaken only with the approval of Community members.

Other events put the British–European differences in further relief. The June 1962 Socialist International meeting at Oslo appeared to approve, however vaguely, the direction of European integrationists. Democratic nations, it suggested, needed to do more to extend co-operative economic development. 'Economic planning', it noted, 'outgrows the borders of nation states. The establishment of regional economic organisations is a recognition of this fact.'[96] Meanwhile, relations deteriorated between Gaitskell and the architects of federalism. On 4 April, Jean Monnet presented his broad outline of EEC philosophy to the XYZ Club, but his address failed to satisfy Gaitskell's detailed questions on British entry and the gap between rich and poor nations. Told by Monnet that he 'must have faith', Gaitskell reportedly answered 'I don't believe in faith. I believe in reason and you have not shown me any.'[97]

The inevitable clash came at the Brussels meeting of the Contact Committee of the Socialist International in July 1962.[98] To the disappointment of the Belgian Foreign Minister, Paul Henri Spaak, Gaitskell's speech to the conference reiterated the five conditions and added Britain's unwillingness to enter a federated version of Europe. Spaak thought some of

---

[94] P. Shore, 'Planning and the Common Market', RD 268/May 1962. Copy in LPA, National Executive Committee minutes, 27 June 1962. Originally submitted to Home Policy Sub-Committee, 4 June 1962.

[95] The report cited a range of areas where Government control would be threatened, including social service funding, exchange rates and nationalisation policy.

[96] Oslo Declaration, adopted at the Socialist International in Oslo, 22–24 June 1962, p. 3. Copy in LPA, International Department File, Box 816, 'Common Market 1962'.

[97] H. Gaitskell quoted in Williams, *Hugh Gaitskell*, p. 708. Roy Jenkins had invited Monnet to speak before the XYZ Club. Douglas Jay gives a similar account in *Change and Fortune*, p. 282.

[98] Peter Shore regarded this as one of the two primary events that shaped Gaitskell's turn against entry in the summer of 1962. Shore, *Leading the Left*, p. 80.

Gaitskell's points 'valid' but viewed others as 'dangerous' and warned that British entry would not be achieved by undermining European unification.[99] Wilson weighed in with criticism of the expectations among federalists in the Socialist International. British entry on their terms, he asserted, would destroy the Commonwealth and make Britain 'merely a province of Europe'.[100] Bob Edwards, an MP and fellow delegate to the Brussels meeting, sought to assuage concerns about federalist intentions but was rebutted by Gaitskell, who blamed Spaak for pushing an integration agenda ahead of the decision on British entry.[101] 'I don't understand', Spaak repeatedly said of Gaitskell's views,[102] suggesting that their positions were mutually incomprehensible.

In the aftermath, token and largely unsuccessful efforts were made to convert European socialists to the British position. No progress was made at a special meeting of European socialists and participants in the 6–8 September gathering of Commonwealth Labour leaders. Gaitskell's Brighton speech ended with a somewhat empty 'appeal to our Socialist comrades' to help reshape the terms of entry.[103] In November, Barbara Castle and Tom Driberg attended the Congress of European Socialist Parties as observers. But Castle's words to the Congress, in which she quoted liberally from Gaitskell's Brighton speech, were 'clearly contrary to the general tenor of the conference' and listened to in 'regretful sorrow'.[104] Following his 4 December meeting with Gaitskell (see below), Guy Mollet, the French Socialist leader, conceded that Labour and European socialists 'were not on the same wavelength'.[105]

After Brighton

Gaitskell was exercised by charges of nationalism and took exception to a *New York Herald Tribune* editorial that claimed he made socialists

[99] Paul Henri Spaak quoted in *The Times*, 16 July 1962. See also Spaak's comments quoted in the *Daily Express*, 16 July 1962.

[100] Wilson quoted in *The Times*, 17 July 1962.

[101] See R. Edwards to H. Gaitskell, 23 July 1962 (includes his notes on a meeting chaired by Spaak in Brussels, 17–18 June 1962); H. Gaitskell to R. Edwards, 25 July 1962, HG Papers C/256.5.

[102] Shore, *Leading the Left*, p. 80.

[103] Labour Party press release, Hugh Gaitskell speech at party conference, 3 October 1962. W. Carron of the Amalgamated Engineers was among those who felt that Labour's policy emphasis was in danger of undermining the faith of Euro-socialists. *Guardian*, 4 October 1962.

[104] Fifth Congress of Socialist Parties of the Member Countries of the European Community, Paris, 5–6 November 1962. Report by B. Castle and T. Driberg, 13 November 1962, LPA, International Department Files, 'Common Market 1962'. The conference was held every two years and drew approximately 100 delegates and observers.

[105] *The Times*, 5 December 1962.

look foolish by placing them 'squarely in the headquarters of Colonel Blimp'.[106] Those sensitivities notwithstanding, he continued in a patriotic manner. At the time of the Conservative Party conference he claimed that 'The Tories would tear the Union Jack down and trample on it if they were told that was the way to stay in power'.[107] While his 13 October speech to the Cambridge Guildhall eschewed the phrase 'thousand years of history', the theme remained in his argument that Conservative policy had degenerated to the point of contemplating entry on any terms. He deconstructed Macmillan's political argument for entry to demonstrate the inevitability of federalism. Europe, he argued, would develop integrated foreign, defence and fiscal policies as it moved along the logical progression of its 'great power' ambitions. The result, he claimed twice in the speech, would be 'the disappearance of Britain as an independent nation'.[108]

Having forged a politicised template and secured party unity, Gaitskell set about mobilising his challenge to the Government. The first step was a propagation of Labour's policy in pamphlet form. With a donation from Frank Cousins and the Transport and General Workers' Union, one million copies of the conference speeches by Gaitskell and George Brown, along with the statement *Labour and the Common Market* from the National Executive Committee, were published under the title *Britain and the Common Market*.[109] Copies were sent to several Commonwealth Prime Ministers, while Arthur Calwell secured 200 copies for Australian state executives and all members of the House of Representatives.[110]

Gaitskell received and courted tributes from the wider anti-Market movement. He possessed the guest list for the first meeting of Leo Russell's AntiCommon Market Council and was therefore aware of attempts to create a cross-party anti-Market coalition.[111] Arthur Bryant sent him the first published volume of *The Story of England* and wrote

---

[106] Gaitskell responded to a 4 October editorial with a letter to John Hay Whitney, the paper's publisher, complaining that 'Few Americans have ever understood our attitude to the Common Market but I should have thought that you were one of them'. H. Gaitskell to J. H. Whitney, 8 October 1962, HG Papers C/256.5.

[107] H. Gaitskell quoted by the *Daily Express*, 13 October 1962.

[108] Labour Party news release, Hugh Gaitskell speech at the Cambridge Guildhall, 13 October 1962.

[109] Labour Party National Executive Committee, *Britain and the Common Market*. LPA, NEC minutes, 3 October 1962. See also A. L. Williams to H. Gaitskell, 11 October 1962 and H. Gaitskell to F. Cousins, 15 October 1962, in HG Papers C/256.5.

[110] A. Calwell to H. Gaitskell, 16 November 1962, HG Papers C/256.5 Tony Benn, however, claimed that the pamphlets 'sat in packets of a thousand in a thousand committee rooms' and were later dug up by his agent for use in the 1975 referendum campaign. T. Benn quoted in Williams, *Hugh Gaitskell*, footnote, p. 739.

[111] Copy of list, 12 December 1962, in HG Papers C/256.5.

'I wanted you to know how much a humble and, I suppose, incorrigible traditionalist honours you for your faith and courage'. 'It encourages me immensely', Gaitskell replied, 'to know that we are together in what now appears an inevitable battle'.[112] Gaitskell even expressed sympathy with Heathcote-Smith's view of British entry as a contravention of 'human nature' and pledged to incorporate that theme in public statements.[113]

Nonetheless, Gaitskell needed more than pamphlets and plaudits, and bolder measures were taken in support of his new policy emphasis. He continued to regard the intricate economic arguments for and against entry as evenly balanced.[114] But that view did not relieve Labour's need for a coherent policy alternative. Its absence, he conceded, 'is the psychological weakness of our position at present which needs to be repaired'.[115]

For inspiration and activism, Gaitskell turned to an informal grouping of Cambridge economists that included Richard Kahn, Nicholas Kaldor and, in particular, James Meade. In late September 1962, Gaitskell urged the group to share their doubts about the wisdom of Britain's application with the wider public. He proposed, for example, a letter to *The Times* which was eventually drafted by Douglas Jay and signed by Kaldor and Kahn as well as Roy Harrod.[116] Following his speech at the Cambridge Guildhall on 13 October, Gaitskell joined the economists and other sympathisers at a dinner meeting to discuss future plans. In the aftermath, further articles were suggested and Clarissa Kaldor was designated as liaison between Gaitskell and the Cambridge group.[117]

Meade's views had been part of an attempt by party leaders to identify acceptable terms of entry in March 1962.[118] By October, Gaitskell felt he had successfully converted Labour to the arguments forwarded in Meade's *UK, Commonwealth and Common Market* but feared that its author might be wavering. At the time, Meade was engaged in what he called the 'agonisingly difficult' alternative policy draft for the second

---

[112] A. Bryant to H. Gaitskell, undated; Gaitskell to A. Bryant, 15 October 1962, HG Papers, C/256.5.
[113] Correspondence between C. Heathcote-Smith and H. Gaitskell, 17 and 22 October 1962. The basis of the argument was presented in Heathcote-Smith's letter to the *Daily Telegraph*, 1 October 1962.
[114] See for example H. Gaitskell to President Kennedy, 11 December 1962, quoted in Williams, *Gaitskell*, pp. 704–5.
[115] H. Gaitskell to J. Meade, 15 October 1962, HG Papers C/256.5.
[116] Correspondence between H. Gaitskell and R. Kahn, 24 September and 5 October 1962, HG Papers C/256.5. Letter to *The Times*, 15 October 1962.
[117] H. Gaitskell to C. Kaldor, 15 October 1962, HG Papers C/256.5.
[118] Williams, *Hugh Gaitskell*, p. 710. In Parliament, Gaitskell used the work of Meade and Donald MacDougall to combat the pro-entry arguments that Britain required entry for economic reasons. *Parliamentary Debates*, Commons, 5th Series, vol. 661, 6 June 1962, col. 513.

edition of his pamphlet.[119] In an attempt to solidify Meade's support, Gaitskell asked him to join Harold Wilson, Denis Healey, James Callaghan and Douglas Jay on an ad hoc alternative policy sub-committee. The meetings, a reluctant Meade was assured, would be private and free from any commitments.[120]

In December 1962 Gaitskell's activities took more dramatic form when he visited French leaders only days before Macmillan's talks with de Gaulle at Rambouillet. Arranged in part by Jacques de Beaumarchais, the Directeur Politique at the Quai D'Orsay,[121] Gaitskell met with Prime Minister Pompidou, the Foreign Minister Couve de Murville and Guy Mollet. Precise details of the meeting are unclear. The text of a report from British Ambassador Pierson Dixon to the Foreign Office reveals that Couve de Murville and Pompidou took a cautious approach and, though noncommittal, spoke in favour of British entry. The development of federal institutions, they claimed, were at least twenty-five to fifty years away. Brief mention was made of a free trade area and the consequences for Europe if the negotiations failed.[122] In any event, Gaitskell used the meetings to aggravate both sides. Roy Jenkins called it a 'nefarious visit', designed to frustrate Macmillan with its implied collusion against Britain's case.[123] But at the same time Gaitskell annoyed Gaullists by emphasising the importance of the Atlantic Alliance.[124]

Beaverbrook personally assigned Alexander Kenworthy to cover Gaitskell's trip to Paris and, on the basis of correspondence from his readers, offered encouraging news of unease in the Tory shires. 'The way is wide open for you and your party', he wrote, 'of that I have no doubt. Opinion against the Common Market in the country is hardening every day.'[125] But Gaitskell would not live to complete his anti-Market plots or reap the rewards of a rising popularity. At the start of the Christmas recess, he was overtaken by disseminated lupus erythematosus and died on 18 January 1963.

---

[119] Correspondence between H. Gaitskell and J. Meade, 15 and 19 October 1962, HG Papers C/256.5.
[120] H. Gaitskell to J. Meade, 24 October and 1 November 1962, HG Papers C/256.5.
[121] Interview with Roy Jenkins, 18 November 1998.
[122] Pierson Dixon to Earl of Home, 4 December 1962, PRO, PREM 11/3857. Dixon also noted that Gaitskell did not meet with de Gaulle. According to the report, Couve de Murville thought de Gaulle would have seen such a meeting as inappropriate.
[123] Jenkins, *A Life at the Centre*, p. 146; interview with Lord Jenkins, 18 November 1998.
[124] Robins, *The Reluctant Party*, p. 41.
[125] Beaverbrook to H. Gaitskell, 6 December 1962, BBK C/139.

Macmillan and the Conservatives

Anti-Market MPs

In his memoirs, Macmillan summarised the anti-Marketeer challenge as a 'complete, and ludicrous failure'.[126] That judgement was at odds with his contemporary assessment. According to Harold Evans, Macmillan was 'desperately worried' in July 1961, fearful that the Government might collapse over Europe, despite assurances to the contrary from the whips.[127] Likewise, Macmillan's diary, though perhaps dramatised for the purposes of future memoirs, forecast wholesale political realignments on the basis of the negotiated terms.[128] In the autumn of 1962, he compared his party unity dilemmas to those of Gaitskell.[129] More often than not, Macmillan framed his predicaments in historic precedents, most notably the conduct of Peel, Disraeli and Lord George Bentinck in 1845 and the general election of 1906.[130]

Macmillan's attitude towards dissent within his own party vacillated between a fear of back-bench revolts and a dismissive attitude towards its likely agents. Having summoned ghosts from the 1840s, he awaited the visitation of a latter-day Disraeli from among two dozen rebel MPs[131] whose primary spokesmen included Anthony Fell, Derek Walker-Smith, R. H. Turton, Peter Walker and Viscount Hinchingbrooke. On that score, Harold Evans predicted, 'one cannot think that when the chips go down people like this will amount to very much'.[132] In confident moments Macmillan shared that view, dismissing Fell as an agent of Beaverbrook, John Biggs-Davison as an imperialist and Walker-Smith and Turton as failed ministers he had justifiably dismissed for incompetence.[133] Macmillan regarded Hinchingbrooke as one of Parliament's last English eccentrics, one he likened to Bentinck rather than Disraeli.[134]

---

[126] Macmillan, *At the End of the Day*, p. 333.

[127] Evans, *Downing Street Diary*, p. 155. On 29 July 1961 Macmillan wrote to Heath, 'I think our chief difficulty at the moment is to carry the House with us'. PRO, PREM 11/3559.

[128] HMD, 9 March, 21 April and 21 September 1962, MS Macmillan dep. d. 45, 47.

[129] HMD, 20 September 1962, MS Macmillan dep. d. 47.

[130] For examples see Evans, *Downing Street Diary*, p. 200; 'Notes of Meeting with De Gaulle at Chateau de Champs, 3 June 1962', PRO, PREM 11/4019; HMD, 7 February, 21 April, 21 August 1962; Macmillan, *At the End of the Day*, pp. 26–7, 128. Macmillan's diary entries for 3 and 9 September 1962 also reveal that he was reading biographies of Disraeli and Peel. The historic precedents were also noted by the press. See for example commentary by Norman Hunt, *Gallery* programme, 15 February 1962, BBC WAC, Film 13/14.

[131] Macmillan, *At the End of the Day*, p. 26.

[132] Evans, *Downing Street Diary*, p. 202.

[133] HMD, 5 August and 30 November 1961, MS Macmillan dep. d. 43, 44.

[134] HMD, 11 June 1962, MS Macmillan dep. d. 46. Hinchingbrooke's record of a conversation with Harold Macmillan, 13 July 1961, quoted in A. Best and J. Sandwich

It is important to note that in Fell, Hinchingbrooke, Biggs-Davison and Paul Williams the anti-Market faction claimed the last of Parliament's remaining Suez rebels. This fact had interrelated consequences. It undoubtedly contributed to Macmillan's perception that he faced implacable enemies in the Commons who, along with Lords Lambton and Salisbury, would oppose his leadership irrespective of the cause.[135] That in turn reinforced a tendency among party leaders to achieve distance from, rather than to silence, their anti-Market critics. Peter Walker, for instance, pursued his anti-Market projects without any interference from party elders.[136] Macmillan played cautiously upon Hinchingbrooke's conscience in an early encounter, complaining of a lack of support for his leadership of the Government.[137] According to Turton, the party was 'friendly' and there were only 'discrete hints ... that I should mellow my opposition'.[138]

Tory dissenters achieved a semblance of unity in June 1961 with the creation of a Conservative Common Market Committee, led by Hinchingbrooke and Turton. Meetings held in parliamentary committee rooms proceeded with full knowledge of the whips and on occasion drew as many as seventy back-benchers.[139] Its membership, which peaked at just over fifty MPs, was subdivided into committees charged with research, drafting parliamentary questions and the creation of an alternative policy.[140] Outright opponents busied themselves with parliamentary motions and conference resolutions that enjoyed varying levels of support.[141] Typical of the parliamentary motions was that submitted in defence of sovereignty by Turton and Walker-Smith in July 1961 and endorsed by approximately thirty MPs.[142]

There were also instances of collaboration between MPs and the wider anti-Market movement. Walker-Smith was featured speaker at the ACML's first public rally, in October 1961. In subsequent months, Biggs-Davison, Fell, Turton, Walker and Paul Williams took their turns on the dais at League events. Ronald Russell, Turton, Walker and Walker-Smith

---

(eds), *Hinch: A Celebration of Viscount Hinchingbrooke MP, 1906–1995* (London, 1997), p. 133.

[135] HMD, 5 August 1961, 6 February 1962 and 17 February 1964, MS Macmillan dep. d. 43, 45, 48.

[136] Interview with Peter Walker, 23 February 1998.

[137] Hinchingbrooke's record of a conversation with Harold Macmillan, 13 July 1961, quoted in Best and J. Sandwich, *Hinch*, pp. 133–4.

[138] R. Turton to A. Eden, 20 November 1962, AP 23/64/14.

[139] Interview with Peter Walker, 23 February 1998.

[140] R. Turton to A. Eden, 20 November 1962 and 25 January 1963, AP 23/64/14 and AP 23/64/15.

[141] For a brief discussion of the 1960–62 party conferences, see A. Gamble, *The Conservative Nation* (London, 1974), pp. 188–95.

[142] Lieber, *British Politics*, p. 205, Pfaltzgraff, *Britain Faces Europe*, pp. 41, 94, 113.

also contributed to the ACML's collection of essays *Britain Not Europe*.[143] The *Sunday Express* devoted extensive coverage to evidence of Conservative dissent and its leader page secured the services of Hinchingbrooke on at least four occasions.[144] Beaverbrook took a particular interest in Peter Walker and helped him arrange a Commonwealth tour during which the young MP spoke out against Common Market entry, in India, Australia, New Zealand and Canada. 'Lord Beaverbrook and the *Daily Express*', Macmillan noted in his diary, 'are making tremendous efforts to get hold of our chaps. Some (I fear) have fallen into the spider's web.'[145]

The Tory rebels were also unified by a devotion to national sovereignty. But they were no more sophisticated than their extra-parliamentary counterparts in offering a definition. As elsewhere, the concept was bound to the imagination of national identity. Sovereignty, wrote Biggs-Davison, was 'easier to understand than define' but facilitated the 'aspiration to a complete identity and free will'.[146] Walker-Smith called national sovereignty 'the essence of independent nationhood, achieved in the early dawn of our history and resolutely safeguarded ever since'.[147] Those assumptions encouraged celebrations of national uniqueness. In its most extreme cases, the 'us' and 'them' differentiation was evident in Hinchingbrooke's notorious remark that 'we don't want to be with a lot of Frogs and Huns'.[148] More typical was Walker-Smith's assertion that the Common Market suited the needs of Europeans but was untenable for Britain 'because we have a special and separate position, different history, different tradition, and, of course, we have a unique association with the Commonwealth'.[149] 'Their evolution', he told the Commons, 'has been Continental and collective. Ours has been insular and imperial.'[150]

---

[143] Corbet, *Britain Not Europe*, pp. 12–15, 45–8, 49–51, 63–5.

[144] Viscount Hinchingbrooke's *Sunday Express* articles included 'Are the Tories Leading Us to Ruin?', 5 November 1961; 'The Gathering Forces that Menace Britain', 17 December 1961; 'Is This Why the Tories Are on the Slide?', 13 May 1962; 'Can the Tory Rebels Still Save Britain?', 23 September 1962.

[145] Macmillan, *At the End of the Day*, p. 31. References to Beaverbrook and *Express* coverage feature throughout Macmillan's diaries. For examples, see HMD, 24 March, 19, 22 May, 5, 6, 10 August, 27 September, 12, 13 October and 18 December 1961; 3 February, 10 April, 1, 6 and 13 June, 3, 7 and 20 July, 21 August, 14, 16 and 21 September, 15 October, and 23 and 26 December 1962, MS Macmillan dep. d. 41–48.

[146] J. Biggs-Davison, *The Walls of Europe* (London, 1962), p. 14. See also his letter to *The Times*, 5 August 1961, and speech in *Parliamentary Debates*, Commons, 5th Series, vol. 645, 28 June 1961, col. 575.

[147] Walker-Smith, 'British Sovereignty and the Common Market', p. 12.

[148] Hinchingbrooke interviewed by ABC television, quoted in the *Daily Express*, 26 April 1962.

[149] Walker-Smith interviewed on the *Gallery* programme, 1 February 1962, BBC WAC, Film 13/14.

[150] Walker-Smith speech, *Parliamentary Debates*, Commons, 5th Series, vol. 645, 2 August 1962, col. 1512.

The Commonwealth, by virtue of its prominence in equations of national interest, provided a thematic focus for those seeking Common Market alternatives. Those plans generally lacked specificity and could therefore absorb the devotions of Empire nostalgia and New Commonwealth realism alike. Furthermore, alternative plans engendered broad support by allowing MPs to register their concerns in a constructive fashion at a time when failure at Brussels looked increasingly likely. Though Patrick Jenkin derided Empire Free Trade as 'moonshine'[151] at the 1962 party conference, 'freer trade' variations on that theme and calls for amendment of the GATT gathered momentum. In a December 1962 letter to *The Times*, twenty-four signatories proposed a relationship between Britain, Europe and the wider world, drawn from the visions of 'Smuts, Leo Amery and Ernest Bevin'. Accordingly, Britain would associate with Europe outside the Common Market framework while enhancing ties between EFTA and the Commonwealth. They suggested the creation of a Sterling Area Board, Commonwealth Payments Union and an Export Council to strengthen 'special trading arrangements' while serving the needs of debtor nations.[152] Similar sentiments motivated a parliamentary motion calling for an alternative policy at the end of December 1962 that drew forty-seven Conservative signatures. One of Turton's sub-committees, furthermore, drafted a nine-point plan that was eventually submitted to Harold Macmillan, Iain Macleod and the Dominion Prime Ministers in the aftermath of de Gaulle's veto.[153]

By the end of 1962 the *Daily Telegraph* counted no less than four distinct approaches to the Commonwealth trade alternative.[154] But, as the *Sunday Times* observed, those plans were fettered by the dissonant voices for free trade or protection and, more importantly, by the absence of reciprocal interest within the Commonwealth.[155] Fractures inside the Conservative Party were magnified by variable interpretations of what the evolving Commonwealth meant to Britishness and Conservatism. Peter Walker, author of the most ambitious scheme, cited Burke, Chamberlain, Disraeli and Leo Amery as his primary influences.[156] 'Britain', his plan concluded, 'is still heart and centre of the Commonwealth connection. This position is both a heritage, which we of this generation have no right to dissipate and a trust which we have no right to disregard.'[157] Walker and

---

[151] Gamble, *Conservative Nation*, p. 193.
[152] Letter to *The Times*, 6 December 1962.
[153] R. Turton to A. Eden, 13 February 1963, AP 23/64/16.
[154] *Daily Telegraph*, 9 December 1962.
[155] *Sunday Times*, 6 January 1963. Macmillan emphasised the latter point in a letter to John Biggs-Davison, 31 July 1961, BD Papers 23.
[156] P. Walker, *Staying Power: An Autobiography* (London, 1991), pp. vii, 30; Walker and Walker-Smith, *A Call to the Commonwealth*, pp. 1–3.
[157] Walker and Walker-Smith, *A Call to the Commonwealth*, p. 30. See also P. Walker, 'Boosting the Commonwealth', *Crossbow*, 5:19 (spring 1962), pp. 16–17.

Walker-Smith's *A Call to the Commonwealth,* however, was crafted with an overriding concern for the New Commonwealth that set Walker and a group of Young Conservative dissidents[158] apart from those who were motivated by 'kith and kin' versions of Commonwealth relations. It was indeed a 'left-wing case' against entry,[159] one that bore closer resemblance to the arguments of James Meade and Denis Healey than the nostalgia of Beaverbrook. Biggs-Davison had also cited Disraeli, celebrated 'the diversity of peoples', argued against 'Little Europe' and urged the necessity of links between Britain, Commonwealth and Continent. If terms compatible with Commonwealth development and the maintenance of national sovereignty could be secured, he favoured Common Market membership.[160]

Hinchingbrooke, whose views were more sophisticated than his Colonel Blimp image suggested, was also a disciple of Disraeli and Burke and an unrepentant Tory reformer.[161] But his interpretation of the Disraelian legacy intertwined with the Chamberlainite view of Empire and therefore led to a more explicit rejection of Europe. Britain, he asserted, faced a choice between 'associating with the old maritime countries which she herself created or the new Continental complex devised by foreigners for themselves'.[162] His views, moreover, were motivated as much by a frustration with Government policy as by the prevailing state of Conservatism itself. The Liberals, he told the BBC, had in effect wielded power in Britain since 1905. 'We haven't had, as I conceive it, a real Tory administration in all those years.'[163]

A facade of unity thus concealed the fact that Conservative anti-Marketeers formed less of a bloc than a coalition. As with Labour, philosophical differences among Conservative opponents were in turn manifest in the tactics of dissent. As leader of the anti-Market committee, Turton found himself presiding over a split between 'extremists' who opposed the Government 'at every opportunity' and those who preferred to keep their critiques within the confines of the committee rooms. It was, he admitted to Anthony Eden, an 'uneasy balance'.[164]

---

[158] A 14 July 1961 letter to *The Times* signed by former Young Conservative national chairmen Walker, Andrew Bowden and Geoffrey Finsberg, the sitting chairman, Terence Wray, and its vice-chair, Nicholas Scott, called for a 'more positive and dynamic' Commonwealth policy. The Commonwealth's many virtues, they argued, included stability because it was neither 'racial nor regional'.

[159] Walker, *Staying Power,* p. 34.

[160] Biggs-Davison, *The Walls of Europe,* see especially pp. 12–14, 77–87. See also, Biggs-Davison, letters to *The Times,* 2 June, 20 July and 5 August 1961. Copies in BD Papers 23.

[161] Hinchingbrooke had supported the Beveridge report and founded the Tory Reform Group in 1943 along with Quintin Hogg and Peter Thorneycroft.

[162] Hinchingbrooke, 'Can the Tory Rebels Still Save Britain?'

[163] Hinchingbrooke interviewed on the *Gallery* programme, 28 June 1962, BBC WAC, Film 13/14.

[164] R. Turton to A. Eden, 20 November 1962, AP 23/64/14.

Anthony Fell set the tone for the attacking group in the inaugural Common Market debate by calling for Macmillan's resignation. 'Is the Prime Minister aware', he asked, 'that this decision to gamble with sovereignty in Europe, when 650 million people of the British Commonwealth depend upon his faith and leadership, is the most disastrous thing that any Prime Minister has done for generations past?'[165] Fell maximised his nuisance value by carrying his attack to the constituencies. His speeches, delivered without the approval of local party agents and incorporating robust attacks on the Prime Minister, brought complaints to Central Office, where one internal memo asked 'Can nothing be done to restrain this gentleman please?'[166]

Tactically, however, Fell was isolated. Though twenty-two Conservatives had abstained on the vote approving Britain's decision to apply, Fell cast the lone Tory vote against, making him an unlikely partner with Michael Foot, Konni Zilliacus, Emrys Hughes and S. O. Davies. Fell was irritated by the failure of '"the right" to make any visible progress'. He criticised both Hinchingbrooke and Biggs-Davison for leaning towards the 'wait and see' position and urged opponents to 'torpedo the present talks by all means possible'.[167]

Other protagonists were uncomfortable playing the role of dissenters. Turton described himself as 'a most reluctant rebel' and, in November 1962, feared compromising the Government's standing at a time when it faced daunting obstacles in Brussels.[168] Walker was equally 'uncomfortable' with a rebellious reputation.[169] Hinchingbrooke was resigned to the fact that post-war MPs had become 'too docile' before the control of the party whips. It was a development he attributed to wartime experience and loyalty to Churchill. But he also thought it an intrinsic feature of Conservatism, which, in its natural state, stood for constitutionality, 'continuity and changelessness'.[170] Only a volcano, he wrote in the *Express*, could shift the 'bedrock' of back-bench Tory loyalty.[171]

In any event there were no seismic shifts. Macmillan, who recognised the profound significance of his 31 July 1961 announcement to the Commons, was pleased by its reception on both sides of the House.[172] The

---

[165] *Parliamentary Debates*, Commons, 5th Series, vol. 645, 31 July 1962, cols 934–5. For Fell's obituary see the *Guardian*, 25 March 1998.

[166] COO to chairman, 30 August 1962; R. J. Webster to Central Office, 1 October 1962, CPA, CCO 500/31/3.

[167] A. Fell to J. Biggs-Davison, 18 April 1962, BD Papers 23.

[168] R. Turton to A. Eden, 5 July 1961 and 20 November 1962, AP 23/64/4 and AP 23/64/14.

[169] Walker, *Staying Power*, pp. 32, 34.

[170] Hinchingbrooke interviewed by R. McKenzie, *Gallery* programme, 28 June 1962, BBC WAC, Film 13/14.

[171] Hinchingbrooke, 'Can the Tory Rebels Still Save Britain?'

[172] HMD, 5 August 1961, MS Macmillan dep. d. 43.

numerous questions put to Macmillan, Heath and Macleod during their visits to the party's back-bench 1922 Committee were submitted without acrimony.[173] At the party's 1961 Brighton conference both Hinching-brooke and Walker-Smith defended sovereignty and the Commonwealth as inviolable national priorities, but to little effect. Only forty delegates from an assembly of some 4,000 voted in favour of Walker-Smith's amendment. The results were similar the following year at Llandudno, when the conference overwhelmingly approved the Government's handling of the negotiations in Brussels.[174] The BBC proclaimed it a triumph for Heath, while the anti-Market motion had mustered only ten further votes over the previous year.[175] The anti-Market group, Turton conceded, had been 'well trampled upon'.[176]

Ironically, by laying claim to a patriotic and political high ground, Gaitskell's Brighton speech helped solidify Conservative support for the Government's Common Market policy.[177] Frustration among Tory rebels was palpable in the comments of Hinchingbrooke, who accused Gaitskell of allowing personal patriotic biases to cloud his judgement. 'Rarely', he told the BBC, 'does one come across a man who within minutes of delivering himself from the strictures of fringe lunacy, goes on to draw so deeply on all the forces which have slanted his own outlook from cradle to maturity'.[178]

This had been an unexpected outcome and once again highlighted the disparity between Macmillan's contemporary fears and hindsight interpretation. Macmillan took initial comfort from the knowledge that Labour would not attack his application announcement in the Commons[179] and, in retrospect, downplayed Gaitskell's 'clever' tactics.[180] But the threat that Labour might harden its position had weighed heavily

[173] P. Goodhart, *The 1922: The Story of the Conservative Backbenchers' Parliamentary Committee* (London, 1973), pp. 179, 184–5. Macmillan felt relieved after his visit to the 1922. See HMD, 15 July 1961, MS Macmillan dep. d. 42. For notes of 1922 Committee discussions during the visits of Ian Macleod on 17 November 1961 and 22 March 1962, and of Ted Heath on 29 March 1962, see R. A. Butler Papers, H/96. For a summary of Ted Heath's visit on 22 June 1961, see K. Cunningham to PM, undated, PRO, PREM 11/3563.

[174] See 'Rout of the Common Market Critics', *The Times*, 12 October 1962.

[175] Gamble, *The Conservative Nation*, pp. 190–5. For BBC coverage of the party conferences see *10 O'Clock* programme, 12 October 1961 and 11 October 1962, BBC WAC, Film T 539/540, 541/542. For Macmillan's reaction see HMD, 13 October 1961, and 11 and 15 October 1962, MS Macmillan dep. d. 43 and 47.

[176] R. Turton to A. Eden, 18 October 1962, AP 23/64/11.

[177] A. Eden to R. Turton, 22 October 1962, AP 23/64/11A; Lieber, *British Politics*, p. 183.

[178] Hinchingbrooke interviewed on the *10 O'Clock* programme, 3 October 1962, BBC WAC, Film T541/542.

[179] HMD, 29 July 1961, MS Macmillan dep. d. 43.

[180] Macmillan, *At the End of the Day*, pp. 130, 132, 137–40.

on British negotiators. Gaitskell's speech to the Spaak Committee, Heath told the Cabinet, had done 'great damage' at a 'critical phase' in the negotiations by undermining Britain's *communautaire* reputation with talk of economic and social policies crafted on a 'purely national basis'.[181] Labour's objections to the terms voiced at the time of the Common-wealth Prime Ministers' Conference and at Brighton also heightened tensions. Harold Evans' diary entry for 7 October 1962 noted that 'the PM had the private office clearing the decks for resignation and an election. Ted Heath had said that if the Labour Party declared an intention to repudiate it would be impossible for him to continue to negotiate.'[182]

Tory grandees

Macmillan survived the challenges offered up by dissenting MPs. But the juxtaposition of his initial apprehension against eventual relief was emblematic of the confrontation with the wider anti-Market movement. Ironically, Macmillan took fright from but eventually survived domestic dissent precisely because it was manifest in a series of ill winds rather than in a single storm. As with the Tory rebels in the Commons, challenges from the Lords and by-election politics were defined and either undermined or successfully weathered by virtue of the unique circumstances attached to each.

In their quest for legitimacy, anti-Marketeers hoped to graft the names of former Prime Ministers to their cause. An August 1962 edition of the *Forward Britain Movement Bulletin*, for instance, claimed that Eden and Churchill had joined Attlee in alignment against British entry.[183] In fact, the opinions of the ex-premiers contained more nuances than Forward Britain claimed and, with little to gain from advocacy of a hardened position, they were reluctant participants.

Compared with Attlee, Eden was more reticent and David Dutton overstates the case when ascribing him a 'key role'[184] in opposing the Common Market. Health problems were a partial hindrance to political activism. Eden departed for the upper house as Lord Avon on those grounds in the summer of 1961 and sympathised with Beaverbrook's depiction of this forum as the House of 'make-believe'.[185] But there were other compelling reasons. Early on, at least, correspondence with Beaverbrook and Salisbury suggested that Eden awaited the terms of

---

[181] E. Heath report to Cabinet, PRO, CAB 128/36 Part II CC 48(62), 19 July 1962.

[182] Evans, *Downing Street Diary*, p. 221.

[183] *Forward Britain Movement Bulletin*, 23 August 1962.

[184] D. Dutton, 'Anticipating Maastricht: The Conservative Party and Britain's First Attempt to Join the European Community', *Contemporary Record*, 7:3 (1993), p. 528.

[185] Correspondence between Beaverbrook and A. Eden, 3, 5 and 11 July 1961, AP 23/8/45 and 45D.

entry before taking a parliamentary stand. He therefore chose to 'hold my fire' during the first Lords debates.[186] It is also crucial to note that Eden regarded his views as neither Europhobic[187] nor deviating from the traditions of Churchillian Conservatism. Federation, he had said in a frequently quoted 1952 speech, was 'something we know in our bones we cannot do'.[188] Like Churchill, he believed that federalism was a logical step for Europe but favoured British association on the basis of intergovernmental co-operation. He was therefore frustrated during the 1960s to find himself characterised as an 'anti-European ogre', first by Lord Boothby in the 2 August 1962 Lords debate and later in the memoirs of both Lord Kilmuir and Harold Macmillan.[189]

Eden's standing and loyalty to the Conservative Party made open criticism of the Government unlikely. In fact, were it not for Boothby's attack on his reputation, he would have remained silent during the 2 August debate. On that occasion Eden's only Common Market remark was in praise of the British negotiating team's desire to secure safeguards for British interests.[190] What is more, he avoided formal links with hardened Tory dissenters. He had side-stepped Beaverbrook's invitation to write *Sunday Express* articles in the spring of 1961[191] and showed no inclination to do so thereafter. He also turned down offers from Turton that included patronage of the Monday Club, membership of the Conservative anti-Market committee and, later, presidency of the Commonwealth Industries Association.[192]

Eden's initial musings were therefore rendered not in Parliament or press but before a June 1961 rally of the Yorkshire Area Young Conservatives. In anticipation of the application, he offered a statement of conditions rather than opposition, a reminder of the nation's outstanding obligations to EFTA, farmers and, like Attlee, to the Commonwealth in particular. With a nod to freer trade imperatives, he nonetheless warned against any 'association' that failed the ongoing interests and bequest of the 'British Commonwealth'. He defended 'those who have stood

---

[186] Beaverbrook to A. Eden, 15 May 1961, AP 23/8/40A; Salisbury to A. Eden, 11 August 1961, AP 23/60/67; A. Eden to Salisbury, 26 July 1961, AP 23/60/64.
[187] Dutton, 'Anticipating Maastricht', p. 530.
[188] Speech at Columbia University, excerpted in A. Eden, *Full Circle* (London, 1960), p. 36.
[189] A. Eden to Beaverbrook, 13 April 1964, AP 23/8/88; A. Eden to Macmillan, 8 April 1969, AP 23/49/96. Boothby's criticism roused Eden to reply during the 2 August 1962 Lords debate. *Parliamentary Debates*, Lords, 5th Series, vol. 243, 2 August 1962, cols 437–43. For an assessment of Eden's reputation on European issues, see Chapter 10 in D. Dutton, *Anthony Eden: A Life and Reputation* (London, 1977), especially pp. 279–81, 310–13.
[190] *Parliamentary Debates*, Lords, 5th Series, vol. 243, 2 August 1962, cols 444–5.
[191] A. Eden to Beaverbrook, 20 April 1961, AP 23/8/36A.
[192] Correspondence between A. Eden and R. Turton, 29 March 1962, AP 23/64/6; 22 November 1962, AP 23/64/14A; 6 and 27 May 1964, AP 23/64/20 and 20D.

by us in good times and bad, with a loyalty beyond compare in the history of the world. These nations practise the reality of parliamentary self-government which we are proud to think is Britain's legacy to mankind.'[193] One year later, before another Young Conservative gathering, he added federalism to the mix, linking it to the plight of the Dominions, in whose interests 'we are unlikely to be able to accept federation, at least in the near future'.[194]

In the months between those speeches, Eden was under increasing pressure to adopt a more public posture. Lord Salisbury urged him to do so on the grounds that 'warnings in private are, I'm afraid, no use with Harold. It is only publicity he is afraid of.'[195] Amidst the silence, Eden maintained a steady correspondence with Commonwealth defenders and anti-Marketeers. Beaverbrook, though kept at arm's length, could still be relied upon for sympathetic interpretations of Suez and favourable book reviews.[196] Peter Walker, an acquaintance from Young Conservative circles, forwarded a copy of *A Call to the Commonwealth* in June 1962.[197] That same month Eden thanked Australian Prime Minister Bob Menzies for reminding both 'our negotiators' and 'foreigners' of the relevance and misunderstood significance of the Commonwealth relationship.[198] Turton, particularly in the second half of 1962, sent frequent updates of anti-Market affairs among MPs. Eden reiterated his position in those letters, telling Turton 'I do not think it is right for this country to federate with France, Germany and Italy as the political outlook is today'.[199] He also posted copies of his Young Conservative speeches to Arthur Bryant, along with a letter emphasising Dominion interests and the ultimate goal of Atlantic federation. The ambitions of the Six, he repeated, 'should be federation' but British participation in that project would forever alter 'the character of our relationship with the Commonwealth'.[200]

Eden's preferred role outside the spotlight produced its potentially dramatic moment in a 29 July 1962 meeting with de Gaulle. Their forty-minute discussion, recorded in notes rather than full transcript, ranged over a variety of topics, including the predicament of wheat, meat and

---

[193] A. Eden, speech to Yorkshire Area Young Conservatives, 10 June 1961, copy in AB Papers H/4.

[194] A. Eden speech to Midlands Area Young Conservatives, 21 July 1962, copy in AB Papers H/4.

[195] Salisbury to A. Eden, 29 November 1961, AP 23/60/84B.

[196] See correspondence in AP 23/8/1–29. Eden was grateful when his book was given a positive review by Oliver Lyttleton, Lord Chandos, in the Beaverbrook press. A. Eden to Beaverbrook, 22 November 1962, AP 23/8/63A.

[197] P. Walker to A. Eden, 29 June 1962, AP 23/65/16. Eden had become President of the Young Conservatives in 1959.

[198] A. Eden to R. Menzies, 9 June 1962, AP 23/51/23A.

[199] A. Eden to R. Turton, 22 October 1962, AP 23/64/11A.

[200] A. Eden to A. Bryant, 21 August 1962, AB Papers H/4.

dairy products from Australia and New Zealand. De Gaulle was moved only far enough to ask what Britain would do if the Common Market negotiations failed. Eden replied that 'we would have to go on as we were'. De Gaulle, perhaps rhetorically, then asked 'That would not be too bad would it?'[201] Private attempts to influence Macmillan were in vain, as Salisbury had warned. In July 1961, Eden complained of difficulties in getting information from the Prime Minister about the Government's 'fateful' position, this despite the fact that they had met two months earlier to discuss policy after another of Eden's visits to de Gaulle.[202] On 4 October 1962, Lord Chandos and Lord Boyd of Merton were deputised to carry anxieties about federalism to Downing Street. But, to Eden's surprise, they returned with their fears allayed.[203] Six days later Eden met Macmillan for lunch, but in the diary entry that followed the Prime Minister summarily dismissed Eden's world-view as outdated.[204]

Eden's remaining option, then, was a Lords speech, and this was delivered on 8 November. Appropriately enough he preceded Attlee, who called the statements 'remarkable'.[205] In establishing a Commonwealth–federalism threat matrix, in raising the case of underdeveloped nations and in hailing parliamentary democracy as 'our donation to what we may like to call Western Civilisation', Eden was on common ground with his Labour counterpart. Yet while this was his strongest address, Eden's presentation was not so much the case against entry as the case against entry at any cost. Implicit in this was a belief that the terms might be too high and he begged for 'clarity' in the Government's assessment of the political and economic consequences. 'Salvation', he warned, 'will not be found in concessions to placate others, if we know in our hearts these are not fair to the Commonwealth, to our EFTA friends and to ourselves'.[206]

Health was also an issue for Winston Churchill, who, aged eighty-seven, was neither physically nor philosophically inclined to take sides in the debate. True, Churchill was an imperial icon and friend of Beaverbrook, a relationship Ernest Bevin likened to the 'man who's married a whore; he knows she's a whore but he loves her just the same'.[207] But

---

[201] Notes on a meeting between Lord Avon and General de Gaulle, 29 July 1962, A. Eden undated memo to Foreign Office, AP 23/24/9.

[202] Eden to Salisbury, 21 July 1961, AP 23/60/63. Macmillan and Eden had met to discuss the French on 30 May following Eden's visit with de Gaulle. H. Macmillan to A. Eden, 2 June 1961, AP 23/48/33A.

[203] Dutton, 'Anticipating Maastricht', pp. 534–5.

[204] HMD, 10 October 1962, MS Macmillan dep. d. 47.

[205] *Parliamentary Debates*, Lords, 5th Series, vol. 244, 8 November 1962, col. 425.

[206] *Ibid.*, cols 421–2, 425.

[207] Chester and Fenby, *The Fall of the House of Beaverbrook*, p. 24. For a brief summary of their relationship during this period see K. Young, *Churchill and Beaverbrook: A Study in Friendship and Politics* (London, 1966), pp. 320–6.

there is no evidence to suggest that Beaverbrook tried to lure Churchill into the fray. In fact, Churchill had perched himself atop the fence in an August 1961 letter to his constituency chair at Woodford. Though an advocate of Continental unity, he thought the terms of entry paramount, given Britain's EFTA and Commonwealth obligations, and he supported the application insofar as it was the only 'way by which we can find out exactly whether the conditions of membership are acceptable'.[208]

Ambiguities intrinsic to Churchill's 'with but not of' sentiments on Europe offered succour to the ambitions of Common Market advocates and opponents alike. Macmillan thought the application an opportunity to 'crown' Churchill's 'work as founder of the European Movement'.[209] On the other hand, indiscreet remarks by Lord Montgomery of Alamein appeared to place Churchill in the sceptical camp. On 15 August 1962, Montgomery created a minor press sensation by revealing that the hospitalised Churchill had responded 'no' when asked if he favoured the Common Market. But the disclosure, as Eden remarked, 'made a muddle of things'[210] and generated an instant backlash. Churchill was reportedly outraged[211] and Montgomery begged forgiveness in letters of apology.[212] To fellow travellers, however, he maintained that he had merely repeated Churchill's answer. 'One day', he wrote to Arthur Bryant:

> I will tell you the inside story of all the excitement about my talk with Winston. I would prefer not to write it. The Governmental and party machine went into action very quickly and put him back on the fence!! The old man is not allowed to say what he thinks: publicly.[213]

Ironically, Montgomery had been enlisted as one of Beaverbrook's anti-Market celebrity contributors since June,[214] even though the *Express* had targeted him for a similar gaffe in March 1962. On that occasion Montgomery leaked details of Suez-related comments made by Eden. John Gordon's opinion column recorded the incident as 'one more proof

---

[208] W. Churchill to D. Moss, 14 August 1961, in PRO, PREM 11/3785. Reprinted in *The Times* and *Daily Express*, 15 August 1962.

[209] HMD, 5 August 1961, quoted in Macmillan, *End of the Day*, p. 24.

[210] A. Eden to Beaverbrook, 17 August 1962, AP 23/8/59A.

[211] M. Gilbert, *Winston S. Churchill: Vol. 3, Never Despair, 1945–65* (Boston, 1988), p. 1337.

[212] Montgomery to W. S. Churchill and Lady Churchill, 24 August 1962, Department of Documents, Imperial War Museum, London, Papers of Field Marshal Viscount Montgomery of Alamein (hereafter cited as Montgomery Papers), Ancillary Collections, Letters to Lady Clementine Churchill, No. 27.

[213] Montgomery to A. Bryant, 19 August 1962, Montgomery Papers, Ancillary Collections 8, Sir A. Bryant 2. See also Montgomery to Beaverbrook, 16 August 1962, BBK/C248.

[214] Montgomery to A. Bryant, 1 June 1962, Montgomery Papers, Ancillary Collections 8, Sir A. Bryant 2.

that Monty has become not merely a garrulous old man, but a menace to those that trusted him'.[215] Like Attlee, therefore, 'Meddlesome Monty'[216] was another unlikely ally in the *Express* corps of strange bedfellows.

Whatever doubts surrounded his powers of discretion, Monty's commitment to the pro-Commonwealth, anti-Market cause was unquestioned. Attlee reviewed his book *Three Continents* for the *Sunday Express*[217] and even A. J. P. Taylor confessed to some shared 'political views'.[218] In Montgomery's correspondence with Arthur Bryant there were mutual opinions, praise and copies of speeches and articles. He took particular interest in Bryant's work on the plan for a Common Market alternative and personally forwarded a signed copy of *A Choice for Destiny* to de Gaulle in November 1962. Both men subsequently received handwritten replies from the General.[219]

In addition, there was much common ground with the *Express* representation of Britain and the wider world. Like Beaverbrook, Montgomery was a Protestant outsider, a self-described 'Irishman of Scottish descent' who belonged to a geographically transcendent 'England'. In a 1963 speech he defined the nation:

> Fear God, honour the Queen. It means family life, good comradeship, a square deal for everybody, laws based on moral code, freedom from oppression and restrictions, and the absolute right of the individual within the law to live his own life and go his own way.[220]

Commonwealth attitudes overlapped as well. 'I call it Empire', he told Edward R. Murrow, 'I'm old fashioned you see'.[221] He played heavily on racial themes. His 1962 book *Three Continents* proposed a Commonwealth destiny that required unity among people alternately referred to as the 'Anglo-Saxons', 'the conquering race', 'blood brothers' and the 'white English speaking group'. There was also a shared conspiratorial tone in the suggestion that American support for British entry obscured its desire to absorb Canada.[222]

---

[215] *Sunday Express*, 1 April 1962. See also, *Daily Express*, 30 March 1962, which labelled him an untrustworthy 'nuisance'.

[216] *Daily Express*, 27 December 1961.

[217] *Sunday Express*, 14 October 1962.

[218] A. J. P. Taylor to Beaverbrook, 10 October 1961, BBK C/305.

[219] Montgomery to A. Bryant, 3 November 12 and 18 December 1962, Montgomery Papers, Ancillary Collections 8, Sir Arthur Bryant 2.

[220] Montgomery, speech to Alamein Reunion, 25 October 1963, copy in letter to A. Bryant, 27 October 1963, Montgomery Papers, Ancillary Collections 8, Sir A. Bryant 2.

[221] Transcript of filmed conversation between Montgomery and Edward R. Murrow, 5 January 1961, Montgomery Papers, Deposit 29.

[222] Viscount Montgomery of Alamein, *Three Continents* (London, 1962), pp. 254–6.

His relative symmetry with the *Express* view on Europe was high-lighted by the fact that the editors made but minor revisions to his draft articles.[223] His first Common Market piece appeared in the *Sunday Express* opinion page under the title 'I Say We Must Not Join Europe'.[224] His argument posited that Britain should maintain its independence on strategic and military grounds, with the Commonwealth serving as a guarantor of international stability. But his case was carried by language dripping in 'blood and belonging' motifs. He cited 'intense nationalism' as the factor undermining European unity and added 'We British are a great people.... Let us continue to rely upon our own strength and judgement. Let the Mother of Nations gather her children about her in obedience to the call of common kindred.' Those sentiments only hinted at the detailed evocation of motherhood to come in a second article, 'My Plea to the Women of Britain'. In a hearth-and-home vein, Montgomery explored kinship and contrasted the Queen as Commonwealth matri-arch against the dysfunctional family of Europe. On the topic of entry as a betrayal of blood sacrifice he wrote:

> Your men whose bodies lie buried in *some corner of a foreign field that is forever England* cry out against such a monstrous and infamous act. Do not forget that they gave their all for Britain and the British peoples.... Rise up and demand that you be consulted before our leaders chuck the Commonwealth overboard.... Thus will the Government be prevented from breaking up the Commonwealth and the expansion of the British race – upon which rests the best hope for the future of the free world.[225]

Beaverbrook called it a 'splendid production' and took extra satisfaction from its appearance as a topic of discussion in the *Daily Mail*'s leader column.[226]

The most important dissent among peers, then, was from those, like Beaverbrook, who rarely entered the Lords or others, like Attlee, Montgomery and Hinchingbrooke, who registered their opinions outside its chamber. Others waited in the wings, adding occasional speeches but little direct activism. Lord Alexander of Hillsborough, leader of the Labour peers since 1955, offered reasoned statements on Europe. But behind these lurked paranoid Protestant visions of a Britain subservient to the Vatican and European Catholics.[227] For an ageing Tory fringe, alienated by the trends of contemporary Conservatism,

---

[223] For draft copies see Montgomery Papers, 'Common Market 1962, Manuscripts of articles for the *Sunday Express*'.

[224] Montgomery, 'I Say We Must Not Join Europe', *Sunday Express*, 3 June 1962.

[225] Montgomery, 'My Plea to the Women of Britain', *Sunday Express*, 1 July 1962.

[226] Beaverbrook to Montgomery, 2 July 1962, BBK C/248.

[227] Alexander to Beaverbrook, 3 May 1963, and other relevant correspondence in BBK C/2.

Europe was one point in an accumulated catalogue of frustrations. Lord Salisbury's letters betrayed a lingering anger over Suez and disaffection with colonial policy, the pay pause and Macmillan's leadership.[228] Lord Lambton also disliked Macmillan and, though a contributor to both the *Express* and *Evening Standard*, his pieces were often rejected on the grounds that their vitriol would offend Conservative readers.[229] Charles Wintour, the *Standard*'s editor, even feared Lambton could become 'an embarrassment' at election time.[230] Likewise, Lord Balfour of Inchyre, who referred to Lord Gladwyn as the 'Member for Versailles', also railed at his party's suicidal desire to 'placate the theorists and the money changers'.[231] But Macmillan appeared more resigned to than troubled by the intractable opposition of a group whose plots he associated with Rhodesia and colonial policy rather than the Common Market.[232]

By-elections

Anti-Market forces played a relatively minor role in the Macmillan Government's poor by-election results. While that was indicative of the marginal position occupied by opponents of entry, it was equally representative of the reluctance of major parties to engage the Common Market as a partisan issue. Unresolved negotiations, Labour's 'wait and see' stance and the allegiance of Conservative MPs to their party line shaped domestic Common Market politics. What is more, the greatest beneficiary of voter dissatisfaction was a Liberal Party wedded to an unambiguous pro-entry agenda.

But it was also the case that, as one member of the 1922 Committee noted of Orpington, 'people voted Liberal for odd reasons, even those against the Common Market and against any immigration. It could not be said that this was a vote for the Liberals; it was a vote against us.' At the same meeting two back-bench MPs mentioned the Common Market factor and though Iain Macleod thought the pay pause a most important factor, he too conceded that it was 'difficult to sell our policies as long

---

[228] For Salisbury's views on the Common Market and other topics see Salisbury to A. Bryant, 19 September 1962, AB Papers H/4; correspondence with A. Eden in AP 23/60 and Welensky in MSS Welensky, 665/1–5.

[229] Beaverbrook to Lambton, 3 July and 17 August 1962, BBK C/200; C. Wintour to Beaverbrook, 4 July 1962, BBK H/268. For more on Lambton's views see correspondence in AP 23/43; his article 'Mac's Vital Need: 40 Labour Rebels', *Evening Standard*, 18 September 1962; and interview with Susan Barnes in *Sunday Express*, 7 October 1962.

[230] C. Wintour to Beaverbrook, 20 December 1962, BBK H/268.

[231] Balfour to Beaverbrook, undated but June 1961, BBK C/22. See also his article 'This Common Market Double Talk', *Daily Express*, 8 March 1962.

[232] HMD, 25 February, 24 March, 4 May, 21 June, 9 September, 18 December 1961, 17 February, 24 March 1962, 17 February 1963, MS Macmillan dep. d. 41–2, 43, 45, 48.

as there was a lack of finality about the Common Market decision'.[233] After Labour's Brighton conference, moreover, Europe became an increasingly contentious political topic. A BBC report on the campaign in Northamptonshire, for instance, described the Common Market as 'the great issue' in an election nearly won by the anti-Market Labour candidate Ivan Wilde.[234]

Anti-Market politics typically fell to independent activists rather than party mavericks. In addition to John Dayton's bid at Oswestry (Chapter 4), there were also the candidacies of A. Taylor at Lincoln, R. Gregory at Derbyshire West and K. Coleman at Norfolk Central that drew 1.1, 4.1 and 2.6 per cent of the vote, respectively.[235] Others such as John Lee at Reading, Peter Bessell at Bodmin[236] and John Paul at Bexley were developing anti-Market challenges that featured in the 1964 elections.

The one notable success for the opponents of entry occurred at South Dorset,[237] where a convergence of anti-Marketeers and idiosyncratic local politics unseated the Conservatives for the first time since 1906. South Dorset entered the November by-election framework following Hinchingbrooke's elevation to the Earldom of Sandwich in June 1962. In response, the Conservatives put forward Angus Maude, who in many regards was an ideal candidate. His credentials included service as an army officer and a prisoner of war in North Africa, Deputy Director of Political and Economic Planning and Director of the Conservative Political Centre from 1951 to 1955. He was MP for Ealing South from 1950 to 1958. Thereafter, journalistic interests carried him to chief editorship of the *Sydney Morning Herald*. The fact that Maude had been a Suez rebel appealed to the *Sunday Express*, which endorsed him as 'fair compensation' for the loss of Hinchingbrooke.[238] But Beaverbrook was less enthusiastic. He had opposed Charles Wintour's bid to hire Maude

---

[233] Notes from Iain Macleod's visit to the 1922 Committee, 22 March 1962, pp. 3–4, 6–7, R. A. Butler Papers, H/96.

[234] *Gallery* programme, 22 November 1962, BBC WAC, Film 13/14. Wilde received 14,004 votes (38.6 per cent) but lost to the Conservative, A. A. Jones, who tallied 14,921 votes (41.2 per cent). Craig, *British Parliamentary Election Results*.

[235] Lincoln, Derbyshire West and Norfolk Central by-elections cited by Lieber, *British Politics*, p. 213. Candidates and statistics from Craig, *British Parliamentary Election Results*.

[236] Lee requested support from Beaverbrook and duly received coverage in the *Sunday Express* 'Crossbencher' column on 1 July 1962. Bessell, a Liberal, was the subject of the article 'A Liberal Speaks for Empire Family', *Sunday Express*, 16 September 1962. Bessell won at Bodmin in 1964 and again in 1966. For an anecdotal account of Beaverbrook's support for Bessell see A. Watkins, 'Lapsed Calvinist', in L. Gourlay (ed.), *The Beaverbrook I Knew* (London, 1984), pp. 237–8.

[237] For a detailed consideration of the issues, candidates and outcomes see Crowson, 'Lord Hinchingbrooke', pp. 43–64.

[238] 'Crossbencher' suggested that a Maude victory 'could help restore the Government's prestige'. *Sunday Express*, 22 July 1962.

in January 1962, on the grounds that he 'just wants to make an easy living off the *Evening Standard*'. Moreover, when Wintour suggested that Butler and Macleod were providing South Dorset as a safe seat, Beaverbrook retorted 'nobody gets an offer of a safe seat unless he is absolutely front rank in Parliament and Maude was never that'.[239]

Maude and his advisors prepared for a conventional contest, with plans to contrast Conservatism against an outdated and divided Labour Party and a 'radical' and 'ineffective' Liberalism. 'It will not be a defensive campaign', they promised.[240] His policy statement accentuated the virtues of prosperity and good government. On the Common Market he pledged 'I promise not to support entry unless I am satisfied that the terms we are offered are on balance to our advantage'.[241] A preliminary report from the local Central Office Agent described the constituency as a 'somewhat sleepy part of the world', with few local issues, and predicted that, with sufficient effort, the Conservatives could 'just hang on'.[242]

The entry of Sir Piers Debenham as an independent anti-Market candidate in October 1962 changed the complexion of the campaign. Debenham's credentials paled in comparison to those of Maude, but he was well known locally by virtue of participation in Dorset's Conservative politics and government throughout the 1950s.[243] Of greater importance, however, were the activities of Hinchingbrooke, whose preferences quickly became clear. When asked to provide a supporting statement for Maude's campaign leaflet, Hinchingbrooke described him as a 'good chap' but told voters that the Common Market issue might force them to cast their votes for a different candidate.[244]

Hinchingbrooke's subsequent endorsement of Debenham infuriated local Conservatives[245] while attracting the support of the anti-Market

---

[239] Soundscriber messages from Beaverbrook to C. Wintour, 15 January 1962, BBK H/268.

[240] Minutes of a meeting to discuss Maude's election strategy, 26 September 1962, CPA, CCO 500/18/62.

[241] Campaign leaflets, 'Introducing Angus Maude, Conservative' and 'Policy Statement', CPA, CCO 500/18/62.

[242] P. R. G. Horton to COO, 25 June 1962, CPA, CCO 500/18/62.

[243] In addition to his farming interests, Debenham had worked at the Economic Advisory Council in 1930 and the Economic Section of the Cabinet Office until 1941. He was in the army but saw no active service during the war. He was a member of the Control Commission for Germany in 1944 and attended the Hague conference of the European Movement in 1948. He unsuccessfully ran for election at Sparkbrook in 1950 as a Unionist candidate. In the 1950s he was an active member of the Wareham and Purbeck District Council and Dorset County Council. 'Piers Debenham' campaign leaflet, 31 October 1962, CPA, CCO 500/18/62.

[244] S. A. Walker to General Director, 23 October 1962, CPA, CCO 500/18/62.

[245] See statement issued by Wessex Area Conservative Council condemning both Debenham and Hinchingbrooke. General Director to COO, 2 November 1962, CPA, CCO 500/18/62.

movement and its attendant patriotism. Arthur Bryant provided Debenham with an election message that called Common Market entry a 'betrayal' of the Commonwealth, EFTA, farmers and democracy.[246] ACML volunteers campaigned on Debenham's behalf.[247] The *Express* leapt aboard with tributes to 'bold Sir Piers', a knight crusading on behalf of British principles.[248] Debenham obliged his supporters and defined his populist cause as a fight 'to preserve our way of life'.[249] His campaign literature exposed the Treaty of Rome as a comprehensive threat to 'our system of Government', world peace, the Commonwealth and British standards of living.[250]

Faced with betrayal from Hinchingbrooke, splits among local Conservatives, an anti-Market onslaught and the attentions of the national press, Maude's cautious approach yielded to frustration. Hinchingbrooke's treachery, he complained, was a transgression of friendship and good 'manners'.[251] In speeches Maude called Debenham a 'megalomaniac moron', a 'slightly scatty stooge' and 'the Ham in the Sandwich'. A Hinchingbrooke–Debenham alliance, he alleged, intended to surrender the constituency to Labour on behalf of Beaverbrookian principles.[252]

Maude and the local party agent willingly ceded the 'lunatic right wing fringe' to Debenham. But they were 'nervous' about the efforts of the *Express* and the ACML and the resonance of their 'dear food' cry among 'ordinary Conservative housewives'.[253] Reports to Central Office spoke of personalities overtaking election issues and organisational problems but nonetheless predicted victory for Maude.[254] Harold Macmillan was less optimistic, however, and two weeks before the election feared the seat would be lost.[255] In the end Debenham's intervention proved decisive. He polled 12.3 per cent, or 5,057 votes, leaving Maude with 13,079 and Labour candidate Guy Barnet victorious with 13,778.

---

[246] A. Bryant to P. Debenham, 9 November 1962, AB Papers H/4.
[247] ACML bulletin, undated, AB Papers H4. J. Paul to Beaverbrook, 9 November 1962, BBK C/269.
[248] See 'The Bold Sir Piers Stirs Things Up In Dorset', *Sunday Express*, 11 November 1962; 'Sir Piers Puts Tories In a Tizzy', *Daily Express*, 17 November 1962; 'Sir Piers Goes Shopping to Woo the Voters' and 'Their Big Chance', *Sunday Express*, 18 November 1962.
[249] *Sunday Express*, 11 November 1962.
[250] Sir Piers Debenham, campaign leaflet, 31 October 1962, in CPA, CCO 500/18/62.
[251] *Sunday Express*, 11 November 1962.
[252] A. Maude quoted in the *Dorset Evening Echo*, 13 November 1962, and *Daily Express*, 17 November 1962. See also *Gallery* programme, 22 November 1962, BBC WAC, Film 13/14.
[253] P. R. G. Horton, Report No. 2, 5 November 1962, CPA, CCO 500/18/62.
[254] P. R. G. Horton to COO, 5, 9, 17 November 1962, CPA, CCO 500/18/62.
[255] HMD, 7 November 1962. See also 25 November 1962 for Macmillan's reaction to the result. MS Macmillan dep. d. 47.

As much of the press and the Conservative post-mortem rightly noted, the circumstances and personalities of the South Dorset contest were unlikely to be replicated elsewhere.[256] Nonetheless, the anti-Marketeers were jubilant. *Express* headlines proclaimed the by-election results a '"Little Election" Shock' and 'Black Day for Mac', with South Dorset representing a warning shot at Tory Common Market policy.[257] Maude's subsequent bitterness reinforced their claims. He blamed the Beaverbrook newspapers for frightening voters with 'imaginary fears'.[258] The 'clever' and 'unscrupulous' forces, he wrote in the *Spectator*, had provided a 'textbook illustration' of how anti-Market politics could succeed under the right conditions.[259]

As Nick Crowson has convincingly demonstrated, the South Dorset election result was largely determined by local circumstances and a badly orchestrated Conservative campaign,[260] but two important points must be made with regard to the wider national context. First, though the Hinchingbrooke factor was pre-eminent, Debenham had successfully turned the election into a single-issue contest over the Common Market. In exorcising banal or 'imaginary fears' and by standing as an independent candidate, Debenham and his supporters provided a focus for the sort of protest votes that had gone to the Liberals at other by-elections. Second, despite Maude's complaints, Debenham's result was achieved without the fully co-ordinated engagement of the anti-Market movement. R. H. Turton chose not speak out at South Dorset, for fear of its effect on party unity.[261] Peter Walker actively supported Maude's campaign, a decision that infuriated Beaverbrook and effectively ended their relationship.[262] The ACML, John Paul reckoned, could have magnified the results if Debenham had requested their support two weeks earlier. Beaverbrook likewise claimed he could have provided a dozen canvassers as well as a motor car with loudspeakers if only Debenham had asked.[263] In other words, Debenham's tally could have been higher had he entered the race earlier and made use of additional support.

---

[256] By-election final report, P. R. G. Horton to COO, 30 November 1962, CPA, CCO 500/18/62; *Gallery* programme, 22 and 29 November 1962, BBC WAC, Film 13/14.

[257] The *Express* was also referring to the declines in Conservative support at Norfolk Central, South Northants, Chippenham and Woodside. *Daily Express*, 23 and 24 November 1962.

[258] A. Maude quoted in the *Daily Express*, 23 November 1962.

[259] A. Maude, 'Over to the Offensive', *Spectator*, 7 December 1962, p. 889.

[260] Crowson, 'Lord Hinchingbrooke', pp. 56–8.

[261] R. Turton to A. Eden, 20 November 1962, AP 23/64/14.

[262] See 'Crossbencher', *Sunday Express*, 11 November 1962; Walker, *Staying Power*, p. 33; interview with Peter Walker, 23 February 1998.

[263] Correspondence between Beaverbrook and J. Paul, 24 and 28 November 1962, BBK C/269.

Politics of propaganda:
government publicity and the anti-Marketeers

Avoiding the issues

According to the enduring allegation levelled by Eurosceptics, the Macmillan Government and its successors deceived the British public in their pursuit and presentation of pro-European policy.[264] It was a common refrain among anti-Marketeers. Turton, for instance, accused the Government of evading the sovereignty topic. 'Never in the course of history', he told an ACML audience, 'has so little been known by so many about so much'.[265] Irrespective of those charges, there was a direct correlation between the Government's fear of an adverse domestic reaction and the public face of its European policy. Indeed, Macmillan's belief that the application represented a 'momentous decision' and a 'historic' moment[266] contrasted with a muted advocacy of entry and a studious avoidance of controversial details.[267]

Government reticence was compounded by a variety of extenuating circumstances. From the start, Macmillan believed the odds were stacked against reaching agreement in Brussels.[268] That, combined with the identification of de Gaulle as the primary barrier to entry, diminished the incentive to sell domestic political opinion on an unpredictable foreign policy. In any event, the contingency of the application and the complex negotiating points impeded the presentation of the issues. As Frederick Bishop noted in June 1961, tabulation and official publication of cost–benefit analyses were impossible given the unknown consequences awaiting British agriculture and Commonwealth trade.[269] A year later the Conservative Research Department contended that it was unable to compute a 'simple balance sheet' on Commonwealth safeguards. It would be a difficult proposition even if the terms were available, the memo complained, and 'at this stage it would be more likely to cause harm rather than help the Government's case'.[270]

British negotiators, it should be noted, distinguished between the Commonwealth as a source of diplomatic wrangling and as a topic

---

[264] See for example Shore, *Separate Ways*, pp. 4–28.

[265] R. Turton, quoted in the *Daily Express*, 28 November 1961. See also Lord Lambton, letter to *The Times*, 2 October 1962.

[266] HMD, 22 July and 9 August 1961, MS Macmillan dep. d. 42, 43; Macmillan, *At the End of the Day*, p. 16.

[267] For a critical assessment of the Government's diplomatic and domestic approach see N. Piers Ludlow, 'A Mismanaged Application: Britain and the EEC, 1961–63', in A. Deighton and A. Milward (eds), *Widening, Deepening and Acceleration: The European Economic Community, 1957–63* (Baden-Baden, 1999), pp. 271–85.

[268] Macmillan, *At the End of the Day*, p. 17.

[269] F. Bishop to H. Macmillan, 27 June 1961, PRO, PREM 11/3563.

[270] Conservative Research Department, memo, 2 May 1962, CPA, CRD 2/43/1.

of domestic resonance. On the eve of the negotiations Macmillan predicted Commonwealth needs would provide the most contentious debating points in Brussels.[271] Rightly or wrongly, however, the Common Market Negotiations Committee believed that the pledges to safeguard the Commonwealth's 'essential' interests had drawn the domestic sting. 'This seems to have satisfied public opinion here', the Committee minutes noted, 'and the really difficult question for decision will not arise until it appears (if it does) that such safeguards are not obtainable from the Six'.[272]

Unresolved negotiations were routinely cited as the barrier to what Conservative MP Peter Kirk described as a 'full blooded' pro-entry campaign.[273] But the frequency with which that complaint featured in Cabinet during the second half of 1962[274] suggests that it may have also provided cover for an increasingly troubled policy. It was on those grounds, for instance, that the Cabinet initially resisted publication of a White Paper in August 1962 on the state of negotiations.[275] In fact, only three days before de Gaulle's veto, Macmillan was still awaiting a final agreement before unleashing 'a great pro-European propaganda'.[276]

The underlying basis for Government unease, however, was its fear of volatile domestic opinion. From the beginning, ministers dreaded the possibility that the public might react negatively or prove malleable to emotive arguments. In May 1961 the Cabinet derived some consolation from evolving support for entry among industrialists and 'informed' opinion. But memories of the 'emotional reactions' that accompanied decolonisation led the warning that 'a great weight of sentiment could easily be aroused' if Common Market entry appeared to betray the Commonwealth or British agriculture.[277] At its 20 April 1961 meeting the Cabinet conceded that:

> Political association with the Six might ultimately involve a significant surrender of national sovereignty.... A major effort of presentation would

---

[271] H. Macmillan to E. Heath, 14 September 1961, PRO, PREM 11/3560.

[272] Minutes of the Common Market Negotiations Committee, 26 September 1961, PRO, PREM 11/3560.

[273] *Gallery* programme, 2 August 1962, BBC WAC, Film 13/14.

[274] See for example PRO, CAB 128/36 Part II CC 44, 56, 57, 61(62), 5 July, 13 September, 20 September and 23 October 1962.

[275] Government ministers were urged to refrain from making any promises of a White Paper. There appears to have been a preference instead for issuing a series of progress reports on the developing negotiations. See PRO, CAB 128/36 Part II CC 51(62), 31 July 1962. In any event, a White Paper entitled *The United Kingdom and the European Communities*, Cmnd 1882, was eventually published in November 1962.

[276] HMD, 11 January 1963, MS Macmillan dep. d. 48. Quoted in Macmillan, *At the End of the Day*, p. 364.

[277] PRO, CAB 128/35 Part I CC 24(61), 4 May 1961.

be needed to persuade the British public to accept the encroachments on national sovereignty.[278]

That awareness, however, precluded rather than encouraged Government propagandising in favour of its policy, especially in the twelve months following Macmillan's announcement.

The nub of the Government's public relations dilemma was a perception that its approach to the Treaty of Rome required tailoring to suit the diametrically opposed interests of diplomatic and domestic audiences. Initial uncertainty surrounded the question of how much public or private enthusiasm Britain ought to display. Heath, for instance, advised against making any suggestion that Britain would sign the Rome Treaty without first negotiating terms. 'Such a declaration', he told the Cabinet, 'would involve us in political difficulties in this country; it would also leave us less room for manoeuvre in the negotiation'.[279] But in Freddie Bishop's estimation, the negotiations required a spirit of 'maximum goodwill' and he counselled against treating submission to each of the Treaty's tenets as British concessions. 'In applying to join a club', he wrote to Macmillan, 'you cannot expect a reduction in the entrance fee because you are prepared to accept some of the rules'.[280]

The Government thus walked a public relations tightrope between the poles of European expectation and domestic opinion, while shouldering the needs of Commonwealth and British agriculture. As a result, calculated caution accompanied its expressions of intent. Heath's speech to the WEU, coinciding as it did with Macmillan's announcement in the Commons, was carefully constructed to 'show reasonable enthusiasm toward the Europeans' without 'giving hostages to fortune' in the Commons.[281] Likewise, Cabinet support had been secured not for a bold entry policy but rather 'for the purpose of enabling negotiations to take place with a view to ascertaining' whether entry could accommodate the 'special needs' of Britain, the Commonwealth and EFTA.[282]

Government apprehensions were also evident in the reluctance to publish official assessments of the prospects for or consequences of British entry. As Leader of the Lords, and facing a rising tide of Common Market questions from the upper house, Hailsham suggested the release of a White Paper or brief from Conservative Central Office.[283] But Macmillan, according to his private secretary Philip de Zulueta, feared that such a document could only present:

---

[278] PRO, CAB 128/35 Part I CC 22(61), 20 April 1961.
[279] E. Heath quoted in PRO, CAB 128/35 Part I CC 24(61), 4 May 1961.
[280] F. Bishop to Macmillan, 5 September 1961, PRO, PREM 11/3560.
[281] Correspondence between E. Heath and H. Macmillan, 29 July 1961, PRO, PREM 11/3559.
[282] CAB 128/35 Part II CC 44(61), 27 July 1961.
[283] Hailsham to H. Macmillan, 14 June 1961, PRO, PREM 11/3563.

the positive aspects of the Treaty of Rome, all of which would be more or less unpopular. It would not be possible to explain our view that in fact many of the paper provisions will prove to be less onerous in practice than they are in theory. Nor could we frankly argue the case in favour of our joining. So the Prime Minister will try to resist publishing anything.[284]

In the meantime, the Foreign Office compiled a confidential thirty-four-page draft that was shelved following review by the Prime Minister and a 10 July consultation with the Cabinet. It was decided instead that copies of the Treaty of Rome would be 'made available' to MPs.[285]

The Government side-stepped demands for a White Paper in July only to confront the issue again three months later. On 10 October Heath opened Britain's application negotiations with a formal presentation to ministers of the Six in Paris. The full statement, crafted by Whitehall and approved by the Cabinet but withheld from Commonwealth governments, balanced Britain's need for 'satisfactory arrangements' with an acceptance of the Treaty's 'aims and objectives'.[286] According to Macmillan's diary, there was agreement that details of the speech would be treated as confidential.[287] The following month, however, the text was leaked to the Americans. The *Express* pounced on the disclosure as evidence of the Government's contempt for Commonwealth brotherhood, a betrayal of 'kith and kin' in favour of 'foreigners'.[288] This in turn occasioned a flurry of activity at the Foreign Office, with Heath and others drafting a press release that smothered the story in most corners of Fleet Street.[289] Though it was held to be a minor affair even at the time, there were consequences. For one thing, the press reaction forced the Government to publish Heath's statement as a White Paper.[290] Among conspiracy theorists, moreover, the incident appeared to validate anti-Marketeer claims of Government duplicity and Commonwealth sell-out. Most importantly, Macmillan took the leak as evidence of a French plot to undermine Britain's application by fomenting discontent within the Commonwealth and British public opinion.[291]

The Cabinet's taciturn approach in turn circumscribed the capacity of Conservative Central Office to provide Common Market publicity. Early

---

[284] P. de Zulueta to F. Bishop, 15 June 1961, PRO, PREM 11/3563.

[285] P. de Zulueta to M. Fraser, 11 July 1961, PRO, PREM 11/3563.

[286] PRO, CAB 128/35 Part II CC 53(61), 5 October 1961.

[287] HMD, 24 November 1961, MS Macmillan dep. d. 44.

[288] 'The Empire Is Placed Last', *Daily Express*, 25 November 1961.

[289] Evans, *Downing Street Diary*, pp. 173–4.

[290] *The United Kingdom and the European Economic Community*, Cmnd 1565 (London, 1961).

[291] HMD, 24 November 1961, MS Macmillan dep. d. 44. Macmillan's brief account of the incident in his memoirs omitted mention of his suspicions of the French. *At the End of the Day*, p. 30.

policy presentations were thus designed largely for internal audiences. In a domestic re-enactment of the summer's ministerial tours to Commonwealth capitals, Central Office dispatched Cabinet ministers Heath, Soames, Maudling, Thorneycroft and Hare to regional meetings of party representatives between 16 and 23 September 1961.[292] Those missions did little, however, to stem requests for Common Market information. Between September 1961 and July 1962 alone the CRD received more than twenty-eight queries from MPs and Conservative Associations.[293] In a November 1961 letter to Sir Michael Fraser, the General Director of Central Office, the Conservative Research Department's Peter Minoprio highlighted constituency demands for party materials describing the background 'simply and in plain language'. In February 1962 the Conservative Central Board of Finance requested a concise summary of the Rome Treaty. The document, it complained, 'is frequently mentioned but few know its contents'.[294] In May, Heath's defensive response to BBC questions about the Government's reluctant lead suggested that the Common Market had received more public scrutiny than any other post-war issue.[295] Yet by September even the Cabinet conceded that the public was 'still insufficiently informed of our case for entry'.[296]

At the same time, Central Office allowed anti-Market propaganda to flow unchallenged, on the grounds that official responses gave publicity to the critics.[297] Privately, however, it monitored anti-Market organisations and personalities and circulated opposition propaganda to the Foreign Office and 10 Downing Street.[298] Annoyance at the tactics of their opponents compelled the Research Department to draft replies for internal circulation. This included a memo refuting each of the six questions raised in the ACML's 'Common Market Quiz'. 'It would be hard to imagine a more dishonest representation', the memo had complained.[299]

The *Daily Express* campaign evoked stronger reactions, as indicated by Foreign Office efforts to deconstruct its pamphlet *You and*

---

[292] Organisation Department meeting notes, 3 July 1961; Memo from General Director, 11 August 1961, CPA, CCO 500/31/2. Dates and locations of meetings listed in CPA, CCO 4/8/94.

[293] Copies of letters, including those from the general public, can be found in CPA, CRD 2/43/1,2,3.

[294] P. Minoprio to M. Fraser, 23 November 1961; General Williams to M. Fraser, 20 February 1962, CPA, CRD 2/43/1.

[295] *Conference* programme, 17 May 1962, BBC WAC, Film T88.

[296] PRO, CAB 128/36 Part II CC 57(62), 20 September 1962.

[297] See for example M. Fraser to G. Sayers re *A Call to the Commonwealth*, 31 June 1962, CPA, CRD 2/43/1.

[298] For copies of anti-Market letters and materials circulated throughout Central Office see CPA, CCO 500/31/3. Central Office maintained files on individual anti-Market pressure groups, with varying levels of completeness. See relevant 'Outside Organisation' files, CPA, CCO 3/6.

[299] CRD memo, undated but probably July 1962, CPA, CRD, 2/43/1.

the Common Market. In forwarding the confidential critique to Central Office, Edward Heath wrote:

> *You and the Common Market* can hardly be described as an objective document. It contains a number of straightforward misstatements of fact (though these are relatively few), further misstatements implied rather than directly expressed, and assertions which are in fact opinions but are presented as if they were facts; it also employs selectivity in presenting facts. It is, however, sometimes difficult to draw a line between factual errors and what we would consider errors of opinion.[300]

A proliferation of page 1 'propaganda boxes' in April and May 1962 drove Central Office to draft 'Q and A on the *Daily Express*', a leaflet written by George Christ. But this exposed a fundamental problem, that of using logic to combat sentiment. One official warned that by providing 'rational' responses to the claims made by the *Express*, 'we were to some extent admitting an element of truth'.[301]

Losing the battle

Ironically, the Government's decision to eschew a campaign in support of the application contributed to precisely the sort of negative public reaction it sought to avoid. In the absence of official rebuttal, anti-Marketeers registered their protests almost unopposed. The Government perhaps hoped that, by virtue of political extremism or sentimental extravagance, anti-Marketeers would subvert their own claims. But by the summer of 1962, impressionistic evidence suggested that the opponents of entry were shaping the domestic debate. The pro-entry Common Market Campaign, for instance, warned that emotional appeals were obscuring facts. More ominously, it noted that Douglas Jay and William Pickles had elevated the intellectual credibility of a cause previously dominated by xenophobes.[302]

In the Cabinet, anxiety surfaced in April 1962 with Heath's warning that 'public opinion would be unduly influenced by the other side' if ministers failed to openly address the Common Market's advantages. In May it was suggested that American support for entry was heightening public suspicions of European federalism.[303] In July, Cabinet discussions concluded:

> There has been a noticeable swing in public opinion in this country against United Kingdom membership of the Common Market. There had

---

[300] E. Heath to M. Fraser, 28 February 1962, CPA, CRD 2/43/2.
[301] G. Christ to P. Minoprio, undated but May 1962; M. Fraser quoting Miss Branston in a letter to P. Minoprio, 21 May 1962, CPA, CRD 2/43/1.
[302] *Common Market Broadsheet*, No. 6 (July 1962) and No. 7 (August 1962).
[303] PRO, CAB 128/36 Part I CC 28(62) and 31(62), 17 April and 3 May 1962.

always been a body of opinion, particularly among farmers, which held that the advantages of membership must be doubtful until the conditions of entry were known; but more recently this had been replaced by a feeling, no doubt inspired by propaganda in the anti-Common Market newspapers and magazines, that it would be wrong in principle for the United Kingdom to join the Common Market on any conditions. Up to now anxiety had centred on the effect on Commonwealth trade. But in the long run anxieties about the effect on our domestic agriculture might be even more important. It was among farmers that the propaganda against the Common Market seemed to be having most effect.[304]

Religious issues, the discussions also noted, had surfaced, with claims by Nonconformist agitators that the UK would be merging with Catholic Europe.

Quantifiable proof of the hardening of opinion had been provided by opinion polls. Two Gallup surveys in June 1962 registered approval for entry at 36 and 37 per cent, a decrease from 47 per cent in May and the low ebb of favourable opinion for the entire period. According to the same polls, sentiment against entry had risen to 31 per cent, the highest level since announcement of the application.[305] More dramatic evidence of anti-Market incursions was suggested by a *Daily Mail* poll in the last week of June 1962. Responses to the question 'Are you for or against Britain joining the Common Market?' showed opinion in favour of entry at 28.2 per cent, down from 47.1 per cent in April, and opinion against at 43.2 per cent, up from 25.0 per cent in April. It was a development the *Express* attributed to its campaign,[306] though its own June poll had shown a more modest split in opinion, of 28.5 per cent for entry and 33.5 per cent against.[307]

The Government's decision to undertake opinion polls of its own exposed the most compelling indications of anti-Marketeer influence. In mid-August Central Office instructed its Area Agents to canvass local opinions and submit reports on attitudes towards Common Market entry. Summary versions of their findings, 'Common Market Public Opinion Report No. 1' and 'No. 2' were compiled by Central Office on 28 August and 12 September, respectively. Awareness of anti-Market rhetoric was apparent in Central Office's request that its missioners survey six contentious themes: 'sovereignty', 'constitutional questions',

---

[304] PRO, CAB 128/36 Part II CC 44(62), 5 July 1962.
[305] Social Surveys (Gallup Poll) Ltd, 'British Attitudes', p. 49.
[306] *Daily Mail* poll results and excerpts from *City Press* article 'Beaverbrook's Triumph', reprinted in the *Daily Express*, 4 July 1962.
[307] For a summary of *Express* poll results for June–September 1962 see *Daily Express*, 11 September 1962. For other summaries of its own and other poll results see *Daily Express*, 29 August and 30 December 1961, 28 February, 24 March, 11 and 25 September, 6 October, 21 December 1962 and 22 January 1963.

'Commonwealth', 'agriculture', 'labour questions' and 'professional questions'. Secrecy was paramount, since 'bad public relations' would inevitably accompany press exposure of a '"national enquiry"'. The survey was thus entrusted to the 'most reliable and secure agents' who could proceed without detection on a 'casual' basis.[308]

Individual area reports[309] supplied varying levels of anecdotal detail and blurred the lines of enquiry, particularly on the 'sovereignty' issue and 'constitutional questions'. But this was less a failure of the agents than a reflection of confused public perceptions and the expansive contours of anti-Market objections. 'Report No. 1' acknowledged a tendency towards 'broad and superficial generalities' but added 'comment is bound to be superficial where knowledge is so'.[310]

Those limitations notwithstanding, the summary reports revealed a comprehensive and ongoing erosion of favourable public opinion. Pro-Common Market sentiment, it was thought, 'probably' held sway but there was no doubt that opinion against entry was gathering strength.[311] There was no uncertainty about the forces shaping public views. Beaverbrook and the *Express* had featured in eight of twelve area reports submitted in August, while the ACML was cited in four of the replies. Central Office thus ascribed the hardening of opinion 'partly to the campaign of the Beaverbrook newspapers; partly to the anti-Common Market group and partly to the opposition of prominent people (e.g. Lord Attlee, Field Marshal Montgomery, Sir Arthur Bryant, etc.)'.[312]

Area Agents detailed public reaction to the anti-Marketeers' 'emotional' and 'sentimental' messages on sovereignty and Empire. Among the older generation, trade unionists and ex-service personnel in particular, the propaganda resonated with latent fears of 'others'. In September, for instance, the deputy Central Office Agent for Yorkshire reported that:

> insularity is a potent emotion with many people and they are on principle suspicious of all foreigners. Conservatives have been brought up for so long on Disraeli maxims that even the more open minded find that it goes against the grain to think of Britain as a part of Europe.[313]

---

[308] COO to Area Agents, 16 August 1962, CPA, CCO 500/31/2. On the need for secrecy see also COO to deputy chairman, 12 September 1962, CPA, CCO 500/31/2.
[309] See collection of individual area reports used in the compilation of 'Common Market Public Opinion Report No. 1' (August 1962) in CPA, CCO 500/31/2, and 'Report No. 2' (September 1962) in CPA, CCO 500/31/4.
[310] 'Common Market Public Opinion – Report No. 1', COO to chairman, 28 August 1962, CPA, CCO 500/31/2.
[311] 'Common Market Public Opinion – Report No. 2', C. F. R. Bagnall to chairman, General Director, 12 September 1962, CPA, CCO 500/31/2.
[312] 'Common Market Public Opinion – Report No. 1'.
[313] Miss V. B. Petherick, deputy Central Office Agent (COA) Yorkshire to COO, 6 September 1962, CPA, CCO 500/31/4.

In some quarters of Newcastle, meanwhile, trepidation of links with the Italians extended to fears of eventual association with Greeks, Turks and Swedes.[314] The Central Office summary noted that 'there is, as always in England, a deep distrust of foreigners on the "wogs start at Calais" principle'. Dislike of the French, suspicion of American motives, loyalty to the Old Commonwealth and fears about an influx of foreign labour suggested that 'popular feeling is with the xenophobes'.[315] The summary also warned that while the claims of the Nonconformist 'lunatic fringe' seemed 'funny', they had featured in a number of area reports, including those covering Wessex, Cambridgeshire, Cheshire, Liverpool and the Western Area.[316]

Greater significance was attached to the impact of the anti-Market campaign outside the patriotic lobby and, in particular, its resonance among what the deputy Central Office Agent for Home Counties North described as 'our good solid citizens' and the 'man in the street'.[317] Agents from Central England reported that the *Express* was influencing undecided opinion in the East Midlands, small farmers in the West Midlands and 'doing damage among small businessmen and poorly informed workers' in Birmingham.[318] In the Eastern Area, moreover, the *Daily Express* had been 'foremost in formulating opinion'.[319] But the 'most noteworthy' aspect of the deteriorating situation, 'Report No. 1' concluded,

> is that opinion seems to be hardening in the middle classes against entry on the grounds that the cost of food and living will go up against those on fixed incomes. This is a very real fear and it is noteworthy that this is the very class of people who are already opposed to the Government and 'going Liberal'. This is a serious development … the anti-Marketeers are much more articulate than those who favour entry, and the argument that not much can be said whilst negotiations are going on is ceasing to have any great force with the public.[320]

Unanimous depiction of public confusion and criticism of the Government's failure to provide information accompanied the reports of *Daily Express* influence. The Central Office Agent for Wessex described the general sentiment as either 'we don't know enough' or worse, the

---

[314] Miss B. L. Hamley, COA Area B to COO, 24 August 1962, CPA, CCO 500/31/2.
[315] 'Common Market Public Opinion – Report No. 1'.
[316] Mr Horton to COO, 23 August 1962; B. T. Powell to COO, 27 August 1962, CPA, CCO 500/31/2; P. G. Gower to COO, 5 September 1962, B. T. Slinn to COO, 10 September 1962, CPA, CCO 500/31/4.
[317] S. R. Newman to COO, 28 August 1962, CPA, CCO 500/31/2.
[318] G. C. Hearn to COO, 27 August 1962; J. Galloway to COO, 27 August 1962, CPA, CCO 500/31/2.
[319] B. T. Powell to COO, 7 September 1962, CPA, CCO 500/31/4.
[320] 'Common Market Public Opinion – Report No. 1'.

perception that information was 'being withheld deliberately or by neglect of the general public'.[321] The Western Area Central Office Agent wrote of 'general bewilderment', while her counterpart in London complained that 70 per cent of the electorate 'knew little' of the issues and therefore 'fall ready victims' of the Beaverbrook press.[322] It was on those points that both summary reports concluded, the first pleading for 'much more Government initiative' and the second warning that 'until some measurement of enlightenment and information is forthcoming ... the position may well deteriorate'.[323]

On the surface, the Macmillan Government's failure to engage the public led to what a Home Counties representative described as 'losing by default to a well sustained and somewhat unscrupulous attack' from the *Express*.[324] But there were more subtle factors at work as well. In fact, frailties in the quality, as much as the quantity, of Conservative information facilitated anti-Market gains. In other words, the strengths of anti-Market propaganda were magnified because they confronted the issue at points where Conservative presentation was weakest.

The crux of the problem was the inability of Government publicity to connect in a positive fashion with the *Express*' 'every man' figure in the 'back streets of Derby' and 'on the Rhyl Promenade' (see Chapter 2). This was, in effect, a structural flaw on two levels. First, there was a weakness born of what Peter Minoprio described as a gap between 'the words and phraseology of the House of Commons reproduced in party literature and the anxieties of men in the street'. In a letter to Michael Fraser outlining the weaknesses of Conservative propaganda, he wrote:

> Up to now we have used 'statesmen's language'; talked about 'economic divisions', 'political advantages', 'changing patterns of trade'. Such phrases mean very little to the average man and as we enter into the final phase of the period leading up to the ratification debate we must stop using them wherever possible.... A case can, it seems to me, be made for concentrating on a less erudite (and cheaper) form of publicity which would without doubt reach a wider market and might in practice prove popular to party workers.... Our publications must therefore be comprehensive as well as comprehensible.[325]

---

[321] Mr Horton, COA Wessex to COO, 23 August 1962, CPA, CCO 500/31/2.

[322] Miss B. A. Cribb, deputy COA Western Area, to COO, 27 August 1962; Miss E. A. Salisbury, deputy COA London, to COO, 27 August 1962, CPA, CCO 500/31/2. See also S. Curtis, Area Publicity Officer for Home Counties, to COO, 11 September 1962, CPA, CCO 500/31/4.

[323] COO to chairman, 28 August 1962; and COO to deputy chairman, 12 September 1962, CPA CCO 500/31/2.

[324] S. Curtis, Area Publicity Officer for Home Counties to COO, 11 September 1962, CPA, CCO 500/31/4.

[325] P. Minoprio to M. Fraser, 6 September 1962, CPA, CRD 2/43/2.

The second defect, as Central Office perceived it, was that rational assessments of the impulse for entry made the application appear as if it sprang from political and economic desperation. In his advice to R. A. Butler on the eve of the 1962 party conference, Sir Michael Fraser warned:

> The logic of such an analysis leads one so inevitably to our application for membership that the Party can hardly be blamed if they feel we have no alternative. This is depressing and contributes to the feeling of national inferiority complex which is a political factor (particularly in the Labour Party). It seems to me we should do our best to avoid this. We want them to see it as a new chapter in our destiny.[326]

This was an inescapable burden because, as Freddie Bishop wrote to Macmillan in June 1961, 'the real argument for our going into Europe is based on our apprehensions' about Britain's future political and economic standing.[327]

There was, moreover, a defensive posture in the Government's confrontation with the signature themes of the anti-Market campaign. This was evident, for instance, in Macmillan's speeches. He knew that the rhetoric of his opponents, no matter how exaggerated, posed dangers[328] and his initial parliamentary defence of the application anticipated public anxieties rooted in the 'long tradition of isolation' and 'suspicion of foreigners'. He described sovereignty as an issue of the 'highest importance' but added that it was 'perhaps, a matter of degree'. The Six, he noted, were not 'losing their national identity because they have delegated a measure of sovereignty'.[329] But with his opponents peddling sovereignty as an absolute proposition, Macmillan was forced to revisit the issue in his February 1962 party political broadcast. Without making explicit reference to the Common Market, he counselled viewers not to confuse membership of alliances with the abandonment of identity and nationhood.[330]

By the autumn of 1962, Macmillan found himself clarifying and in some cases conceding the claims of anti-Marketeers. 'I want to make one thing clear', he told his audience in a further broadcast. 'We ... reject altogether the view that Britain is faced with a choice between the Commonwealth and Common Market.'[331] In November his opponents'

---

[326] M. Fraser to R. A. Butler, 28 September 1962, CPA, CRD 2/43/2.

[327] F. Bishop to H. Macmillan, 27 June 1961, PRO, PREM 11/3563.

[328] HMD, 4 October 1962, Ms Macmillan dep. d. 47.

[329] Macmillan, *At the End of the Day*, pp. 19, 23. See also *Parliamentary Debates*, Commons, 5th Series, vol. 645, 2 August 1961, cols 1482, 1490–1.

[330] Conservative party political broadcast, 24 January 1962, BBC WAC, Film 35/36.

[331] Conservative party political broadcast, 20 September 1962, BBC WAC, Film 35/36.

continued exploitation of 'dear food' wrested a confession that Common Market entry would indeed lead to 'some increase in the price of food'.[332] Macmillan's vulnerability on patriotic themes was indicated by his urge to renounce Dean Acheson's infamous speech. In a memo to his secretaries he called it a 'rare' opportunity, 'which can be seized with great internal political advantage. It might be a turning point in our fortunes which are low at the moment.'[333]

The belated campaign for entry

Defensive tendencies were both responsible for and compounded by the Government's faltering approach towards an information campaign in 1962. In July, Bill Deedes was appointed Minister Without Portfolio and charged with co-ordinating the official information services and, in particular, issues relating to the Common Market. His appointment, however, did not coincide with a Cabinet mandate for a pro-entry information campaign. Indeed, whatever urgency lay behind the Cabinet's desire, expressed in a meeting on 5 July, for initiatives that presented membership in a 'fairer light' was tempered by a willingness to do so 'when practicable'.[334]

It was only in the immediate aftermath of the Commonwealth Prime Ministers' Conference that members of the Government showed a unified determination to promote entry. At this point Harold Evans, Bill Deedes and the Chief Whip believed that 'the boats were burnt and that the time had come to argue for Common Market entry without inhibitions'.[335] Macmillan's political broadcast at the conclusion of the Commonwealth conference was printed for publication and distributed in October under the title *Britain, the Commonwealth and Europe*.[336] Speeches by Government ministers, particularly at the 1962 party conference, advocated entry with more force and detail. On that occasion Butler assured his audience that 'British policy is opposed to any extinction of national identity',[337] while Heath defended the Government's political and economic rationale. On 22 October, Deedes also convened the first meeting of

---

[332] Conservative party political broadcast, 14 November 1962, BBC WAC, Film 35/36.
[333] H. Macmillan to T. Bligh and P. de Zulueta, 7 December 1962, PRO, PREM 11/4057. In his public response Macmillan suggested that Acheson had 'appeared to denigrate the resolution and will of the British people ... an error which has been made by quite a lot of people ... including Philip of Spain, Louis the Fourteenth, Napoleon, the Kaiser and Hitler'. H. Macmillan to Lord Chandos, also used as a press release, 7 December 1962, PRO, PREM 11/4057.
[334] PRO, CAB 128/26 Part II CC 44(62), 5 July 1962.
[335] Evans, *Downing Street Diary*, p. 215.
[336] H. Macmillan, *Britain, the Commonwealth and Europe* (London, 1962).
[337] *The Times*, 12 October 1962.

a Parliamentary Group on the Common Market, which discussed ideas for pamphlets and provided links to the back-benches.[338]

Those charged with public relations, however, laboured under considerable burdens. Foremost among these was the fact that Cabinet had approved an extension to 'the scope of limited publicity'[339] rather than the initiation of a full propaganda campaign. But there were practical limits as well. Deedes, for instance, was prohibited from developing 'propaganda' in favour of entry because the Information Office used taxpayer money.[340] In discussions with the Prime Minister, moreover, Oliver Poole, a former Chair of the Conservative Party Organisation, had suggested that the pro-Market forces be consolidated through existing channels.[341] That meant information would be disseminated primarily in publications from the Conservative Research Department, such as *Notes on Current Politics* and *Pocket Politics*, with the addition of occasional leaflets or pamphlets from the Central Office Publicity Department or Conservative Political Centre.[342] If this speeded production, it nonetheless tended to limit the audience to MPs and party activists.

The greatest obstacle, however, was the fact that delays in presenting the Government's case for entry forced Conservative publicists into a debate whose terms had already been dictated by the anti-Marketeers. In August, Central Office's public opinion 'Report No. 2' had concluded with a list of factors harming the case for entry. These overwhelmingly reflected public unease and included 'distrust' of 'foreigners' and 'political hook-ups', 'fear' of increased living costs, 'cheap competition', the Commonwealth's fate, 'cheap foreign labour', 'agricultural dumping', the unresolved negotiations and the *Express* campaign.[343] Central Office reacted by devoting a September issue of the fortnightly *Pocket Politics* to 'Common Market Misconceptions'.[344] In the following months it published nine pamphlets in a series entitled 'Common Market Common Sense'. Pamphlet No. 3, 'The Commonwealth', denied that Britain faced a choice between Europe and the 'great Commonwealth'. No. 5, 'Employment Prospects', dismissed fears of a southern Italian migration as 'nonsense'. No. 7, entitled 'Would Britain Get Pushed Around?', denied

[338] In addition to Deedes, the committee included thirteen MPs and a representative from the Conservative Research Department. Minutes of relevant meetings are in CPA, CRD 2/42/8.

[339] PRO, CAB 128/36 Part II CC 57(62), 20 September 1962.

[340] W. Deedes, *Dear Bill: W. F. Deedes Reports* (London, 1997), pp. 154–5.

[341] HMD, 23 September 1962, MS Macmillan dep. d. 47.

[342] P. Minoprio to M. Fraser, 6 September 1962, CPA, CRD 2/43/2; P. Minoprio to M. Reed, 16 January 1963, CPA, CRD 2/43/3. For examples see Conservative Political Centre series, No. 250, *The Commonwealth and the Common Market*, and No. 252, *National Sovereignty and the European Community*, in CPA, CCO 4/9/152.

[343] 'Common Market Public Opinion – Report No. 2'.

[344] W. Deedes to deputy chairman, 6 August 1962, CPA, CRD 2/42/8.

Britain would be ruled by foreigners, while No. 8, 'European Stability', argued against isolationism. No. 9, 'Religious Freedom', counselled that the Common Market 'has nothing to do with religion ... the Pope or the Vatican. The treaty just happened to be signed in Rome.'[345]

The minutes of the Parliamentary Group on the Common Market revealed a preoccupation with fears and ignorance among the party faithful. As late as October, it was suggested that back-benchers needed 'fact sheets' to deal with Common Market speeches and questions. In November Central Office was trying to compile a list of MPs whom it thought capable of arguing the Common Market case. In December, only weeks before the veto, it was publishing a broadsheet entitled *The Common Market: How It Works*.[346] Women, it was believed, were particularly concerned with the 'cost of living' issue.[347] As a result Deedes organised monthly meetings of a Women's Advisory Committee on Europe at the Treasury[348] and secured the support of the National Council of Women for the distribution of party literature.

Stalled negotiations, ambiguities in the Government's public approach to Europe and the successful intrusion of anti-Market propaganda put Deedes in the unenviable position of fighting a rearguard battle in an uphill campaign. During a December 1962 lunch with the editor of Beaverbrook's *Evening Standard*, Deedes conceded that the anti-Market crusade was having a 'tremendous impact'.[349] Pessimism over the outcome in Brussels was evident the previous month amidst Parliamentary Group queries about 'what line to take' if the negotiations failed. Worse yet was Peter Kirk's suggestion that the Government's belated information effort had so confused the public with minute reasoning that 'they often forgot the main object of our joining the EEC'.[350] After the veto, Deedes confessed that when the country had needed a 'medicine man' he had only been able to supply 'placebos'.[351]

---

[345] CCO pamphlets in the series 'Common Market Common Sense': No. 1, 'The Economic Case'; No. 2, 'The Political Case'; No. 3, 'The Commonwealth'; No. 4, 'Cost of Living'; No. 5, 'Employment Prospects'; No. 6, 'The Farmers'; No. 7, 'Would Britain Get Pushed Around?'; No. 8, 'European Stability'; No. 9, 'Religious Freedom'. For copies see R. A. Butler Papers F/124.

[346] Minutes of the Parliamentary Group on the Common Market, 22 October, 5 November and 3 December 1962, CPA, CRD 2/48/2.

[347] This was a recurring theme in the meetings of Deedes' parliamentary committee. See Minutes of the Parliamentary Group on the Common Market, 12 and 19 November, 10 and 17 December 1962, CPA, CRD 2/48/2.

[348] Deedes, *Dear Bill*, p. 155.

[349] W. Deedes quoted by C. Wintour in a letter to Beaverbrook, 20 December 1962, BBK H/268.

[350] Minutes of the Parliamentary Group on the Common Market, 26 November and 17 December 1962, CPA, CRD 2/48/2.

[351] Deedes, *Dear Bill*, p. 157.

Conclusion

The veto

Awareness that French intransigence might undermine Britain's application failed to assuage the Macmillan Government's frustration when de Gaulle's veto arrived. According to a BBC report, the 14 January 1963 Elysée press conference left the British delegation 'very depressed' and resigned to a 'bitterly disappointing outcome'.[1] The negotiators forged ahead in vain until the abandonment of talks two weeks later. Macmillan's diary entry for 28 January compared the General's ambitions for European 'hegemony' to those of Louis XIV and Napoleon. 'All our policies at home and abroad', he lamented, 'are in ruins'.[2] Deedes described 29 January as 'one of the worst days I remember in or out of politics'. The veto, he added, 'did more damage to the Government than anything else'.[3]

Meanwhile, the *Express* printed its 'Hallelujah' headline and praised de Gaulle's recognition of Britain's 'unique history and conditions of life and her world-wide commitments'.[4] Grateful readers thanked Beaverbrook for 'helping keep Britain Great' and for single-handedly 'saving us from the disgustingly servile Macmillan, Heath, Thorneycroft and Sandys'.[5] Yet Beaverbrook's reaction, as we have seen, was ambivalent and there were no victory celebrations.

---

[1] *Gallery* programme, 17 January 1963, BBC WAC, Film No. 13/14.
[2] HMD, 28 January 1963, quoted in *At the End of the Day*, p. 367. For more reactions and critiques of de Gaulle's motives see *At the End of the Day*, pp. 365–78; Charlton, *The Price of Victory*, pp. 299–302; Horne, *Macmillan*, pp. 444–51; and G. Wilkes, 'Eye-Witness Views of the Brussels Breakdown', in *Britain's Failure to Enter*, pp. 213–56.
[3] Deedes, *Dear Bill*, p. 156.
[4] *Daily Express*, 30 January and 15 January 1963.
[5] Mr Moyse to Beaverbrook, 4 February 1963, A. J. F. MacDonald to Beaverbrook, 9 February 1963, and other examples in BBK F/4.

In fact, relief rather than jubilation typified the response among anti-Marketeers. Attitudes were shaped, above all, by the expectation of future applications. Hinchingbrooke, the new President of the ACML, told its members to 'remain on guard', while Montgomery predicted 'round 2 may follow, it must be hit for six'.[6] Alexander of Hillsborough warned that Heath and Lord Gladwyn still posed a danger 'from the now permanent Common Market HQ in London'.[7] Beaverbrook, like Lambton, viewed the Common Market as a 'standing threat' and advocated maintaining the campaign apparatus for a future 'day of betrayal'.[8]

But celebrations were also muted by a recognition that it was ultimately an outsider who, as Lord Balfour wrote, 'saved us from an act of folly'.[9] The ACML, after equating the pro-entry 'defeated "Establishment"' with the appeasers of Hitler, credited 'a few foreign friends with a true realisation of Britain's destiny'.[10] The FBM was less generous, portraying the EEC as 'anti-British' and de Gaulle as a front for the policies of 'French monopolists'.[11] In addition, despite the favourable outcome, Conservative opponents recognised the damage done to their party. An immediate withdrawal from the negotiations, the *Express* advised, would end dissent and unite the Tories, while bringing 'harmony and purpose' to Britain.[12] The Government was in 'serious difficulty', Eden wrote. 'I never could see how the pledges to our own agriculture and Commonwealth could be met.... It is a woeful business.'[13] The veto, moreover, exposed the failure of anti-Marketeers to construct alternatives that were economically or politically viable. As Beaverbrook knew, Empire Free Trade was a lost cause. Turton's policy committee continued its work. Yet his immediate hope was that Eden might guide the nation through the letter page of *The Times*.[14] Meanwhile, neither the Government nor Labour heeded Walker and Walker-Smith's *Call to the Commonwealth*. In place of plans arose vague assertions about joining the path to national renewal. Attlee wrote 'Britain Can Still Be Great' but this amounted to a counselling exercise against 'defeatism'.[15] Similar platitudes about 'national confidence' infused *Express* opinion columns under titles such as 'The Whole World Her Market', 'A Time for Faith' and 'Now It's Time to Step Back to Glory'.[16]

---

[6] *AntiCommon Market League Newsletter*, 9 February 1963; Montgomery to Beaverbrook, 5 March 1963, BBK C/248.
[7] Alexander to Beaverbrook, undated 1963, BBK C/2.
[8] Beaverbrook to Lambton, 4 April 1963, BBK C/200.
[9] Balfour to Beaverbrook, 29 January 1963, BBK C/22.
[10] *AntiCommon Market League Newsletter*, 9 February 1963.
[11] *Forward Britain Movement Bulletin and Digest*, No. 27 (11 July 1963).
[12] *Daily Express*, 15 January 1963.
[13] A. Eden to Beaverbrook, 29 March 1963, AP 23/8/65B.
[14] R. Turton to A. Eden, 25 January, 13 February 1963, AP 23/64/15,16.
[15] Attlee, 'I Say Britain Can Still Be Great', *Sunday Express*, 4 February 1963.
[16] See *Daily Express* opinion columns, 15, 16, 28 and 30 January 1963.

The anti-Market impact

While the forces aligned against Britain's application to the EEC achieved less than their most combative advocates hoped, the influence of the anti-Marketeers was more pronounced than their dismissive critics allowed. More significantly, that mixed result was both a reflection and a consequence of their overwhelming reliance upon national identity issues. Nationalism in the hands of anti-Marketeers was a double-edged sword. Thus, while the invocation of Britishness and construction of a patriotic discourse, banal or otherwise, was a primary source of strength, it was simultaneously a source of weakness.

The ironic twist in the veto lay in the fact that a French nationalist had terminated Macmillan's bid in the language of British nationalism. This prompted little comment at the time, with the notable exception of the failed Conservative candidate at South Dorset. De Gaulle, Angus Maude observed, 'used virtually the same words as the anti-Marketeers'.[17] Comparisons were apt, given that the General's speech was structured around the incompatibility of British and European interests. These included the divergent systems of agricultural support as well as Britain's outstanding ties to EFTA and the Commonwealth. Suspicions of America featured in his suggestion that Britain's application amounted to a Trojan horse carrying US interests in its belly. De Gaulle even invoked 'dear food' by questioning whether British consumers would willingly sacrifice cheap imports from the Commonwealth and America.

National identification, however, was the pervasive theme, as evident in de Gaulle's contention that the British were insufficiently European. His rhetoric mimicked that of British patriots:

> England in effect is insular, she is maritime, she is linked through her exchanges, her market, her supply lines to the most diverse and often the most distant countries; she pursues essentially industrial and commercial activities, and only slight agricultural ones. She has in all her doings very marked and very original habits and traditions. In short, the nature, the structure, the very situations that are England's differ profoundly from those of the continentals.[18]

His conclusion, echoing Bryant's 'inevitability of gradualness' (see Chapter 3), asserted that only through 'evolution' could England 'transform herself' and perhaps one day 'moor alongside the Continent'.

Analysis of the veto includes conjecture that its tenor was partly fashioned by chauvinism or a desire to humiliate the British government.[19]

---

[17] *Gallery* programme, 17 January 1963, BBC WAC, Film 13/14.

[18] *The Times*, 15 January 1963.

[19] This line of analysis features most prominently in the biographies by Horne, *Macmillan*, pp. 447, 451, and J. Lacouture, *De Gaulle: Vol. 2, The Ruler, 1945–70*

But two additional considerations must be added. On the one hand, it is possible that de Gaulle, like the anti-Marketeers, adhered to typologies of nationhood and utilised that sentiment for political advantage. The General, Horne noted, had used similar terms in discussions with Macmillan at Rambouillet.[20] But there had been earlier hints as well. A memo from the Foreign Office to its European representatives at the end of May 1962 attributed de Gaulle's attitude to a 'well known predilection for Delphic utterances' and an 'inadequate understanding of how European we had become'.[21] It was an impression reinforced by frequent Government complaints about the General's single-minded devotion to the glories of France and supremacy in Europe.[22]

On the other hand, the language and tone might also be attributed to contacts between the French leadership and the anti-Marketeers. Eden met with the General in May 1961 and July 1962, while Pompidou and Couve de Murville hosted Gaitskell during his December 1962 trip to Paris. De Gaulle had corresponded with Viscount Montgomery and, after receiving *A Choice for Destiny*, Arthur Bryant.[23] Peter Walker claimed that de Gaulle had followed his speeches, and after reading *A Call to the Commonwealth* 'communicated' that he opposed British entry 'for the same reasons'.[24] Thus, in their strident assertions about British uniqueness, the anti-Marketeers may have bolstered the pretext for the veto and at the same time provided a ready-made rhetorical context.

Anti-Marketeer influence was also evident in other contexts. It is entirely plausible to conclude that the opponents constrained Britain's negotiating position in Brussels, either by forcing its diplomats to honour Government pledges on safeguards or by narrowing the terms that might be acceptable to an increasingly sceptical public.[25] Likewise, the suggestion that the anti-Marketeers and Gaitskell in particular had

---

(London, 1991), p. 360. It is also a component in the veto analyses of Camps, *Britain and the European Community*, pp. 367–506, and Beloff, *The General Says No*, pp. 148–78.

[20] Horne, *Macmillan*, p. 445.

[21] 'Britain and the EEC: France's Attitude', FO telegram no. 220, 31 May 1962, PRO, PREM 11/4019.

[22] For examples see A. Rumbold to P. Dixon, 9 January 1962, and P. Dixon to FO, undated, PRO, PREM 11/4019; HMD, 29 November 1961, 19 and 27 May, 1, 5 and 16 December 1962, 12 and 28 January 1963, Ms Macmillan dep. d. 44, 46, 48; H. Macmillan, party political broadcast, 30 January 1963, BBC WAC, Film 35/36.

[23] 'Write to him in English and begin "My dear General"', Monty advised. 'He likes it thus and not "Dear Mr. President."' Montgomery to A. Bryant, 3 and 12 December 1962; de Gaulle to A. Bryant, 1 December 1962, AB Papers H/4.

[24] Interview with Peter Walker, 25 February 1998. For personal reasons, Walker refused to elaborate on how de Gaulle's response had been 'communicated' to him.

[25] See, for example, Denman, *Missed Chances*, p. 224; Dutton, 'Anticipating Maastricht', p. 537; George, *An Awkward Partner*, p. 34, Lieber, *British Politics*, pp. 183, 215; Ludlow, 'A Mismanaged Application', p. 281.

assisted de Gaulle's strategy by raising doubts about Britain's enthusiasm for membership[26] is consistent with Heath's professed fears about
Labour's attitude and the negotiating position in Brussels. Camps took
this critique further, blaming de Gaulle for listening to the views of Avon,
Montgomery, Attlee and Gaitskell when 'what counted – or should have
counted – was not what the British people thought and felt but what the
British Government was prepared to accept'.[27]

The difficulty with Camps' conclusion is that it trivialises the relevance of domestic opinion while simultaneously citing its influence
abroad. The contradiction reflects a tendency in the 'missed bus' thesis
to judge the anti-Marketeers through a high political or foreign policy
prism. But a complete understanding of the opposition requires that the
movement be viewed upwards, from its roots. From that perspective the
campaign against entry assumes greater importance precisely because
so many of its agents operated outside the corridors of power. Thus,
opposition to Britain's first application is significant less in its influence
over de Gaulle's veto than in its notable success in grafting a host of
emotive and enduring patriotic meanings to a foreign policy issue for the
purposes of domestic consumption.

In quantitative terms, anti-Market endeavour clearly contributed to
the hardening of opinion against entry, particularly from the spring of
1962. As the polls showed, those gains drew primarily from 'undecided'
ranks. Conservative Central Office's secret surveys in August and
September 1962 confirmed the trend. In addition, they showed that,
apart from outright conversions, agitation also produced questions to
which uncommitted opinion increasingly desired answers. Moreover,
the reports' qualitative details spoke to the influence of Beaverbrookian
techniques by identifying the *Express* as the most potent vehicle of
anti-Market sentiment, with the ACML and prominent dissenters
playing a secondary role. Though on the cusp of decline in the early
1960s, the *Express* claimed the second highest circulation in Britain
and was uniquely defined by its crusading instincts. Hence the opinion
registered by the Royal Commission on the Press whose *1961–62 Report*
concluded,

> Campaigns conducted over a long period may have their effect: thus the
> campaign conducted – quite frankly (and legitimately) for the purpose of
> propaganda – by Beaverbrook Newspapers Ltd. in support of the ideals

---

[26] For contemporary examples see P. Dixon, *Double Diploma: The Life of Sir Pierson Dixon* (London, 1968), p. 295, and comment by C. Layton, MP, on the *Gallery* programme, 17 January 1963, BBC WAC, Film 13/14. For this view in subsequent analysis see Robins, *The Reluctant Party*, pp. 41–2, and Pfaltzgraff, *Britain Faces Europe*, p. 152.

[27] Camps, *Britain and the European Community*, pp. 504–5.

of the British Empire and more recently their opposition of the Common Market may not have achieved all that Lord Beaverbrook would have wished, but it would be impossible to suppose that they had no result.[28]

Whether or not anti-Market pressure groups evoked public sympathy on the basis of their 'amateur' methods[29] is debatable. But their propaganda achievements were impressive given the limits imposed by funding. In terms of volume alone, the ACML had matched the efforts of Conservative Central Office. It is worth remembering, moreover, that organised anti-Market sentiment extended beyond the confines of single-issue groups. Thus, while the ACML claimed 30,000 members, so too did the Communist Party of Great Britain, which protested against entry with equal vigour.

Apart from its impact on undecided opinion, the anti-Market message appeared to resonate because the movement was, in large measure, preaching to the converted. On the basis of existing evidence it is difficult to profile its supporters with precision. Not all Beaverbrook's readership embraced the cause. One complaint against its crusade preoccupations begged 'Please start being a newspaper again and stop playing the same old tune'.[30] But as a January 1963 survey discovered, support for Common Market membership was lower among *Express* readers than among those of any of Fleet Street's other major papers.[31] The bulk of those who wrote to Beaverbrook or the *Express* voiced unconditional support for the campaign. John Junor imagined such readers 'were in the main patriotic people who'd fought in the war and they were believers in Britain and what was then termed the British Empire'. Peter Walker offered a similar assessment of the crowds who gathered for his speeches.[32] Anti-Market letters in the archived papers of Bryant, Gaitskell and Conservative Central Office[33] reinforce those impressions. The preponderance of ex-servicemen and their wives among the correspondents, many of whom recalled Beaverbrook's original Empire Crusade, indicated the presence of an ageing, frustrated group for whom the Common Market application was yet another blow to an imperial version of imagined Britishness. Abandonment of the

---

[28] *Report – Royal Commission on the Press, 1961–62*, p. 18.

[29] Windlesham, *Communication and Political Power*, p. 178.

[30] J. Croom to *Daily Express*, 22 May 1962.

[31] According to the poll, 36 per cent supported membership, with only the *Daily Herald*, at 34 per cent, posting a lower level. Yet those numbers were not far removed from the national averages. *NOP Political Bulletin*, January 1963, cited in Spence, 'Movements in the Public Mood', p. 22.

[32] Interviews with Sir John Junor, 19 November 1996, and Peter Walker, 25 February 1998.

[33] AB Papers Box 69, F/21; HG Papers C 256.6, files 1–5; CPA, CRD 2/43/1,2,3 and CCO 4/8/94.

Commonwealth, xenophobia, charges of Government duplicity, and protests against public ignorance and apathy featured prominently. Their
words, replete with quotations from the Bible, Shakespeare, Blake and
Kipling, among others, betrayed a sense of helplessness and fear before
a rapidly changing world. One veteran asked 'What has happened to our
faith and pride in ourselves as a nation and as a mother of Empire?'[34] If
the anti-Marketeers spoke most loudly for this constituency, it was one
that needed no convincing.

The manifestations of an anti-Market impact on Westminster politics
were more dramatic. As we have seen, both Gaitskell and Macmillan
tailored non-confrontational if not evasive positions on Europe precisely
because they feared the opponents of entry might compromise party
stability. Later, the realisation of anti-Market gains facilitated Gaitskell's
partisan turn at Brighton and summoned a reluctant Conservative
Government into a propaganda game it was ill-prepared to contest. More
importantly, the degree to which the opponents had managed to shape
the debate around the contours of national identity was demonstrated in
Gaitskell's patriotic speeches and the topics addressed by Conservative
campaign literature.

Thus, intentionally or not, de Gaulle had squared the anti-Market
circle. Britishness, defined in the broadest terms, dominated the case
against entry. Its centrality was expedited by overlapping motivations.
On the one hand, identity was incorporated or manipulated to service
the arguments against entry. In its starkest formulations the means were
indistinguishable from their ends. In fact, a signature success of the
anti-Market movement was its ability to promote the deliberations from
a 'condition of England' question to an 'existence of England' question.
On the other hand, patriotism was more than a convenience or a 'refuge
of the scoundrel'. Nationalism was paramount because Common Market
membership challenged existing suppositions about the nature of British
identity. A pro-entry *Crossbow* article published shortly after the veto
posited that 'The British way of life does not depend on the maintenance
of particular and unique institutions of Government. These are the
results of our Britishness rather than its causes.'[35] But few participants in
the debate raised, let alone accommodated, such distinctions. In fact, a
near consensus among the anti-Marketeers held that identity and institutions were inseparable.

Patriotic responses were also assisted by the circumstances surrounding the Government's application and, in particular, perceptions
that the negotiations were complex and secretive. The lack of resolved
terms of entry or official projections of its consequences invited simplistic and emotive criticisms. Evidence for EEC supra-nationalism,

---

[34] J. A. Sandom to Beaverbrook, 21 February 1962, BBK F/4.
[35] Pears, 'A Question of National Identity', p. 39.

however remote, also played into the hands of the patriot lobby. Federalist omens were foretold on the basis of the Treaty, the statements of its architects and the creation of the CAP and institutions such as the Commission. The Government's reluctance to bolster its application with a campaign for domestic support compounded those tendencies. In this regard the application was indeed 'mismanaged',[36] perhaps more so than previously suggested.

In their quest to secure the commanding heights of Britishness, anti-Marketeers waged their offensive without Government rebuttal until the latter half of 1962. Macmillan's pledges to secure terms acceptable for EFTA, the Commonwealth and British agricultural interests provided a measure of protection. But the chink in its armour was the failure to address controversial topics relating to federalism, sovereignty and therefore identity. That raised suspicions about the Treaty's ultimate aims and provided ammunition for those who equated secrecy not only with a Commonwealth betrayal but also with a subversion of the popular will and due democratic process.

Ultimately, the European question provoked nationalist reactions not merely because it confronted British identity in a political void, but because it also resonated with mechanisms responsible for the construction and ongoing imagination of Britishness. In particular, responses were powered by reflexive 'us' and 'them' distinctions that habitually cast Europeans in the role of 'others'. That dichotomy was magnified by the proximity of the Common Market application to decolonisation and therefore imperial sensitivities. In other words, the 'Commonwealth not Common Market' equation evolved atop the foundation stones of British identity. As a result, the opponents engaged the Common Market not on its own terms, but in the shadows of the 'waved' and banal 'unwaved' flags of Britain's uniqueness.

National identification had profound consequences for the shape and content of the anti-Market case. There were advantages to arguing against entry on a patriotic basis because those themes were attuned to the argumentative strengths of Europe's detractors. The populist historicism of Bryant and Taylor, 'bread and butter' points raised by trade unionists and farmers, village hall meetings of pressure groups, and above all the Rhyl and Derby focus of the *Express* put the anti-Marketeers in touch with the grievances of a volatile 'common man' constituency. It was a body aptly described by Iain Macleod as the 'faceless men of politics'.[37] Furthermore, the triumph of sentiment over technicality appeared to absolve opponents from the responsibility of attaching either detail or alternative policies to their arguments. In fact,

---

[36] Ludlow, 'A Mismanaged Application', pp. 271–85.
[37] I. Macleod speaking to the 1922 Committee, 22 March 1962, meeting notes in R. A. Butler Papers, H/96.

the rarity of textual references to the Treaty of Rome suggested that few had bothered to read the document. Roseate constructions of the past serviced attacks on the Government's failure to uphold the spirit and material bases of British greatness. Those sentiments were also used to cloud discomforting manifestations of Britain's diminished standing.

But a propensity for emotive nationalism also risked compromising legitimate aspects of the anti-Market case. Defining Britishness against 'otherness' was a negative process and a veneer of political debate failed to obscure deep-seated prejudices. Germanophobia, in particular, was pervasive across the political spectrum, with the EEC portrayed as an instrument of Teutonic ambitions. Religious biases, though less common, featured in overt anti-Catholic tirades and the coded anti-Semitic references to 'international financiers', 'cosmopolitans' and 'bankers'. John Paul bemoaned the damage done to the movement's political ambitions by 'independent cranks'.[38] But the fact remained that even sophisticated arguments, raised for instance in Harrod's letters to Macmillan or Pickles' articles on sovereignty, routinely abandoned analysis for instinctive delineation of national character.

Diatribes of the 'Frogs' and 'Huns' variety provided ammunition for those keen to renounce the anti-Marketeers as 'ginger groups' or the 'lunatic fringe'. In Parliament, for instance, Nigel Birch accused the Beaverbrook press of using *'suppressio veri, suggestio falsi,* xenophobia, chauvinism, and plain damned nonsense'.[39] Wary of being tarred with a pejorative 'nationalist' label, the anti-Marketeers invariably cast themselves as 'patriots'. But by playing up national stereotypes, they played into their own caricatures. For critics of the right in particular, rhetorical excesses verified the reputations of Hinchingbrooke as Colonel Blimp, Suez rebels as embittered imperialists and Beaverbrook as cartoon Crusader. Moreover, by confessing to 'old fashioned' sensibilities, the likes of Attlee, Eden, Carrington, Bryant and Montgomery confirmed the generation gap evident at the core of anti-Market public opinion. With exceptions such as Peter Walker, the Monday Club, the Young Socialists and a clutch of dissenting Young Conservatives, anti-Market Britishness was coloured by those born to the late Victorian age. Nowhere was this more evident than in the Commonwealth question. As one *Express* reader complained to Beaverbrook, 'I cannot help feeling that your views have become an old man's vendetta, an *idée fixé*, that you cannot grow old gracefully and admit that you are wrong'.[40]

The strengths and limits of the patriotic case were also evident in the structure of anti-Market ranks. On the one hand, a genuine 'nation before party' spirit brought a measure of harmony to disparate factions.

---

[38] J. Paul to Beaverbrook, 12 December 1962, BBK C/269.
[39] *The Times*, 2 August 1962.
[40] R. A. Mason to Beaverbrook, 28 January 1963, BBK F/4.

If anti-Market sentiments were of diversified origin and therefore cacophonous, they were nonetheless based upon allegiance to the same nation. Hence the 'strange bedfellows' scenarios that for example put articles by Attlee, Wilson and Taylor on the *Express* opinion page, the LEL and FBM on shared platforms and Foot and Hinchingbrooke on the same side of parliamentary debates. But that rapport should not be overstated. Insofar as it existed, a facade of unity was partly imposed by *Express* dominance. Yet Beaverbrook loathed sharing the spotlight and the crusade was designed to serve his Fleet Street interests. The comparative insignificance of umbrella organisations such as the AntiCommon Market Union was symptomatic of deep divisions. This was partly a matter of incompatible personalities but political orientations also imposed limits. MPs, for instance, organised within parliamentary party confines. Likewise, at pressure-group level, the non-partisan ambitions of the ACML, FBO and KBO belied affinities with values and symbols of their respective Conservative, Labour and Liberal traditions.

The ascendancy of banal nationalism in particular made sovereignty and Commonwealth the primary motifs of opposition to Europe. But that tendency conferred benefits and liabilities in equal measure. Mundane or vague expositions of those causes provided the movement with platforms of common assent. Yet symmetry could be achieved only in generalities, because Britishness fractured in its component details.

Consensus was evinced most powerfully in the defence of national sovereignty defined loosely and absolutely as a matter of 'independence', 'controlling our own affairs' or preserving 'our way of life'. This reverberated with a devotion to British institutions as well as an assumption that the Common Market was more a political device than an economic project. Parliament in particular invited comparisons with Continental traditions that were deemed inferior because they lacked historic stability and heralded constitutional rigidity. Beyond this, anti-Marketeers argued that entry would compromise both the unique and the mundane facets of British custom and culture. The efficacy of banal nationalism was revealed in its capacity to bring the consequences of remote diplomacy home to the exercise of daily existence.

In its specifics, however, sovereignty evinced variegated if not contradictory attachments culled from the 'thousand years of history'. Disraelian maxims in celebration of institutions and Tory values co-existed with Labour's defence of national planning. The human face of institutional identity was a miscellany that cast yeoman farmers, housewives, trade unionists, shopkeepers, 'trouble-makers' and policemen, among others, as paragons of Britishness. Likewise, in the formula perfected by the *Express*, 'our way' was equally a matter of 'you' and 'your way'. Thus, while there was unifying power in the articulation of collective belonging, its claims were limited by the diverse situational and subjective interpretations of imagined Britishness.

If the 'British way of life' encapsulated banal conceptions of sovereignty and the inward-looking component of national character, its outward-looking counterpart was the 'British way' of Empire and Commonwealth. Here, too, broad assumptions raised points of agreement. Foremost among these was a belief that Common Market entry would fundamentally alter the character of the Commonwealth relationship. It was aligned, moreover, with a conviction that the experience of Empire, and latterly its dissolution, endowed Britain with superior wisdom. Accordingly a Commonwealth prototype, 'misunderstood by outsiders' and historically evolved along British lines, offered lessons if not models for global interaction.

But it was not simply the case, as Dean Acheson contended, that Britain had 'lost an Empire' and failed to locate a commensurate 'role'.[41] Rather, introspection of the early 1960s revealed just how many different roles had been ascribed within assessments of Britain's imperial past and its Commonwealth future. Compared with sovereignty, Commonwealth allegiances were less prone to absolute definition. True, an equation reduced to 'Commonwealth or Common Market' presented an irrevocable choice. But anti-Marketeers of a 'wait and see' disposition willingly contemplated safeguards or advantageous terms of association for Britain's former dependencies. Deeper rifts were manifest in the conceptualisation of a Commonwealth identity and trading relationship. Beaverbrook's crusade, for example, was composed on the increasingly tired theme of Chamberlainite protectionism. C. E. Carrington, by way of contrast, venerated Adam Smith, loose imperial bonds and, like Oliver Smedley and S. W. Alexander, paid tribute to the nation of shopkeepers and the virtues of free trade. James Meade, Roy Harrod, Peter Walker and much of the Labour leadership evaluated the Commonwealth with an eye to trade liberalisation as a bridge between the developed and underdeveloped worlds. Likewise, while all Commonwealth defenders invoked Dominion allegiances, this was a matter of degree. On the right, in particular, ethno-linguistic ties drove Dominion priorities, while the left tended to envisage the Commonwealth in its multiracial entirety.

There were disconnections between the anti-Market visualisation of the Commonwealth relationship and the reality of its shifting commercial and diplomatic trajectories. With regard to alternative trading systems, what the anti-Marketeers failed to comprehend or chose to ignore was the fact that, as *The Times* suggested, 'The Commonwealth does not want it'.[42] An additional quandary was posed by Commonwealth identity. The entry of new members had raised open questions about the linkages between Britain and what Menzies called the 'Crown Commonwealth'. 'Many of us', he complained to Macmillan, 'have great

[41] For text of Acheson's speech at West Point see *The Times*, 11 December 1962.
[42] *The Times*, 6 January 1963.

anxiety about the Commonwealth and the disappearance of so many of its old characteristics'.[43] But while Dominion Britishness was fading, its imagined multicultural equivalent had yet to materialise. A Commonwealth Unity Group plan drafted by Clifford Heathcote-Smith in 1959 cited the 'lack of an all-Commonwealth team-spirit or patriotism' as a fundamental weakness. 'Is it practical politics', he wrote, 'to expect those not racially akin to share a common patriotism? Unless they do, there can be no lasting integral Commonwealth.'[44] It was a dilemma best summarised by a young anti-Marketeer who asked Arthur Bryant 'How do you appeal on the Commonwealth's behalf without sounding like a nostalgic empire builder? I wish I knew.'[45]

From Anti-Marketeers to Eurosceptics?

The lines of descent from the anti-Marketeers to the Eurosceptics demand further research. For the moment, it is worth noting that those links are largely indirect because the ambiguities that accompanied the anti-Market movement's structure, philosophies and impact are also manifest in its legacy. These are evident for instance in the Eurosceptics' regard for the contribution of the original anti-Marketeers. Not surprisingly, Gaitskell's Brighton speech appears to have attracted the most attention.[46] In *The Eurosceptical Reader*,[47] it features as the initial and indeed the only entry from the first application debate. A less likely development was the decision of the Bruges Group to reprint a series of A. J. P. Taylor's *Sunday Express* articles in pamphlet form under the title *Professor A. J. P. Taylor on Europe: The Historian Who Predicted the Future*. The foreword, by a former Beaverbrook writer, hailed Taylor for citing the threat posed by Germany and Brussels with 'total clarity'.[48] By way of contrast, Andrew Roberts' Thatcherite revisionism castigated Arthur Bryant for doing 'more harm than good' in presenting the anti-Market case.[49]

---

[43] R. Menzies to H. Macmillan, 15 January 1962, PRO, PREM 11/3663.

[44] Commonwealth Unity Group, draft plan by C. Heathcote-Smith, 'Evolving Commonwealth Unity from Weakness', in R. Turton to A. Eden, 18 June 1959, AP 23/64/1,1A.

[45] J. Boyden to A. Bryant, 14 June 1962, AB Papers, F/21.

[46] Hugo Young described it as 'the chief rallying point for Euroscepticism'. Young, *This Blessed Plot*, p. 170.

[47] M. Holmes, *The Eurosceptical Reader* (Basingstoke, 1996).

[48] J. Collett (ed.), *Professor A. J. P. Taylor on Europe: The Historian Who Predicted the Future*, Bruges Group Occasional Paper No. 26 (London, 1997). As previously suggested, however (see Chapter 3), *Sunday Express* editor John Junor may well have dictated the content of Taylor's articles.

[49] Roberts, 'Patriotism', p. 320. If Thatcher's correspondence with Bryant is any indication, she is unlikely to have shared this view. See AB Papers, E/64.

De Gaulle's veto was the pre-emptive conclusion to an incomplete debate. It neither vindicated the opponents nor resolved the questions they had raised. Many of their arguments appeared in almost identical form in 1967 and, to a lesser extent, in the 1970–72 debates over entry.[50] But much had changed in the interim. The deaths of Gaitskell, only days after the veto, and Beaverbrook in 1964, robbed the anti-Market campaign of its most powerful exponents. Dramatic shifts occurred in their absence. Victorious in the 1964 and 1966 general elections, the previously sceptical Harold Wilson fronted Labour's bid for membership in 1967. The *Express*, meanwhile, went into inexorable decline under Max Aitken's stewardship and was resigned to Common Market membership by the time of the 1975 referendum. Empire Free Trade vanished with Beaverbrook.

Greater sophistication characterised subsequent debates on Europe, partly because membership debunked the inflated claims of economic benefit presented by the supporters of entry as well as the doomsday political scenarios of its opponents. It was also necessary to tailor the arguments around changing assessments of Britain's economic performance and its international standing. But the evolution of the European project was equally significant. In fact, supranational overtones that attended the progression from Common Market to European Union magnified the sovereignty issue, thereby making it the most enduring feature of the anti-Market case.

Rigorous debates aside, the sovereignty dialogue among sceptics on both the right and left remained tied to broad definitions. Those concepts blurred national and parliamentary independence, so much so that sovereignty set in the European context had itself become banal. When criticised by Sicco Mansholt in April 1972 for deserting the 'socialist family' in favour of patriotic impulse, Tony Benn replied 'the banner we have hoisted is not labelled "nationalism" but "democracy"'.[51] Sovereignty was carried forth most prominently in the long-standing positions of Enoch Powell, Michael Foot and Peter Shore, but was reinvigorated by the Thatcherite embrace. Her speech at Bruges provided an archetype for a generation of Eurosceptics nursed on the precepts of neo-Conservatism. Yet it was predicated on the traditional assumption that the drive for economic harmonisation was a precursor of political union. As a result the speech bore similarities not only to de Gaulle's

---

[50] See for example AntiCommon Market League, *Joining the Common Market or What the Treaty of Rome Means* (London, 1967, revised August 1970); D. Jay, *Towards a Lesser Britain* (London, 1971); W. Pickles, *Britain and Europe: How Much Has Changed?* (London, 1967) and 'Political Hopes and Political Realities', in D. Evans (ed.), *Destiny or Delusion: Britain and the Common Market* (London, 1971), pp. 109–21; R. Turton, *Why I Voted Against the Common Market* (London, 1972).

[51] Correspondence between S. Mansholt and T. Benn, 12 and 28 April 1972, LPA, MF Papers C/2.

concept of a *'Europe des patries'* and Gaitskell's speech at Brighton, but also to elements of the anti-Marketeer defence of sovereignty in cultural terms. After claiming 'We have not rolled back the frontiers of the state in Britain only to see them re-imposed' by a 'super-state' in Brussels, she added,

> Europe will be stronger precisely because it has France as France, Spain as Spain, Britain as Britain, each with its own customs, traditions and identity. It would be folly to try to fit them into some sort of identikit European personality.[52]

If the more recent examples of the UK Independence Party slogan 'Save our Sovereignty, Save our Sterling' and the No Euro campaign's use of Hitler in its 2002 video are any indication, those banalities will be central to future debates, whether they relate to the single currency, the Treaty of Lisbon or the overriding question of British participation in the European Union.

The suggestion that 'nothing' in the ideological make-up of the anti-Marketeers foreshadowed a fusion between Euroscepticism and liberal Conservatism[53] holds for analysis confined to party politics and a search for direct links. But libertarian strands were evident at the extra-parliamentary and unorthodox edges of anti-Marketeerism. This was most obvious in the arguments of Oliver Smedley and S. W. Alexander, who, despite their isolation, were torchbearers for a version of Cobdenism that surfaced in Eurosceptical thought.[54] Predictably, Smedley paid tribute in the 1980s to Thatcher, Keith Joseph, Professor von Hayek and Enoch Powell,[55] conspicuous absentees from the first application debate. In its championship of individual material gain, cheap food and defence of sovereignty, the *Express* had hinted at later developments. In fact, Powell, who characterised Beaverbrook as '"evil"', contacted John Junor after 'the Proprietor's' death in 1964, pledging both his sympathy with many *Sunday Express* causes and a willingness to write articles.[56]

---

[52] M. Thatcher, *The Downing Street Years* (London, 1993), pp. 744–5.

[53] Tratt, *The Macmillan Government and Europe*, p. 202.

[54] Howe, *Free Trade and Liberal England*, p. 275. Smedley had helped found the Institute of Economic Affairs, an organisation whose Hobart Papers published James Meade's *UK, Commonwealth and Common Market* in 1962. Indeed, both Meade and E. J. Mishan were cited by the Institute in its twentieth anniversary 'roll of honour'. See R. Harris and A. Seldon (eds), *Not from Beneveolence: Twenty Years of Economic Dissent*, Hobart Paperback No. 10 (London, 1977), pp. 146–7.

[55] Smedley, *Out!*, p. 21. Powell served in the Macmillan Government as Minister of Health. For a brief discussion of his views during this period see R. Shepherd, *Enoch Powell* (London, 1996), pp. 247–51.

[56] Junor respected Powell's intellect but questioned 'whether he was always completely in charge of his trolley'. Junor, *Memoirs*, pp. 164–5, 168.

Elsewhere, compelling but superficial links between anti-Marketeers and Eurosceptics are attributable to structure and rhetorical style. Current pressure group ranks include veterans of the first application debate such as the AntiCommon Market League, the British Housewives' League and the Monday Club.[57] Among Fleet Street's press magnates it is probably coincidental that Conrad Black and Rupert Murdoch, Beaverbrook's Eurosceptic successors, are themselves sons of the Dominions. But Beaverbrook's directive that opposition to Europe provided an opportunity to 'make news'[58] is an accepted tabloid formula, as evident during the Beef War, the ongoing Anglo-German football pantomime and recent debates over the single currency. Perhaps, as Roy Greenslade wrote in the *Observer*, 'The British newspaper is a nationalist enterprise', beset by the realisation that 'its own power is threatened by greater European integration'.[59]

What all of this suggests is that the construction of a Eurosceptic genealogy should begin not with linear political anatomies, but rather with comparisons of the abstract questions raised by contemporary national perceptions. It is tempting to view the dissonance between Britishness and European integration as a contest between ossified assumptions and the ascendant forces of a post-modern age. In point of fact, the question of independence and interdependence is as old as the system of nation states. The prospects for Europe, Julian Amery wrote in 1968, posed the dilemma confronted earlier by Joseph Chamberlain, 'the problem of how sovereign states can unite and yet preserve their individual personalities'.[60] In other words, as a catalyst for those tensions, European membership resonates with Britain's self-regard and fundamental questions about its place in the world. Anti-Marketeers and Eurosceptics therefore are ultimately united by an instinctive reaction to integration, a perception that aspects of European unity are incompatible with a set of achievements and characteristics that they believe define Britain as a unique nation among nations.

---

[57] For links to the AntiCommon Market League see Campaign for an Independent Britain at www.bullen.demon.co.uk. For the British Housewives' League see www. housewives.freeuk.com.
[58] Beaverbrook to M. Aitken, 24 August 1962, BBK H/221.
[59] *Observer*, 28 April 1996.
[60] J. Amery, *Joseph Chamberlain and the Tariff Reform Campaign, 1903–68* (London, 1969), p. 1054.

Bibliography

Primary sources

Manuscript sources

Bodleian Library of Commonwealth and Africa Studies at Rhodes House, Oxford

Sir Roy Welensky Papers (MSS Welensky)
MSS Welensky, Parts 5–7
522/2 and 522/9 – 'Commonwealth and Empire Groups and Political Parties'
654/1 and 665/1–5 – 'Personal Files of Correspondence'
743/3 and 765/3 – 'Correspondence with Individuals and Institutions, 1964–81'

British Broadcasting Corporation Written Archives Centre, Caversham, Reading (BBC WAC)
BBC radio scripts
BBC television talks scripts

Department of Documents, Imperial War Museum, London

Papers of Field Marshal Viscount Montgomery of Alamein
Lord Montgomery Deposit
Montgomery Ancillary Collections – 'Letters, Sir Arthur Bryant', 'Letters, Lady Clementine Churchill'

Department of Special Collections and Western Manuscripts, Bodleian Library, Oxford

Conservative Party Archives (CPA)
Conservative Central Office (CCO)
CCO 3/6 – 'Agent's Clubs, Labour, Women's, Youth and Outside Organisations, January 1960 – July 1965'
CCO 4/8/94 – 'European Common Market, 1958–61'
CCO 4/9/152 – 'European Common Market, 1961–66'
CCO 500/18/62 – 'South Dorset By-election, November 1962'
CCO 500/31/2,4 – 'Organisation Dept. – EEC General, 1959 – August 1962' and 'September 1962 – December 1962'

Conservative Research Department (CRD)
CRD 2/42/8 – 'Parliamentary Group on the Common Market'
CRD 2/43/1–3 – 'Peter Minoprio Letter Books – Common Market Correspondence' (September 1961–February 1964)

Harold Macmillan Diaries (HMD)
MS Macmillan dep. d. 41–8 (12 October 1960–16 March 1963)

House of Lords Records Office, London

Lord Beaverbrook Papers (BBK)
Series C – 'Special Correspondence, 1911–64'
Series F – 'Campaigns, Propaganda, Speeches, 1918–62'
Series H – 'Newspaper and Business Correspondence, 1912–64'

John Biggs-Davison Papers (BD Papers)
BD 23 – 'Common Market, 1957–63'
BD 25 – 'Commonwealth, 1955–67'

Labour History Archive and Study Centre, National Museum of Labour History, Manchester

Michael Foot Papers (MF Papers)
M2 – 'MP's Papers – 1946–70'
C2 – 'Common Market Debate Material – 1962–72'
P4 – '*Daily Herald* Articles'

Labour Party Archives (LPA)
Commonwealth Department Files
International Department Files – 'EEC Correspondence', 'EEC Memoranda, etc.', 'Common Market 1962'
National Executive Committee Files – 'Minutes'
Pamphlets Box 328.5101 – 'Europe – 1961–75', 'Labour Party Research Department Publications'

Liddell Hart Centre for Military Archives, King's College, London

Sir Arthur Bryant Papers (AB Papers)
Section C – 'Correspondence and Related Papers, 1919–84'
Section E – 'Correspondence with Individuals'
Section F – 'Fan Letters and Other Correspondence About Bryant's Books and Articles'
Section H – 'Political, 1943–82'
Section M – 'Manuscripts'

Modern Manuscripts Collection, Wren Library, Trinity College, Cambridge

R. A. Butler Papers
F/124 – 'Common Market – Misc. Pamphlets, Speeches, etc.'
H/96 – '1922 Committee Minutes'
L/110 – 'RAB Books – March 1961 to 8 June 1962'

Public Record Office, Kew, London (PRO)

Cabinet Files (CAB)
CAB 128 – 'Cabinet: Minutes (CM and CC Series) 1945–74'

Prime Minister's Files (PREM)
PREM 11 – 'Prime Minister's Office: Correspondence and Papers, 1951–64'

Special Collections, University of Birmingham Library

Lord Avon Papers (AP)
AP 23 – 'Post-resignation Correspondence with Notable People'

Special Collections, University College London Library

Hugh Gaitskell Papers (HG Papers)
C – 'Political Career'

Official publications

Parliamentary Debates, Commons, 5th Series.
Parliamentary Debates, Lords, 5th Series.
The United Kingdom and the European Economic Community, Cmnd 1565 (London, 1961).
Report – Royal Commission on the Press, 1961–62, Cmnd 1811 (London, 1962).
The United Kingdom and the European Communities, Cmnd 1882 (London, 1962).

Interviews and correspondence

Robert Edwards, written correspondence, 8 November 1996
Michael Foot, 27 October 1998
Lord Jenkins of Hillhead, 18 November 1998
Sir John Junor, 19 November 1996
Chapman Pincher, written correspondence, 31 May 1998
Lord Walker of Worcester, 25 February 1998
Garry H. Weston, 24 September 1998
Lord Windlesham, 18 March 1998

Newspapers and periodicals

AntiCommon Market League Newsletter
Candour
Common Market Broadsheet
Crossbow
Daily Express
Daily Telegraph
The Economist
Evening Standard
Forward Britain Movement Bulletin and Digest
Guardian
Illustrated London News
Listener
Observer

Spectator
Statist
Sunday Express
Sunday Times
The Times

Printed primary sources and memoirs

Alexander, S. W., *Save the Pound – Save the People: Montagu Norman versus Beaverbrook, Keynes, Boothby, and the Political Pygmies* (London, 1978).
AntiCommon Market League, *Conservatives and the Common Market* (October 1961).
—— *British Sovereignty and the Common Market*, Pamphlet No. 2 (undated).
—— *Britain's Offer of Free Trade to Canada*, Pamphlet No. 6 (undated).
—— *The Common Market and British Law*, Pamphlet No. 7 (undated).
—— *Joining the Common Market or What the Treaty of Rome Means* (London, 1967, revised August 1970).
Attlee, C., *Empire into Commonwealth* (London, 1961).
—— 'I Say "Halt!"' Britain Must Not Merely Become a Part of Europe', *Sunday Express*, 12 August 1962.
—— 'Are We Barring the Right People From Britain?', *Sunday Express*, 4 November 1962.
—— 'Yes, We're Still a First Class Power', *Daily Express*, 7 December 1962.
—— 'I Say Britain Can Still Be Great', *Sunday Express*, 4 February 1963.
Australian League of Rights, *The Common Market Threat to the British Commonwealth* (Melbourne, 1962).
—— *The Suppressed Truth About the Common Market* (Melbourne, 1962).
Baldwin, S., *On England and Other Addresses* (London, 1926).
Balfour, Lord, 'This Common Market Double Talk', *Daily Express*, 8 March 1962.
Beaverbrook, Lord, *My Case for Empire Free Trade* (London, 1930).
—— *Resources of the British Empire* (London, 1934).
—— *Don't Trust to Luck* (London, 1954).
—— *The Divine Propagandist* (London, 1962).
—— 'A Statement by Lord Beaverbrook', *Sunday Express*, 11 February 1962.
—— 'This is Why I Believe What I Believe', *Sunday Express*, 6 May 1962.
—— 'The Man Who Likes to Stir Things Up', *Sunday Express*, 21 October 1963.
Benians, L. E., Butler, Sir J. and Carrington, C. E. (eds), *The Cambridge History of the British Empire: Vol. 3, The Empire – Commonwealth 1870–1919* (Cambridge, 1959).
Best, A. and Sandwich, J. (eds), *Hinch: A Celebration of Viscount Hinchingbrooke, MP, 1906–1995* (London, 1997).
Bevan, J. S., leaflet, *The European Common Market and the Jesuit Menace* (Bristol, 1962).
Biggs-Davison, J., *The Walls of Europe* (London, 1962).
Bowman, D., *The Alternative to the Common Market* (London, 1961).
Brown, G., *In My Way* (London, 1971).
Bryant, A., *The Spirit of Conservatism* (London, 1929).
—— *The National Character* (London, 1934).
—— *English Saga: 1840–1940* (London, 1940).
—— *Unfinished Victory* (London, 1940).
—— *The Years of Endurance: 1793–1802* (London, 1942).
—— *The Story of England: Makers of the Realm* (London, 1954).

—— *A Choice for Destiny: Commonwealth or Common Market* (London, 1962).

—— 'The British Nations and Their Heritage', *Sunday Times*, 24 June 1962.

—— 'An Historian Protests', *The Director*, January 1963, pp. 79–81.

Campaign for Nuclear Disarmament, *The Bomb and You* (London, 1962).

Carrington, C. E., *The Liquidation of the British Empire* (London, 1961).

—— 'Commonwealth or Common Market?', *Statist*, 15 December 1961, pp. 1204–5.

—— 'Between the Commonwealth and Europe', *International Affairs*, 38:4 (October 1962), pp. 449–59.

—— 'Commonwealth or Common Market?', in R. H. Corbet (ed.), *Britain Not Europe. Commonwealth Before Common Market* (London, 1962), pp. 36–40.

—— *The British Overseas: Exploits of a Nation of Shopkeepers* (Cambridge, 1968).

Carter, A., *The Common Market – A Challenge to Unilateralists* (London, 1962).

Castle, B., 'Planning and the Common Market – The Anti-Socialist Community', *New Statesman and Nation*, 13 March 1962.

Chesterton, A. K., *The Menace of World Government* (London, 1955).

—— *Britain's Graveyard: Dangers of the Common Market* (London, 1957).

—— *Empire or Eclipse: Grim Realities of the Mid-Twentieth Century* (London, 1965).

—— *The New Unhappy Lords: An Exposure of Power Politics* (London, 1965).

Christiansen, A., *Headlines All My Life* (London, 1981).

Church of the Nazarene, *The Flame*, 27:2 (March–April 1962), p. 16.

City Press and Free Trade League, *The Common Market – The Alternative* (undated), reprint of C. T. Brock, *The Moral Case for Free Trade* (1935).

Commonwealth Fellowship, *The Commonwealth Fellowship* (Crowborough, 1962).

Commonwealth First Society, *Common Market – What This Means to You* (Warrington, 1962).

Commonwealth Republic Party, leaflet, *A Call to Youth* (1962).

Conservative Central Office, 'Common Market Common Sense', Nos 1–9 (London, 1962).

Conservative Political Centre, *The Commonwealth and the Common Market*, No. 250 (London, 1962).

—— *National Sovereignty and the European Community*, No. 252 (London, 1962).

Corbet, R. H. (ed.), *Britain Not Europe. Commonwealth Before Common Market* (London, 1962).

Critchley, J., 'The Flat Earthers', *Spectator*, 25 May 1962, p. 677.

Cummings, M., *These Uproarious Years: A Pictorial Post War History* (London, 1954).

—— *On the Point of My Pen: The Best of Cummings* (Portsmouth, 1985).

Daily Express, You and the Common Market (London, 1962).

Deedes, W., *Dear Bill: W. F. Deedes Reports* (London, 1997).

Dixon, P., *Double Diploma: The Life of Sir Pierson Dixon* (London, 1968).

Draper, A., *Scoops and Scandals: Memoirs of a Fleet Street Journalist* (London, 1988).

Driberg, T., *Beaverbrook: A Study of Power and Frustration* (London, 1956).

Drummond-Wolff, H., *The Commonwealth* (London, 1962).

—— *The Commonwealth Priority* (London, 1963).

Eden, A., *Full Circle* (London, 1960).

Edgar, D., *Express '56: A Year in the Life of an Express Journalist* (London, 1981).

Edwards, R., *Goodbye Fleet Street* (London, 1988).

Evans, H., *Downing Street Diary: The Macmillan Years, 1957–63* (London, 1981).

Fairlie, H., 'The Earl of Sandwich's Crew', *Spectator*, 31 August 1962, p. 296.

—— 'Mr. Gaitskell's Fatal Words', *Spectator*, 28 September 1962, p. 427.

—— 'Mr. Gaitskell on the Rock', *Spectator*, 12 October 1962, p. 548.

Farrer, D., *G – For God Almighty: A Personal Memoir of Lord Beaverbrook* (London, 1969).

Foot, M., 'Beelzebub', in L. Gourlay (ed.), *The Beaverbrook I Knew* (London, 1984), pp. 79–95.

Forward Britain Movement, *Common Market Realities* (London, April 1962).

—— *Britain Should Stay Out: Report of the Proceedings of the Britain–Commonwealth–EFTA Conference* (London, 1962).

General Council of the Press, *The Press and the People: The 9th Annual Report of the General Council of the Press* (London, 1962).

Gourlay, L. (ed.), *The Beaverbrook I Knew* (London, 1984).

Harrod, R., 'Debate on Sterling: The Case Against Devaluation', *Statist*, 8 December 1961, pp. 1122–4.

—— 'Britain, the Free World and the Six', *The Times*, 2 January 1962.

—— 'Britain, the Free World and The Six', in R. H. Corbet (ed.), *Britain Not Europe. Commonwealth Before Common Market* (London, 1962), pp. 32–5.

—— 'The Case Against Signing the Treaty of Rome', *The Director*, 15:6 (December 1962), pp. 444–5.

Healey, D., 'The Crisis in Europe', *International Affairs*, 38:1 (April 1962), pp. 145–55.

—— *The Time of My Life* (London, 1990).

—— *When Shrimps Learn to Whistle* (London, 1990).

Heathcote-Smith, C., 'American Influence in European Union', in R. H. Corbet (ed.), *Britain Not Europe. Commonwealth Before Common Market* (London, 1962), pp. 16–19.

Hetherington, A., *Guardian Years* (London, 1981).

Hinchingbrooke, Viscount, 'Are the Tories Leading Us to Ruin?', *Sunday Express*, 5 November 1961.

—— 'The Gathering Forces That Menace Britain', *Sunday Express*, 17 December 1961.

—— 'Is This Why the Tories Are on the Slide?', *Sunday Express*, 13 May 1962.

—— 'Can the Tory Rebels Still Save Britain?', *Sunday Express*, 23 September 1962.

Howard, P., *Beaverbrook: A Study of Max the Unknown* (London, 1964).

Howson, S. (ed.), *The Collected Papers of James Meade: Vol. 3, International Economics* (London, 1988), pp. 274–84.

Jay, D., *Towards a Lesser Britain* (London, 1971).

—— *Change and Fortune: A Political Record* (London, 1980).

Jay, D. and Jenkins, R., *The Common Market Debate* (London, 1962).

Jenkins, R., 'From London to Rome', *Encounter*, 17:3 (September 1961), pp. 5–8.

—— *A Life at the Centre* (London, 1991).

Junor, J., *Memoirs: Waiting For a Midnight Tram* (London, 1990).

Junor, P., *Home Truths: Life Around My Father* (London, 2002).

Kebbel, T. E. (ed.), *Selected Speeches of the Late Right Honourable the Earl of Beaconsfield, Vol. 2* (London, 1882).

Labour Party National Executive Committee, *Britain and the Common Market* (London, 1962).

Lambton, Lord, 'Mac's Vital Need: 40 Labour Rebels', *Evening Standard*, 18 September 1962.

Leighton, R., *What Next for Britain?* (London, 1963).

McLaren, H., 'Anti-Market: Profile of a Lobby', *Crossbow*, 6:21 (October–December 1962), pp. 13–14.

Macmillan, H., *Britain, the Commonwealth and Europe* (London, 1962).

—— *Pointing the Way, 1959–61* (London, 1972).

—— *At the End of the Day, 1961–63* (London, 1973).

Maude, A., 'Over to the Offensive', *Spectator*, 7 December 1962, p. 889.

Meade, J., *UK, Commonwealth and Common Market*, Hobart Paper No. 17, 1st edn (London, 1962).

—— 'The Common Market. Is There an Alternative?', Prologue to 2nd edn of *UK, Commonwealth and Common Market*, Supplement to Hobart Paper No. 17 (London, 1962).

—— 'A Time To Be Radical', letter to *The Times*, 1 February 1963.

Mishan, E. J., 'The Economic Case Against Joining the Common Market', *Listener*, 14 September 1961, pp. 371–3.

—— *Twenty-One Popular Economic Fallacies* (London, 1969).

Monday Club, *Winds of Change or Whirlwind* (London, 1961).

—— *Policy and Aims* (London, 1962).

Montgomery of Alamein, Viscount, *Three Continents* (London, 1962).

—— 'I Say We Must Not Join Europe', *Sunday Express*, 3 June 1962.

—— 'My Plea to the Women of Britain', *Sunday Express*, 1 July 1962.

Mosley, N., *Rules of the Game. Beyond the Pale: Memoirs of Sir Oswald Mosley and Family* (Elmwood Park, Illinois, 1991).

Pears, G., 'A Question of National Identity', *Crossbow*, 6:22 (January–March 1963), pp. 37–9.

Pickles, W., 'Will the Common Market Ever Work', *Sunday Express*, 6 August 1961.

—— 'The Inglorious Revolution', *Daily Express*, 13 November 1961.

—— 'Keep Out of Europe.... The Political Case', *Statist*, 17 November 1961, p. 882.

—— 'Stuck – in Plaster of Paris', *Daily Express*, 1 January 1962.

—— *Not With Europe: The Political Case for Staying Out*, Fabian Tract No. 336 (London, April 1962).

—— 'Political Power in the EEC', *Journal of Common Market Studies*, 2 (1963), pp. 63–84.

—— *Britain and Europe: How Much Has Changed?* (London, 1967).

—— 'Political Hopes and Political Realities', in D. Evans (ed.), *Destiny or Delusion: Britain and the Common Market* (London, 1971), pp. 109–21.

Pincher, C., *Pastoral Symphony* (Shrewsbury, 1993).

Pitman, R., *British Trade Unions and the Common Market* (London, 1962).

Protestant Alliance and Lord's Day Observance Society, *The Common Market and the Common Man* (1962).

Rose, R., 'Tensions in Conservative Philosophy', *Political Quarterly*, 32 (1961), pp. 275–83.

Rowse, A. L., *Historians I Have Known* (London, 1995).

Sampson, A., *Anatomy of Britain* (London, 1962).

Shay, M., 'The Conservative Europeans', in R. H. Corbet (ed.), *Britain Not Europe. Commonwealth Before Common Market* (London, 1962), pp. 25–7.

Shore, P., *Leading the Left* (London, 1993).

—— *Separate Ways: The Heart of Europe* (London, 2000).

Slessor, H., 'The Common Market and the Common Law', *Listener*, 23 August 1962, pp. 267–9.

Smedley, O., 'Our Freedom Is What They Want to End', *Sunday Express*, 25 February 1962.

—— *Out! UK in EEC Spells Disaster* (London, 1986).

Social Surveys (Gallup Poll) Ltd, 'British Attitudes to the EEC, 1960–63', *Journal of Common Market Studies*, 5 (1966), pp. 49–61.

Spears, E., 'Britain the Loser', in R. H. Corbet (ed.), *Britain Not Europe. Commonwealth Before Common Market* (London, 1962), pp. 8–11.

Taylor, A. J. P., *The Course of German History* (London, 1945).

—— *The Struggle for Mastery of Europe 1848–1918* (Oxford, 1954).

—— *The Trouble Makers: Dissent Over Foreign Policy 1792–1939* (London, 1957).

—— 'Are We Being Told the Whole Truth?', *Sunday Express*, 2 July 1961.

—— 'Are We Being Fair to the Russians?', *Sunday Express*, 19 November 1961.

—— 'Why Do We Stir Up Trouble in the Family?', *Sunday Express*, 3 December 1961.

—— 'Must We Always Take Orders From America?', *Sunday Express*, 31 December 1961.

—— 'Must de Gaulle's Enemies Drag Us Down Too?', *Sunday Express*, 11 February 1962.

—— 'I Say Ormseby-Gore Should Be Recalled', *Sunday Express*, 13 May 1962.

—— 'Why Do I Write For This "Awful Newspaper"?', *Sunday Express*, 27 May 1962.

—— 'Macmillan Has Not Found the Answer Yet', *Sunday Express*, 15 July 1962.

—— 'Will Menzies Speak for Britain?', *Sunday Express*, 9 September 1962.

—— 'Why Don't These "Top People" Think for Themselves?', *Sunday Express*, 21 October 1962.

—— 'The Bitter Truth About Britain's Unemployed', *Sunday Express*, 2 December 1962.

—— 'Why Don't We Have an Election Now?', *Sunday Express*, 27 January 1963.

—— *English History 1914–1945* (Oxford, 1965).

—— *A Personal History* (New York, 1983).

Thatcher, M., *The Downing Street Years* (London, 1993).

Tozer, D., 'Real Meaning of the Common Market', *Intelligence*, 1:15 (June–July 1961), p. 7.

Turton, R., 'Agriculture: The Vital Issues', in R. H. Corbet (ed.), *Britain Not Europe. Commonwealth Before Common Market* (London, 1962), pp. 63–5.

—— *Why I Voted Against the Common Market* (London, 1972).

Utley, T. E., 'Will Parliament Lose Its Sovereignty?', *Daily Telegraph*, 30 September 1962.

Vines, C. M., *A Little Nut Brown Man: My Three Years with Lord Beaverbrook* (London, 1968).

Walker, P., 'Boosting the Commonwealth', *Crossbow*, 5:19 (spring 1962), pp. 16–17.

—— *Staying Power: An Autobiography* (London, 1991).

Walker, P. and Walker-Smith, D., *A Call to the Commonwealth: The Constructive Case* (London, 1962).

Walker-Smith, D., 'British Sovereignty and the Common Market', in R. H. Corbet (ed.), *Britain Not Europe. Commonwealth Before Common Market* (London, 1962), pp. 12–15.

Webster, J., *The Express Years: A Golden Decade* (Edinburgh, 1994).

Wilson, H., 'A New Deal Now for the Commonwealth', *Sunday Express*, 26 February 1962.

—— 'I Say There Is Still Time to Save the Empire', *Sunday Express*, 10 June 1962.

—— 'Macmillan Must Call an Election Now', *Sunday Express*, 16 September 1962.

—— 'Is Macmillan Ready to Drop His Bluff At Last?', *Sunday Express*, 14 October 1962.
—— 'Danger!... The German Finger Is Reaching for the H-Bomb Trigger', *Sunday Express*, 13 January 1963.
Wood, A., *The True History of Lord Beaverbrook* (London, 1965).

Secondary sources

Books and articles

Allen, R., *Voice of Britain: The Inside Story of the Daily Express* (Cambridge, 1983).
Amery, J., *Joseph Chamberlain and the Tariff Reform Campaign, 1903–68* (London, 1969), Vol. 6 of J. L. Garvin and J. Amery, *The Life of Joseph Chamberlain* (London, 1932–69).
Anderson, B., *Imagined Communities: Reflections on the Origins and Spread of Nationalism* (London, 1983).
Baker, D., *Ideology of Obsession: A. K. Chesterton and British Fascism* (London, 1996).
Baker, D. and Seawright, D. (eds), *Britain For and Against Europe: British Politics and the Question of European Integration* (Oxford, 1998).
Barberis, P., McHugh, J., Tyldesley, M., with Pendry, H., *Encyclopaedia of British and Irish Political Organisations* (London, 2000).
Barnet, A., 'After Nationalism', in R. Samuel (ed.), *Patriotism: The Making and Unmaking of British National Identity* (London, 1989), vol. 1, pp. 140–55.
Beckett, F., *Clem Attlee* (London, 2000).
Beloff, N., *The General Says No: Britain's Exclusion from Europe* (London, 1963).
Bentley, M. and Stevenson, J. (eds), *High and Low Politics in Modern Britain* (Oxford, 1983).
Billig, M., *Banal Nationalism* (London, 1995).
Bogdanor, V. (ed.), *Liberal Party Politics* (Oxford, 1983).
Brivati, B., *Hugh Gaitskell* (London, 1996).
Brivati, B. and Jones, H. (eds), *From Reconstruction to Integration: Britain and Europe Since 1945* (London, 1993).
Brockliss, L. and Eastwood, D. (eds), *A Union of Multiple Identities, the British Isles c. 1750 – c. 1850* (Manchester, 1997).
Bulmer, S., 'Britain and European Integration: Of Sovereignty, Slow Adaptation and Semi-Detachment', in S. George (ed.), *Britain and the European Community: The Politics of Semi-Detachment* (Oxford, 1992), pp. 1–29.
Burk, K., *Troublemaker: The Life and History of A. J. P. Taylor* (London, 2000).
Byrne, P., *The Campaign for Nuclear Disarmament* (London, 1988).
Cameron, N. M. de S., *Dictionary of Scottish Church History and Theology* (Edinburgh, 1993).
Campbell, B., *The Iron Ladies: Why Do Women Vote Tory?* (London, 1987).
Camps, M., *Britain and the European Community, 1955–1963* (London, 1964).
Cannadine, D., 'British History as a "New Subject"', in A. Grant and J. K. Stringer (eds), *Uniting the Kingdom?, The Making of British History* (London, 1995), pp. 12–28.
—— *History in Our Time* (London, 1998).
Charlton, M., *The Price of Victory* (London, 1983).
Chester, L. and Fenby, J., *The Fall of the House of Beaverbrook* (London, 1979).
Chisolm, A. and Davie, M., *Beaverbrook: A Life* (London, 1992).

Cole, R., *A. J. P. Taylor: The Traitor Within the Gates* (London, 1993).

Collett, J. (ed.), *Professor A. J. P. Taylor on Europe: The Historian Who Predicted the Future*, Bruges Group Occasional Paper No. 26 (London, 1997).

Colley, L., 'Britishness and Otherness: An Argument', *Journal of British Studies*, 31:4 (October 1992), pp. 309–29.

—— *Britons: Forging the Nation, 1707–1837* (New Haven, 1992).

Colls, R. and Dodd, P. (eds), *Englishness: Politics and Culture, 1880–1920* (London, 1986).

Cook, C., *Sources in British Political History, 1900–1951: Vol. 1, A Guide to the Archives of Selected Organisations and Societies* (London, 1975).

Craig, F. W. S., *British Parliamentary Election Results, 1950–1970* (Chichester, 1971).

—— (ed.), *Minor Parties at British Parliamentary Elections, 1885–1974* (London, 1975).

Crowson, N. J. 'Lord Hinchingbrooke, Europe and the November 1962 South Dorset By-election', *Contemporary British History*, 17:4 (winter 2003), pp. 43–64.

—— *The Conservative Party and European Integration Since 1945* (New York, 2007).

Davies, N., *Europe: A History* (Oxford, 1996).

—— *The Isles: A History* (Oxford, 1999).

Deighton, A. and Ludlow, N. P., '"A Conditional Application": British Management of the First Attempt to Seek Membership of the EEC, 1961–63', in A. Deighton (ed.), *Building Postwar Europe: National Decision Makers and European Institutions, 1948–63* (London, 1995), pp. 107–26.

Deighton, A. and Milward, A. (eds), *Widening, Deepening and Acceleration: The European Economic Community, 1957–63* (Baden-Baden, 1999).

Dell, E., *The Schuman Plan and British Abdication of the Leadership of Europe* (Oxford, 1995).

Denman, R., *Missed Chances: Britain and Europe in the Twentieth Century* (London, 1996).

Dutton, D., 'Anticipating Maastricht: The Conservative Party and Britain's First Application to Join the European Community', *Contemporary Record*, 7:3 (1993), pp. 522–40.

—— *Anthony Eden: A Life and Reputation* (London, 1997).

Eley, G., 'Culture, Britain and Europe', *Journal of British Studies*, 31:4 (October 1992), pp. 390–414.

Ellison, J., *Threatening Europe: Britain and the Creation of the European Community, 1955–58* (Basingstoke, 2000).

Evans, D., *While Britain Slept: The Selling of the Common Market* (London, 1975).

Finer, S. E., *Anonymous Empire: A Study of the Lobby in Great Britain* (London, 1966).

Forster, A. *Euroscepticism in Contemporary British Politics* (London, 2002).

Gamble, A., *The Conservative Nation* (London, 1974).

—— 'Liberals and the Economy', in V. Bogdanor (ed.), *Liberal Party Politics* (Oxford, 1983), pp. 191–216.

Gellner, E., *Nations and Nationalism* (Oxford, 1983).

George, S. (ed.), *Britain and the European Community: The Politics of Semi-Detachment* (Oxford, 1992).

—— 'The Awkward Partner: An Overview', in B. Brivati and H. Jones (eds), *From Reconstruction to Integration: Britain and Europe Since 1945* (Leicester, 1993), pp. 179–90.

—— *An Awkward Partner: Britain in the European Community*, 2nd edn (Oxford, 1994).

Gilbert, M., *Winston S. Churchill: Vol. 3, Never Despair, 1945–65* (Boston, 1988).

Goodhart, P., *The 1922: The Story of the Conservative Backbenchers' Parliamentary Committee* (London, 1973).

Gowland, D. A. and Turner, A., *Reluctant Europeans: Britain and European Integration, 1945–1998* (Harlow, 2000).

Grant, A. and Stringer, K. J. (eds), *Uniting the Kingdom? The Making of British History* (London, 1995).

Green, E. H. H., 'The Battle of Books: Book Clubs and Conservatism in the 1930s', in *Ideologies of Conservatism* (Oxford, 2002), pp. 135–56.

Greenwood, J. and Stancich, L., 'British Business: Managing Complexity', in D. Baker and D. Seawright (eds), *Britain For and Against Europe* (Oxford, 1998), pp. 130–47.

Greenwood, S. (ed.), *Britain and European Integration Since the Second World War* (Manchester, 1996).

Harris, K., *Attlee* (London, 1982).

Harris, R. and Seldon, A. (eds), *Not from Benevolence: Twenty Years of Economic Dissent*, Hobart Paperback No. 10 (London, 1977).

Haseler, S., *The English Tribe: Identity, Nation and Europe* (London, 1996).

Hassner, P., 'Beyond Nationalism and Internationalism: Ethnicity and World Order', *Survival*, 35:2 (summer 1993), pp. 49–65.

Hastings, A., *The Construction of Nationhood: Ethnicity, Religion and Nationalism* (Cambridge, 1997).

Hedetoft, U., 'The State of Sovereignty in Europe: Political Concept or Cultural Self-Image', in S. Zetterholm (ed.), *National Cultures and European Integration* (Oxford, 1994), pp. 13–48.

Hinton, J., 'Militant Housewives: The British Housewives League and the Attlee Government', *History Workshop*, 38 (autumn 1994), pp. 129–56.

Hobsbawm, E., *Nations and Nationalism Since 1780* (Cambridge, 1992).

Hobsbawm, E. and Ranger, T. (eds), *The Invention of Tradition* (Cambridge, 1983).

Holmes, M., *The Eurosceptical Reader* (Basingstoke, 1996).

Horne, A., *Macmillan: Vol. 2, 1957–1986* (London, 1989).

Howe, A., *Free Trade and Liberal England, 1846–1946* (Oxford, 1997).

Howe, S., 'Labour Patriotism, 1939–83', in R. Samuel (ed.), *Patriotism: The Making and Unmaking of British National Identity* (London, 1989), vol. 1, pp. 127–39.

Jenkins, B. and Sofos, S. (eds), *Nation and Identity in Contemporary Europe* (London, 1996).

Jowell, R. and Hoinville, G. (eds), *Britain into Europe: Public Opinion and the EEC, 1961–75* (London, 1976).

Kaiser, W., 'Using Europe and Abusing Europeans: The Conservatives and the European Community, 1957–1994', *Contemporary Record*, 8:2 (1994), pp. 381–99.

—— *Using Europe, Abusing Europeans: Britain and European Integration, 1945–63* (London, 1996).

Kaiser, W. and Staerck, G. (eds), *British Foreign Policy, 1955–64: Contracting Options* (London, 2000).

Kandiah, M., 'British Domestic Politics: Conservatives and Foreign Policy', in W. Kaiser and G. Staerck (eds), *British Foreign Policy, 1955–64: Contracting Options* (London, 2000), pp. 61–88.

Kearney, H., *The British Isles: A History of Four Nations* (Cambridge, 1989).

Kitzinger, U., *The Second Try: Labour and the EEC* (Oxford, 1968).

Lacouture, J., *De Gaulle: Vol. 2, The Ruler, 1945–70* (London, 1991).

Layton-Henry, Z., 'Labour's Lost Youth', *Journal of Contemporary History*, 11 (1976), pp. 275–308.

Lieber, R. J., *British Politics and European Unity: Parties, Elites and Pressure Groups* (Berkeley, 1970).

Ludlow, N. P., *Dealing With Britain: The Six and the First UK Application to the EEC* (Cambridge, 1997).

—— 'A Mismanaged Application: Britain and the EEC, 1961–63', in A. Deighton and A. Milward (eds), *Widening, Deepening and Acceleration: The European Economic Community, 1957–63* (Baden-Baden, 1999), pp. 271–85.

Lunn, K., 'Reconsidering "Britishness": The Construction and Significance of National Identity in Twentieth Century Britain', in B. Jenkins and S. Sofos (eds), *Nation and Identity in Contemporary Europe* (London, 1996), pp. 83–100.

MacKenzie, J. M., *Propaganda and Empire: The Manipulation of British Public Opinion, 1880–1960* (Manchester, 1984).

—— 'The Popular Culture of Empire in Britain', in J. M. Brown and W. R. Louis (eds), *The Oxford History of the British Empire: Vol. 6, The Twentieth Century* (Oxford, 1999), pp. 213–31.

Maguire, G. E., *Conservative Women: A History of Women and the Conservative Party, 1874–1997* (London, 1998).

Mandler, P., *History and National Life* (London, 2002).

Marquand, D., 'How United Is the Modern United Kingdom?', in A. Grant and K. J. Stringer (eds), *Uniting the Kingdom? The Making of British History* (London, 1995), pp. 277–91.

May, A. (ed.), *Britain, the Commonwealth and Europe: The Commonwealth and Britain's Application to Join the European Communities* (Basingstoke, 2001).

Milward, A., *The European Rescue of the Nation State* (London, 1992).

—— *The UK and European Community: Vol. 1, The Rise and Fall of a National Strategy 1945–1963*, Government Official History Series (London, 2002).

Moon, J., *European Integration in British Politics, 1950–63: A Study of Issue Change* (Aldershot, 1985).

Morgan, K. O., 'The Second World War and British Culture', in B. Brivati and H. Jones (eds), *From Reconstruction to Integration: Britain and Europe Since 1945* (London, 1993), pp. 33–46.

—— *Britain Since 1945: The People's Peace*, 3rd edn (London, 2001).

Moxon-Browne, E., *Nation, Class and Creed in Northern Ireland* (London, 1983).

Nairn, T., *The Left Against Europe?* (London, 1973).

—— *The Break-Up of Britain: Crisis and Neo-Nationalism* (London, 1977).

Newman, M., *Socialism and European Unity* (London, 1983).

Nicholas, S., 'The Construction of National Identity: Stanley Baldwin, "Englishness" and the Mass Media in Inter-War Britain', in M. Francis and I. Zweiniger-Bargielowska (eds), *The Conservatives and British Society, 1880–1990* (Cardiff, 1996), pp. 126–46.

Nugent, N. and King, R., *The British Right: Conservative and Right Wing Politics in Britain* (Farnborough, 1977).

O'Brien, P. K., 'The Costs and Benefits of British Imperialism 1846–1914', *Past and Present*, 120 (August 1988), pp. 163–200.

Orwell, G., *The Lion and the Unicorn: Socialism and the English Genius* (1941, London, 1982 edn).

Pfaltzgraff, R. L., Jr., *Britain Faces Europe* (Philadelphia, 1969).

Phelps Brown, H., 'Sir Roy Harrod: A Biographical Memoir', *Economic Journal*, 90:357 (March 1980), pp. 1–33.

Philip, A. B., 'The Liberals and Europe', in V. Bogdanor (ed.), *Liberal Party Politics* (Oxford, 1983), pp. 217–40.
—— 'British Pressure Groups and the European Community', in S. George (ed.), *Britain and the European Community: The Politics of Semi-Detachment* (Oxford, 1992), pp. 149–71.
Pocock, J. G. A., 'British History: A Plea for a New Subject', *Journal of Modern History*, 47:4 (December 1975), pp. 601–28.
Potter, A. M., *Organised Groups in British National Politics* (London, 1961).
Rainer, E. (ed.), *Stereotypes in Contemporary Anglo-German Relations* (London, 2000).
Reynolds, D., 'Britain and the New Europe: The Search for Identity Since 1940', *Historical Journal*, 31:1 (1988), pp. 223–39.
Robbins, K., *History, Religion and Identity in Modern Britain* (London, 1993).
—— *Great Britain: Identities, Institutions and the Idea of Britishness* (London, 1998).
Roberts, A., 'Patriotism: The Last Refuge of Sir Arthur Bryant', in *Eminent Churchillians* (London, 1994), pp. 287–322.
Robins, L. J., *The Reluctant Party: Labour and the EEC, 1961–75* (Ormskirk, 1979).
Roll, E., *Where Did We Go Wrong? From the Gold Standard to Europe* (London, 1995).
Rosamund, B., 'The Integration of Labour? British Trade Union Attitudes to European Integration', in D. Baker and D. Seawright (eds), *Britain For and Against Europe* (Oxford, 1998), pp. 130–47.
Said, E., *Orientalism* (New York, 1978).
Samuel, R. (ed.), *Patriotism: The Making and Unmaking of British National Identity*, 3 vols (London, 1989).
—— *Theatres of Memory* (London, 1994).
Seldon, A. and Ball, S. (eds), *Conservative Century* (Oxford, 1994).
Seyd, P., 'Factionalism Within the Conservative Party: The Monday Club', *Government and Opposition*, 7:4 (autumn 1972), pp. 464–87.
Shepherd, R., *Enoch Powell* (London, 1996).
Sisman, A., *A. J. P. Taylor: A Biography* (London, 1994).
Smith, A. C. H., *Paper Voices: The Popular Press and Social Change, 1935–65* (London, 1975).
Smith, A. D., *National Identity* (London, 1991).
—— 'National Identity and the Idea of European Unity', *International Affairs*, 68:1 (1992), pp. 55–76.
—— *Nations and Nationalism in a Global Era* (Cambridge, 1995).
Solow, R. M., 'James Meade at Eighty', *Economic Journal*, 97:388 (December 1987), pp. 986–8.
Spence, J., 'Movements in the Public Mood: 1961–75', in R. Jowell and G. Hoinville (eds), *Britain into Europe: Public Opinion and the EEC, 1961–75* (London, 1976), pp. 19–23.
Stephenson, J., 'Britain and Europe in the Later Twentieth Century: Identity, Sovereignty, Peculiarity', in M. Fulbrook (ed.), *National Histories and European History* (London, 1993), pp. 230–54.
Street, P., *Arthur Bryant: Portrait of a Historian* (London, 1979).
Taylor, A. J. P., *Beaverbrook* (London, 1972).
Thayer, G., *The British Political Fringe: A Profile* (London, 1965).
Tratt, J., *The Macmillan Government and Europe: A Study in the Process of Policy Development* (London, 1996).
Ward, S., 'Anglo-Commonwealth Relations and EEC Membership: The Problem of the Old Dominions', in G. Wilkes, (ed.), *Britain's Failure to Enter the*

European Community, 1961–63: Crises in European, Atlantic and Common-wealth Relations (London, 1997), pp. 178–99.

—— 'A Matter of Preference: Britain, Europe and the Erosion of the Old Common-wealth Relationship', in A. May (ed.), *Britain, the Commonwealth and Europe: The Commonwealth and Britain's Application to Join the European Communities* (Basingstoke, 2001), pp. 156–80.

—— *Australia and the British Embrace: The Demise of the Imperial Ideal* (Melbourne, 2001).

Watkins, A., 'Lapsed Calvinist', in L. Gourlay (ed.), *The Beaverbrook I Knew* (London, 1984), pp. 231–40.

Wilkes, G. (ed.), *Britain's Failure to Enter the European Community, 1961–63: Crises in European, Atlantic and Commonwealth Relations* (London, 1997).

—— 'The Commonwealth in British European Policy: Politics and Sentiment, 1956–63', in A. May (ed.), *Britain, the Commonwealth and Europe: The Commonwealth and Britain's Application to Join the European Communities* (Basingstoke, 2001), pp. 53–81.

—— and Wring, D., 'The British Press and Integration: 1948 to 1996', in D. Baker and D. Seawright (eds), *Britain For and Against Europe: British Politics and the Question of European Integration* (Oxford, 1998), pp. 185–205.

Williams, P. M., *Hugh Gaitskell* (Oxford, 1982).

Williamson, P., *Stanley Baldwin: Conservative Leadership and National Values* (Cambridge, 1999).

Windlesham, Lord, *Communication and Political Power* (London, 1966).

Young, H., *This Blessed Plot: Britain and Europe From Churchill to Blair* (London, 1998).

Young, J. W., *Britain and European Unity, 1945–1992* (London, 1993).

Young, K., *Churchill and Beaverbrook: A Study in Friendship and Politics* (London, 1966).

Young, W., *Harrod and His Trade Cycle Group* (New York, 1989).

Zetterholm, S. (ed.), *National Cultures and European Integration* (Oxford, 1994).

Zweineger-Bargielowska, I., 'Explaining the Gender Gap: The Conservative Party and the Women's Vote, 1945–64', in M. Francis and I. Zweineger-Bargielowska (eds), *The Conservatives and British Society, 1880–1990* (Cardiff, 1996), pp. 194–223.

Unpublished theses

Bromund, T., 'From Empire to Europe: Material Interests, National Identities and British Policies Towards European Integration, 1956–63' (unpublished PhD dissertation, Yale University, 1999).

Index